*I*n the early years of our career, we designed and made mostly appliqué quilts. As beginners, we thought that all those little pieces in a pieced quilt would take far more time and attention than we could give. Looking at the pro-

cedures required to make a pieced quilt, we were convinced that we'd never finish one—templates had to be made for every pattern piece, and cutting was a major ordeal. Accuracy was essential. But the pieces that we cut with scissors never seemed to fit together properly.

The introduction of rotary cutting and quick piecing opened up a whole new world of quilts to us. Developed by talented professionals, these tools and techniques are among the greatest innovations of all time for quiltmakers.

Using these methods, we were surprised how quickly we could cut out and sew all those little pieces together. Now we approach piecing with a new attitude.

Our lifestyle today usually does not allow us the time we'd like to spend on quilting. But with the techniques in this book, we save time and get the quality results our grandmothers expected. You'll find a variety of designs—bed quilts for young and old, wall hangings, holiday projects, baby quilts, pillows, and tablecloths.

Each project employs one or more of five quick-piecing techniques. **Basics & Beyond** introduces each technique in detail, with step-by-step photos. If you are just learning these methods, practice will lead to accuracy—it doesn't take long to become proficient, and the time spent will yield spectacular results. Also see **How to Use These Instructions** on page 34—this explains how the instructions are formatted and some rules of thumb that apply throughout.

Whichever project you choose, we hope to make your quilting a faster, more rewarding experience with projects that you will be proud to give as gifts or treasure for yourself for years to come.
Happy quilting!

*Pam Bono*     *Robert Bono*

# Contents

## Basics and Beyond

20

122

60

# Rotary Cutter Quilt Collection

**128**

**154**

**149**

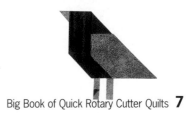

226

275

246

**237**

**290**

**174**

# Basics and Beyond

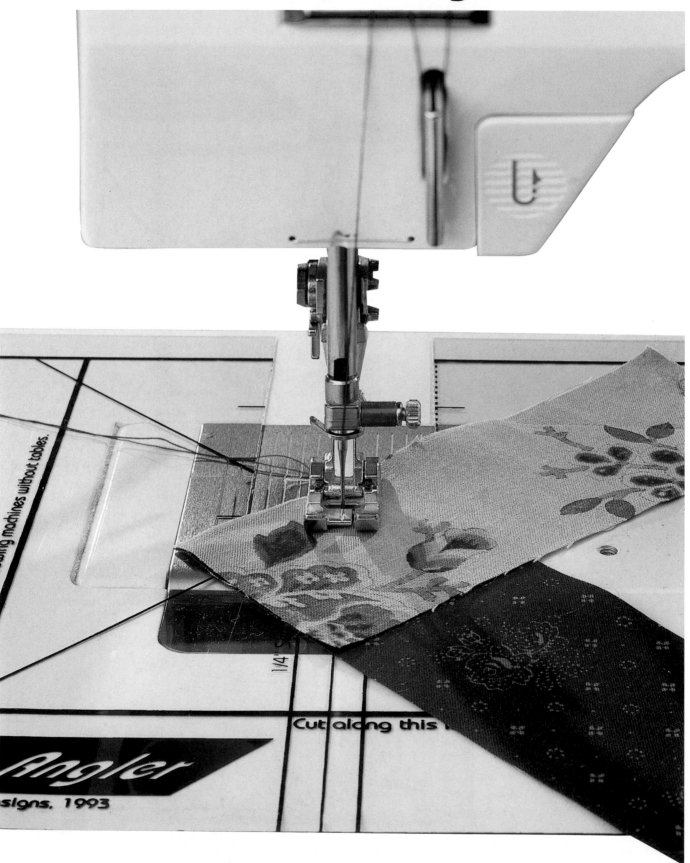

# Fabric

Lightweight, 100%-cotton fabric is the best choice for quilts. Sturdy and durable, cotton is neither stretchy nor tightly woven and it takes a crease well, so seams are easy to press. When you use good-quality fabric, your quilt looks nice and lasts a long time.

## Selecting Fabric

Choosing fabrics seems to bring out the insecurities in many quilt-makers. Will my quilt look as good as the one in the picture? If I change the color to blue, will my quilt look as nice as the green one?

**Trust Your Instincts.** Go with the fabrics *you* like. You can ask for help from family, friends, and helpful shop staff, but the final choice is yours.

Fabric manufacturers offer sets of coordinated prints and solids that can take some of the pain out of the fabric selection process. If such a group of fabrics works for you, that's fine. But coordinated fabrics leaves no room for personal creativity and preferences.

Take your book with you to the fabric store—having the picture in front of you is helpful and enables the shop staff to make suggestions.

Make the most of the people at your favorite shop. Take down as many bolts as you need to try different fabric combinations. Group your choices on a large table and then—this is very important—step back and *squint*. This lets you preview the mix of value and texture. If a fabric doesn't blend, replace it and try again. And again. And again, until you're satisfied.

**Choose a Color Scheme.** Don't limit yourself to the color schemes presented here. True, we list the materials needed by color for ease of identification, but you can pencil in your own choices

The choice of fabric colors and patterns affects the mood of any design. The soft pastels of *Formal Garden* (page 290) evoke gentle spring breezes and delicate flowers. The same design in bright, strong colors will convey a very different mood. It's up to the quiltmaker to establish the quilt's personality.

Look at *Safari Path* (page 310) for another example. Rich browns and golds suggest African plains. The same design is a fantasy if you make pink elephants and purple lions on a background of sky blue.

Even if you're working on a Christmas project, you can still vary the mood. Bright red and green with sparkling white looks crisp and new. Soft beige, rich burgundy, and forest green suggest a country or Victorian atmosphere.

A design has an Amish look when you combine bright solid fabrics with black. Big floral prints are excellent for Victorian and English Country looks. Don't be afraid to cut big prints into little pieces, as they create interesting texture.

## How Much to Buy

Each materials list gives the amount of fabric needed to make the quilt as shown. Yardages are based on 43"-wide fabric after prewashing.

**The Fabric Bug.** Anyone who loves fabric eventually gets the fabric bug. Once bitten, you are compelled to buy fabric even when you don't need it. Try to balance the limits of your purse and space with the inalienable right to have fun. Don't let guilt keep you from building a nice inventory. Then you can use fabrics from your stockpile with new fabric to make more quilts.

**Finders Keepers.** When buying any fabric, remember that you may never find it again. If you see a fabric that you *really* like, buy a lot! Chances are, if you need more, it will be gone. That fabric may *never* be available again. It's better to have extra than not enough. All the *Friends* dolls (page 230) were made from scraps leftover from other pink and blue projects.

Buy a ¼ yard if the fabric is something you just want to have. If a fabric is a good accent, you might want 1 yard. Get 3 yards if the fabric will make a great background

minimize raveling. Wash light and dark colors separately in cool water. Use mild detergent or Orvus Paste, a mild soap available at quilt shops.

**Dry and Press.** Dry prewashed fabrics at a medium or permanent-press setting in the dryer until they're just damp. Then press them dry. Iron out all creases and folds so you have smooth, straight fabric with which to work.

## Grain Lines

The interwoven lengthwise and crosswise threads of a fabric are grain lines. Cotton fabric can be stable or stretchy, depending on how it is cut.

**Selvage.** The lengthwise finished edges of the fabric are selvages (Grain Diagram). These edges are more tightly woven than the body of the fabric. *Always trim selvage from the ends of a strip before cutting pieces for your quilt.*

**Straight Grain.** Lengthwise grain, parallel to the selvage, has the least give. Long strips for sashing and borders are best cut lengthwise for more stability.

Crosswise grain, perpendicular to the selvage, has a little more give. Most strips are cut on the crosswise grain. For small patchwork pieces, either direction is acceptable.

**Bias.** True bias is at a 45° angle to the selvages, on the diagonal between lengthwise and crosswise grains. Bias-cut fabric has the most stretch. At least one edge of a triangle is bias. Handle a bias edge carefully, as it can stretch out of shape, warping the patchwork.

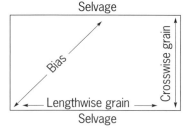

Grain Diagram

and 6 yards if the fabric is on sale and it's a sure-fire candidate for major design elements and borders.

**Directional Prints.** Buy extra when using stripes or directional prints—cutting them to keep the direction consistent can be wasteful. (If the stripes don't go in the right direction, your quilt can have a chaotic appearance.) It's best not to use a directional print as a background fabric.

## Prewashing

Wash, dry, and iron fabrics before cutting. Use the washer and detergent that you'll use to wash the finished quilt. Washing removes excess dye and sizing from the fabric and may shrink it slightly. If you prewash, there's less chance of damage occurring later.

Before you put the fabric in the washing machine, snip a triangle from each corner of the piece to

# Tools & Supplies

Selection of quiltmaking tools is a personal choice. What works for one person may not be the best equipment for someone else. Choose the tools that are most comfortable for you. This list is by no means all-inclusive. There are many wonderful gadgets available today. We've listed those that are most necessary to help you make quilts quickly, easily, and accurately.

## Cutting Tools

**Rotary Cutter.** A rotary cutter has a round blade attached to a handle. If possible, experiment with different shapes and sizes of cutters to find the one that is most comfortable in your hand, as it will spend a lot of time there. Some quilters feel a curved handle puts less strain on their wrists.

Change the cutter's blade at the first sign of dullness. A dull blade tends to skip and be less accurate. Make it a habit to retract the blade after each cut—this protects the blade as well as everyone's fingers. Keep the cutter out of the reach of small children and pets.

To keep a rotary cutter blade running smoothly, lubricate it occasionally by loosening the tension screw and placing a drop of sewing machine oil between blade and sheath. Wipe away any excess oil with a clean cloth.

**Cutting Mat.** Always use a heavy-duty, self-healing cutting mat. A 24" x 36" mat is a good, all-purpose size, especially for cutting strips from yardage. Smaller mats require you to move largee fabric pieces too frequently but they are ideal for cutting scraps. Most mats are marked in a 1" grid with two 45° angles. Always store a mat flat and avoid exposing it to heat.

**Rulers.** Rulers used with rotary cutters are made of clear, ⅛"-thick acrylic. Most are marked in ⅛" increments as well as 45° and 60° angles. The most versatile ruler is 6" x 24", a good length for cutting long strips. A large square ruler (10" to 16" square), used with the 24" ruler, helps to keep cuts straight. You will also need smaller rulers, because a long ruler is awkward for making small cuts.

Other rulers that make cutting easier include those with light print for dark fabrics, rulers with dark print for lighter fabrics, and a 1" x 6" ruler to keep near the sewing machine for checking seam accuracy. An 18"-long plastic ruler is helpful for drawing grids.

To keep your ruler from slipping, cut ⅜" squares of self-sticking sandpaper (available at most hardware stores) and place them on the back of your ruler at the corners.

## Basic Supplies

**Sewing Machine.** Any basic straight-stitch machine is adequate. You will want a more sophisticated machine for machine appliqué or machine quilting.

Keep the machine in good order. The machine should make an evenly locked stitch that looks the same on front and back. If the tension is not properly adjusted, you'll get puckered seams. Clean and oil the machine as directed by the manufacturer and take it to your dealer periodically to be serviced.

Use a throat plate that has a small, round needle hole designed for straight stitching. A wide or oblong needle hole (intended for zigzag stitching) lets the needle push the fabric down into the throat plate as you stitch. Replace the throat plate if necessary.

**Sewing Machine Presser Feet.** Special feet that measure a ¼" seam allowance are available for most machines. If you don't have one, see page 18 for other ways to mark an accurate ¼" seam allowance.

**Sewing Machine Needles.** The needle recommended for machine piecing is size 80/12. If you hear a popping noise when sewing, the needle may be dull. Replace it to maintain stitch quality.

**Sewing Thread.** Use either 100% cotton thread or the stronger cotton-wrapped polyester thread. Use a light neutral color (ivory or taupe) when sewing light fabrics and a dark neutral (gray) thread when piecing dark fabrics.

**Seam Ripper.** This invaluable tool is much more efficient than the tips of small scissors for removing unwanted stitches. A seam ripper is also useful in several of these quilts where you are instructed to remove a square from a pieced sashing strip or border.

**Pins and Pincushions.** Use long, thin dressmaker's pins. Sharp, rust-proof pins with round heads are preferable. Any type of pincushion will do.

**Scissors.** You need sharp dressmaker's shears for cutting the occasional appliqué shape and for trimming batting and backing. Use sharp embroidery scissors or specialized snips for clipping threads. If your project requires a template, you will also need small utility scissors for cutting paper or plastic.

**Iron and Ironing Board.** Use an iron that has both dry and steam settings. For steam, use distilled water to keep your iron clean. An ironing board that adjusts to different heights will make your work more comfortable.

**Fabric Sizing Spray.** If you like your fabric to have body, use a light spray of sizing after prewashing to give the fabric some stiffness. This is helpful when working with bias edges to prevent stretching.

**Zip-top Plastic Bags.** Resealable bags are *essential* for storing cut pieces. One box of sandwich bags should see you through several quilts. See page 17 for more details.

**Pencils and Markers.** Use pencils to mark grids and pattern shapes on fabric. Keep pencils sharp and make thin lines. A good mechanical pencil that holds 0.5-mm (thin) lead is an excellent investment.

For marking quilt tops, try a silver drawing pencil or chalk marker that shows well on both light and dark fabrics and washes out easily. Water-erasable markers are easy to use, but the chemicals from these sometimes remain in the fabric even after a cold water rinse, causing permanent discoloration. Whatever product you choose, test it on scraps first to be sure it will wash out.

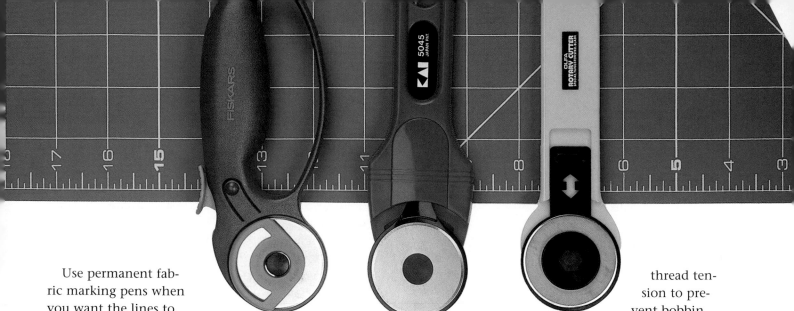

Use permanent fabric marking pens when you want the lines to remain forever. I used three colors of fine-tipped permanent fabric marking pens on the *Friends* quilt and doll. These pens are useful for signing and dating your quilts.

**Template Plastic.** Available in sheets of lightweight plastic, this material is transparent enough to allow you to see the pattern through it and trace the pattern directly onto it. It is thin enough to cut with scissors, but strong enough to withstand repeated use. Templates are used for appliqué shapes and for marking faces on the *Friends* quilt.

**Tear-Away Stabilizer.** This lightweight, nonwoven material is placed under the background fabric to keep it from slipping during machine appliqué.

**Eraser.** A white eraser called Magic Rub is available at most art supply stores. This eraser, used by professional drafters and artists, cleanly removes carbon smudges left by pencil lead without fraying the fabric or leaving eraser crumbs.

**Fabric Glue.** After pressing under ¼" on appliqués, apply a little fabric glue to hold the edges in place while you pin and stitch the fabric.

**Safety Pins.** Purchase rustproof, 1"-long, nickel-plated safety pins to pin-baste quilt layers for machine quilting. You need 350–500 safety pins to baste a large quilt.

**Thimble.** Hand quilting is painful without a thimble on the middle finger of your sewing hand to keep the needle from digging into your fingertip. Use a thin rubber thimble if you want to feel the needle.

**Quilting Needles.** Buy a packaged assortment of "sharps" for general hand stitching and a package of "betweens" for hand quilting. Sharps are longer and have a larger eye than betweens. For hand quilting, select the between that is most comfortable to use. I use a size 10 between for hand quilting, but size 7 or 8 is better for beginners.

**Quilting Thread.** Available in a wide range of colors, quilting thread is heavier than sewing thread and is coated to prevent tangling. Throw away an old spool of thread if it has become brittle.

For machine quilting, load the bobbin with regular sewing thread that matches the backing. For the top thread, use sewing thread that coordinates with the quilt top, or use clear nylon monofilament (which blends with any fabric and tends to camouflage irregularities in the stitching). Adjust the top thread tension to prevent bobbin thread loops from showing.

**Bicycle Clips.** For machine quilting, use these metal or plastic bands to hold the rolled edges of the quilt in place. These clips are sold in quilt shops and fabric stores.

**Walking Foot.** This presser foot is recommended for machine quilting straight lines or grids as well as for applying binding. While it is not essential, this foot certainly makes these tasks easier. It is an even-feed foot; that is, it feeds the top fabric through the machine at the same rate that the feed dogs move the bottom fabric. Some machines have a built-in even-feed feature.

**Quilting Hoops and Frames.** A quilting hoop has deeper sides than an embroidery hoop to accommodate the three thicknesses of a quilt. For hand quilting you can carry anywhere or work in your lap, use the size hoop you find most comfortable or practical. The most popular hoops are 14"–22" in diameter.

A quilting frame is large, heavy, and usually fixed in place while the quilting is in progress (which can be a long time). Inquire at a local quilt shop or look at mail order sources for the best style, price, and size to fit your needs.

# Rotary Cutting

Rotary cutting is fast and easy. It's fast because you measure and cut with one stroke. It's accurate because the fabric stays flat as you cut, instead of being raised by a scissor blade. If rotary cutting is new to you, use these instructions to practice on scraps. It may seem strange at first, but try it—you'll love it!

## Squaring Up the Edge

Fabric off the bolt is likely to have jagged edges or be folded off-center. Prewashing the fabric should eliminate the crease of the fold. To cut straight strips, you should refold the fabric and square up the ends.

**1.** Fold the fabric with selvages matching. Place the fabric on a cutting mat with the fold nearest you. Then fold the fabric in half again, bringing the selvages down almost even with the fold to make four layers (Photo A). This makes fabric only 11" wide—the narrower width is easier to cut accurately than a long piece. The yardage should extend to your right, leaving the end you are cutting on the mat. (Reverse directions if you are left-handed.)

**2.** Align the bottom of a large square ruler with the bottom fold so the left edge of the ruler is approximately 1" from the left edge of the fabric (Photo B). Butt a long ruler against the left side of the square, overlapping the fabric edge. Keeping the long ruler in place, remove the square.

**3.** Release the safety guard on the cutter. Keeping the ruler stable with your left hand, hold the cutter blade against the ruler at the bottom of the mat. *Before you cut,* make sure that the fingertips of your left hand are well away from the ruler's edge where that sharp blade is about to go by. Exerting a firm pressure (not too hard, you don't want to wear yourself out), begin rolling the cutter alongside the ruler until it meets the fabric. With a fluid, continuous movement roll the cutter away from you, cutting through all layers of fabric (Photo C). Keep the ruler stable and the blade firmly against the

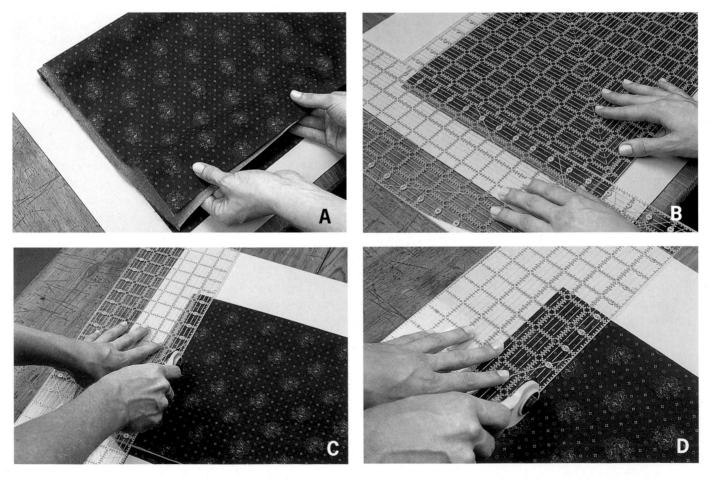

ruler. Do not lift the cutter until it has completely cut through the opposite edge of the fabric.

## First Cut

Rotary cutting often begins with cutting strips of fabric, which are then cut into smaller pieces. In this book, instructions for the first cut (designated by ✱), specify the number and width of strips needed. Unless specified otherwise, cut strips crosswise, selvage to selvage.

Instructions for the second cut (designated by •) state the quantity, size, and unit number of the pieces to cut from these strips. *Seam allowances are included in measurements for all strips and pieces.*

**1.** To measure the strip width, position the ruler on the left edge of the fabric. Carefully align the desired measurement on the ruler with the straight edge of the fabric, checking the line on the ruler from

top to bottom of the fabric. Cut, holding the ruler firmly in place (Photo D). A sharp blade cuts easily through all four layers.

**2.** Examine the cut strip. If the edge of the fabric is not squared up properly, the strip will bow in the middle (Photo E, top). If necessary, square up the edge again and cut another strip.

**3.** Rotary-cut about ½" from the strip ends to remove selvages.

## Second Cut

To cut squares and rectangles from a strip, align the desired ruler measurement with the end of the strip and cut across the strip (Photo F).

For right triangles, instructions may say to cut a square in half or in quarters diagonally (Photo G). This works with rectangles, too. The edges of the square or rectangle are straight grain, so diagonal edge of the triangle is bias. On

these pieces, run a line of stay-stitching ⅛" from the bias edge to keep the fabric from stretching as you work with it.

## Organize Cut Pieces

It's easy to get cut pieces mixed up unless they are neatly stored and organized—especially if, like many people, you are constantly moving your work on and off the dining room table. It's important to be sure which piece is which when you've cut so many.

Place all cut pieces in a zip-top plastic bag, labelled with the unit number (Photo H). You can see the fabric through the bag, which helps you locate pieces as you work. If the sewing takes several weeks, the pieces inside the bags don't get lost, mixed up, or dirty. Keep the bags close to your sewing machine for easy access and remove one piece at a time as you work.

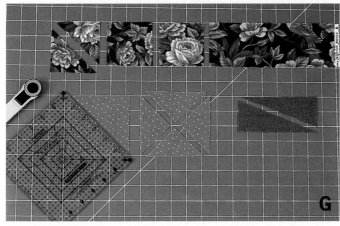

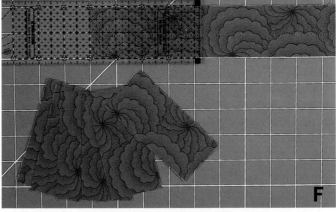

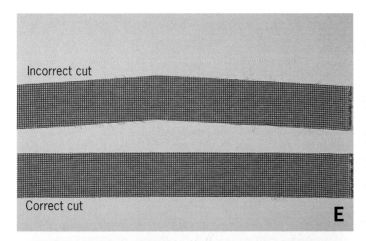

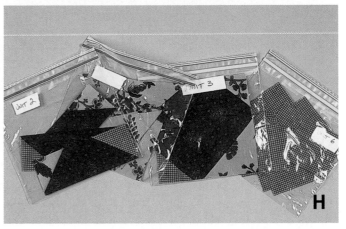

# Machine Piecing

An accurate, consistent ¼" seam allowance is essential for good patchwork. If each seam varies by the tiniest bit, the difference multiplies greatly by the time a block is complete. Before you start a project, be sure your machine is in good order and that you can sew a precise ¼" seam allowance.

## Measure the Seam

On some sewing machines, you can adjust the needle position to make a ¼" seam. If your needle is not adjustable, use a presser foot that is ¼" from the needle to the outside edge of the foot. These feet are available at sewing supply stores.

**Make a Seam Guide.** Another way to gauge a seam is to mark the throat plate. Use a sharp pencil with a ruler to draw a line ¼" from the edge of a piece of paper. Lower the machine needle onto the line, drop the foot, and adjust the paper to parallel the foot (Photo A). Lay masking tape on the throat plate at the edge of the paper; then remove the paper.

Sew a seam, using the guide. Check the seam allowance—if it gets wider or narrower, the tape is not straight. Adjust the tape as needed until the seam is accurate.

## Machine Stitching

Set your sewing machine to 12–14 stitches per inch. Use 100%-cotton or cotton/polyester sewing thread.

Match pieces to be sewn with right sides facing. Sew each seam from cut edge to cut edge of the fabric piece. It is not necessary to backstitch, because most seams will be crossed and held by another.

To piece a block, join small pieces first to form units. Then join units to form larger ones until the block is complete. (See assembly diagrams with quilt instructions.)

**Sew an X.** When triangles are pieced with other units, seams should cross in an X on the back. If the joining seam goes precisely through the center of the X (Photo B), the triangle will have a nice sharp point on the front.

## Press and Pin

To make neat corners and points, seams must meet precisely. Pressing and pinning can help achieve matched seams.

To press, set your iron for cotton. Use an up-and-down motion, lifting the iron from spot to spot. Sliding the iron back and forth can push seams out of shape. First press the seam flat on the wrong side; then open the piece and press the right side.

**Press to One Side.** Press patchwork seam allowances to one side, not open as in dressmaking. If possible, press toward the darker fabric to avoid seam allowances showing through light fabrics.

Press seam allowances in opposite directions from row to row (Photo C). By offsetting seam allowances at each intersection, you reduce the bulk under the patchwork. This is more important than whether seam allowances are pressed toward dark or light.

**Pin Matching.** Use pins to match seam lines. With right sides facing, align opposing seams, nesting seam allowances. On the top piece, push a pin through the seam line

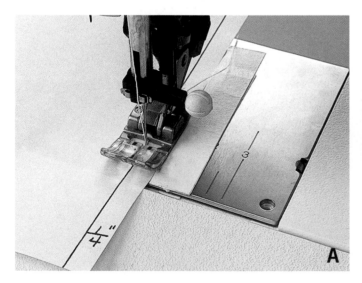

¼" from the edge (Photo D). Then push the pin through the bottom seam and set it. Pin all matching seams; then stitch the joining seam, removing pins as you sew.

## Easing Fullness

Sometimes two units that should be the same size turn out to be slightly different. When joining such units, pin-match the opposing seams so the seam lines with line up. Sew the seam with the shorter piece on top (Easing Diagram). As you sew, the feed dogs ease the fullness on the bottom piece. This is called sewing "with a baggy bottom."

If units are too dissimilar to ease without puckering, check each one to see if the pieces were correctly cut and that the seams are ¼" wide. Remake the unit that varies most from the desired size.

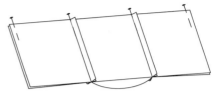

Easing Diagram

C

D

E

## Chain Piecing

Chain piecing is an efficient way to sew many units in one operation, saving time and thread.

Line up several units to be sewn. Sew the first unit as usual, but at the end of the seam do not back-stitch, clip the thread, or lift the presser foot. Instead, feed in the next unit right on the heels of the first. There will be a little twist of thread between units (Photo E).

Sew as many seams as you like on a chain. Keep the chain intact to carry it to the ironing board and clip the threads as you press.

# Quick-Piecing Techniques

You can make any quilt in this book using the methods explained here. These methods are uniquely suited to machine sewing. Combined with rotary cutting, they reduce cutting and sewing time without sacrificing results.

## Strip Piecing

For some projects, you'll join strips of different fabrics to make what is called a strip set. Project directions specify how to cut strips and each strip set is illustrated.

To sew a strip set, match each pair of strips with right sides facing. Stitch through both layers along one long edge (Photo A). When sewing multiple strips in a set, practice "anti-directional" stitching to keep strips straight. As you add strips, sew each new seam in the *opposite* direction from the last one (Diagram 1). This distributes tension evenly in both directions and keeps the strip set from getting warped and wobbly.

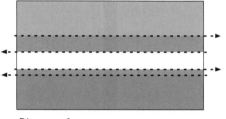

Diagram 1

**Cut Segments.** After a strip set is assembled and pressed, you will cut it into segments. Use a ruler to measure; then make appropriate crosswise cuts to get individual segments (Photo B). Each segment becomes a unit in the design.

This technique is fast and accurate because you assemble and press a unit *before* it is cut from the strip set.

## Diagonal Corners

This technique turns squares into sewn triangles with just a stitch and a snip. It is particularly helpful if the corner triangle is very small, because it's easier to cut and handle a square than a small triangle. By sewing squares to squares, you don't have to guess where seam allowances meet, which can be difficult with triangles. The ease and speed with which you'll sew these corners is delightful.

Project instructions give the size of the fabric pieces needed. The base fabric is either a square or a

A

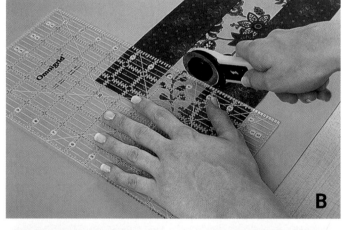

B

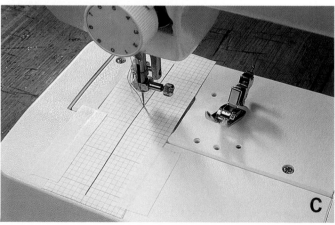

C

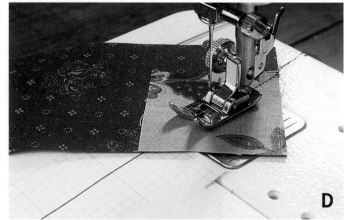

D

rectangle, but the contrasting corner always starts out as a square.

**Make a Seam Guide.** Before sewing, make a seam guide that will enable you to machine-stitch diagonal lines without having to mark the fabric beforehand. (Or see Mail-Order Resources, page 24, for information on purchasing The Angler from Pam Bono Designs.)

Draw a line on graph paper. Place the paper on the sewing machine and bring the needle down through the line (Photo C). Remove the foot if necessary for a good viewpoint. Use a ruler to verify that the line is parallel to the needle. Tape the paper to the throat plate. Trim the paper to leave the needle and presser foot unobstructed.

**1.** With right sides facing, match the small square to one corner of the base fabric.

**2.** Align the top tip of the small square with the needle and the bottom tip with the seam guide. Stitch

a seam from tip to tip, keeping the bottom tip of the square in line with the seam guide (Photo D).

**3.** Press the small square in half at the seam (Photo E).

**4.** Trim the seam allowance to ¼" (Photo F).

Repeat the procedure to add a diagonal corner to two, three, or four corners of the base fabric.

This technique is the same when you add a diagonal corner to a strip set—treat the base fabric as one piece, even if it is already pieced.

When sewing a large diagonal corner, draw or press a stitching line through the center of the corner square.

## Diagonal Ends

This method joins two rectangles on the diagonal and eliminates the difficulty of measuring and cutting a trapezoid. It is similar to the diagonal-corner technique, but

here you work with two rectangles. Project instructions specify the size of each rectangle.

To sew diagonal ends, make a seam guide for your machine as described for diagonal corners.

**1.** Place rectangles perpendicular to each other with right sides facing, matching corners to be sewn.

**2.** Before you sew, pin on the stitching line and check the right side to see if the line is angled in the desired direction.

**3.** Position the rectangles under the needle, leading with the top edge. Sew a diagonal seam to the opposite edge (Photo G).

**4.** Check the right side to see that the seam is angled correctly. Then press the seam and trim excess fabric from the seam allowance.

**5.** As noted in Step 2, the direction of the seam makes a difference (Photo H). Make mirror-image units with this in mind, or you can put different ends on the same strip.

E

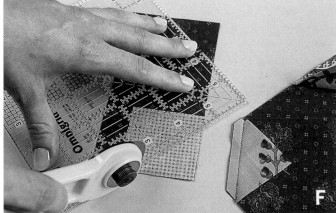

F

G

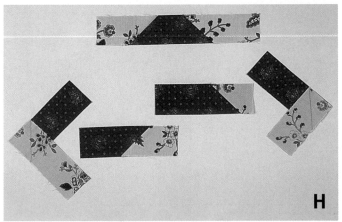

H

# Quick-Pieced Triangles

The triangle is a basic element of patchwork. But cutting and sewing triangles pose unique problems for quilters. These quick-piecing techniques eliminate those difficulties and enable you to create many pre-sewn units with one process—a real time-saver when you're making a large quilt.

## Triangle-Squares

Many patchwork designs are made by joining two contrasting triangles to make a square. I use the grid method of sewing triangle-squares. In these projects, instructions describe a grid that is the basis for making a lot of triangle-squares quickly and easily.

Cutting instructions specify two fabric squares or rectangles for each grid. Spray both pieces with spray starch to keep the fabric from distorting during marking and stitching. Accuracy is important in every step—if your marking, cutting, sewing, and pressing are not precise, your triangle-squares may be lopsided or the wrong size.

**Marking the Grid.** For marking, use a see-through ruler and a fine-tipped fabric pen—a pencil drags on the fabric, making an inaccurate line and stretching the fabric.

**1.** Let's say, for example, instructions call for a 2 x 4 grid of 2⅛" squares. This describes a grid of eight squares, drawn two down and four across (Diagram 1). Draw the grid on the *wrong* side of the lighter fabric. The fabric size allows a margin of at least 1" around the grid, so align the ruler parallel to one side of the fabric, 1" from the edge, and draw the first line.

**2.** Draw the second line exactly 2⅛" from the first. Continue in this manner, using the ruler's markings to position each new line. Take care to make lines accurately parallel and/or perpendicular—the size and shape of your triangle-squares depend on it.

**3.** When the grid is complete, draw a diagonal line through each square (Diagram 2). Alternate direction of diagonals in adjacent squares.

**Stitching the Grid.** With right sides facing, match all edges of the two fabric pieces.

**1.** Start at an outside point near the top left corner of the grid (blue arrow, Diagram 3).

**2.** Sewing a ¼" seam allowance, stitch alongside the diagonals

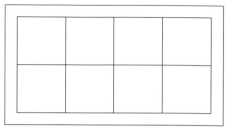

Diagram 1

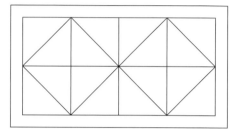

Diagram 2

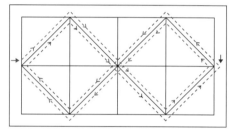

Diagram 3

indicated by the blue line (Diagram 3). At the end of one line, stitch into the margin as shown. Keep the needle down, but raise the foot and pivot the fabric so you can stitch along the next line. When you return to the starting point, you'll have stitched on one side of all diagonal lines.

A

B

**3.** Begin again at another outside point (red arrow on sample grid). Repeat stitching on the opposite side of the diagonal lines.

**Cutting and Pressing.** When the grid is completely stitched, press the fabric to smooth the stitching.

**1.** Rotary-cut on *all* the drawn lines to separate the triangle-squares (Photo A). Each grid square yields two triangle-squares, so our previous example would produce 16 units.

**2.** Press each triangle-square open, pressing the seam allowance toward the darker fabric.

**3.** Trim points from ends of each seam allowance (Photo B).

In our example, we're working toward a desired finished size of 1¼" square. The grid squares are drawn ⅞" larger than the finished size. After the grid is sewn, the cut and pressed square is ½" larger than the finished size (1¾").

## Four-Triangle Squares

You can quick-piece squares made of four triangles using an expanded version of the grid method above that produces two-triangle squares. Marking and stitching the grid is the same, except that you start with grid squares 1¼" larger than the desired finished size.

Project instructions specify how to mark and sew a grid and how many triangle-squares will result.

**1.** On the wrong side of one triangle-square, draw a diagonal line through the center, bisecting the seam (Photo C).

**2.** Match the marked square with another triangle-square, with right sides facing. Position the squares with *contrasting* fabrics together (Photo D).

**3.** Stitch ¼" seam on both sides of the drawn diagonal line (Photo E).

**4.** Cut units apart on the drawn line (Photo F). Press units open and trim points from seam allowances.

 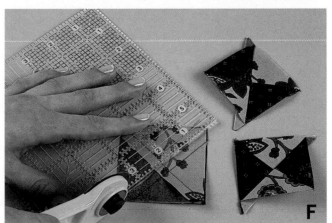

# Joining Blocks

The easiest way to join blocks is in rows, either diagonally, vertically, or horizontally. All the quilts in this book are pieced in this manner.

## Sew by the Row

Lay out your blocks on the floor or a large table. Identify the pieces in each row and verify the position of each block. Moving blocks around to find the best balance of color and value can be great fun. Don't start sewing until you're happy with the placement of each block.

**Pin-match.** As you join blocks in each row, pick up one block at a time to avoid confusion. Pin-match adjoining seams. Re-press a seam if necessary to offset seam allowances. If some blocks are larger than others, pinning may help determine where easing is required. A blast of steam from the iron may help fit the blocks together.

**Pressing.** When a row is assembled, press seam allowances between blocks in the same direction. For the next row, press seam allowances in the opposite direction (Diagram 1).

In an alternate set, straight or diagonal, press seam allowances between blocks toward setting squares or triangles (Diagram 2). This creates the least bulk and always results in opposing seam allowances when adjacent rows are joined.

Sashing eliminates cares about opposing seam allowances. Assemble horizontal rows with sashing strips between blocks; then press the new seam allowances toward the sashing (Diagram 3). If necessary, ease the block to match the length of the sashing strip. Assemble the quilt top with rows of sashing between block rows, always pressing seam allowances toward the sashing strips.

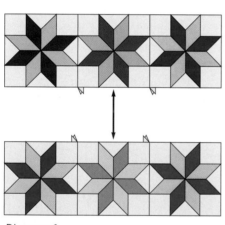

Diagram 1

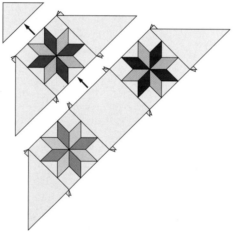

Diagram 2

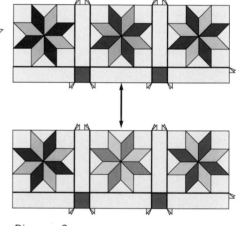

Diagram 3

# Mail-Order Resources

The Angler™ (pictured on page 10) is a sewing guide designed especially for the quick-piecing techniques described in this book. Easy to use with any sewing machine, it is available from *Pam Bono Designs* at www.pambonodesigns.com or telephone 800-970-5426.

Quiltmaking supplies are available at many craft and fabric stores, especially quilting specialty shops.

Consult your local telephone directory to find a shop in your area.

If you prefer to have things delivered to your door, order supplies from a mail-order source or internet web site. These are good suppliers of fabric, batting, stencils, notions, books, and other quilting supplies. Each has a toll-free telephone numbers and will mail you a catalog at no charge.

*Keepsake Quilting*
800-865-9458
www.keepsakequilting.com

*The Quilt Farm*
800-435-6201
www.quiltfarm.com

*Hancock's of Paducah*
800-845-8723
www.hancocks-paducah.com

# Borders

Most quilts have a wide border or several narrow ones that frame the design. In this book, all quilts are made with square border corners (not miters). Before you sew , measure and trim borders to fit properly.

## Measuring

It's common for one side of a quilt top to be a slightly different measurement than its opposite side. No matter how careful your piecing, tiny variables add up. You want to sew borders of equal length to opposite sides to square up the quilt.

Cutting instructions for borders include extra length to allow for piecing variations.

**1.** Measure the quilt from top to bottom *through the middle* of the quilt (Photo A). (For a large quilt, use a 10-foot measuring tape.) Trim both side border strips to this measurement. Sew borders to quilt sides, easing as needed.

**2.** For top and bottom borders, measure from side to side through the middle of the quilt (Photo B). Trim and sew borders as before.

This example joins side borders first, and then top and bottom borders. Sometimes it is practical to reverse the sequence. Instructions specify the order in which you should sew borders.

## Contrasting Corners

If you plan to add a contrasting corner, measure and trim all four borders *before* sewing side borders to the quilt. Stitch a contrasting block to the ends of the top and bottom border strips. When sewn to the quilt, the seams of the blocks should align with the side border seams.

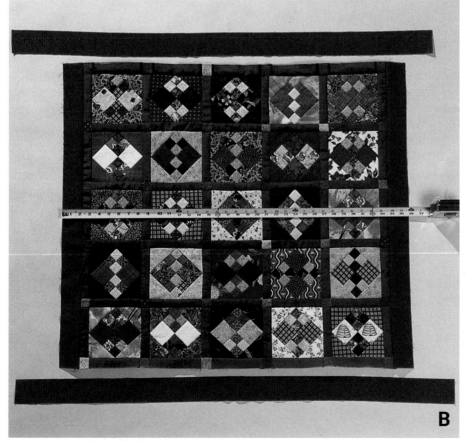

# Getting Ready to Quilt

The quilting design is an important part of any quilt, so choose it with care. The hours you spend connecting the layers of your quilt create shadows and depths that bring the quilt to life, so make the design count.

## Marking

Most quilters mark a quilting design on the quilt top before it is layered and basted. To do this, you need marking pencils, a long ruler or yardstick, stencils for quilting motifs, and a smooth, hard surface on which to work. Press the quilt top thoroughly before you begin.

**Test Markers.** Before using any marker, test it on scraps to be sure marks will wash out. Don't use just any pencil because that's what your grandmother used. There are many

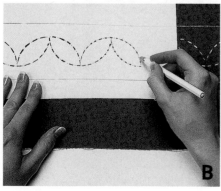

fine-line pencils and chalk markers available that are designed to wash out. No matter what marking tool you use, lightly drawn lines are easier to remove than heavy ones.

**Stencils.** Many beautiful quilting designs are available in stencils (see Mail-Order Resources, page 24). To transfer a design to the quilt top, position the stencil on the quilt and mark through the slits in the stencil (Photo A). Connect the lines after removing the stencil.

To make a stencil, trace a design onto freezer paper or template plastic. Use a craft knife to cut little slots along the lines of the design. Place the stencil on the fabric and mark in each slot (Photo B).

**Marking a Grid.** Many quilts feature a grid of squares or diamonds as a quilting design in the background areas of the quilt. Use a rotary-cutting ruler to mark a grid, starting at one border seam and working toward the opposite edge. Mark parallel lines, spacing them as desired (usually 1" apart), until background areas are marked as desired.

**Quilting Without Marking.** Some quilts are quilted in-the-ditch (right in the seams) or outline-quilted (¼" from the seam line). These methods do not require marking.

If you are machine quilting, use the edge of your presser foot and the seam line as guides for outline quilting. If you are hand quilting, use narrow drafting tape as a guideline between the seam and the quilting line.

Another option is stippling—free-style, meandering lines worked closely together to fill open areas. This can be done by hand or by machine, letting your needle go where the mood takes you.

## Making a Backing

The backing should be at least 3" larger than the quilt top on all sides. For quilts up to 40" wide, use a single length of 45"-wide cotton fabric. For a larger quilt, a sensible option is to use 90"- or 108"-wide fabric—it's easier and often saves a lot of waste. But the selection is limited for wide fabrics, so most quilters will piece the backing from 45"-wide fabric.

Most quilt backs have two or three seams to avoid having a seam in the center of the quilt (Backing Options Diagram). Trim selvages and follow instructions for assembling the backing. For large quilts, you will join two or three lengths of fabric to make a backing about 3" larger all around than the quilt top. Press seam allowances open.

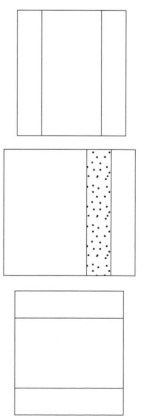

Backing Options Diagram

Choose a light backing for light-colored quilts, because you don't want a dark color to show through. If you want to show off your stitching, select a plain fabric. If you don't want to showcase your quilting, choose a busy print for the backing as camouflage or piece the backing from assorted scraps.

## Batting

When selecting batting, consider loft, washability, and fiber content. Read the package label to decide if a particular batt suits your needs.

Precut batting comes in five sizes. The precut batt listed for each quilt in this book is the most suitable for the quilt's finished size. Some stores sell 90"-wide batting by the yard, which might be more practical for your quilt.

**Loft.** Loft is the thickness of the batting. For a flat look, choose low-loft cotton batting. Polyester batting is usually a medium loft suitable for most quilts. Thick batting is difficult to quilt, but it's nice for a puffy tied comforter.

**Cotton.** Cotton batting has the flat, thin look of an antique. Cotton shrinks slightly when washed, giving it that wrinkled look characteristic of old quilts, so always wash quilts with cotton batting in cold water to prevent excessive shrinking. Cotton batting should be closely quilted, with quilting lines no more than 1" apart.

**Polyester.** Look for the word "bonded" when selecting polyester batting. Bonding keeps the loft of the batt uniform and reduces the effects of bearding (the migration of loose fibers through the quilt top). Polyester batting is easy to stitch and can be machine washed with little shrinkage. Avoid bonded batts that feel stiff.

## Layering

A quilt is a three-layer sandwich held together with quilting stitches. Once your quilt top is complete, it's time to layer it with the batting and backing.

Prepare a large surface where you can spread out—a large table, two tables pushed together, or a clean floor. Take the batting out of its package and unfold it to let it "relax" for a few hours.

Place the backing right side down on your work surface. Secure the edges of the backing to the work surface with masking tape, keeping it wrinkle-free and slightly taut. If the quilt hangs over the table sides, start in the center and work in sections.

Center the batting on the backing, smoothing it as you go (Photo C). Trim batting to match the backing. Then center the ironed quilt top right side up on the batting. Make sure edges of the backing and quilt top are parallel.

## Basting

Basting keeps layers from shifting during quilting. Baste with a long needle and white sewing thread. Start in the center and baste a line of stitches to each corner, making a large X. Then baste parallel lines 6"–8" apart. Finish with a line of basting ¼" from each edge.

**Safety Pins.** Some quilters use safety pins for basting. This is helpful for machine quilting so there are no basting threads to catch on the presser foot. Use 1" nickel-plated safety pins, which can stay in the quilt for a long time without rusting.

Place pins every 2"–3" all over the quilt. Don't close the pins until they are all in place, as the closing action can pucker the backing as you go. When the pins are all in place, remove the masking tape at the quilt edges. Gently, but firmly, tug the backing as you close the safety pins so that you do not pin any pleats underneath.

C

# Quilting

Quilting is the process of stitching the layers of a quilt together, by hand or machine. The choice of hand or machine quilting depends on the design, intended use of the quilt, and how much time you have. Both techniques are functional and attractive.

## Hand Quilting

To quilt by hand, you need a quilting hoop or a frame, quilting thread (which is heavier than sewing thread), quilting needles, and a thimble. If you're not used to a thimble, you'll find it a must for quilting to prevent the needle from digging into your fingertip.

**Preparation.** Put the basted quilt in a hoop or frame. Start with a size 7 or 8 "between," or quilting needle. (As your skill increases, try a shorter between to make smaller stitches. A higher number indicates a shorter needle.) Thread a needle with 18" of quilting thread and make a small knot in the end.

**The Stitch.** The quilting stitch is a small running stitch that goes through all three layers of a quilt.

Stitches should be small (8–10 per inch), straight, and evenly spaced. The number of stitches per inch is less important than the uniformity of stitching. Don't worry if you take only five or six stitches per inch—concentrate on even and straight; tiny comes with practice.

**Pop the Knot.** Insert the needle through the top about 1" from the point where the line of quilting will start. Slide the needle through the batting, without piercing the backing, and pull it out where the first stitch will be. Pull the thread taut and tug gently until the knot pops through the top and lodges in the batting (Knot Diagram). If it does not pop through, use your needle to gently separate the fabric threads to let the knot through.

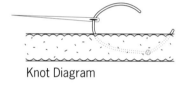

Knot Diagram

**Rock the Needle.** To make a stitch, first insert the needle straight down (Photo A). With your other hand under the quilt, feel for the needle point as it pierces the backing. With practice, you'll be able to find the point without pricking your finger.

Roll the needle to a nearly horizontal position. Use the thumb of your sewing hand and the underneath hand to pinch a little hill in the fabric as you push the needle back through the quilt top.

Rock the needle back to an upright position to take the next stitch in the same manner. Load 3–4 stitches on the needle before pulling it through (Photo B).

**Ending a Thread.** Quilt until you have 6" of thread left. Then tie a knot in the thread close to the quilt surface. Take a backstitch and tug the thread to pop the knot into the batting as you did before. Run the thread through the batting and out the top to clip it.

## Machine Quilting

Choose a small project for your first effort, because the bulk of a large quilt is difficult to manage. Plan simple quilting with continuous straight lines and few changes of direction. Good choices are outline or in-the-ditch quilting and all-over grids. When you are comfortable with machine quilting, try free-motion quilting and more complex designs.

**Preparation.** For quilting straight lines, use an even-feed presser foot or a walking foot. You can

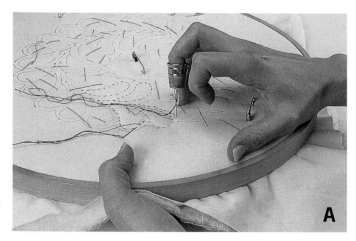

A

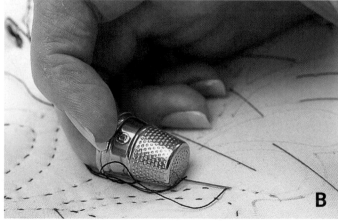

B

# Tying

If you don't have the time for quilting or if you just want a different look, then tying is a fast and easy way to secure the quilt layers. It's the best way to work with thick batting for puffy comforters.

For ties, use pearl cotton, lightweight yarn, floss, or narrow ribbon—anything that will stay in place once tied. You'll also need a sharp needle with an eye large enough to accommodate the ties.

Thread the needle with about 6" of the tie material. Do not knot the ends. Starting in the center of your basted quilt top, take a small stitch through all three layers. Center a 3"-long tail on each side of the stitch (Diagram 1). Tie the tails in a tight double knot (Diagram 2).

Make a tie at least every 6" across the surface of the quilt. Trim the tails of all knots to a uniform length.

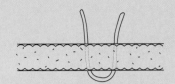

Diagram 1

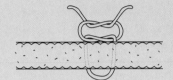

Diagram 2

machine-quilt without this foot, but the work is much easier *with* it.

Thread the machine with .004 monofilament "invisible" thread or regular sewing thread in a color that coordinates with the quilt. For the bobbin, use sewing thread that matches the backing. Set the stitch length at 8–10 stitches per inch. Adjust the tension so that the bobbin thread does not pull to the top.

Roll the sides of the quilt to the middle and secure the rolls with clips. If you're working on a large quilt, extend your work area by setting up tables to the left and behind the machine to support the quilt while you work.

**Straight Lines.** Work in long, continuous lines as much as possible. The block seam lines form a grid of long lines across the quilt—quilt these first, starting at the top center and stitching to the opposite edge. Quilt the next line from bottom to top. Alternating the direction of quilting lines keeps the layers from shifting.

Use your hands to spread the fabric slightly. Gently push the quilt toward the foot to reduce the drag on the fabric (Photo C).

Quilt vertical lines on half the quilt, unrolling it until you reach the edge. Remove the quilt from the machine and reroll it so you can quilt the other half. When all vertical lines are done, reroll the quilt again in the other direction to quilt horizontal lines in the same manner.

**Free-motion Quilting.** Following a curved quilting design is a skill that takes practice to master. Start with a small project that is easy to handle.

Attach a darning foot or free-motion quilting foot to your machine. Lower the feed dogs or cover them. You don't need to adjust stitch length, because you control the stitches by manually moving the fabric.

Position your hands on each side of the presser foot so you can maneuver the fabric (Photo D). To make even stitches, run the machine at a slow, steady speed and move the fabric smoothly and evenly so that the needle follows the design. Do not rotate the quilt; simply move the fabric forward, backward, and side to side.

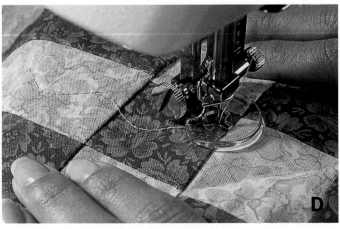

# Binding

These instructions are for double-fold straight-grain binding. Doubled binding is stronger than one layer, so it better protects the edges, where a quilt suffers the most wear. We like straight-grain binding because it is easier to make than bias binding and requires less fabric.

## Making Continuous Binding

Each project specifies the number of cross-grain strips to cut for binding. Cut 3" wide, these strips result in a finished binding ½"–⅝" wide. Make wider binding when using thick batting.

To join two strips end-to-end, match the ends perpendicular to each other with right sides facing. Stitch a diagonal seam across the corner (Photo A). Trim seam allowances to ¼" and press them open.

Join strips end-to-end in this manner to make one continuous strip that is the length specified in the project instructions.

## Applying Binding

**1.** With wrong sides facing, press the binding in half along the length of the strip (Photo B).

**2.** With raw edges aligned, position the binding on the front of the quilt top, in the middle of any side. Leave 3" of binding free before the point where you begin (Photo C).

**3.** Stitch through all layers with a ¼" seam. Stop stitching ¼" from the quilt corner and backstitch (Photo D). (Placing a pin at the ¼" point beforehand will show you where to stop.) Remove the quilt from the machine.

**4.** Rotate the quilt a quarter turn. Fold the binding straight up, away from the corner, and make a 45°-angle fold (Photo E).

**5.** Bring the binding straight down in line with the next edge, leaving the top fold even with the raw edge

of the previously sewn side. Begin stitching at the top edge, sewing through all layers (Photo F). Stitch all corners in this manner.

**6.** Stop stitching as you approach the beginning point. Fold the 3" tail

of binding over on itself and pin (Photo G). The end of the binding will overlap this folded section. Continue stitching through all layers to 1" beyond the folded tail. Trim any extra binding.

**7.** Trim the batting and backing nearly even with the seam allowance, leaving a little extra to fill out the binding.

**8.** Fold the binding over the seam allowance to the back. When turned, the beginning fold conceals the raw end of the binding (Photo H).

**9.** Blindstitch the folded edge of the binding to the backing fabric (Photo I). Fold a miter into the binding at back corners.

# Care and Cleaning

A quilt's greatest enemies are light and dirt. To keep your quilt in prime condition would mean never using it. But then you'd never get to see it, enjoy it, or share it. Your quilt can last a lifetime if you treat it with care.

## Safekeeping

A quilt is bound to fade over time. But you can reduce the risks by keeping the quilt away from strong sunlight and storing it properly when not in use.

Alternate your quilts every few months to reduce exposure. Store an unused quilt—with as few folds as possible—in a cotton pillowcase. Don't use plastic bags, which trap moisture. To prevent permanent creases, stored quilts should occasionally be aired and refolded. Wads of acid-free paper inside the folds also discourage creases.

## Washing

Wash quilts infrequently. A good airing is usually all that's needed to freshen a quilt. Vacuuming with a hose removes dust. Dry cleaning is bad for quilts because it leaves harmful chemicals in the fabric.

When you must wash a quilt, use a mild soap such as Ensure or Orvis Paste. These soaps (as well as acid-free paper) are available at quilt shops and from mail-order resources (see page 24).

**A Good Soak.** If fabrics are pre-washed, you can wash your quilt in the washing machine if the machine is large enough. Wash an extra-large quilt in the bathtub, letting it soak in warm soapy water for about 15 minutes. Rinse repeatedly to remove the soap.

**Drying.** Squeeze as much water out of the quilt as possible, but don't wring or twist it. Carefully lift the quilt out of the washer or tub, supporting its weight with your arms so that no part of the quilt is pulled or stressed. Place the quilt flat between two layers of towels, and roll it up to remove as much moisture as possible.

Putting a wet quilt in a dryer is not recommended, because heat and agitation can damage fabric and batting.

Dry a damp quilt flat on a floor or table. If you want to dry it outside, pick a shady spot on a sunny day, and place the quilt between sheets to protect it. When the quilt is almost dry, and if it isn't too large, you can put it in the dryer on a cool setting to smooth out wrinkles and fluff it up.

## Hanging

If you want to hang your quilt on a wall, make a hanging sleeve as described on page 138. Do not use pushpins or tacks to hang a quilt, because the metal can leave rust stains on the fabric. Also, the weight of the quilt pulls against the pins, distorting the edge of the quilt and damaging the fibers.

# Measuring Metric and Computing Fractions

If you are accustomed to the metric system, this chart will be helpful in establishing conversions for common measurements. Or, if you are buying fabric in the U.S.A., use the decimals column and your calculator to figure cost. For example, if you're buying 1⅜ yards of $8.50-a-yard fabric, multiply $8.50 by 1.375 to get a cost of $11.69.

| Inches | Fractions | Decimals | Meters |
|--------|-----------|----------|--------|
| ¼" | | .25" | .635 cm |
| ½" | | .5" | 1.27 cm |
| ¾" | | .75" | 1.91 cm |
| 1" | | 1.0" | 2.54 cm |
| 4½" | ⅛ yard | .125 yard | 11.43 cm |
| 9" | ¼ yard | .25 yard | 22.86 cm |
| 13½" | ⅜ yard | .375 yard | .3375 m |
| 18" | ½ yard | .5 yard | .45 m |
| 22½" | ⅝ yard | .625 yard | .563 m |
| 27" | ¾ yard | .75 yard | .675 m |
| 31½" | ⅞ yard | .875 yard | .788 m |
| 36" | 1 yard | 1 yard | .9 m |
| 39⅜" | 1 1/10 yards | 1.1 yards | 1 m |

| When you know: | Multiply by: | To find: |
|----------------|--------------|----------|
| inches | 2.54 | centimeters (cm) |
| yards | .9 | meters (m) |

# ROTARY CUTTER QUILT
# COLLECTION

# How to Use These Instructions

The following notes explain how these instructions are organized. You'll find the quiltmaking easier if you keep these tips in mind.

✻ At the beginning of each project, you'll find a list of quick-piecing techniques used to make that quilt. Before beginning the project, see *Basics and Beyond* for general instructions on each technique.

✻ A color key accompanies each materials list, matching each fabric with the color-coded illustrations given with the project directions.

✻ Cutting instructions are given for each fabric. The first cut, indicated by a ✻, is usually a specified number of crossgrain strips.

✻ Second cuts, indicated by a •, specify how to cut those strips into smaller pieces. The identification of each piece follows in parentheses, consisting of the block letter and unit number that correspond to the assembly diagrams. For pieces used in more than one unit, several unit numbers may be given.

✻ Organize cut pieces in zip-top bags and label each bag with the appropriate unit numbers. This avoids confusion and keeps a lot of pieces stored safely until they're needed.

✻ Large pieces such as sashings and borders are usually cut first to be sure you have enough fabric.

✻ To reduce waste, you may be instructed to cut some pieces from a first-cut strip and then cut that strip down to a narrower width to cut additional pieces.

✻ Cutting lists identify triangle-square units in the same way as for other pieces, but the piece cut is large enough to sew a grid as directed in the project instructions. Each piece allows a margin of 1" of fabric around the grid.

✻ Cutting instructions are given for the whole quilt as shown. If you want to make just one block, see information at right.

✻ Cutting and piecing instructions are given in a logical step-by-step progression. Follow this order in all cases to avoid confusion.

✻ Every project has one or more block designs. Instructions include block illustrations that show the fabric colors and the numbered units.

✻ Individual units are assembled first, using one or more of the quick-piecing techniques described in *Basics and Beyond*.

✻ Strip-set illustrations show the size of the segments to be cut from that strip set. The unit number of the segment is also shown. Keep strip-set segments in a labelled zip-top bag as for other units.

✻ An assembly diagram is given for each block. Each numbered unit is isolated, with + symbols indicating how units are joined. Follow the instructions to join units in the proper sequence. Some blocks are further divided into sections, which are joined according to instructions.

# Rules of Thumb

Here are a few things to keep in mind when making the quilts in this collection. For more detailed quilt-making information, turn to the *Basics and Beyond* chapter, which begins on page 10.

✻ Yardages are based on 45"-wide fabric, allowing for up to 4% shrinkage. 100% cotton fabric is recommended for the quilt top and for backing. Wash, dry, and press fabrics before cutting.

✻ Materials are listed to make each quilt as shown. Select similar fabrics or fabrics in the colors of your choice in the quantities stated.

✻ Read all instructions for the selected project before you begin to cut.

✻ Cut pieces from each fabric in the order in which they are listed, cutting largest pieces first. This ensures efficient use of yardage.

✻ All seam allowances are ¼". Seam allowances are included in all stated measurements and cutting instructions.

✻ Store cut pieces in labelled zip-top bags to avoid getting them mixed up.

✻ The quilts in this book can be made in a relatively short time because of the methods used. But everyone works at his or her own speed—don't feel like you're racing the clock to get your quilt finished. Relax and enjoy the creative process.

✳ Each unit in the assembly diagram is numbered. The main part of the unit is indicated with the number only. A diagonal line represents a seam where a diagonal corner or end is attached. Each diagonal piece is numbered with the main unit number plus a letter (such as 1a).

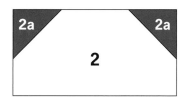

✳ Some units have multiple diagonal corners or ends. When these are the same size and are cut from the same fabric, the identifying letter is the same. But if the unit has multiple diagonal pieces that are different in size and/or color, the letters are different. These pieces are joined to the main unit in alphabetical order.

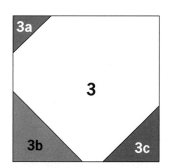

✳ Triangle-squares are shown as assembled, with the unit number in the center of the square.

✳ Practice the quick-cutting and quick-piecing methods with scrap fabrics before beginning a project. Refer to assembly diagrams frequently, following the unit identification system carefully. Organizing your work as suggested will save time and avoid confusion.

✳ Piecing instructions are given for making one block. Make the number of blocks stated in the project instructions to complete the project as shown.

## How to Make One Block

Cutting instructions are given for making the quilt as shown. But sometimes you want to make just one block for a project of your own design. What then?

All you have to do is count. Or divide, if you prefer.

With each cutting list is an illustration of the block(s). The unit numbers in the cutting list correspond to the units in the illustration. Count how many of each unit are in the block illustration. Instead of cutting the number shown in the cutting list, cut the number you need for one block.

If you prefer, you can figure it out just from the cutting list. If the quilt shown has 20 blocks, for example, then divide each quantity by 20 to determine how many pieces are needed for one block.

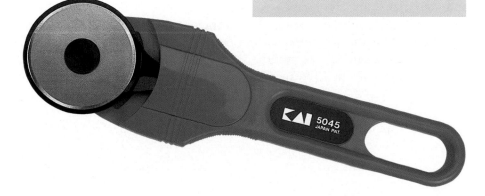

# Chains of *Love*

*The Irish Chain is a best-loved quilt design, and this one takes tradition to heart. Select a luscious floral print for the main fabric and then choose four more fabrics to coordinate.*

## Finished Size
Quilt: 82" x 110"
Blocks: 18 heart blocks, 14" square
       17 chain blocks, 14" square

## Quick-Piecing Techniques
Strip Piecing (see page 20)
Diagonal Corners (see page 20)

## Materials

| | | |
|---|---|---|
| Fabric I (dark plum large print) | 2 yards |
| Fabric II (green print) | 1⅞ yards |
| Fabric III (plum print or solid) | 2¾ yards |
| Fabric IV (pink print) | 2¾ yards |
| Fabric V (white-on-white print) | 2⅜ yards |
| Backing fabric | 6½ yards |
| Precut batting | 90" x 108" |

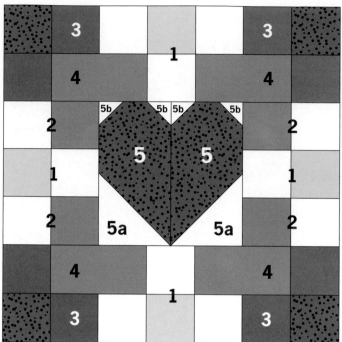

Block A—Make 18.

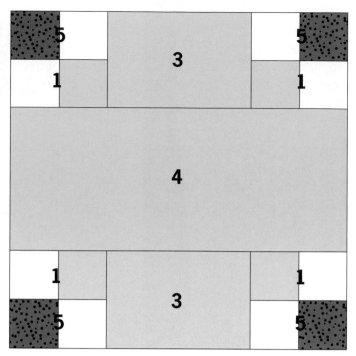

Block B—Make 17.

## Cutting

Cut all strips crossgrain, from selvage to selvage. For best use of yardage, cut pieces in order listed. See diagrams to identify strip sets.

### From Fabric I (dark plum), cut:

* Three 6½"-wide strips. From these, cut:
  * Thirty-six 3½" x 6½" (A5).
* Seventeen 2½"-wide strips. Set aside 10 strips for strip sets 3 and 5. From remaining strips, cut:
  * Six 2½" x 22½" (Border 2).
  * Four 2½" x 20½" (Border 3).
  * Four 2½" x 18½" (Border 1).

### From Fabric II (green), cut:

* Twenty-four 2½"-wide strips. Set aside 10 strips for strip sets 3 and 4. From remaining strips, cut:
  * Fourteen 2½" x 26½" (Border 4).

### From Fabric III (plum), cut:

* Five 4½"-wide strips for Strip Set 4.
* Fifteen 2½"-wide strips. Set aside five strips for Strip Set 2 and 10 strips for outer border.
* Ten 3"-wide strips for binding.

### From Fabric IV (pink), cut:

* Ten 2½"-wide strips for strip sets 1 and 6.
* Ten 6½"-wide strips. From these, cut:
  * Seventeen 6½" x 14½" (B4).
  * Thirty-four 4½" x 6½" (B3).

### From Fabric V (white), cut:

* Twenty-five 2½"-wide strips for strip sets 1, 2, 3, 5, and 6. From ends of 10 of these strips, cut:
  * Ten 2½" squares for middle border.
* Three 3½"-wide strips. From these, cut:
  * Thirty-six 3½" squares (A5a).
* Three 1½"-wide strips. From these, cut:
  * Seventy-two 1½" squares (A5b).

## Units for Block A

Refer to strip set diagrams and Block A Assembly Diagram throughout to identify units. Store units cut from each strip set in labelled zip-top bags. In block assembly, unit numbers will be the same as strip set numbers.

**1.** For Strip Set 1, join strips of fabrics IV and V as shown. Make nine of Strip Set 1. Press seam allowances toward Fabric IV. From these strip sets, cut 140 2½"-wide segments for Unit 1.

**2.** For Strip Set 2, join strips of fabrics III and V as shown. Make five of Strip Set 2. Press seam allowances toward Fabric III. From these strip sets, cut seventy-two 2½"-wide segments for Unit 2.

**3.** For Strip Set 3, join strips of fabrics I, II, and V as shown. Make five of Strip Set 3. Press seam allowances toward Fabric II. From these strip sets, cut seventy-two 2½"-wide segments for Unit 3.

**4.** For Strip Set 4, join strips of fabrics II (2½"-wide) and III (4½"-wide) as shown. Make five of Strip Set 4. Press seam allowances toward Fabric II. From these strip sets, cut seventy-two 2½"-wide segments for Unit 4.

**5.** Use diagonal-corner technique to make two of Unit 5. These are mirror images, so be careful to position each 5a piece in opposite corners as shown.

## Block A Assembly

Assemble this block in sections X, Y, and Z. Each completed section should measure approximately 14½" wide. Refer to Block A Assembly Diagram throughout.

### Sections X and Z

**1.** For Section X, join two pair of units 3 and 4 as shown. Sew combined units to opposite sides of one Unit 1.

**2.** Repeat to make Section Z.

### Section Y

**1.** Join mirror-image Unit 5s to make a heart.

**2.** Sew one of Unit 2 to opposite sides of Unit 1. Make two 2/1/2 units.

**3.** Join 2/1/2 units to opposite sides of heart unit.

### Assembly

Join sections X, Y, and Z to complete block. Make 18 of Block A.

*(continued)*

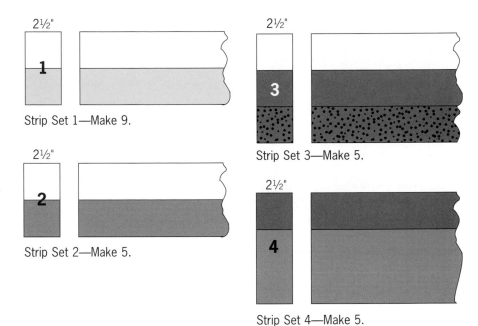

Strip Set 1—Make 9.

Strip Set 2—Make 5.

Strip Set 3—Make 5.

Strip Set 4—Make 5.

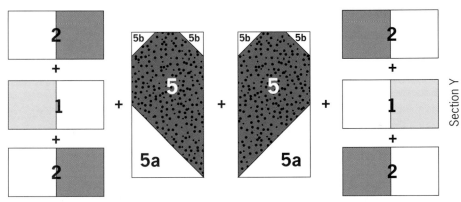

Section X

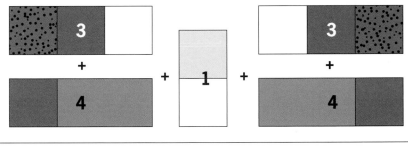

Section Y

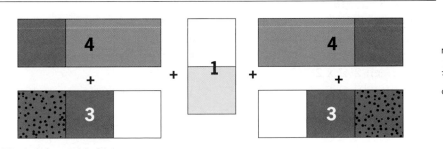

Section Z

Block A Assembly Diagram

## Block B Assembly

Assemble this block in sections X, Y, and Z. Section Y is a single piece, Unit 4. Each completed section should measure 14½" wide. Refer to Block B Assembly Diagram throughout.

### Sections X and Z

**1.** For Strip Set 5, join strips of fabrics I and V as shown. Press seam allowances toward Fabric I. Make four of Strip Set 5. From these strip sets, cut sixty-eight 2½"-wide segments for Unit 5.

**2.** For Section X, join two pair of units 1 and 5 as shown. Sew combined units to opposite sides of one Unit 3.

**3.** Repeat to make Section Z.

### Assembly

Join sections X, Y, and Z to complete block. Make 17 of Block B.

## Quilt Assembly

Refer to Row Assembly Diagram for placement of blocks in rows.

**1.** For Row 1, select three A blocks and two B blocks. Starting with an A block, join blocks as shown, alternating As and Bs. Make four of Row 1.

**2.** For Row 2, select three B blocks and two A blocks. Starting with a B block, join blocks as shown. Make three of Row 2.

**3.** Join rows, starting with Row 1 and alternating rows 1 and 2.

## Borders

The first two borders are pieced to allow the chain design to continue into the border.

### Inner Border

For the first border, make one more strip set. Units from this strip set are pieced with strips 1, 2, and 3 to make inner border. Refer to border diagrams and photo throughout.

**1.** For Strip Set 6, join strips of fabrics IV and V as shown. Press seam allowances toward Fabric IV. From this, cut ten 2½"-wide segments.

**2.** To make border for top edge, join one Unit 6 to both ends of one Border 2 strip (Border Diagram 1). Then sew Border 1 strips to both ends of border as shown. Repeat to make bottom border.

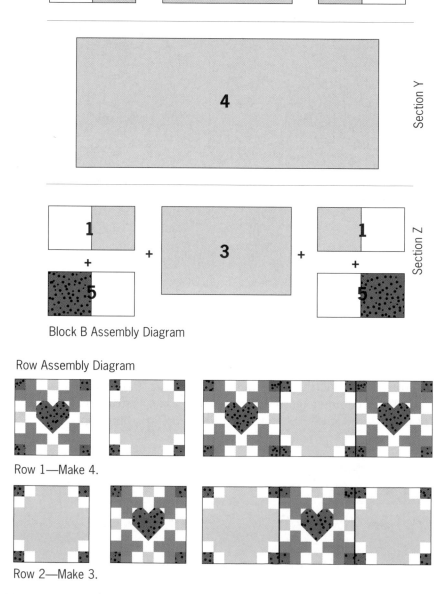

Block B Assembly Diagram

Row Assembly Diagram

Row 1—Make 4.

Row 2—Make 3.

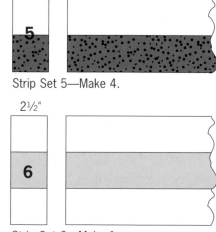

2½"

Strip Set 5—Make 4.

2½"

Strip Set 6—Make 1.

**3.** Pin borders to top and bottom edges of quilt, matching Unit 6 seams with seams of Block B. Stitch borders to quilt, easing as needed.

**4.** To make each side border, join three of Unit 6 and two Border 2 strips as shown (Border Diagram 2). Join a Border 3 strip to both ends to complete each border. Pin borders to quilt sides, matching Unit 6 seams with Block B seams. Stitch borders to quilt, easing as needed.

### Middle Border

**1.** For top border, join one Fabric V square to both ends of a Border 4 strip (Border Diagram 3). Sew Border 4 strips to both ends of border as shown. Repeat for bottom border.

**2.** Pin borders to top and bottom edges of quilt, matching seams of square with center seams of Unit 6 in first border. Stitch borders to quilt. Trim excess length at ends.

**3.** For side borders, repeat Step 1. Then add another Fabric V square and one more Border 4 strip to one end of each border.

**4.** Pin borders to quilt sides, matching seams of square with Unit 6. Stitch borders to quilt sides. Trim excess length at ends.

### Outer Border

**1.** For each side border, join three Fabric III border strips end-to-end. For top and bottom borders, join two strips end-to-end.

**2.** Referring to instructions on page 25, measure quilt from side to side. Trim top and bottom borders to match width. Sew borders to top and bottom edges of quilt.

**3.** Measure quilt from top to

bottom. Trim side borders to match length. Sew borders to quilt sides.

## Quilting and Finishing

**1.** Mark quilting design on quilt top as desired. On quilt shown, patchwork and borders are outline-quilted. Use a commercial stencil to mark the heart motif in B blocks.

**2.** Divide backing into two 3¼-yard lengths. Cut one piece in half lengthwise. Join one narrow panel to each side of wide piece.

**3.** Layer backing, batting, and quilt top. Baste. Quilt as desired.

**4.** From reserved strips, make 11 yards of straight-grain binding. See page 30 for instructions on making and applying binding.

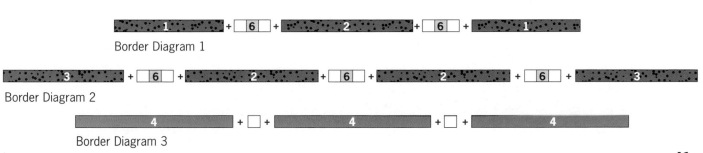

Border Diagram 1

Border Diagram 2

Border Diagram 3

# Flying Home

*This quilt combines original design with time-honored patchwork. A gaggle of seven quick-pieced birds flies across the top of the quilt, with a single straggler breaking formation. Create the look of filtered sunlight with classic flying geese blocks.*

## Finished Size
Quilt: 73½" x 109"
Blocks: 8 geese blocks, 15" square
304 Flying Geese blocks, 2½" x 5"

## Materials

|  |  |  |
|---|---|---|
|  | Fabric I (light blue print) | 6½ yards |
|  | Fabric II (gray solid) | ¼ yard |
|  | Fabric III (black solid) | 1¾ yards |
|  | Fabric IV (white-on-white print) | ⅛ yard |
|  | Fabric V (brown print) | ¾ yard |
|  | Fabric VI (taupe print) | ¾ yard |
|  | Fabric VII (rust print) | 1⅝ yards |
|  | Fabric VIII (tan print) | ⅞ yard |
|  | Fabric IX (gold solid) | ¾ yard |
|  | Fabric X (pale yellow print) | ¾ yard |
|  | Fabric XI (black/brown print) | ⅝ yard |
|  | Backing fabric | 6½ yards |
|  | Precut batting | 120" x 120" |

## Quick-Piecing Techniques
Strip Piecing (see page 20)
Diagonal Corners (see page 20)
Diagonal Ends (see page 21)
Triangle-Squares (see page 22)

## Cutting
Cut all strips crossgrain, from selvage to selvage. For best use of yardage, cut pieces in order listed. Refer to diagrams to identify pieces.

**From Fabric I (light blue print), cut:**
✳ Two 15½"-wide strips.
From one strip, cut:
• One 15½" x 30½" (Spacer F).
• Two 5½" x 10½" (Spacer E).
From second strip, cut:
• One 15½" square (Spacer H).
• One 8" x 10½" (Spacer G).
• One 7½" x 10½" for triangle-squares (A3, A20).
• Four 7⅛" squares. Cut each square in half diagonally to get eight triangles (A15).
✳ Three 5½"-wide strips. From these, cut:
• Eight 5½" x 6¾" (A16).
• One 5½" square (Spacer C).
• Eight 4¼" x 5½" (A23).
• Ten 3" x 5½" (A11, Spacer D).
✳ Four 4¼"-wide strips. From these, cut:
• Eight 4¼" x 10½" (A5).
• Sixteen 4¼" squares (A4, A22).
✳ Forty-six 3"-wide strips. From these, cut:
• 616 3" squares (A12c, B1a).
• Eight 1¾" x 3" (A19).
• Eight 3" x 4¼" (A9).
✳ Twelve 1¾"-wide strips. Set aside 10 strips for inner border. From two strips, cut:
• Eight 1¾" x 5½" (A14a).
• Sixteen 1¾" squares (A1a, A21a).

*(continued)*

**From Fabric II (gray solid), cut:**

✱ Two 3"-wide strips. From these, cut:
  • Eight 3" x 8½" (A12).
  • Four 2⅛" squares. Cut each square in half diagonally to get eight A6 triangles.

**From Fabric III (black solid), cut:**

✱ One 5½"-wide strip. From this, cut:
  • Sixteen 1¾" x 5½" (A1, A21).
  • Four 3⅜" squares. Cut each square in half diagonally to get eight triangles (A13).
✱ Sixteen 3"-wide strips. Set aside nine strips for binding. From seven strips, cut:
  • Thirty-one 3" x 5½" (B1-1).
  • Eight 3" x 3¾" (A12a).
  • Eight 3" squares (A9a).
  • Eight 1¾" squares (A7).

**From Fabric IV (white print), cut:**

✱ One 4¼"-wide strip. From this, cut:
  • Eight 3" x 4¼" (A12b).
  • Four 2⅛" squares. Cut each square in half diagonally to get eight triangles (A8).

**From Fabric V (brown print), cut:**

✱ One 2¼"-wide strip for Strip Set 1 (A10, A17).

✱ One 7½"-wide strip. From this, cut:
  • One 7½" x 10½" for triangle-squares (A3, A20). Use leftover fabric for next cut.
✱ Five 3"-wide strips and two 3" x 30" strips. From these, cut:
  • Sixteen 3" x 4¼" (A2, A18).
  • Thirty 3" x 5½" (B4-1).
✱ Eight 1¾" squares (A19a).

**From Fabric VI (taupe print), cut:**

✱ One 2½"-wide strip for Strip Set 1 (A10, A17).
✱ Three 5½"-wide strips. From these, cut:
  • Thirty-six 3" x 5½" (B5-1).

**From Fabric VII (rust print), cut:**

✱ Three 5½"-wide strips. From these, cut:
  • Twenty-nine 3" x 5½" (B3-1).
✱ Ten 3½"-wide strips for outer border.

**From Fabric VIII (tan print), cut:**

✱ Four 5½"-wide strips. From these, cut:
  • Forty-three 3" x 5½" (B6-1).
✱ Eight 1¾" x 6¾" (A14).

**From Fabric IX (gold solid), cut:**

✱ Four 5½"-wide strips. From these, cut:
  • Forty-four 3" x 5½" (B7-1).

**From Fabric X (yellow print), cut:**

✱ Four 5½"-wide strips. From these, cut:
  • Fifty-one 3" x 5½" (B8-1).

**From Fabric XI (brown print), cut:**

✱ Three 5½"-wide strips. From these, cut:
  • Forty 3" x 5½" (B2-1).

## Making Units for Block A

Refer to Block A Assembly Diagram throughout to identify units.
**1.** On wrong side of 7½" x 10½" piece of Fabric I, draw a 3 x 4-square grid of 2⅛" squares.
**2.** With right sides facing, match marked piece with corresponding piece of Fabric V. Stitch grid as described on page 22. Cut 24 triangle-squares from grid, three for each block (units A3 and A20). Store triangle-squares in a labelled zip-top bag.

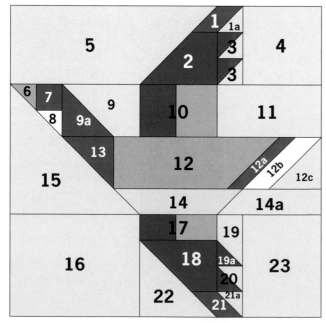

Block A—Make 8.

Block B1—Make 31.

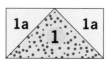

Block B2—Make 40.

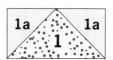

Block B3—Make 29.

Block B4—Make 30.

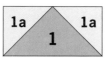

Block B5—Make 36.

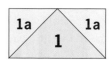

Block B6—Make 43.

Block B7—Make 44.

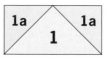

Block B8—Make 51.

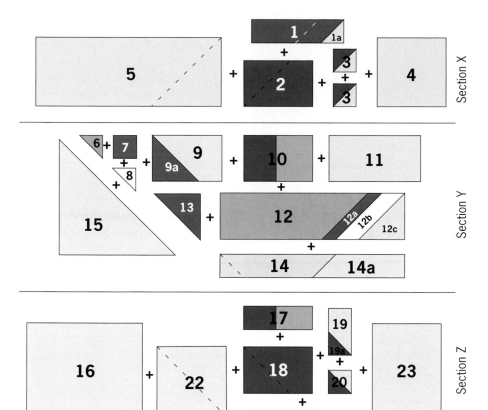

Section X

Section Y

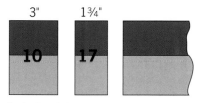

Section Z

Block A Assembly Diagram

Strip Set 1 Diagram—Make 1.

Unit 5 Diagram

## Block A Assembly

Assemble this block in horizontal sections X, Y, and Z. Each completed section should measure approximately 15½" wide. Refer to Block Assembly Diagram throughout.

### Section X

**1.** Join two A3 triangle-squares as shown.
**2.** Sew Unit 2 to left side of joined squares; press seam allowance toward Unit 2.
**3.** Join Unit 1 to top of combined unit.
**4.** Sew Unit 4 to right side of combined unit.
**5.** Use diagonal-end technique to sew Unit 5 to left side of unit (Unit 5 Diagram). Press; then trim excess fabric from seam allowance.

### Section Y

**1.** Join units 6 and 8 to Square 7.
**2.** Add Unit 9 to right side of combined unit.
**3.** Join units 10 and 11 to row as shown.
**4.** Sew Triangle 13 to Unit 12.
**5.** Join 12/13 to bottom of first row, aligning right-hand ends of both rows.
**6.** Add Unit 14 to bottom of combined unit in same manner.
**7.** Sew Triangle 15 to diagonal edge of combined unit. Press; then trim seam allowance to remove excess fabric from Unit 14.

### Section Z

**1.** Join units 17 and 18 as shown.
**2.** Sew Unit 20 triangle-square to bottom of Unit 19.
**3.** Join 19/20 to side of 17/18 as shown. *(continued)*

**3.** Join strips of fabrics V and VI (Strip Set 1 Diagram). From this strip set, cut eight 3"-wide segments (Unit 10) and eight 1¾"-wide segments (Unit 17).
**4.** Use diagonal-corner technique to make one each of units 1, 9, 19, and 21 as shown.
**5.** Using diagonal-end technique, make one of Unit 14.

**6.** Unit 12 combines diagonal-end and diagonal-corner techniques. Use diagonal-end technique to join units 12 and 12a (Unit 12 Diagram). Trim excess fabric from seam allowance and press. Repeat diagonal-end technique to add 12b; trim and press. Use diagonal-corner technique to add 12c as shown.

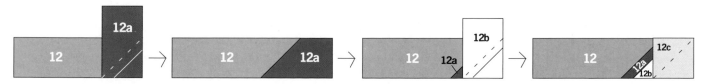

Unit 12 Diagram

Unit 22 Diagram

**4.** Join Unit 21 to bottom of combined unit.

**5.** With right sides facing, align Unit 22 with bottom left corner of combined unit (Unit 22 Diagram). Use diagonal-corner technique to sew Unit 22 as shown. Press. Trim excess fabric from seam allowance.

**6.** Join units 16 and 23 to sides to complete section.

### Assembly

Join sections X, Y, and Z to assemble block. Make eight of Block A.

## Block B Assembly

There are eight color variations of Block B. To avoid getting confused, keep each variation in a separate labeled zip-top bag. All variations are sewn in the same manner (Block B Diagrams).

**1.** For each B1 block, select one Unit 1 of Fabric III and two 1a squares of Fabric I. Use diagonal-corner technique to assemble block as shown. Make 31 of Block B1. For each block, press one seam allowance toward small triangle and the other toward large triangle. (This gives you offset seam allowances when joining blocks. Press all B blocks in same manner.)

**2.** For B2 block, use one Unit 1 of Fabric XI and two 1a squares of Fabric I. Make 40 of Block B2.

**3.** For B3 block, use one Unit 1 of Fabric VII and two 1a squares of Fabric I. Make 29 of Block B3.

**4.** For B4 block, use one Unit 1 of Fabric V and two 1a squares of Fabric I. Make 30 of Block B4.

**5.** For B5 block, use one Unit 1 of Fabric VI and two 1a squares of Fabric I. Make 36 of Block B5.

**6.** For B6 block, use one Unit 1 of Fabric VIII and two 1a squares of Fabric I. Make 43 of Block B6.

**7.** For B7 block, use one Unit 1 of Fabric IX and two 1a squares of Fabric I. Make 44 of Block B7.

**8.** For B8 block, use one Unit 1 of Fabric X and two 1a squares of Fabric I. Make 51 of Block B8.

## Quilt Assembly

Refer to Quilt Assembly Diagram and photo for placement of blocks in rows. Assemble each row from left to right.

### Row 1

**1.** Select four A blocks, three B8 blocks, and one each of spacers C and D.

**2.** Join B8 blocks and Spacer D in pairs. Join pairs as shown; then sew Spacer C to top of combined units.

**3.** Add A blocks as shown to complete Row 1.

### Row 2

**1.** From B blocks, select two B6, seven B7, and 11 B8. Then select one each of Block A, Spacer E, and Spacer F.

**2.** Join three B8 and three B7 blocks in a row as shown.

**3.** Join two B7 and four B8 blocks in a row.

**4.** Join both rows of B blocks. Add Spacer E to right side of row.

**5.** Join two B6, two B7, and four B8 blocks in a row as shown. Add this row to bottom of unit.

**6.** Join Block A to right side of unit; then add Spacer F to complete Row 2.

### Row 3

**1.** From B blocks, select five B5, eight B6, 11 B7, and 11 B8. Then select one each of Block A and spacers D, G, and H.

**2.** Join three B6, two B7, three B8, and two more B7 blocks in a row. Add Spacer D to end of row.

**3.** Join two B5, two B6, three B7, three B8, and one more B7 block in a row.

**4.** Join both rows. Sew Spacer G to right end of combined row.

**5.** Join three B5, three B6, three B7, and five B8 in a row. Join this to bottom of combined row.

**6.** Add Block A and Spacer H as shown to complete Row 3.

### Row 4

**1.** From B blocks, select one B3, four B4, 12 B5, 12 B6, 13 B7, and 14 B8. Then select one each of Block A and Spacer E.

**2.** Join four B5, three B6, three B7, six B8, and two more B7 blocks in a row.

**3.** Join two B4, three B5, four B6, four B7, and five B8 blocks in a row.

Block B1—Make 31.

Block B2—Make 40.

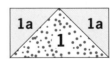
Block B3—Make 29.

Block B4—Make 30.

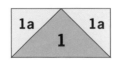
Block B5—Make 36.

Block B6—Make 43.

Block B7—Make 44.

Block B8—Make 51.

**4.** Join both rows; sew Spacer E to right end of combined row.

**5.** Join one B3, two B4, five B5, five B6, four B7, and three B8 blocks in a row. Join this to bottom of combined row.

**6.** Sew Block A to right end of combined row to complete Row 4.

## Row 5

**1.** From B blocks, select three B2, seven B3, eight B4, eight B5, 12 B6, 10 B7, and 12 B8.

**2.** Join two B3, two B4, and four B5 blocks in a row as shown.

**3.** Join one B2, two B3, three B4, and two B5 blocks in a row. Join this to bottom of previous row.

**4.** Join two B2, three B3, and three B4 blocks in a row. Join this to bottom of combined row.

**5.** Add remaining A block to right side of combined row.

**6.** Join two B6, two B7, five B8, and three more B7 blocks in a row as shown.

**7.** Join four B6, three B7, and five B8 blocks in a row. Join this to bottom of previous row.

**8.** Join two B5, six B6, two B7, and two B8 blocks in a row. Join this to bottom of combined row.

**9.** Join unit to right side of Block A to complete Row 5.

## Rows 6–10 and Assembly

**1.** For remaining rows, join B blocks as shown in Quilt Assembly Diagram.

**2.** Join rows as shown.

*(continued)*

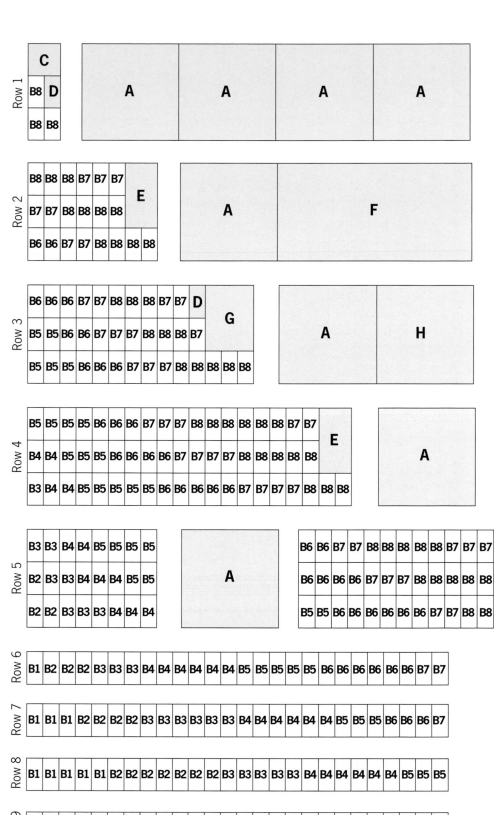

Quilt Assembly Diagram

## Borders

**1.** For inner border, join two 1¾"-wide Fabric I strips end-to-end for top and bottom borders. Join three strips for each side border.

**2.** Referring to instructions on page 25, measure quilt from side to side. Measuring outward from center seam, trim top and bottom borders to match width. Matching centers, sew borders to top and bottom edges of quilt.

**3.** Measure quilt from top to bottom; then trim remaining borders to match quilt length. Sew borders to quilt sides. Press seam allowances toward borders.

**4.** For outer border, piece 3½"-wide strips of Fabric VII in same manner as for inner border. Trim borders to fit. Sew to quilt in same manner.

## Quilting and Finishing

**1.** Mark quilting design on quilt top as desired. Quilt shown is outline-quilted, with two geese outlines quilted in Spacer F. Wavy lines of air currents are quilted around each goose.

**2.** Divide backing into two 3¼-yard lengths. Cut one piece in half lengthwise. Join one narrow panel to each side of wide piece to assemble backing.

**3.** Layer backing, batting, and quilt top. Baste. Quilt as marked or as desired.

**4.** From reserved strips, make 11 yards of binding. See page 30 for instructions on making and applying straight-grain binding.

# Baby Buggies Crib Set

*Personalize each pretty pram in this crib quilt with
bits of ribbon and lace. Coordinating bumper pads (instructions
included) make this sweet set ready for dreamland.*

## Finished Size

Quilt: 48" x 50"
Blocks: 6 buggy blocks, 12" x 14"

## Materials

|  |  |  |
|---|---|---|
|  | Fabric I (peach solid) | 1¼ yards |
|  | Fabric II (dark peach solid) | 1½ yards |
|  | Fabric III (mint green solid) | ¼ yard |
|  | Fabric IV (green print for one buggy, border) | ½ yard |
|  | Fabric V (two peach prints) | ¼ yard each |
|  | Fabric VI (three assorted green prints) | ¼ yard each |
|  | Fabric VII (muslin) | ¼ yard |
|  | Fabric VIII (mint green print) | ⅜ yard |
|  | Backing fabric | 3 yards |
|  | 1½"-wide beaded lace trim | 1½ yards |
|  | ⅝"-wide mint green satin ribbon | ½ yard |
|  | ⅝"-wide peach satin ribbon | 1 yard |
|  | Precut batting | 72" x 90" |

## Quick-Piecing Techniques

Diagonal Corners (see page 20)
Triangle-Squares (see page 22)

## Cutting

Cut all strips crossgrain, from selvage to selvage, except as noted. For best use of yardage, cut pieces in order listed. Refer to block and quilt assembly diagrams to identify pieces.

**From Fabric I (peach solid), cut:**

✱ One 5½"-wide strip. From this, cut:
  • Six 5½" x 6½" (A3, B3).
✱ Ten 2½"-wide strips. Set aside five strips for inner border and horizontal sashing. From remaining strips, cut:
  • Four 2½" x 14½" (sashing).
  • Eighteen 2½" x 3½" (A11, B11).
  • Eighteen 2½" squares (A1a, A4a, B1a, B4a).
✱ Four 1½"-wide strips. From these, cut:
  • Six 1½" x 4½" (A7, B7).
  • Twelve 1½" x 3½" (A5, B5).
  • Forty-eight 1½" squares (A8a, B8a).

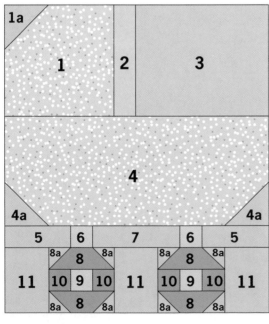

Block A—Make 2.

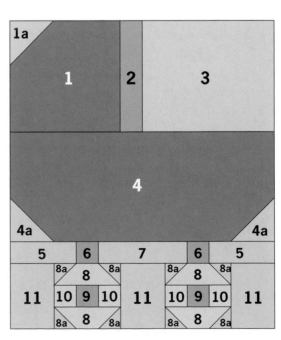

Block B—Make 4.

**From Fabric II (dark peach solid), cut:**

✻ Four 2" x 52" lengthwise strips for outer border.

✻ Four 3" x 52" lengthwise strips for straight-grain binding.

✻ One 7" x 27" lengthwise strip for triangle-squares.

✻ Seven 1½" x 15" strips. From these, cut:
  • Four 1½" x 5½" (B2).
  • Eight 1½" x 3½" (A8).
  • Twenty-four 1½" squares (A10, B6, B9).

**From Fabric III (green solid), cut:**

✻ Three 1½"-wide strips. From these, cut:
  • Two 1½" x 5½" (A2).
  • Sixteen 1½" x 3½" (B8).
  • Twenty-four 1½" squares (A6, A9, B10).

**From Fabric IV (green print), cut:**

✻ One 12½" square. From this, cut:
  • One 5½" x 12½" (B4).
  • One 5½" square (B1).

✻ Eight 2" x 26" strips for middle border.

**From Fabric V (peach prints), cut:**

✻ Two 5½" x 12½" (A4).

✻ Two 5½" squares (A1).

**From Fabric VI (green prints), cut:**

✻ Three 5½" x 12½" (B4).

✻ Three 5½" squares (B1).

**From Fabric VII (muslin), cut:**

✻ One 7" x 27" strip for triangle-squares.

**From Fabric VIII (mint green), cut:**

✻ Ten 4½" squares (pieced sashing).

## Units for Block A

Refer to Block A Assembly Diagram throughout to identify units.

**1.** Use diagonal-corner technique to make one each of units 1 and 4 as shown.

**2.** Use diagonal-corner technique to make four of Unit 8.

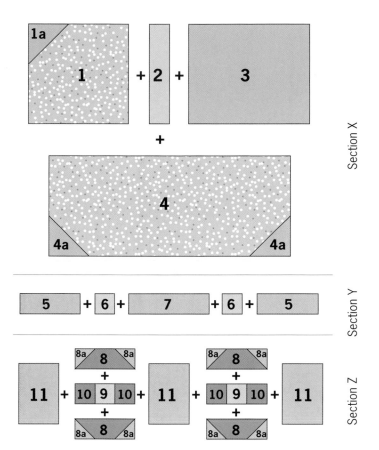

Block A Assembly Diagram

## Block A Assembly

Assemble this block in horizontal sections X, Y, and Z. Each completed section should measure 12½" wide. Refer to Block A Assembly Diagram throughout.

### Section X

**1.** Join Unit 1 to one side of Unit 2.

**2.** Sew Unit 3 to opposite side of Unit 2 as shown. Press seam allowances away from Unit 2.

**3.** Join Unit 4 to bottom of combined unit. Press seam allowance toward Unit 4.

### Section Y

**1.** Join one of Unit 6 to both ends of Unit 7.

**2.** Add one Unit 5 to both ends of row.

**3.** Press seam allowances away from Unit 6.

### Section Z

**1.** Join one of Unit 10 to both sides of Unit 9 as shown. Make two 9/10 units, one for each wheel.

**2.** Sew one of Unit 8 to top edges of both 9/10 units. Repeat for bottom edges. Press seam allowances away from Unit 8.

**3.** Join combined units with three of Unit 11 in a row as shown.

### Assembly

Join sections to assemble block. Make two of Block A.

## Block B Assembly

Refer to Block B Diagram to identify units.

**1.** Use diagonal-corner technique to make one each of units 1 and 4 as shown.

**2.** Use diagonal-corner technique to make four of Unit 8.

**3.** Assemble Block B in same manner as for Block A. Make four of Block B.   *(continued)*

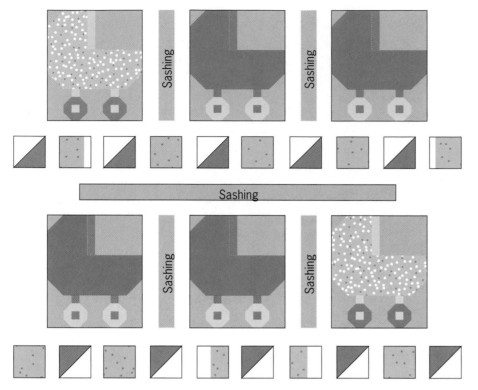

Quilt Assembly Diagram

## Quilt Assembly

Refer to Quilt Assembly Diagram for placement of blocks in rows. Assemble each row from left to right.

**1.** For top row, select one A block, two B blocks, and two 14½"-long sashing strips. Join blocks and sashing strips in a row as shown. In same manner, join remaining blocks and sashing strips for second row. Press seam allowances toward sashing.

**2.** On wrong side of 7" x 27" piece of muslin, draw a 1 x 5-square grid of 4⅞" squares. With right sides facing, match marked piece with corresponding piece of Fabric II. Stitch grid as described on page 22. Cut 10 triangle-squares from grid, five for each row of pieced sashing.

**3.** For top row of pieced sashing, select five triangle-squares and five squares of Fabric VIII. Starting with a triangle-square, join squares in a row, alternating triangle-squares and plain squares as shown.

**4.** For bottom row of pieced sashing, join remaining squares and triangle-squares as shown.

**5.** Join rows from top to bottom as shown, adding horizontal strip of sashing in center as shown.

## Borders

**1.** Referring to instructions on page 25, measure quilt from side to side. Trim two 2½"-wide Fabric I strips to match width. Sew borders to top and bottom edges of quilt.

**2.** Measure quilt from top to bottom; then trim remaining borders to match quilt length. Sew borders to quilt sides. Press seam allowances toward borders.

**3.** For middle border, piece two Fabric IV strips end-to-end to make one strip for each side of quilt. Measure quilt as before; then trim borders to fit and sew to quilt in same manner.

**4.** For outer border, measure quilt and trim Fabric II strips to fit. Sew borders to quilt as before.

## Quilting and Finishing

**1.** Mark quilting design on quilt top as desired. Quilt shown is outline-quilted.

**2.** Divide backing into two 1½-yard lengths. Cut one panel in half lengthwise, discarding one half. Join remaining half panel to full piece to assemble backing with an off-center seam.

**3.** Layer backing, batting, and quilt top. Baste. Quilt as marked or as desired.

**4.** From reserved strips, make 5¾ yards of binding. See page 30 for instructions on making and applying straight-grain binding.

**5.** Cut lace trim into 9" lengths. Turn under 1" at ends of each piece. Tack one piece of trim to edge of each Unit 2 as shown.

**6.** Cut ribbons into 9" lengths. Tie each piece into a bow. Tack one bow center to bottom of each Unit 2 as shown.

## Crib Bumpers

These instructions are for two 8" x 28" bumpers and two 8" x 52" bumpers. Adjust yardage and instructions as necessary to make different sizes.

**To make bumpers that coordinate with the crib quilt, you'll need the following:**

* ¾ yard each of fabrics I, II, and VIII for patchwork.
* 1½ yards of Fabric III for backing and ties.
* ¾ yard of muslin and ⅝ yard of 60"-wide low-loft batting for quilting.
* 1⅛ yards of 60"-wide high-loft batting for padding.

**1.** From Fabric I, cut two 12" x 27" strips for triangle-squares. Cut matching pieces from Fabric II.

**2.** On wrong side of one Fabric I piece, draw a 2 x 5-square grid of

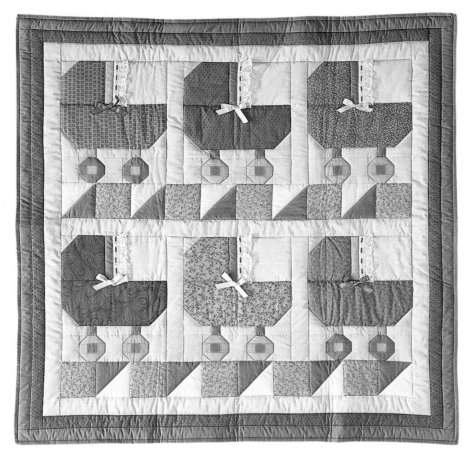

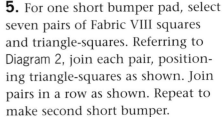

**5.** For one short bumper pad, select seven pairs of Fabric VIII squares and triangle-squares. Referring to Diagram 2, join each pair, positioning triangle-squares as shown. Join pairs in a row as shown. Repeat to make second short bumper.

**6.** Cut four 8½" x 42" strips of muslin. Trim two strips to 8½" x 30" for short bumpers. Piece remainder to get two 8½" x 54" pieces for long bumpers. Cut one piece of low-loft batting to match each muslin strip.

**7.** For each bumper, sandwich batting between pieced front (faceup) and muslin. Outline-quilt patchwork through all layers.

**8.** Cut and piece Fabric III backing in same manner as for muslin (Step 6). Cut two pieces of high-loft batting to match each backing strip.

**9.** With right sides facing, match backing to each quilted bumper. Add two layers of batting and pin. With batting side down, stitch around bumper through all layers, leaving a 7"-wide opening on one long side. Clip corners and turn right side out. Press lightly. Slip-stitch openings closed.

**10.** For ties, cut sixteen 1½" x 21" strips from remaining Fabric III. Press under ¼" on all edges of each strip.

**11.** With wrong sides facing, press each strip in half lengthwise. Top-stitch all pressed edges. Pin center of one tie to back of each bumper corner and topstitch to secure.

4⅞" squares. With right sides facing, match marked piece with Fabric II piece. Sew grid as shown on page 22. Cut 20 triangle-squares from grid. Use remaining pieces to stitch a second grid to get a total of 40 triangle-squares.

**3.** From Fabric VIII, cut forty 4½" squares.

**4.** For one long bumper pad, select 13 pairs of Fabric VIII squares and triangle-squares. Referring to Diagram 1, join each pair, taking care to position triangle-squares as shown. Join pairs in a row as shown. Repeat to make second long bumper.

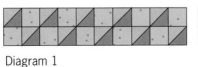

Diagram 1

Diagram 2

# Flowers
## *in the Cabin*

*The time-honored Log Cabin block is new again.
Use different-width strips to create an illusion of
circles without sewing any curves at all. Sashing gives
the quilt an open and airy look.*

### Finished Size
Quilt: 75" x 107"
Blocks: 96 Log Cabin blocks, 7½" square
4 corner blocks, 4" square

### Quick-Piecing Technique
Strip Piecing (see page 20)

### Materials

| | | |
|---|---|---|
| | Fabric I (muslin or white-on-white) | 5⅛ yards |
| | Fabric II (slate blue solid) | 2¾ yards |
| | Fabric III (blue-on-ivory print) | 3⅛ yards |
| | Fabric IV (light blue solid) | ¼ yard |
| | Fabric V (gold print) | ¾ yard |
| | Backing fabric | 6½ yards |
| | Precut batting | 90" x 108" |

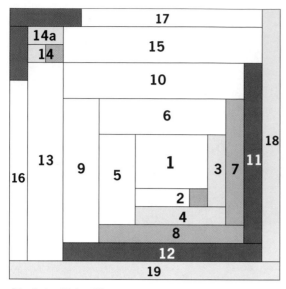

Block A—Make 60.

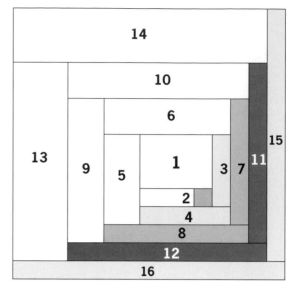

Block B—Make 36.

## Cutting

Cut all strips crossgrain, from selvage to selvage. For best use of yardage, cut pieces in order listed. Refer to block diagrams to identify pieces.

### From Fabric I (muslin), cut:

✳ Four 5½"-wide strips for strip sets 3 and 4.

✳ Twenty-two 2"-wide strips. Set aside three strips for Strip Set 1. From remaining strips, cut:
  • Thirty-six 2" x 7½" (B14).
  • Thirty-six 2" x 6" (B13).
  • Ninety-six 2" x 2½" (A1, B1).

✳ Seventy-two 1½"-wide strips. From these, cut:
  • Thirty-eight 1½" x 15½" for sashing.
  • 120 1½" x 6" (A13, A15).
  • Ninety-six 1½" x 5½" (A10, B10).
  • Ninety-six 1½" x 4½" (A9, B9).
  • Ninety-six 1½" x 4" (A6, B6).
  • Ninety-six 1½" x 3" (A5, B5).
  • Four 1" x 1½" (C3).
  • Four 1" squares (C2).

### From Fabric II (slate blue), cut:

✳ Nine 3"-wide strips for binding.

✳ Two 2½"-wide strips for Strip Set 4.

✳ Two 2"-wide strips for Strip Set 3.

✳ Twenty 1½"-wide strips for borders.

✳ Twenty-eight 1"-wide strips. From these, cut:
  • Ninety-six 1" x 6" (A12, B12).
  • Ninety-six 1" x 5½" (A11, B11).
  • Four 1" x 2½" (C7).
  • Four 1" x 2" (C6).

### From Fabric III (ivory print), cut:

✳ Ten 4½"-wide strips for middle border.

✳ One 2"-wide strip. From this, cut:
  • Four 2" x 4½" (C11).
  • Four 2" x 3" (C10).

✳ Fifty-four 1"-wide strips. Set aside two strips for Strip Set 2. From remaining strips, cut:
  • Ninety-six 1" x 8" (A19, B16).
  • Ninety-six 1" x 7½" (A18, B15).
  • 100 1" x 3" (A4, B4, C9).
  • 100 1" x 2½" (A3, B3, C8).
  • Four 1" x 2" (C5).
  • Sixty-four 1" x 1½" (A14a, C4).

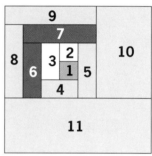

Block C—Make 4.

### From Fabric IV (light blue), cut:

✳ Five 1"-wide strips for strip sets 1 and 2. From ends of these strips, cut:
  • Four 1" squares (C1).

### From Fabric V (gold print), cut:

✳ One 1½"-wide strip. From this, cut:
  • Fifteen 1½" squares for sashing.

✳ Twenty-one 1" x 42" strips. From these, cut:
  • Ninety-six 1" x 4½" (A8, B8).
  • Ninety-six 1" x 4" (A7, B7).

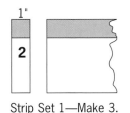

Strip Set 1—Make 3.

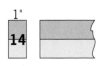

Strip Set 2—Make 2.

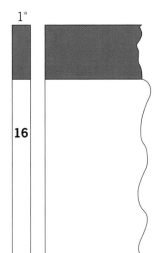

Strip Set 3—Make 2.

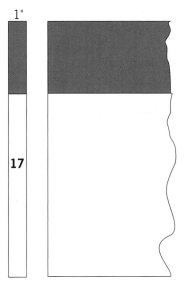

Strip Set 4—Make 4.

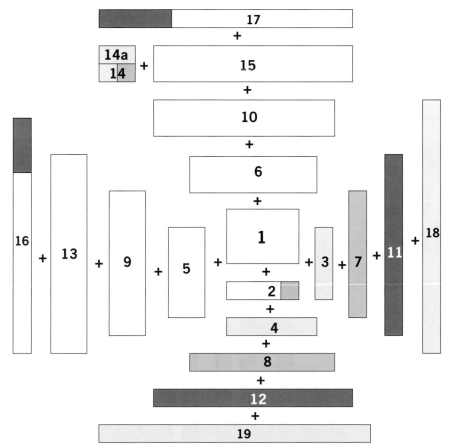

Block A Assembly Diagram

## Strip Sets

Refer to strip set diagrams and Block A Assembly Diagram throughout to identify units. Store units cut from each strip set in zip-top bags.

**1.** For Strip Set 1, join strips of fabrics I and IV as shown. Make three of Strip Set 1. Press seam allowances toward Fabric IV. From these strip sets, cut ninety-six 1"-wide segments for Unit 2.

**2.** For Strip Set 2, join strips of fabrics III and IV as shown. Make two of Strip Set 2. Press seam allowances toward Fabric III. From these strip sets, cut sixty 1"-wide segments for Unit 14.

**3.** For Strip Set 3, join 5½"-wide strip of Fabric I and 2"-wide strip of Fabric II as shown. Make two of Strip Set 3. Press seam allowances toward Fabric II. From these strip sets, cut sixty 1"-wide segments for Unit 16.

**4.** For Strip Set 4, join 5½"-wide strip of Fabric I and 2½"-wide strip of Fabric II as shown. Make two of Strip Set 4. From these, cut sixty 1"-wide segments for Unit 17.

## Block A Assembly

Assemble this block from the center out. Each completed block should measure approximately 8" square. Refer to Block A Assembly Diagram throughout.

**1.** Join units in numerical order as shown. Work around the block up to Unit 13. As strips are added, press seam allowances toward the strip just added.

**2.** Join Unit 14 to 14a. Press seam allowance toward 14a. Join combined Unit 14 to one end of Unit 15, and press seam allowance toward Unit 15. Stitch 14/15 to block as shown.

**3.** Add units 16–19 as shown to complete block.

**4.** Make 60 of Block A.

*(continued)*

## Block B Assembly

Assemble this block like Block A, but without the corner "flower." Each completed block should measure 8" square.

Referring to Block B Assembly Diagram, join units in numerical order as shown. Press seam allowances toward each new strip. Make 36 of Block B.

## Block C Assembly

Positioned in the border corners, this block is a smaller version of Block A. Each completed block should measure approximately 4½" square. Referring to Block C Assembly Diagram, join units in numerical order as shown. Make four of Block C.

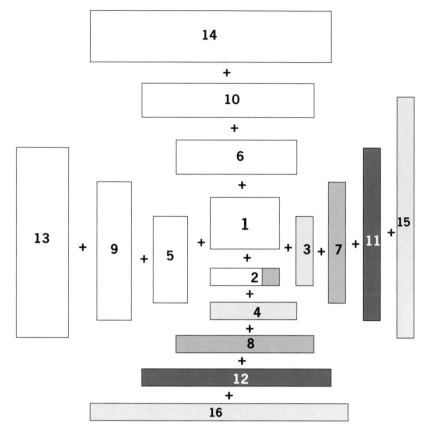

Block B Assembly Diagram

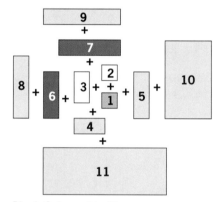

Block C Assembly Diagram

## Quilt Assembly

Refer to Row Assembly Diagram for placement of blocks in rows. Be careful to turn each block as shown for correct position. Assemble each row from left to right.

**1.** For Row 1, select six A blocks, 10 B blocks, and three Fabric I sashing strips. Join blocks in groups of four as shown, making four 15½" squares. Join squares in a row with sashing between squares as shown. Press seam allowances toward sashing strips. Make two of Row 1.

**2.** For Row 2, select 12 A blocks, four B blocks, and three sashing strips. Join blocks in groups of four as shown. Join squares in a row

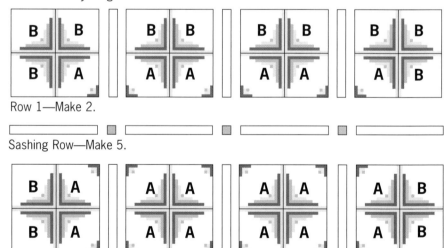

Row Assembly Diagram

Row 1—Make 2.

Sashing Row—Make 5.

Row 2—Make 4.

with sashing strips between squares. Make four of Row 2.
**3.** For Sashing Row, select four sashing strips and three Fabric V sashing squares. Join strips and squares in a row as shown. Press seam allowances toward sashing strips. Make five Sashing Rows.

**4.** Referring to photo, lay out four of Row 2. Position one of Row 1 at top and bottom. Place a Sashing Row between all rows. When satisfied with row placement, join rows.

## Borders

**1.** For inner border, join three 1½"-wide strips of Fabric II end-to-end for each side border. Join two strips for top and bottom borders.

**2.** Referring to instructions on page 25, measure quilt from top to bottom. Measuring outward from center of border strips, trim side borders to match length. Matching centers, sew borders to quilt sides.

**3.** Measure quilt from side to side; then trim remaining borders to match quilt width. Sew borders to top and bottom edges. Press seam allowances toward border.

**4.** For middle border, repeat Step 1 with 4½"-wide strips of Fabric III. Measure quilt from top to bottom and trim longer strips to match length. Measure quilt from side to side and trim shorter borders to match width.

**5.** Stitch shorter borders to top and bottom edges of quilt.

**6.** Referring to photo, join Block C to ends of each side border. Then sew borders to quilt sides.

**7.** For outer border, repeat steps 1 and 2.

## Quilting and Finishing

**1.** Mark quilting design on quilt top as desired. On quilt shown, patchwork is outline-quilted and three concentric circles are quilted around each flower. Centered on the sashing squares, circles are 5¾", 9¾", and 13¾" in diameter. Look for plates, bowls, pots, or other objects that can be ready-made templates for marking circles.

**2.** Divide backing into two 3¼-yard lengths. Cut one piece in half lengthwise. Join one narrow panel to each side of wide piece.

**3.** Layer backing, batting, and quilt top. Baste. Quilt as marked or as desired.

**4.** From Fabric II strips, make 10½ yards of straight-grain binding. See page 30 for instructions on making and applying binding.

# Pinwheels

*This updated version of the traditional Drunkard's Path has no curved seams. Quick-piecing eliminates the difficulty of cutting and sewing curves. Choose two shades of your favorite color to make your own all-new classic quilt.*

## Finished Size
Quilt: 81" x 99"
Blocks: 36 pinwheel blocks, 9" square

## Materials

| | | |
|---|---|---|
| | Fabric I (burgundy print) | 5⅛ yards |
| | Fabric II (rose print) | 3⅛ yards |
| | Fabric III (white-on-white print) | 2⅜ yards |
| | Backing fabric | 6 yards |
| | Precut batting | 90" x 108" |

## Cutting
Cut all strips crossgrain, from selvage to selvage, except as noted. For best use of yardage, cut pieces in order listed. Refer to block diagrams to identify pieces.

### From Fabric I (burgundy print), cut:
✳ Two 9½" x 83" lengthwise strips and two 9½" x 65" lengthwise strips for border.
✳ Four 2¾"-wide strips. From these and fabric left over from border, cut:
  • 124 2¾" squares (B1a).

## Quick-Piecing Techniques
Diagonal Corners (see page 20)

✳ Forty-two 1¼"-wide strips. From these, cut:
  • 288 1¼" x 2¾" pieces (A3).
  • 288 1¼" x 2" pieces (A2).
  • 288 1¼" squares (A1a).
✳ Nine 3"-wide strips for binding.

### From Fabric II (rose print), cut:
✳ Eight 9½" x 42" strips. From these, cut:
  • Thirty-one 9½" squares (B1).
✳ Fourteen 2"-wide strips. From these, cut:
  • 288 2" squares (A4).

### From Fabric III (white-on-white print), cut:
✳ Thirty-two 2"-wide strips. From these, cut:
  • 144 2" x 2¾" pieces (A6).
  • 288 2" squares (A1).
  • 288 1¼" x 2" pieces (A5).
✳ Nine 1¼"-wide strips. From these, cut:
  • 288 1¼" squares (A4a).

*(continued)*

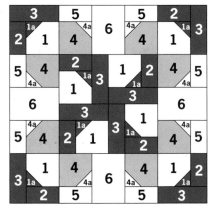

Block A—Make 36.

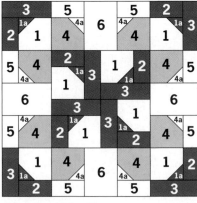

Block B—Make 31.

## Units for Block A

Refer to Block A Assembly Diagram throughout to identify units.

**1.** Use diagonal-corner technique to make eight of Unit 1.

**2.** Use diagonal-corner technique to make eight of Unit 4.

## Block A Assembly

Assemble this block in sections X, Y, and Z. Each completed section should measure approximately 9½" wide. Refer to Block A Assembly Diagram throughout.

## Sections X and Z

Assemble Section X from left to right. Make Section Z with the same units in the same manner.

**1.** Join units 1 and 2. Press seam allowance toward Unit 2.

**2.** Add Unit 3 to top of combined unit as shown. Press seam allowances toward Unit 3.

**3.** Make a second 1/2/3 unit in same manner.

**4.** Join Unit 5 to top of Unit 4 as shown. Make a second 4/5 unit. Press seam allowances toward Unit 5.

**5.** To complete Section X, join combined units in a row as shown, with Unit 6 in middle of row. Press joining seam allowances away from 4/5 units.

**6.** Repeat steps 1–5 above to assemble Section Z.

## Section Y

Assemble the center of the section first; then the outer rows.

**1.** Follow steps 1 and 2 above to make four 1/2/3 units.

**2.** Join four units as shown. Press joining seams toward Unit 3s.

**3.** Join a Unit 5 to one Unit 4. Make four 4/5 units.

**4.** Sew a 4/5 unit to opposite sides of Unit 6. Make two 4/5/6 units.

**5.** Join 4/5/6 units to opposite sides of center as shown to complete section.

## Assembly

Join sections X, Y, and Z to complete block. Make 36 of Block A.

## Block B Assembly

Use diagonal-corner technique to make one block as shown. Make 31 of Block B.

## Quilt Assembly

Refer to Row Assembly Diagram for placement of blocks in rows. Assemble each row from left to right.

**1.** Set aside four A blocks for border.

**2.** For Row 1, select four A blocks and three B blocks. Starting with an A block, join blocks as shown, alternating As and Bs. Make five of Row 1.

**3.** For Row 2, select three of Block A and four of Block B. Starting with a B block, join blocks as shown, alternating Bs and As. Make four of Row 2.

**4.** Join rows, starting with Row 1 and alternating rows 1 and 2.

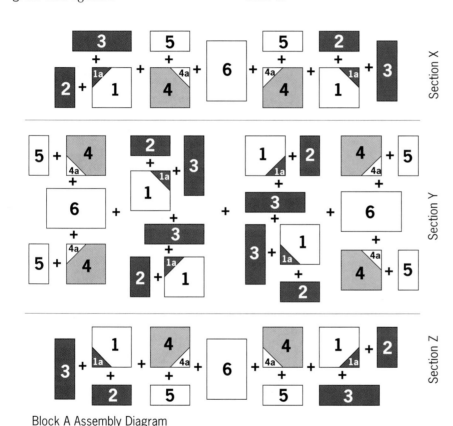

Block A Assembly Diagram

Row Assembly Diagram

Row 1—Make 5.

Row 2—Make 4.

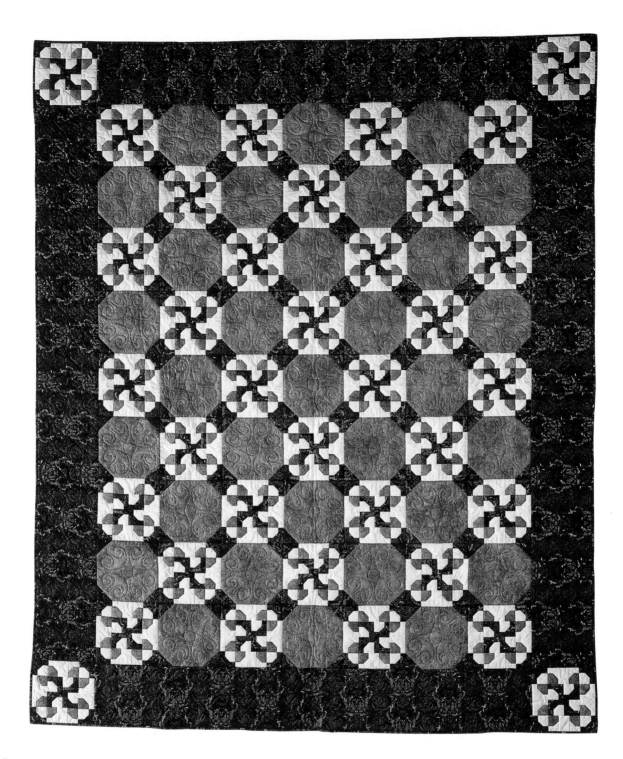

## Borders

**1.** Referring to instructions on page 25, measure quilt from top to bottom. Trim 83"-long border strips to match length.

**2.** Measure quilt from side to side. Trim 65"-long borders to match quilt width.

**3.** Sew longer borders to quilt sides. Press seam allowances toward borders.

**4.** Join A blocks to both ends of each remaining border. Press seam allowances away from blocks.

**5.** Sew pieced borders to top and bottom edges of quilt.

## Quilting and Finishing

**1.** Mark quilting design on quilt top as desired. On quilt shown, patchwork is outline-quilted and a wave pattern is quilted in borders.

**2.** Divide backing into two 3-yard lengths. Cut one piece in half lengthwise. Join one narrow panel to each side of wide piece to assemble backing.

**3.** Layer backing, batting, and quilt top. Baste. Quilt as marked or as desired.

**4.** From Fabric I strips, make 10¼ yards of straight-grain binding. See page 30 for instructions on making and applying binding.

# *Counting* **Sheep**

*Sweet dreams come to one who sleeps with these
little lambs. Use three quick-piecing methods to make the flock and flowers,
and you'll be counting sheep in no time.*

## Finished Size
Quilt: 68¼" x 105"
Blocks: 6 white sheep blocks, 13½" x 15"
      7 black sheep blocks, 9¾" x 13½"
      38 flower blocks, 5¼" x 6"

## Materials

| | | |
|---|---|---|
| ■ | Fabric I (black solid) | 2½ yards |
| □ | Fabric II (white-on-white) | 1¼ yards |
| ▨ | Fabric III (light green solid) | 2¼ yards |
| ▨ | Fabric IV (gray print) | ⅜ yard |
| ▨ | Fabric V (yellow print) | 3 yards |
| ▨ | Fabric VI (gold print) | ½ yard |
| ▨ | Fabric VII (olive print) | ⅝ yard |
| ▨ | Fabric VIII (dark green print) | ¾ yard |
| | Backing fabric | 6½ yards |
| | Precut batting | 90" x 108" |

## Quick-Piecing Techniques
Strip Piecing (see page 20)
Diagonal Corners (see page 20)
Diagonal Ends (see page 21)

## Cutting
Cut all strips crossgrain, from selvage to selvage. For best use of yardage, cut pieces in order listed. Refer to diagrams to identify pieces.

**From Fabric I (black), cut:**

✳ Thirteen 3½"-wide strips. Set aside 10 strips for borders. From remaining strips, cut:
- Seven 3½" x 5¾" (C7).
- Twenty-eight 2¾" x 3½" (C12).

✳ One 2¾"-wide strip. From this, cut:
- Fourteen 2¾" squares (C13).

✳ Two 2"-wide strips. From these, cut:
- Six 2" x 3½" (A1, B1).
- Twelve 2" x 2½" (A12, B12).
- Twenty 1¼" x 2" (A4, B4, C4a).

✳ Six 1¼"-wide strips. From these, cut:
- Fourteen 1¼" x 3½" (C3).
- Thirteen 1¼" x 2¾" (A14a, B14a, C9).
- 110 1¼" squares (A5a, B5a, A6b, B6b, A7a, B7a, A8a, B8a, C2b, C5a, C8a).

✳ Nine 3"-wide strips for binding.
*(continued)*

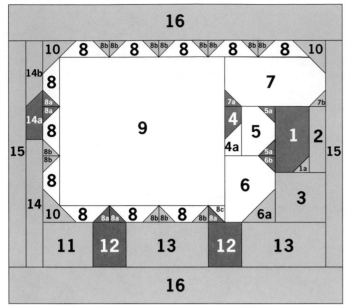

Block A—Make 3.

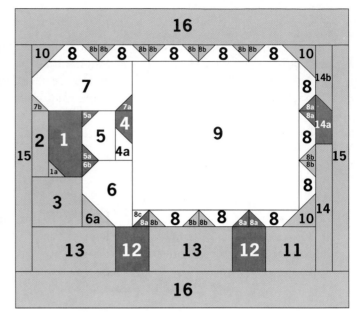

Block B—Make 3.

**From Fabric II (white), cut:**

* One 8"-wide strip. From this, cut:
  * Six 7¼" x 8" (A9, B9).
* Five 2¾"-wide strips. From these, cut:
  * Six 2¾" x 5" (A7, B7).
  * Seven 2¾" x 4¼" (C6).
  * Six 2¾" x 3½" (A6, B6).
  * Twenty 2" x 2¾" (A5, B5, C2).
  * Sixty-six 1¼" x 2¾" (A8, B8).
  * Six 1¼" x 2" (A4a, B4a).
* Four ⅞"-wide strips for Strip Set 1.
* Twelve 1⅝"-wide strips. From these, cut:
  * 152 1⅝" x 2" (D5).
  * 152 1¼" x 1⅝" (D2a).
  * Six 1¼" squares (A8c, B8c).

**From Fabric III (light green), cut:**

* One 11¾"-wide strip. From this, cut:
  * Two 11¾" x 14" (Spacer E).
  * Six 1¼" x 14" (Spacer F).
* Three 3⅛"-wide strips. From these, cut:
  * Eight 3⅛" x 14" (Spacer G).
* Three 2¾"-wide strips. From these, cut:
  * Twenty-seven 2¾" squares (A3, B3, C10).
  * Fourteen 2" x 2¾" (C11).
* Six 2⅛"-wide strips. From these, cut:
  * Twelve 2⅛" x 15½" (A16, B16).

* Two 2½"-wide strips. From these, cut:
  * Twelve 2½" x 4¼" (A13, B13).
  * Six 2½" x 2¾" (A11, B11).
* Fifteen 1¼"-wide strips. From these, cut:
  * Twelve 1¼" x 10¾" (A15, B15).
  * Fourteen 1¼" x 10¼" (C14).
  * Six 1¼" x 6¼" (A14, B14).
  * Twelve 1¼" x 3½" (A2, A14b, B2, B14b).
  * Fourteen 1¼" x 2" (C1).
  * 174 1¼" squares (A1a, A7b, A8b, B1a, B7b, B8b, C2a, C6a, C12b, C13a).
* From scraps, cut:
  * Fifty-two 2" squares (A6a, B6a, A10, B10, C12a).

**From Fabric IV (gray print), cut:**

* One 3½"-wide strip. From this, cut:
  * Fourteen 2" x 3½" (C8).
  * Two 1¼" x 10" strips. From these, cut fourteen 1¼" squares (C6b).
* One 2¾" strip. From this, cut:
  * Seven 2¾" squares (C5).
  * Fourteen 1¼" x 2¾" (C4).

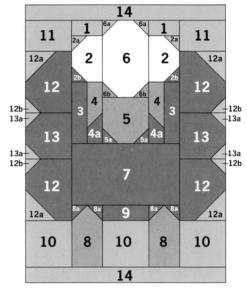

Block C—Make 7.

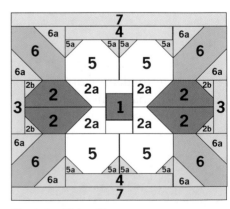

Block D—Make 38.

## From Fabric V (yellow print), cut:

✳ Nine 5¾"-wide strips. From these, cut:
  - Twenty-four 5" x 5¾" (Sashing 3).
  - Forty 4¼" x 5¾" (Sashing 2).
  - Twelve 3⅛" x 5¾" (Sashing 1).
✳ Two 6½"-wide strips. From these, cut:
  - Seventy-six ⅞" x 6½" (D7).
✳ Ten 1⅜" strips. From these and scraps, cut:
  - 304 1⅜" squares (D6a).
✳ Eleven 1"-wide strips. From these, cut:
  - 456 1" squares (D2b, D5a).
✳ Ten ⅞"-wide strips. From these, cut:
  - Seventy-six ⅞" x 3½" (D4).
  - Seventy-six ⅞" x 2" (D3).

## From Fabric VI (gold print), cut:

✳ Two 1¼"-wide strips for Strip Set 1.
✳ Nine 1¼"-wide strips. From these, cut:
  - 152 1¼" x 2⅜" (D2).

## From Fabric VII (olive print), cut:

✳ Eight 2"-wide strips. From these, cut:
  - 152 2" squares (D6).

## From Fabric VIII (dark green), cut:

✳ Four 5¾"-wide strips. From these, cut:
  - Twenty-four 5¾" squares for sashing.

## Units for Block A

Refer to Block A Assembly Diagram throughout to identify units.
**1.** Use diagonal-corner technique to make one each of units 1, 5, 6, and 7. Be sure to place appropriate fabric in each corner as shown.
**2.** Use diagonal-corner technique to make 11 of Unit 8. Make two units with one 8a corner, three units with one 8b corner, four units with two 8b corners, and two units with one each of 8a and 8b corners (see diagram for fabric placement).

**3.** Place one 8a and one 8c together with right sides facing. Stitch a diagonal seam through center, like a diagonal corner. Trim excess fabric from seam allowance and press to get a triangle-square as shown.
**4.** Use diagonal-end technique to make one each of units 4 and 14.

## Block A Assembly

Refer to Block A Assembly Diagram throughout to identify units. Each completed block should measure approximately 14" x 15½".
**1.** Join units 1 and 2. Add Unit 3 to bottom of 1/2 unit.
**2.** Join units 4 and 5. Add Unit 6 to bottom of 4/5 unit.
**3.** Join combined unit 1/2/3 to right side of unit 4/5/6.
**4.** Join Unit 7 to top of combined unit to complete head section.
**5.** For bottom of Unit 9, select three of Unit 8—one with one 8a corner, one with two 8b corners, and one with 8a/8b corners. Referring to diagram, join three units in a horizontal row. Join Unit 8a/8c to right end as shown. Sew row to bottom of Unit 9.
**6.** For side of Unit 9, select three of Unit 8—one with one 8a corner, one with one 8b corner, and one with 8a/8b corners. Join units in a vertical row as shown. Sew row to left side of Unit 9.
**7.** Join 8/9 unit to head section.
**8.** Join five remaining Unit 8s in a horizontal row. Sew row to top of combined body section.
**9.** Sew Unit 10 to three corners of body section as shown.
**10.** Join units 11, 12, and 13 in a row as shown. Sew row to bottom of body section.
**11.** Sew units 14 and 15 to left side of body section. Sew Unit 15 to right side.
**12.** Sew Unit 16s to top and bottom edges to complete block.
**13.** Make three of Block A.

*(continued)*

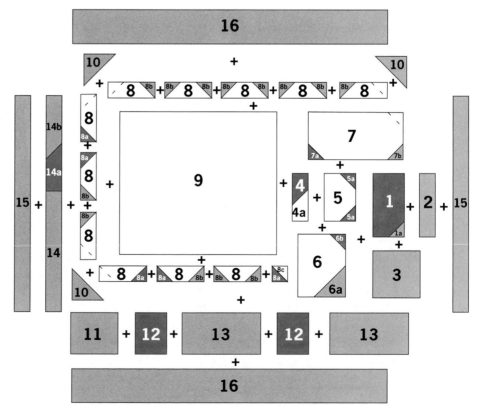

Block A Assembly Diagram

## Block B Assembly

Block B is a mirror image of Block A. Make most units exactly the same as for Block A, but reverse angles of diagonal corners and diagonal ends. Refer to Block B Diagram carefully when making units 1, 4, 6, 7, 8, and 14. Make three of Block B.

## Units for Block C

Refer to Block C Assembly Diagram throughout to identify units.

**1.** Use diagonal-corner technique to make one each of units 5 and 6. Make two each of units 8 and 13.

**2.** Use diagonal-corner technique to make two of Unit 2. Note that the second unit is a mirror image, so refer to diagram carefully to position pieces correctly.

**3.** Use diagonal-corner technique to make four of Unit 12. Note that two units are mirror images.

**4.** Use diagonal-end technique to make two of Unit 4. The second unit is a mirror image.

## Block C Assembly

Assemble this block in vertical sections X and Y. Refer to Block C Assembly Diagram throughout to identify units. Each completed block should measure approximately 10¼" x 14".

### Section X

**1.** Join both pair of units 3 and 4 as shown.
**2.** Join units 1, 2, and 3/4 in two vertical rows as shown.
**3.** Join units 5 and 6.
**4.** Sew units 1/2/3/4 to sides of unit 5/6.
**5.** Join Unit 7 to bottom of combined unit.
**6.** Sew Unit 9 to one of Unit 10.
**7.** Join Unit 8 to sides of unit 9/10. Sew 8/9/10 to bottom of Unit 7.

### Section Y

**1.** Referring to left side of diagram, join units 10, 11, 12, and 13 in a vertical row as shown.

**2.** For right side of block, join remaining units 10, 11, 12, and 13 in a row as shown.

### Assembly

Join Y sections to sides of Section X to complete block. Make seven of Block B.

## Units for Block D

Refer to Block D Assembly Diagram throughout to identify units.

**1.** Referring Strip Set 1 Diagram, join ⅞"-wide strips of Fabric II to both sides of 1¼"-wide strip of Fabric VI. Make two of Strip Set 1. From these, cut thirty-eight 1¼"-wide segments for Unit 1.

Strip Set 1—Make 2.

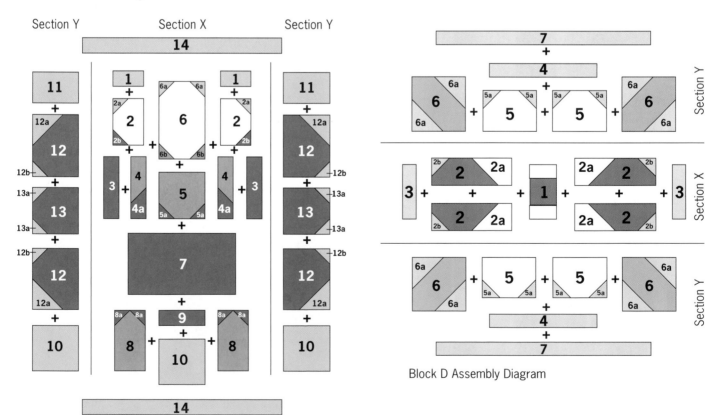

Block C Assembly Diagram

Block D Assembly Diagram

**2.** Use diagonal-end technique to sew piece 2a to piece 2. Complete Unit 2 by adding diagonal corner 2b as shown. Make another of Unit 2 in same manner; then make two mirror-image units.

**3.** Use diagonal-corner technique to make four each of units 5 and 6.

## Block D Assembly

This block is assembled in horizontal sections X and Y. Refer to Block D Assembly Diagram throughout to identify units. Each completed block should measure approximately 5¾" x 6½".

### Section X

**1.** Join mirror-image Unit 2s in pairs as shown.

**2.** Join Unit 2 pairs to opposite sides of Unit 1.

**3.** Sew a Unit 3 to each end of combined unit.

### Section Y

**1.** Referring to top of assembly diagram, join two of Unit 5.

**2.** Sew Unit 4 to top of combined Unit 5s.

**3.** Join a Unit 6 to each end of 4/5 unit.

**4.** Make bottom Y section in same manner.

### Assembly

Join Y sections to Section X. Sew Unit 7 to top and bottom edges to complete block. Make 38 of Block D. *(continued)*

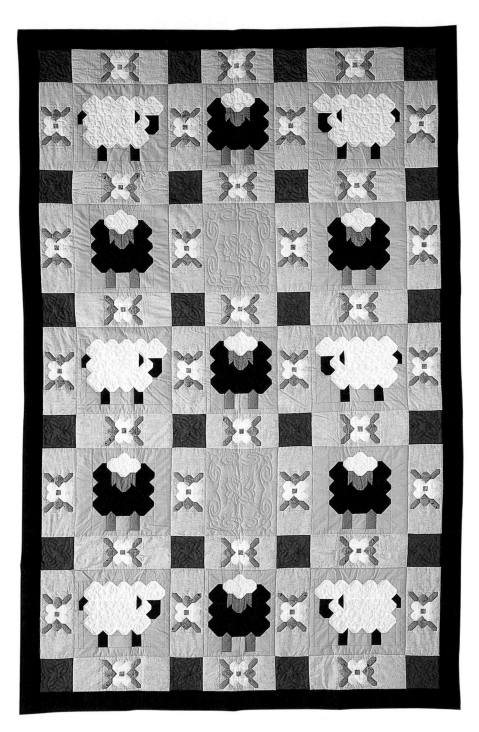

## Quilt Assembly

Refer to Row Assembly Diagram for placement of blocks in rows. Assemble each row from left to right.

### Row 1

**1.** Select one each of blocks A, B, and C. Also select four of Block D, two of Spacer F, and eight of Sashing 2.
**2.** To make sashing units, join Sashing 2 to opposite sides of each D block.
**3.** Sew Spacer F to sides of Block C.
**4.** Join blocks and sashing units in a horizontal row as shown.
**5.** Make three of Row 1.

### Sashing Row

**1.** Select three of Block D, four of Sashing 3, two of Sashing 1 and four Fabric VIII sashing squares.
**2.** To make sashing units, join Sashing 3 to opposite sides of two D blocks. Join Sashing 1 to sides of remaining D block.
**3.** Join sashing units and squares in a horizontal row as shown.
**4.** Make six Sashing Rows.

### Row 2

**1.** Select two C blocks, four D blocks, four of Spacer G, and eight of Sashing 2.
**2.** Join Sashing 2 to opposite sides of each D block.
**3.** Sew Spacer G to sides of both C blocks.
**4.** Join blocks and sashing units in a horizontal row as shown.
**5.** Make two of Row 2.

Row Assembly Diagram

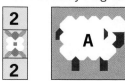

Row 1—Make 3.

Row 2—Make 2.

Sashing Row—Make 6.

### Assembly

**1.** Referring to photo, lay out rows. Start with a Sashing Row and alternate rows 1 and 2 with sashing rows between them.
**2.** When satisfied with row placement, join rows.

## Borders

**1.** Join three Fabric I strips end-to-end for each side border. Join two strips for top and bottom borders.
**2.** Referring to instructions on page 25, measure quilt from top to bottom. Measuring outward from center of border strips, trim side borders to match length. Matching centers, sew borders to quilt sides.
**3.** Measure quilt from side to side; then trim remaining borders to match quilt width. Sew borders to top and bottom edges. Press seam allowances toward border.

## Quilting and Finishing

**1.** Mark quilting design on quilt top as desired. On quilt shown, patchwork is outline-quilted, with additional swirls quilted in the sheep bodies to represent wooly fleece. Use a stencil to mark a design of your choice in spacer blocks.
**2.** Divide backing into two 3¼-yard lengths. Cut one piece in half lengthwise. Join one narrow panel to both sides of wide piece to assemble backing.
**3.** Layer backing, batting, and quilt top. Baste. Quilt as marked or as desired.
**4.** From Fabric I strips, make 10 yards of straight-grain binding. See page 30 for instructions on making and applying binding.

# Crows *in the* Corn

When the corn is as high as an elephant's eye, it's picnic time.
Dress your table for a summer feast with this patchwork tablecloth that's full of
charm. If you like things corny, add wider borders to make a twin-sized quilt.

## Finished Size
Tablecloth: 56" x 83"
Blocks: 36 crow blocks, 4" x 4½"
6 corn blocks, 6" x 16"

## Materials

| | | |
|---|---|---|
| | Fabric I (white solid) | 3⅜ yards |
| | Fabric II (green check) | 2¼ yards |
| | Fabric III (gold print) | ½ yard |
| | Fabric IV (yellow solid) | ⅜ yard |
| | Fabric V (black solid) | ½ yard |
| | Fabric VI (gray print) | ⅜ yard |
| | 90"-wide backing fabric | 1¾ yards |
| | Low-loft batting (optional) | 72" x 90" |
| | Gold embroidery floss | 1 skein |

## Quick-Piecing Techniques
Strip Piecing (see page 20)
Diagonal Corners (see page 20)
Diagonal Ends (see page 21)

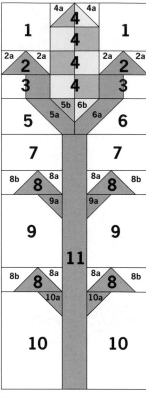

Block A—Make 6.

## Cutting
Cut all strips crossgrain, from selvage to selvage. For best use of yardage, cut pieces in order listed. Refer to diagrams to identify pieces.

### From Fabric I (white solid), cut:
* One 16½"-wide strip. From this, cut:
  * One 16½" x 33½" (M).
  * Two 5½" x 6½" (I).
* One 10½"-wide strip. From this, cut:
  * Four 10½" squares (D1).
* Two 9½"-wide strips. From these, cut:
  * Four 9½" x 13½" (H).
  * Four 4½" x 9½" (G).
* One 8½"-wide strip. From this, cut:
  * Two 8½" x 21½" (L).
* Three 4½"-wide strips. From these, cut:
  * Two 4½" x 11½" (K).
  * Eight 4½" squares (E).
  * Twelve 3" x 4½" (A10).
  * Twelve 1" x 4½" (F).

* Four 3½"-wide strips. From these, cut:
  * Thirty-six 3½" squares (B4, C4).
  * Thirty-six 1" x 3½" (B1, C1).
* One 3"-wide strip. From this, cut:
  * Twelve 3" x 3½" (A9).
* Three 2½"-wide strips. Set aside two strips for Strip Set 3. From remaining strip, cut:
  * Two 2½" x 3½" (J).
  * Twelve 2½" squares (A1).
* Two 2¼"-wide strips for Strip Set 3.
* Three 2"-wide strips. From these, cut:
  * Twenty-four 2" x 3" (A5, A6, A7).
  * Twenty-four 1½" x 2" (A8b).
* Six 1½"-wide strips. Set aside two strips for strip sets 1 and 4. From remaining strips, cut:
  * Ninety-six 1½" squares (A2a, A4a, A8a, B2a, C2a).
* Two ¾"-wide strips for Strip Set 3.

### From Fabric II (green check), cut:
* Eight 4½"-wide strips for Borders 1 and 2.
* Seven 3"-wide strips for binding.

* One 2"-wide strip. From this, cut:
  * Twelve 2" x 2½" (A5a, A6a).
* Six 1½"-wide strips. Set aside one strip for Strip Set 1. From remaining strips, cut:
  * Six 1½" x 11" (A11).
  * Thirty-six 1½" x 2½" (A2, A8).
  * Twenty-four 1½" squares (A9a, A10a).

### From Fabric III (gold print), cut:
* Six 1½"-wide strips. Set aside five strips for strip sets 2 and 4. From remaining strip, cut:
  * Six 1½" squares (A5b).
  * Thirty-six 1" squares (B1a, C1a). *Note:* If necessary, cut two or three squares from strip for Strip Set 4.
* Four ¾"-wide strips for Strip Set 3.

### From Fabric IV (yellow solid), cut:
* Five 1½"-wide strips. Set aside four strips for Strip Set 2. From remaining strip, cut:
  * Six 1½" squares (A6b).

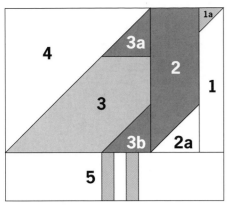

Block B—Make 18.

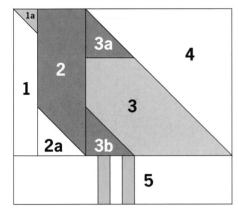

Block C—Make 18.

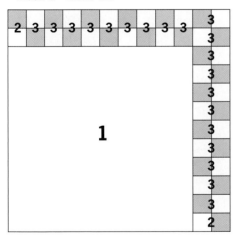

Block D—Make 4.

## From Fabric V (black solid), cut:

✻ Eight 1½"-wide strips. From these, cut:
  • Seventy-two 1½" x 3½" (B2, B3a, C2, C3a).
  • Thirty-six 1½" squares (B3b, C3b).

## From Fabric VI (gray print), cut:

✻ Three 2½"-wide strips. From these, cut:
  • Thirty-six 2½" x 3½" (B3, C3).

## Units for Block A

Refer to strip set diagrams and Block A Assembly Diagram throughout to identify units.

**1.** For Strip Set 1, join 1½"-wide strips of fabrics I and II. Press seam allowances toward Fabric II. From this strip set, cut twelve 1½"-wide segments for Unit 3.

**2.** For Strip Set 2, join 1½"-wide strips of fabrics III and IV. Make four strip sets. Press seam allowances toward Fabric III. From these strip sets, cut twenty-four 1½"-wide segments for Unit 4. Set aside remainder for Block D.

**3.** Use diagonal-corner technique to add 4a corners to one Unit 4 segment.

**4.** Use diagonal-corner technique to make two each of units 2, 9, and 10.

**5.** Use diagonal-end technique to join 5a to piece 5. Then add diagonal corner 5b. Make Unit 6 in same manner, making sure angle of diagonal end is a mirror image of Unit 5.

**6.** Join diagonal end 8b to two of Unit 8; then add diagonal corner 8a. Make two more of Unit 8 that are mirror-image units, with angles of diagonal ends and diagonal corners opposite those of first pair.

## Block A Assembly

Assemble this block in two sections. Each completed section should measure approximately 6½" wide. Refer to Block A Assembly Diagram throughout.

### Section X

**1.** For each side of this section, join units 1, 2, and 3 in a row.
**2.** Join four of Unit 4 in a vertical row as shown, placing unit with corners at top.
**3.** Sew 1/2/3 units to sides of Unit 4 row.
**4.** Join units 5 and 6.
**5.** Sew unit 5/6 to bottom of combined 1/2/3/4 unit.

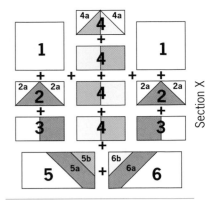

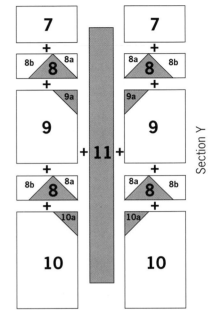

Block A Assembly Diagram

Strip Set 1—Make 1.

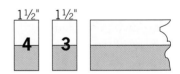

Strip Set 2—Make 4.

### Section Y

**1.** Join units 7, 8, 9, and 10 in a row for each side of block. Position mirror-image Unit 8s as shown.
**2.** Sew combined units to both sides of Unit 11.

### Assembly

Join sections X and Y to complete corn block. Make six of Block A.

*(continued)*

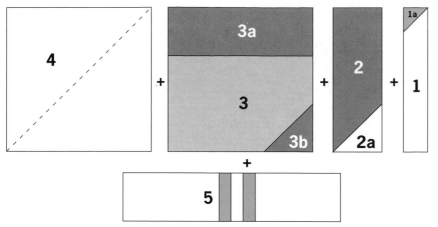

Block B Assembly Diagram

## Units for Block B

Refer to strip set diagrams and Block B Assembly Diagram throughout to identify units.

**1.** For Strip Set 3, join ¾"-wide strips of fabrics I and III as shown. Then join 2¼"-wide and 2½"-wide strips of Fabric I to top and bottom edges. Make two strip sets. Press seam allowances away from center. From these strip sets, cut thirty-six 1½"-wide segments for Unit 5.

**2.** Use diagonal-corner technique to make one each of units 1 and 2.

**3.** Join strip 3a to one edge of piece 3 as shown. Use diagonal-corner technique to add 3b.

## Block B Assembly

**1.** Join units 1, 2, and 3 in a row as shown.

**2.** Use diagonal-corner technique to sew Unit 4 to left end of row.

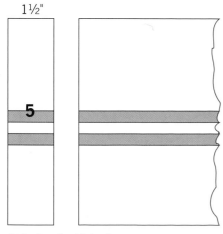

Strip Set 3—Make 2.

Press; then trim excess fabric from seam allowance.

**3.** Add Unit 5 to bottom of block, positioning wider Fabric I strip under Unit 3.

**4.** Make 18 of Block B.

## Block C Assembly

Block C is a mirror image of Block B. Units are the same, but diagonal corners are reversed. Referring to block diagram, make 18 of Block C.

## Block D Assembly

Block D is the corner of the tablecloth. Each completed block should measure approximately 12½" square.

**1.** For Strip Set 4, join 1½"-wide strips of fabrics I and III. From this strip set, cut eight 1½"-wide segments for Unit 2. Cut and set aside four more segments for tablecloth assembly.

**2.** From remainder of Strip Set 2, cut eighty 1½"-wide segments for Unit 3. Cut and set aside two more segments for tablecloth assembly.

**3.** Join nine of Unit 3 in a row, alternating fabrics as shown (Block D Assembly Diagram). Add one Unit 2 to left end of row. Join row to square D1.

**4.** Join 11 of Unit 3 in a row as shown, adding one Unit 2 to bottom of row. Join row to adjacent side of D1 as shown.

**5.** Make four of Block D.

## Tablecloth Assembly

Assemble the tablecloth in three sections—two of Section X and one of Section Y. Refer to bottom half of Tablecloth Assembly Diagram to assemble sections (top half is the same, but upside-down).

### Section X

**1.** Join two B blocks side-by-side.

**2.** Sew one E and one F to sides of another B block.

**3.** Sew E/B/F row to top edge of joined B blocks.

**4.** Sew G to top edge of combined unit.

**5.** Join assembled unit to one side of Block D as shown.

**6.** Repeat steps 1 and 2 to join three C blocks. Sew combined C blocks to one side of H.

**7.** Join both units as shown to complete corner.

**8.** Repeat steps 1–7 to make another corner in same manner.

**9.** Join I to top of Block A.

**10.** Sew corners to both sides of A/I unit.

**11.** Repeat to make second Section X.

Strip Set 4—Make 1.

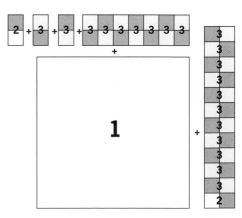

Block D Assembly Diagram

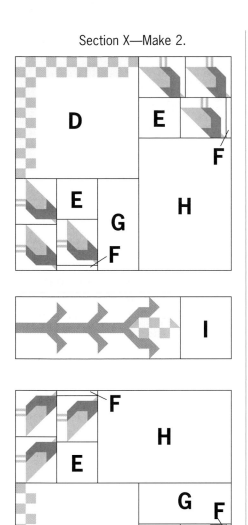

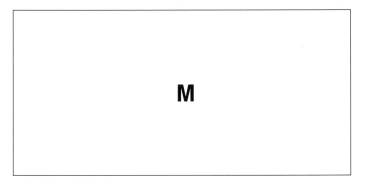

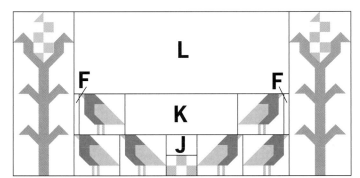

Tablecloth Assembly Diagram

## Section Y

**1.** Join two Strip Set 4 segments to sides of one Strip Set 2 segment as shown. Add J to top of combined segments.

**2.** Join two B blocks; then join two C blocks. Sew each pair to sides of J unit as shown.

**3.** Sew one C block and one B block to both ends of K. Add Fs to both ends of row as shown.

**4.** Join both assembled rows as shown. Then sew L to top edge.

**5.** Add an A block to both sides of center unit.

**6.** Repeat steps 1–5 to make a second center unit.

**7.** Sew center units to both sides of M.

## Assembly

Sew one Section X to both sides of Section Y.

## Borders

**1.** For each border, join two 4½"-wide strips of Fabric II end-to-end.

**2.** Referring to instructions on page 25, measure length of table-cloth. Trim two borders to match length. Sew these to long sides of tablecloth.

**3.** Measure width of tablecloth. Measuring from center seam, trim remaining border to match width. Sew borders to shorter edges of tablecloth. Press seam allowances toward borders.

## Quilting and Finishing

**1.** Mark quilting design on quilt top as desired. On tablecloth shown, patchwork is outline-quilted. If desired, draw curls of wavy corn silk at top of each ear of corn.

**2.** Layer backing and quilt top (low-loft batting is optional for tablecloth). Baste. Quilt as marked or as desired.

**3.** Use two strands of embroidery floss to quilt corn silk.

**4.** From Fabric II strips, make eight yards of straight-grain binding. See page 30 for instructions on making and applying binding.

# Intersection

*Strip piecing combines with log cabin-type construction to make this project. Chains of dark squares march in diagonal rows across the surface of this quilt, marked with nine-patch blocks at each junction.*

## Finished Size

Quilt: 69" x 99"
Blocks: 24 blocks, 12" square

## Quick-Piecing Technique

Strip Piecing (see page 20)

## Materials

| | | |
|---|---|---|
| | Fabric I (ivory print) | 2⅝ yards |
| | Fabric II (blue solid) | 2⅞ yards |
| | Fabric III (tan-and-blue print) | 2¾ yards |
| | Fabric IV (rust print) | 1½ yards |
| | Backing fabric | 6 yards |
| | Precut batting | 90" x 108" |

## Cutting

Cut all strips crossgrain, from selvage to selvage. For best use of yardage, cut pieces in order listed. Refer to diagrams to identify pieces.

### From Fabric I (ivory print), cut:

* Sixteen 3½"-wide strips. Set aside five strips for strip sets 1 and 2. From remaining strips, cut:
  * Four 3½" x 24½" (Sashing Strip E).
  * Three 3½" x 21½" (Sashing Strip D).
  * Twenty-two 3½" x 9½" (Sashing Strip C).
  * Two 3½" x 12½" strips for Row 1.
* Nine 2"-wide strips for inner border.
* Seven 1½"-wide strips for strip sets 3 and 4.

### From Fabric II (blue solid), cut:

* Four 3½"-wide strips. Set aside three strips for Strip Set 2. From remaining strip, cut:
  * Eight 3½" sashing squares.
* Nine 3"-wide strips for binding.
* Eight 1½"-wide strips for strip sets 3 and 4.
* Twenty 2"-wide strips for second and outer borders.

### From Fabric III (tan print), cut:

* Forty-seven 1½"-wide strips. Set aside six strips for Strip Set 5. From remaining strips, cut:
  * Thirty-two 1½" x 11½" (A12, A13).
  * Thirty-two 1½" x 9½" (A14a, B8, B11b).
  * Thirty-two 1½" x 8½" (A8, B7, B11a).
  * Sixty-four 1½" x 7½" (A4, A5, A9a, B4, B9b).
  * Thirty-two 1½" x 6½" (A3, B3, B9a).
* Nine 2"-wide strips for third border.

### From Fabric IV (rust print), cut:

* Two 3½"-wide strips for Strip Set 1.
* Twenty-four 1½"-wide strips. Set aside three strips for Strip Set 5. From remaining strips, cut:
  * Thirty-two 1½" x 9½" (A7, A10).
  * Thirty-two 1½" x 8½" (A11a, B6, B10b).
  * Thirty-two 1½" x 7½" (A6, B5, B10a).

*(continued)*

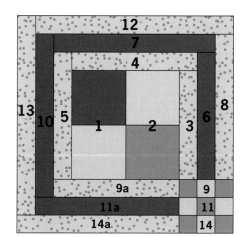

Block A—Make 16.

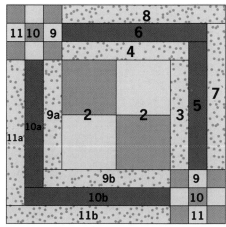

Block B—Make 8.

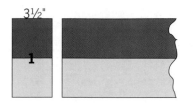

3½"

**1**

Strip Set 1—Make 2.

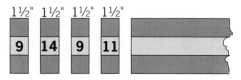

1½" 1½" 1½" 1½"

**9** **14** **9** **11**

Strip Set 3—Make 3.

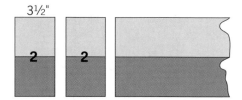

3½"

**2** **2**

Strip Set 2—Make 3.

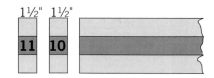

1½" 1½"

**11** **10**

Strip Set 4—Make 2.

## Strip Piecing for Blocks A and B

Refer to strip-set diagrams and block assembly diagrams to identify units. Store strip-set segments in labelled zip-top bags.

**1.** For Strip Set 1, join 3½"-wide strips of fabrics I and IV as shown. Make two of Strip Set 1. Press seam allowances toward Fabric IV. From these strip sets, cut sixteen 3½"-wide segments for Unit A1.

**2.** For Strip Set 2, join 3½"-wide strips of fabrics I and II as shown. Make three of Strip Set 2. Press seam allowances toward Fabric II. From these strip sets, cut thirty-two 3½"-wide segments for units A2 and B2.

**3.** For Strip Set 3, join 1½"-wide strips of fabrics I and II as shown. Make three of Strip Set 3. Press seam allowances toward Fabric II. From these strip sets, cut sixty-four 1½"-wide segments for units A9, A14, B9, and B11.

**4.** For Strip Set 4, join 1½"-wide strips of fabrics I and II as shown. Make two of Strip Set 4. Press seam allowances toward Fabric II. From these strip sets, cut thirty-two 1½"-wide segments for units A11 and B10.

## Block A Assembly

Assemble this block from the center out. Each completed block should measure approximately 12½" square. Refer to Block A Assembly Diagram throughout.

**1.** Join units in numerical order as shown. Work around block to Unit 8. As strips are added, press seam allowances toward strip just added.

**2.** Join Unit 9 to 9a. Press seam allowance toward 9a. Join combined Unit 9 to bottom of block.

**3.** Add Unit 10 to left side of block as shown.

**4.** Join Unit 11 to 11a. Press seam allowances toward Unit 11. Join combined Unit 11 to bottom of block.

**5.** Add units 12 and 13 as shown.

**6.** Join Unit 14 to 14a. Press seam allowances toward 14a. Join combined Unit 14 to bottom of block.

**7.** Make 16 of Block A.

## Block B Assembly

Make Block B in the same manner as for Block A. Referring to Block B Assembly Diagram, join units 2–11 in numerical order as shown. As strips are added, press seam allowances toward strip just added. Make eight of Block B.

*(continued)*

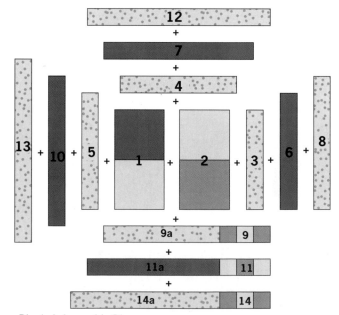

Block A Assembly Diagram

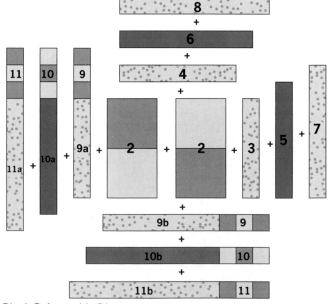

Block B Assembly Diagram

## Quilt Assembly

Make sashing units as described below. Refer to Row Assembly Diagram for placement of blocks and sashing units in rows.

**1.** For Strip Set 5, join 1½"-wide strips of fabrics III and IV as shown. Make three of Strip Set 5. Press seam allowances toward Fabric IV. From these strip sets, cut thirty-two 3½"-wide segments for sashing units.

3½"

Strip Set 5—Make 3.

Sashing Unit—Make 24.

**2.** Referring to Sashing Unit Diagram, sew one segment from Strip Set 5 to one end of each C and E sashing strip. Sew a segment to both ends of each D strip.

**3.** For Row 1, select four A blocks, one 3½" x 12½" strip, and two C sashing units. Positioning nine-patch corner of each block as shown, join blocks and sashing in a row. Make two of Row 1.

**4.** For Row 2, select two Cs, 1 D, and two Fabric II sashing squares. Join units in a row as shown. Make three of Row 2.

**5.** For Row 3, select two each of blocks A and B, and three C units. Join blocks and sashing as shown. Make two of Row 3.

**6.** For Row 4, join two E sashing units and one sashing square as shown. Make two of Row 4.

**7.** For Row 5, select two A blocks, two B blocks, and three C units. Join blocks and sashing as shown. Make two of Row 5.

**8.** Join rows 1–5 in numerical order to assemble half the quilt. Join second set of rows 1–5 in same manner. Referring to photo on page 79, turn second half upside down. Join halves with remaining Row 2 between them.

## Borders

**1.** For Fabric I inner border, cut one strip in half. For each side border, join a strip to both ends of each short piece. For top and bottom borders, join two strips end-to-end.

**2.** Referring to instructions on page 25, measure quilt from top to bottom. Trim longer borders to match quilt length. Sew borders to quilt sides. Press seam allowances toward borders.

**3.** Measure quilt from side to side. Trim remaining borders to match width. Sew borders to top and bottom edges of quilt.

**4.** For second border, repeat steps 1–3 with Fabric II strips.

**5.** For third border, join three Fabric III strips end-to-end for each side and two strips for top and bottom borders. Measure and sew borders to quilt as before.

**6.** For outer border, repeat Step 5 with Fabric II strips.

## Quilting and Finishing

**1.** Mark quilting design on quilt top as desired. On quilt shown, patchwork is outline-quilted.

**2.** Divide backing into two 3-yard lengths. Cut one piece in half lengthwise. Join one narrow panel to each side of wide piece to assemble backing.

**3.** Layer backing, batting, and quilt top. Baste. Quilt as marked or as desired.

**4.** From Fabric II strips, make 9¾ yards of straight-grain binding. See page 30 for instructions on making and applying binding.

Row Assembly Diagram

  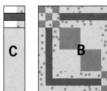 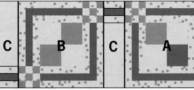

Row 1—Make 2.

Row 2—Make 3.

  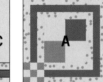 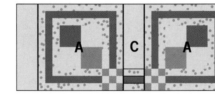

Row 3—Make 2.

Row 4—Make 2.

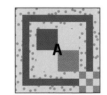   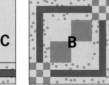 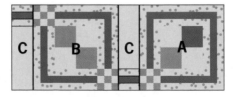

Row 5—Make 2.

# Old Bones

*The king of dinosaurs, Tyrannosaurus Rex, roars for attention on this colorful quilt that's sure to please young paleontologists. If your child is thrilled by Godzilla, he'll love blue Brachiosaurus and green Triceratops. Quick piecing lets you sew with speed, make no bones about it!*

## Finished Size

Quilt: 65½" x 93½"

Blocks: 15 dinosaur blocks, 15½" x 16½"
16 bone blocks, 4" x 16½"

## Quick-Piecing Techniques

Diagonal Corners (see page 20)
Diagonal Ends (see page 21)

## Materials

| | | |
|---|---|---|
| ☐ | Fabric I (white solid) | 2⅛ yards |
| ☐ | Fabric II (blue-green print) | 1¾ yards |
| ☐ | Fabric III (light blue solid) | 1½ yards |
| ☐ | Fabric IV (dark green print) | ⅜ yard |
| ☐ | Fabric V (bright green solid) | ¾ yard |
| ☐ | Fabric VI (orange print) | 1¼ yards |
| | Fabric VII (blue-green dot) | 1⅛ yards |
| | Backing fabric | 5¾ yards |
| | Precut batting | 81" x 96" |
| | Fine-tipped black fabric marker (optional) | |

## Cutting

Cut all strips crossgrain, from selvage to selvage. For best use of yardage, cut pieces in order listed. In some cases, you'll need to trim a strip to a narrower width to cut remaining pieces listed or use fabric left over from cutting larger pieces. Refer to block diagrams to identify pieces.

### From Fabric I (white), cut:

✱ One 17"-wide strip. From this, cut:
  • Sixteen 1¼" x 17" (A12, B12, E15, F15).
  • Two 11" squares (E1, F1).
  • Six 3" x 5½" (A10, B10).
  • Two 1½" x 5½" (E13, F13).
✱ Two 6½"-wide strips. From these, cut:
  • Six 6½" x 8" (A2, B2).
  • Two 6½" x 7" (E12, F12).
  • Two 2" x 3½" (E9, F9).
  • Six 1" x 3½" (A8, B8).
  • Six 3" squares (A3a, B3a).

✱ Three 5"-wide strips. From these, cut:
  • Six 5" x 12½" (A1, B1).
  • Six 5" x 6½" (A11, B11).
  • Two 2" x 4½" (E3b, F3b).
  • Two 1½" x 3½" (E7, F7).
✱ Two 2½"-wide strips. From these, cut:
  • Two 2½" x 9" (E4, F4).
  • Six 2½" x 3" (A6b, B6b).
  • Six 2½" squares (A6a, B6a).
  • Eight 2" x 2½" (A4, B4, E3a, F3a).
  • Two 1" x 2½" (E5, F5).
✱ Three 2"-wide strips. From these and scraps, cut:
  • Eight 2" squares (A7a, B7a, E11a, F11a).
  • Sixty-four 1¾" x 2" (G2).
✱ Seven 1½"-wide strips. From these, cut:
  • Sixteen 1½" x 10" (G4).
  • Four 1½" x 2" (E8a, E10a, F9a, F10a).
  • Eighty 1½" squares (A9a, B9a, E2a, E6a, F2a, F6a, G3a).

### From Fabric II (blue-green), cut:

✱ One 8"-wide strip. From this, cut:
  • Six 6½" x 8" (A3, B3).
✱ Three 2¾"-wide strips. From these, cut:
  • Thirty-two 2¾" x 3½" (G1).
✱ Four 2½"-wide strips. From these, cut:
  • Six 2½" x 8½" (A7, B7).
  • Six 2½" x 6½" (A6, B6).
  • Six 2½" x 3½" (A9, B9).
  • Eighteen 2½" squares (A5, A11a, B5, B11a).
✱ Nine 1½"-wide strips. From these and scraps, cut:
  • Thirty-two 1½" x 10" (G3).
  • Fourteen 1½" squares (A1a, A2a, B1a, B2a, E13a, F13a).
✱ Sixteen 1"-wide strips. From these, cut:
  • Thirty-two 1" x 17" (G5).
  • 128 1" squares (G2a).

### From Fabric III (light blue), cut:

✱ One 8¾"-wide strip. From this, cut:
  • Seven 5" x 8¾" (C10, D10).
  • Seven 1" x 7" (C2, D2).
✱ One 6½"-wide strip. From this, cut:
  • Seven 4¾" x 6½" (C7, D7).

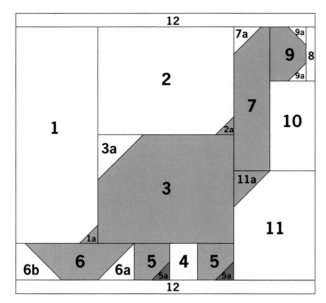

Block A—Make 3.

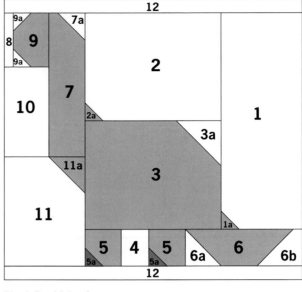

Block B—Make 3.

✱ Four 3¾"-wide strips. From these, cut:
  • Seven 3¾" x 17" (C16, D16).
  • Seven 3¾" x 4½" (C4, D4).
✱ Five 2½"-wide strips. From these, cut:
  • Seven 2½" x 6¼" (C1, D1).
  • Fourteen 2½" x 3" (C12, C15a, D12, D15a).
  • Thirty-five 2½" squares (C5a, C11, C13, C15b, D5a, D11, D13, D15b).
✱ One 2"-wide strip. From this, cut:
  • Seven 2" x 4" (C3b, D3b).
  • Seven 2" squares (C3a, D3a).
✱ From scraps, cut:
  • Seven 3" squares (C9a, D9a).

**From Fabric IV (dark green), cut:**
✱ Three 2½"-wide strips. From these, cut:
  • Seven 2½" x 6½" (C8, D8).
  • Seven 2½" x 4½" (C5, D5).
  • Fourteen 2½" squares (C6a, C12a, D6a, D12a).
✱ One 1½"-wide strip. From this, cut:
  • Twenty-eight 1½" squares (C6b, C7a, C14a, D6b, D7a, D14a).

**From Fabric V (bright green), cut:**
✱ Three 4½"-wide strips. From these, cut:
  • Seven 4½" x 6½" (C9, D9).
  • Seven 4½" x 5½" (C6, D6).
  • Fourteen 1½" squares (C8b, C11a, D8b, D11a).
✱ Three 2½"-wide strips. From these, cut:
  • Seven 2½" x 6½" (C15, D15).
  • Twenty-one 2½" squares (C8a, C14, D8a, D14).
  • Seven 2" x 5" (C3, D3).

*(continued)*

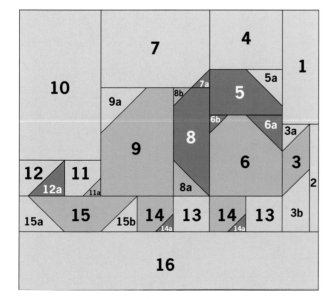

Block C—Make 4.

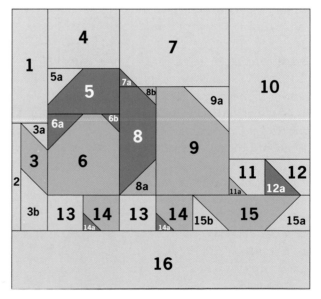

Block D—Make 3.

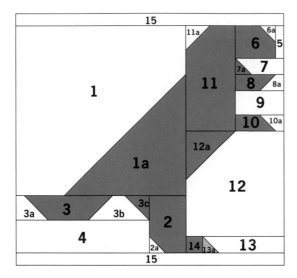

Block E—Make 1.

Block F—Make 1.

## From Fabric VI (orange), cut:

* One 8"-wide strip. From this, cut:
  * Two 8" squares (E1a, F1a).
  * One 4½" x 26" strip and one 3½" x 26" strip. From these, cut:
    * Four 4½" squares for border corners.
    * Two 3½" x 7" (E11, F11).
    * Two 3½" squares (E12a, F12a).
    * Sixteen 1½" squares (A5a, B5a, E7a, E14, F7a, F14).
* One 2½"-wide strip. From this, cut:
  * Two 2½" x 4" (E2, F2).
  * Two 2½" x 3" (E6, F6).
  * Two 2" x 6" (E3, F3).
  * Two 2" squares (E3c, F3c).
  * Four 1½" x 3" (E8, E10, F8, F10).
* Eight 3"-wide strips for binding.

## From Fabric VII (blue-green dot), cut:

* Eight 4½"-wide strips for borders.

## Units for Block A

Refer to Block A Assembly Diagram throughout to identify units.

**1.** Use diagonal-corner technique to make two of Unit 5 and one each of units 1, 2, 3, 7, 9, and 11.

**2.** Use diagonal-corner technique to add 6a to Unit 6 and diagonal-end technique to add 6b.

## Block A Assembly

Assemble this block in sections X and Y. Refer to Block A Assembly Diagram throughout.

**1.** Join units 2 and 3. Add Unit 1 to side of combined units.

**2.** Join units 4, 5, and 6 in a row as shown.

**3.** Sew 4/5/6 row to bottom of 1/2/3 unit to complete Section X.

**4.** Join units 8 and 9. Add Unit 10 to bottom of 8/9 unit.

**5.** Sew Unit 7 to side of 8/9/10 unit.

**6.** Sew Unit 11 to bottom to complete Section Y.

**7.** Join sections X and Y.

**8.** Sew Unit 12 to top and bottom edges of block.

**9.** Make three of Block A.

## Block B Assembly

Block B is a mirror image of Block A. Make units in the same manner, but reverse angles of diagonal end and diagonal corners. Referring to Block B Diagram, make three of Block B.

## Units for Block C

Refer to Block C Assembly Diagram throughout to identify units.

**1.** Use diagonal-corner technique to make two of Unit 14 and one each of units 5, 6, 7, 8, 9, 11, and 12.

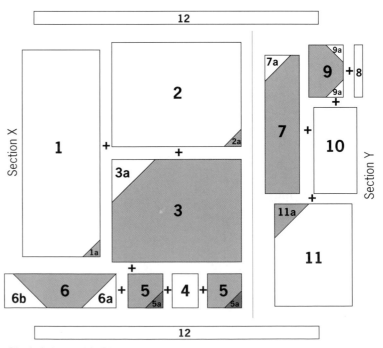

Block A Assembly Diagram

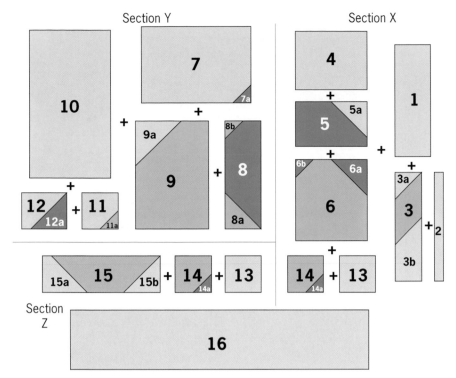

Block C Assembly Diagram

## Block D Assembly

Block D is a mirror image of Block C. Make units in the same manner, but reverse angles of diagonal corners. Referring to Block D Diagram, make three of Block D.

## Units for Block E

Refer to Block E Assembly Diagram throughout to identify units.
**1.** Use diagonal-corner technique to make one each of units 1, 2, 6, 7, 11, 12, and 13.
**2.** Use diagonal-end technique to make one each of units 8 and 10.
**3.** For Unit 3, use diagonal-end technique to add 3a and 3b to sides of Unit 3. Use diagonal-corner technique to add 3c to 3b.

**2.** Use diagonal-end technique and diagonal-corner technique to make one each of units 3 and 15.

## Block C Assembly

Assemble this block in sections X, Y, and Z. Refer to Block C Assembly Diagram throughout.

### Section X
**1.** Join units 2 and 3. Then add Unit 1 to top of 2/3 unit.
**2.** Join one each of units 13 and 14. Then join units 4, 5, 6, and 13/14 in a row as shown.
**3.** Join both rows to complete Section X.

### Section Y
**1.** Join units 8 and 9. Then add Unit 7 to top of 8/9 unit.
**2.** Join units 11 and 12. Then add Unit 10 to top of 11/12 unit.
**3.** Join 7/8/9 unit and 10/11/12 unit to complete Section Y.

### Section Z
Join units 13, 14, and 15 in a row as shown.

## Assembly
**1.** Join Section Z to bottom of Section Y.
**2.** Sew Section X to right side of block.
**3.** Add Unit 16 to bottom to complete block.
**4.** Make four of Block C.

## Block E Assembly

Assemble this block in sections X and Y. Refer to Block E Assembly Diagram throughout.

### Section X
**1.** Join units 3 and 4. Then sew Unit 2 to side of 3/4 unit.
**2.** Sew Unit 1 to top of 2/3/4 unit.

*(continued)*

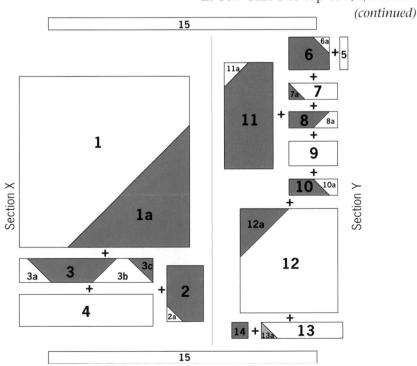

Block E Assembly Diagram

## Section Y

**1.** Join units 5 and 6.
**2.** Join units 5/6, 7, 8, 9, and 10 in a row as shown.
**3.** Sew Unit 11 to side of combined row as shown.
**4.** Add Unit 12 to bottom of combined units.
**5.** Join units 13 and 14. Sew 13/14 to bottom of Unit 12.

### Assembly

**1.** Join sections X and Y.
**2.** Sew Unit 15 to top and bottom of block.
**3.** Make one of Block E.

## Block F Assembly

Block F is a mirror image of Block E. Make units in the same manner, but reverse angles of diagonal corners. Referring to Block F Diagram, make one of Block F.

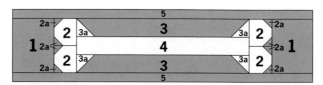

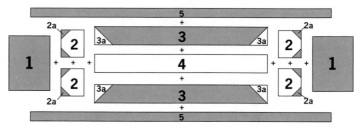

Block G—Make 16.

Block G Assembly Diagram

## Block G Assembly

Refer to Block G Assembly Diagram throughout.

**1.** Use diagonal-corner technique to make four of Unit 2 and two Unit 3.
**2.** Join units 3 and 4 as shown.
**3.** Join two of Unit 2. Sew combined units to one side of 3/4 unit as shown. Join second pair of Unit 2s in same manner and join to opposite side of 3/4 unit.

**4.** Sew Unit 1 to both ends of block as shown.
**5.** Sew Unit 5 to top and bottom of block.
**6.** Make 16 of Block G.

## Quilt Assembly

Refer to photo and Row Assembly Diagram for placement of blocks in each row.

**1.** If desired, use fine-tipped marker to draw smiles and dots for eyes on each dinosaur before assembly.
**2.** For Row 1, join three G blocks and two border corners as shown. Make two of Row 1.
**3.** Trim ½" from both short sides of remaining G blocks to get ten 4½" x 16" bone blocks for remaining rows.
**4.** For Row 2, join one each of blocks A, B, and C as shown. Sew G blocks to both sides of row. Make two of Row 2 as shown. Then make another row, putting a D block in place of C.
**5.** For Row 3, join one each of blocks C, D, and E as shown. Sew G blocks to both sides of row. Make one of Row 4 as shown. Then make another row, putting an F block in place of E.
**6.** Referring to photo, join rows in 1-2-3-2-3-2-1 sequence.

Row Assembly Diagram

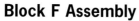

Row 1—Make 2.

Row 2—Make 2 with Block C and 1 with Block D.

Row 3—Make 1 with Block E and 1 with Block F.

## Borders

**1.** For borders, trim a 7"-long piece from ends of two Fabric VII border strips. For each side border, join a full-length strip to both ends of a 7" piece. For top and bottom borders, join two 35"-long strips.

**2.** Referring to instructions on page 25, measure quilt from top to bottom. Measuring from center, trim longer border strips to match length. Sew borders to quilt sides.

**3.** Measure quilt from side to side; then trim remaining borders to match quilt width. Sew borders to top and bottom edges of quilt. Press seam allowances toward borders.

## Quilting and Finishing

**1.** Mark quilting design on quilt top as desired. On quilt shown, patchwork is outline-quilted. The background of each block is machine stipple-quilted.

**2.** Divide backing into two 2⅞-yard lengths. Cut one piece in half lengthwise. Join one narrow panel to each side of wide piece to assemble backing.

**3.** Layer backing, batting, and quilt top. Baste. Quilt as marked or as desired.

**4.** From Fabric VI strips, make 9¼ yards of straight-grain binding. See page 30 for instructions on making and applying binding.

# It's Okay to Be Different

*This quilt goes to show that different can be splendid. A long-time favorite in appliqué, Sunbonnet Sue now makes her pieced debut. Scrap fabrics make sunbonnet fashions as cute as ever. What else is different? Look for one little girl going against the crowd.*

## Finished Size
Quilt: 59" x 93¾"
Blocks: 20 blocks, 10" x 12¼"

## Quick-Piecing Techniques
Diagonal Corners (see page 20)
Diagonal Ends (see page 21)

## Materials

| | | |
|---|---|---|
| | Fabric I (yellow solid) | 3⅛ yards |
| | Fabric II (peach solid) | ¼ yard |
| | Fabric III (purple solid or pindot) | ¾ yard |
| | Fabric IV (turquoise print) | 2½ yards |
| | Fabric V (assorted purple and pink prints) | scraps |
| | Fabric VI (green prints) | scraps |
| | Fabric VII (green solid) | ⅛ yard |
| | Fabric VIII (red solid) | ⅛ yard |
| | 108"-wide backing fabric | 2 yards |
| | Precut batting | 81" x 96" |
| | ½"-wide flat lace trim | 2½ yards |
| | Pink and violet ⅜"-wide satin ribbon | 2¼ yards each |
| | Pink and violet ½"-wide rickrack | 2 yards each |
| | Green ribbon and rickrack | ¼ yard each |

## Cutting

Cut all strips crossgrain, from selvage to selvage. For best use of yardage, cut pieces in order listed. Refer to diagrams to identify pieces.

### From Fabric I (yellow solid), cut:

✳ Two 6½"-wide strips. From these, cut:
- Ten 6¼" x 6½". From these, cut 20 triangles (A6, B6) and 20 mirror-image triangles (A11, B11) as shown in Diagram 1. Store triangles in separate bags to avoid confusion.

✳ Two 5¼"-wide strips. From these, cut:
- Twenty 2½" x 5¼" (A1, B1).
- Twenty 1¾" x 5¼" (A5, B5).

✳ One 5"-wide strip. From this, cut:
- Eleven 2⅜" x 5". Cut 10 of these in half to get 19 (and one extra) of triangle A2 (Diagram 2). Cut one in half as shown to get one B2 triangle (and one extra).

✳ Six 3¼"-wide strips for sashing.

✳ Three 3"-wide strips. From these, cut:
- Twenty 3" squares (A15, B15).
- Twenty 2½" x 3" (A14, B14).
- Twenty 1¼" squares (A13a, B13a).

✳ Four 2"-wide strips for inner border.

✳ Twenty 1¾"-wide strips. From these, cut:
- Twenty 1¾" x 12¾" (A17, B17).
- Twenty 1¾" x 8" (A16, B16).
- Twenty 1¾" x 2¼" (A3, B3).
- Eighty 1¾" squares (A4a, A12, B4a, B12).
- Forty-six 1¾" x 4¼" for rick-rack borders.

### From Fabric II (peach solid), cut:

✳ Two 2¼"-wide strips. From these, cut:
- Forty 1¾" x 2¼" (A9, B9).

### From Fabric III (purple pindot), cut:

✳ Twelve 1¾"-wide strips. From these, cut:
- Ten 1¾" x 3½" (A13).
- Ninety-two 1¾" x 4¼" for rick-rack borders.
- Four 1¾" x 8" for border corners.

### From Fabric IV (turquoise print), cut:

✳ Six 1¾"-wide strips. From these, cut:
- Forty-two 1¾" x 4¼" for rick-rack borders.
- Eight 1¾" x 8" for border corners.

✳ Eight 6"-wide strips for outer border.

✳ Eight 3"-wide strips for binding.

### From Fabric V (purple and pink prints), cut:

*Note:* Cut pieces for nine pink blocks and 10 purple blocks.

✳ Six 6¼" x 6½" (three purple, three pink). Cut two each of triangles A6 and A11 from each piece (Diagram 1), enough for two blocks from each fabric. Cut a total of 20 purple triangles and 18 pink triangles. Discard extras.

✳ Nineteen 4¼" x 5¼" (A4).

✳ Nineteen 1¼" x 5½" (A7).

✳ Ten 2⅜" x 5" (five purple, five pink). Cut each piece in half as shown at left in Diagram 2 to get two A2 triangles for a total of 10 purple and nine pink triangles. Discard extra triangle.

✳ Nineteen 2¼" x 3" (A8).

✳ Nineteen 1¾" x 2¼" (A10).

### From Fabric VI (green scraps), cut:

✳ One 6¼" x 6½". Cut as shown in Diagram 1 to get one each of triangles B6 and B11. Discard extra triangles.

✳ One 4¼" x 5¼" (B4).

✳ One 1¼" x 5½" (B7).

✳ One 1¾" x 2¼" (B10).

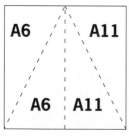

Diagram 1

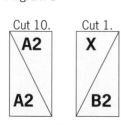

Diagram 2

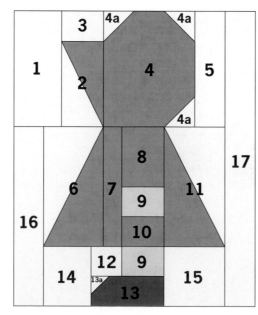

Block A—Make 19.

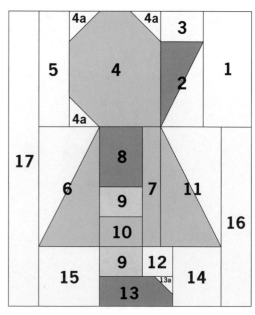

Block B—Make 1.

### From Fabric VII (green solid), cut:

* One 1¾" x 3½" (B13).
* One 2¼" x 3" (B8).
* One 2⅜" x 5" (B2). Cut in half as shown in Diagram 2 to get one A2 triangle and one extra.

### From Fabric VIII (red solid), cut:

* One 1¾"-wide strip. From this, cut:
  * Nine 1¾" x 3½" (A13).

## Units for Block A

Refer to Block A Assembly Diagram throughout to identify units.

**1.** Use diagonal-corner technique to make one each of units 4 and 13.

**2.** For Unit 2, select one triangle each of fabrics I and V. Before you sew, trim 1" from the tip of each triangle (Diagram 3). Then join

triangles to make one of Unit 2 as shown. Press seam allowances toward Fabric V.

**3.** For units 6 and 11, trim 1" from triangle tips in same manner (Diagram 3). Then join triangles to make one of each unit.

Diagram 3

## Block A Assembly

Assemble this block in sections X, Y, and Z. Refer to Block A Assembly Diagram throughout to identify units and sections. Each completed block should measure approximately 10½" x 12¾".

### Section X

**1.** Join units 2 and 3 as shown.
**2.** Join units 1, 2/3, 4, and 5 in a row as shown.

### Section Y

**1.** Join units 8, 9, and 10 in a vertical row. Press seam allowances away from Unit 9.
**2.** Join units 6, 7, 8/9/10, and 11 in a horizontal row as shown.

### Section Z

**1.** Join units 9 and 12 as shown.
**2.** Sew Unit 13 to bottom of combined unit 9/12.
**3.** Join units 14 and 15 to sides of combined unit.

### Assembly

**1.** Join sections Y and Z as shown. Add Unit 16 to left side of combined sections.
**2.** Sew Section X to top of combined sections.
**3.** Join Unit 17 to right side of block.
**4.** Make nine of Block A with pink fabrics and 10 blocks with purple fabrics.
**5.** For each block, cut 4" of flat lace and 7" of rickrack. Tack rickrack in place ½" from skirt seam. Machine-stitch lace to edge of hat brim.

## Block B Assembly

Block B is a mirror image of Block A. Make units in the same manner, but reverse angles of diagonal-corners. Referring to Block B Diagram, make one of Block B.

*(continued)*

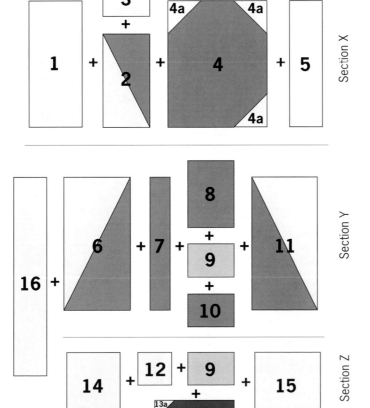

Block A Assembly Diagram

Row Assembly Diagram

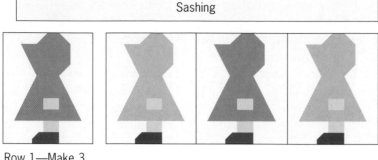

Row 1—Make 3.

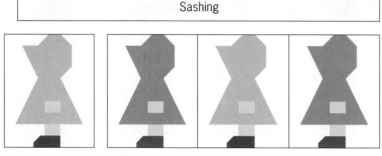

Row 2—Make 2.

## Quilt Assembly

Refer to photo and Row Assembly Diagram for placement of blocks in rows.

**1.** For each row, select two purple blocks and two pink blocks. Lay out row, alternating block colors as shown. Lay out three of Row 1, starting with a purple block, and two of Row 2, starting with a pink block. Position Block B as desired between any two purple blocks.

**2.** When satisfied with block placement, join blocks in each row.

**3.** Join a sashing strip to top edge of each row. Trim sashing even with row. Then join rows as shown in photo. Add last sashing strip to bottom of quilt.

## Borders

**1.** Referring to instructions on page 25, measure quilt from top to bottom. Join two 2"-wide strips of Fabric I end-to-end to make a border for each quilt side. Measuring

out from center, trim borders to fit quilt length. Sew borders to quilt sides.

**2.** For first row of rickrack border, select forty-six 1¾" x 4¼" pieces of Fabric III and 46 matching pieces of Fabric I.

**3.** For top border, join nine Fabric III pieces and eight Fabric I pieces in a continuous diagonal end (Diagram 4). Start with a Fabric III piece and alternate fabrics as shown (Top and Bottom Border Diagram). With right sides facing, align Fabric I edge of border with top edge of quilt, matching centers, and sew. Trim border even with edge of quilt as necessary. Assemble and join bottom border to quilt in same manner.

**4.** Begin and end each side border with a 1¾" x 8" piece of Fabric III. Add 15 pieces of Fabric I and 14 pieces of Fabric III in a continuous diagonal end as shown (Side Borders Diagram). Make two side borders. Matching centers, stitch borders to quilt sides. Trim excess length at both ends as necessary.

**5.** Make next row of rickrack border in same manner. For top border, begin and end with a 1¾" x 8" piece of Fabric IV and add eight 1¾" x 4¼" pieces of Fabric III and seven pieces of Fabric IV, alternating fabrics as shown (Top and Bottom

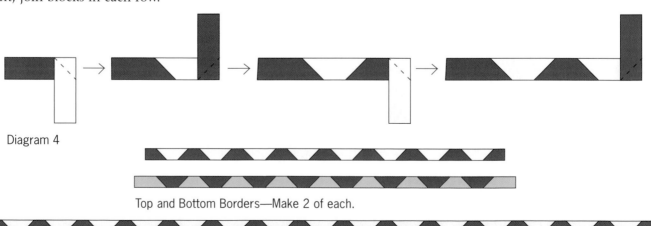

Diagram 4

Top and Bottom Borders—Make 2 of each.

Side Borders—Make 2 of each.

Borders Diagram). Make bottom border in same manner. Center borders on top and bottom edges of quilt, and stitch.

**6.** Begin and end each side border with an 8" piece of Fabric IV, adding 15 pieces of Fabric III and 14 pieces of Fabric IV as shown. Center borders on side edges of quilt and stitch.

**7.** From 6"-wide strips of Fabric IV, cut four 26"-long strips. Join two pieces each for top and bottom borders. Referring to instructions on page 25, measure quilt from side to side and trim borders to match quilt width. Sew borders to top and bottom edges of quilt.

**8.** For each side border, sew two 6"-wide strips to opposite ends of a leftover 16"-long strip. Measure quilt from top to bottom and trim borders to match quilt length. Sew borders to quilt sides. Press seam allowances toward outer borders.

## Quilting and Finishing

**1.** Mark quilting design on quilt top as desired. On quilt shown, patchwork is outline-quilted and a row of 4"-high hearts is quilted in the border.

**2.** Layer backing, batting, and quilt top. Baste. Quilt as marked or as desired.

**3.** From Fabric IV strips, make 9 yards of straight-grain binding. See page 30 for instructions on making and applying binding.

**4.** For each block, cut 7" of ribbon. Tie each piece in a bow. Tack bow securely at bottom of hat brim.

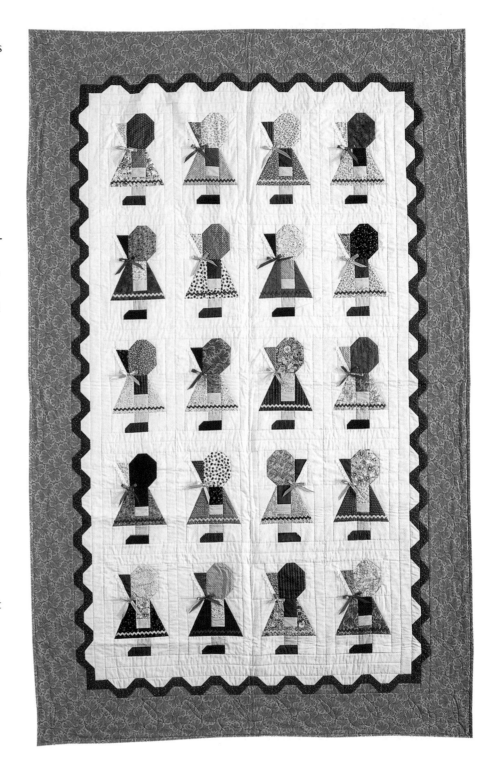

# Primrose

*Pretty in pink, this lovely bed of roses has the grace of appliqué, but it's pieced. Versatile quick-piecing techniques let us make lovely, traditional quilts like this with a speed that our grandmothers would envy.*

## Finished Size
Quilt: 88½" x 112"
Blocks: 12 primrose blocks, 16½" square
36 rosebud blocks, 4½" square

## Quick-Piecing Techniques
Strip Piecing (see page 20)
Diagonal Corners (see page 20)
Diagonal Ends (see page 21)

## Materials

| | | |
|---|---|---|
| Fabric I (white solid) | | 4⅞ yards |
| Fabric II (pink print) | | 4⅛ yards |
| Fabric III (dark pink print) | | 2½ yards |
| Fabric IV (yellow print) | | 1⅛ yards |
| Fabric V (green solid) | | 1⅛ yards |
| 108"-wide backing fabric | | 3½ yards |
| Precut batting | | 120" x 120" |

# Cutting

Cut all strips crossgrain, from selvage to selvage. For best use of yardage, cut pieces in order listed. Refer to diagrams to identify pieces.

## From Fabric I (white solid), cut:

✳ Four 17"-wide strips. From these, cut:
- Six 17" squares for setting squares.
- Twenty-four 2¾" x 17" strips for sashing.

✳ Five 5"-wide strips. From these, cut:
- Two 5" x 16⅞" (C4).
- Two 5" x 10½" (C6).
- Four 5" squares (C5).
- Twenty-eight 4½" x 5" (C3).

✳ Eighteen 2"-wide strips. From these, cut:
- Ninety-six 2" x 3½" (A1).
- Four 2" x 12¼" (C9).
- Four 2" x 12" (C10).
- Twenty-eight 2" x 9" (C7).
- Two 2" x 6½" (C8).

✳ Thirty 1¼"-wide strips. Set aside nine strips for Strip Set 1. From remaining strips, cut:
- 696 1¼" squares (A2a, A3a, A5a, A9a, A16a, B3a, B5a, B9a, B16a).

## From Fabric II (pink print), cut:

✳ Two 21½"-wide strips. From these, cut:
- Three 18½" squares. Cut each square in quarters diagonally to get 10 C1 setting triangles and two extra.
- Two 11" squares. Cut each square in half diagonally to get four C2 setting triangles.
- Sixty-eight 2" squares (C7a, C8a, C9a, C10a).

✳ Twelve 3½"-wide strips for outer borders.

✳ Six 2¾"-wide strips. From these, cut:
- Eighty-four 2" x 2¾" (A8, B8).
- Forty-eight 1¼" x 2¾" (A17).

## From Fabric III (dark pink print), cut:

✳ Eleven 2"-wide strips. Set aside two strips for Strip Set 4. From remaining strips, cut:
- Four 2" x 6" (C7c).
- Four 2" x 4½" (C7b).
- Ninety-six 2" x 3½" (A2).

✳ Sixteen 1¼"-wide strips. Set aside four strips for strip sets 2 and 3. From remaining strips, cut:
- 132 1¼" x 2" (A6, A14, B6).
- 192 1¼" squares (A10a).

## From Fabric III (dark pink print), cut:

✳ Ten 3"-wide strips for binding.

✳ Nine 2¾"-wide strips. From these, cut:
- Ninety-six 2¾" squares (A10).
- Eighty-four 1¼" x 2¾" (A9, B9).

✳ Nineteen 1¼"-wide strips. Set aside four strips for strip sets 2 and 3. From remaining strips, cut:
- Eighty-four 1¼" x 3½" (A5, B5).
- 252 1¼" squares (A6a, A7, A8a, B6a, B7, B8a).

## From Fabric IV (yellow print), cut:

✳ Thirty 1¼"-wide strips. Set aside six strips for strip sets 2, 3, and 4. From remaining strips, cut:
- Twenty-four 1¼" x 17" (A19).
- Twenty-four 1¼" x 15½" (A18).

## From Fabric V (green solid), cut:

✳ Eight 2¾"-wide strips. From these, cut:
- 168 2" x 2¾" (A3, A16, B3, B16).

✳ Nine 1¼"-wide strips for Strip Set 1.

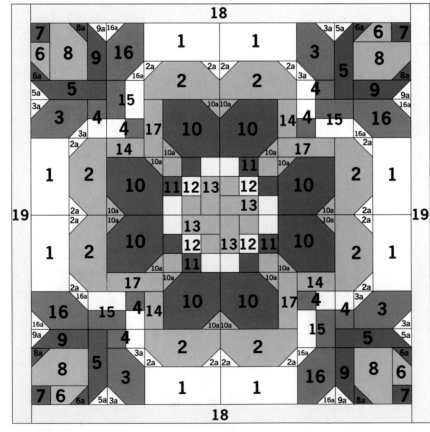

Block A—Make 12.

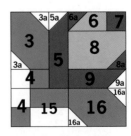

Block B—Make 36.

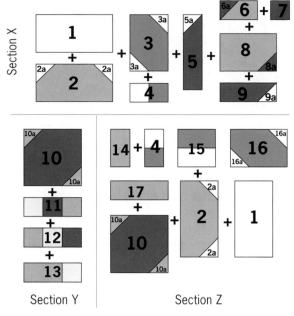

Section X

Section Y          Section Z

Quarter-Block Assembly Diagram

## Units for Block A

Refer to Quarter-Block Assembly Diagram and strip-set diagrams to identify units. Store strip-set segments and assembled units in labelled zip-top bags.

**1.** For Strip Set 1, join 1¼"-wide strips of fabrics I and V as shown. Make nine strip sets. Press seam allowances toward Fabric V. From these strip sets, cut 168 1¼"-wide segments for Unit 4 and eighty-four 2"-wide segments for Unit 15.

**2.** For Strip Set 2, join 1¼"-wide strips of fabrics II, III, and IV as shown. Make two strip sets. Press seam allowances toward center strip. From these strip sets, cut forty-eight 1¼"-wide segments for Unit 11.

**3.** For Strip Set 3, join 1¼"-wide strips of fabrics II, III, and IV as

shown. Make two strip sets. Press seam allowances away from center strip. From these strip sets, cut forty-eight 1¼"-wide segments for Unit 12.

**4.** For Strip Set 4, join 1¼"-wide strip of Fabric IV and 2"-wide strip of Fabric II as shown. Make two strip sets. Press seam allowances toward Fabric II. From these strip sets, cut forty-eight 1¼"-wide segments for Unit 13.

**5.** Use diagonal-corner technique to make two each of units 2 and 10.

**6.** Use diagonal-corner technique to make one each of units 3, 5, 6, 8, 9, and 16.

## Block A Assembly

Assemble this block in four quarter-block units. Make each quarter-block in sections X, Y, and Z. Refer

to Quarter-Block Assembly Diagram throughout. Each completed block should measure approximately 17" square.

### Section X

**1.** Join units 1 and 2 as shown.
**2.** Join units 3 and 4 as shown.
**3.** Join units 6 and 7 as shown.
**4.** Sew unit 6/7 to top of Unit 8. Join Unit 9 to bottom of Unit 8.
**5.** Join units 1/2, 3/4, 5, and 6/7/8/9 in a horizontal row as shown.

### Section Y

Join units 10, 11, 12, and 13 in a vertical row as shown.

### Section Z

**1.** Join units 14, 4, 15, and 16 in a horizontal row as shown.
**2.** Sew Unit 10 to bottom of Unit 17.
**3.** Join units 10/17, 2, and 1 in a horizontal row as shown.
**4.** Join rows to complete section.

### Assembly

**1.** Join Section Y to left side of Section Z.
**2.** Sew Section X to top of Y/Z to complete quarter-block.
**3.** Make four quarter-blocks for each block.
**4.** Referring to Block A Diagram, lay out four quarter-blocks in a square, placing rosebuds in corners. Join quarter-blocks in pairs; then join pairs.
**5.** Join Unit 18 to top and bottom edges of block. Then sew Unit 19 to sides to complete block.
**6.** Make 12 of Block A.

## Block B Assembly

Referring to Block B Diagram, assemble units 3, 4, 5, 6, 7, 8, 9, 15, and 16 in same manner as for Block A. Make 36 of Block B for rosebud border.

*(continued)*

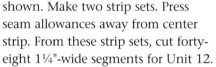

1¼"    1¼"    2"

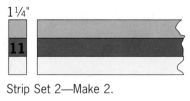

1¼"

Strip Set 1—Make 9.

Strip Set 2—Make 2.

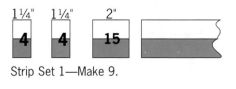

1¼"

1¼"

Strip Set 3—Make 2.

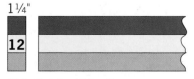

Strip Set 4—Make 2.

Quilt Assembly Diagram

## Quilt Assembly

Join blocks and setting squares in diagonal rows. Setting triangles C1 and C2, with sashing strips, fill in at sides and corners. Refer to Quilt Assembly Diagram throughout.

**1.** Referring to Sashing Diagram, join sashing strips to two sides of each C1 triangle and long edge of each C2 triangle. Trim ends of sashing even with triangle edges as shown.

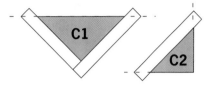

Sashing Diagram

**2.** For Row 1, join C2 unit to one side of Block A. Then sew two C1 units to opposite sides of block.
**3.** For Row 2, join two A blocks to opposite sides of one setting square. Press seam allowances toward square. Add C1 units to ends of row.
**4.** Join blocks, setting squares, and triangle units in diagonal rows. Complete rows 3–6 as shown.
**5.** Join rows in numerical order.

## Borders

There are three borders on this quilt—a rosebud border, a scallop border, and an outer border of Fabric II. Refer to Border Diagrams throughout.

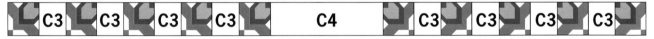

Side Rosebud Border—Make 2.

Top and Bottom Rosebud Border—Make 2.

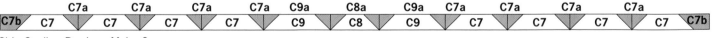

Side Scallop Border—Make 2.

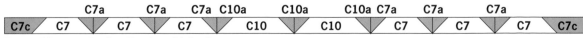

Top and Bottom Scallop Border—Make 2.

## Rosebud Border

**1.** For side border, select 10 B blocks, eight C3, and one C4. Lay out units in a row, positioning rose-buds as shown. Join units in a row. Make two side borders.

**2.** Match center of border with center of quilt side. If border doesn't match quilt side at ends, adjust C4 seams as necessary. Sew borders to quilt sides.

**3.** For top border, select eight B blocks, six C3, two C5, and one C6. Join units in a row, positioning rosebuds as shown.

**4.** Match center of border with center of quilt's top edge. Adjust C6 seams as necessary to make ends match. Sew border to quilt.

**5.** Repeat steps 3 and 4 to make bottom border.

## Scallop Border

**1.** Use diagonal-corner technique to make two of Unit C8 and four each of units C9 and C10 as shown.

**2.** Use diagonal-corner technique to make 20 of Unit C7 with two corners. Make eight more of Unit C7 with one corner.

**3.** Referring to diagram, join a C9 unit to each end of C8. Add three C7s to both ends of row; then add a one-corner C7 to row ends. To complete side border, use diagonal-end technique to add a C7b at each end of row. Note that these are mirror-image units. Make two side borders.

**4.** With right sides facing, pin side borders to quilt sides. Align C7 seams (between Fabric II corners) with centers of C3 units of rosebud borders. Sew borders to quilt sides.

**5.** Referring to diagram, join two C10 units. Add two C7s to both ends of row; then add a one-corner C7 to row ends. To complete bor-der, use diagonal-end technique to add a C7c at each end of row. Make two borders. Pin and sew borders to top and bottom edges of quilt as you did for side borders.

## Outer Border

**1.** For each border, join three 3½" strips of Fabric II end-to-end. Make four borders.

**2.** Referring to instructions on page 25, measure quilt from top to bottom. Measuring out from center, trim two border strips to match length. Sew borders to quilt sides.

**3.** Measure quilt from side to side. Trim remaining borders to match quilt width. Sew borders to top and bottom edges of quilt. Press seam allowances toward borders.

## Quilting and Finishing

**1.** Mark quilting design on quilt top as desired. On quilt shown, patchwork is outline-quilted. If desired, make a stencil of Block A outline and mark block design in setting squares and rosebuds in C1 triangles and Fabric I border units.

**2.** Layer backing, batting, and quilt top. Baste. Quilt as marked or as desired.

**3.** From Fabric III strips, make 11⅝ yards of straight-grain binding. See page 30 for instructions on making and applying binding.

# Grandmother's Violets

*Grace and elegance bloom in this bed of pieced posies. In old-fashioned lavender or bright scrap fabrics, the medallion setting guarantees a bold effect. A scallop-like outer border sets this quilt apart from garden-variety patchwork.*

## Finished Size
Quilt: 81" x 109½"
Blocks: 26 violet blocks, 9" square
　　　　48 leaf blocks, 9" square

## Quick-Piecing Techniques
Strip Piecing (see page 20)
Diagonal Corners (see page 20)
Diagonal Ends (see page 21)
Four-Triangle Squares (see page 23)

## Materials

| | | |
|---|---|---|
| ☐ | Fabric I (white-on-white print) | 5¼ yards |
| ▨ | Fabric II (green print) | 3 yards |
| ▨ | Fabric III (solid navy) | 1⅛ yards |
| ▨ | Fabric IV (purple solid) | ⅞ yard |
| ▨ | Fabric V (lavender solid) | 2⅜ yards |
| ☐ | Fabric VI (yellow solid) | ¼ yard |
| | Backing fabric | 6½ yards |
| | Precut batting | 120" x 120" |

## Cutting
Cut all strips crossgrain, from selvage to selvage. For best use of yardage, cut pieces in order listed. Refer to diagrams to identify pieces.

### From Fabric I (white), cut:
* Three 9½"-wide strips. From these, cut:
  * Three 9½" squares (D).
  * Sixteen 5½" x 9½" (C3).
* Ten 5½"-wide strips. Set aside eight strips for strip sets 2 and 4. From remaining strips, cut:
  * Sixteen 4½" x 5½" (C2).
* Four 4½"-wide strips for Strip Set 3.
* Three 4¼"-wide strips. From these, cut:
  * Fifty-two 2" x 4¼" (A2).

* Four 4"-wide strips for Strip Set 3.
* Nine 3"-wide strips. Set aside six strips for Strip Set 4. From remaining strips, cut:
  * Thirty-two 3" squares (C1a).
* Three 1½"-wide strips for Strip Set 1.
* Eight 1¼"-wide strips. From these, cut:
  * 260 1¼" squares (A1a, A3a, A8b, A10b, A11a).
* From scraps, cut:
  * Fifty-two 1¾" squares (A11b).
  * Twenty-six 1" x 3½" (A9).

### From Fabric II (green), cut:
* One 34" square for bias binding.
* Two 4½"-wide strips. From these, cut:
  * Sixteen 4½" squares (C1).

* Three 3¼"-wide strips. From this and scraps from previous steps, cut:
  * Fifty-two 2⅜" x 3¼" (A11).
* Twenty-one 2"-wide strips. Set aside 16 strips for strip sets 3, 4, 5, and 6. From remaining strips, cut:
  * Two 2" x 8" (E5).
  * Sixteen 2" x 6½" (E4).
  * Twenty-six 2" squares (A1).
* Eight 1¼" strips. Set aside five strips for strip sets 1 and 2. From remaining strips and scraps, cut:
  * 104 1¼" squares (A3b, A10a).

*(continued)*

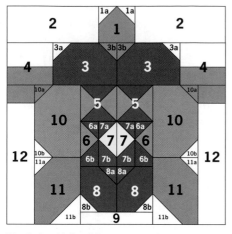

Block A—Make 26.

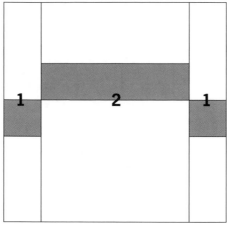

Block B—Make 32.

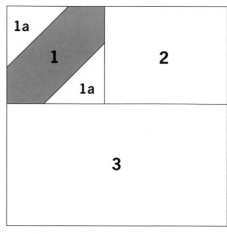

Block C—Make 16.

## From Fabric III (navy), cut:

✱ One 7½"-wide strip. From this, cut:
- One 7½" x 21¼" for triangle-squares (A5).
- Six 1¼" x 21¼" strips. From these, cut:
- Fifty-two 1¼" x 1⅝" (A7b).

✱ Four 1¼"-wide strips. From these and scraps from previous steps, cut:
- 156 1¼" squares (A6a, A7a, A8a).

✱ Ten 2"-wide strips for inner border.

## From Fabric IV (purple), cut:

✱ One 7½"-wide strip. From this, cut:
- One 7½" x 21¼" for triangle-squares (A5).
- Four 1¼" x 21¼" strips. From these, cut:
- Fifty-two 1¼" x 1⅝" (A6b).

✱ Three 2⅜"-wide strips. From these, cut:
- Fifty-two 2" x 2⅜" (A8).

✱ Four 2¼"-wide strips. From these, cut:
- Fifty-two 2¼" x 3⅛" (A3).

## From Fabric V (lavender), cut:

✱ One 7½"-wide strip. From this, cut:
- Two 7½" x 21¼" for triangle-squares (A5).

✱ Seventeen 3½"-wide strips. Set aside three strips for Strip Set 6 and eight strips for middle border. From remaining strips, cut:
- Two 3½" squares (E1).
- Fifty-two 2⅜" x 3½" (A10).

✱ Five 2"-wide strips. Set aside three strips for Strip Set 5. From remaining strips, cut:
- Fifty-two 1¼" x 2" (A6).

## From Fabric VI (yellow), cut:

✱ Two 2"-wide strips. From these, cut:
- Fifty-two 1¼" x 2" (A7).

## Units for Block A

Refer to strip set diagrams and Block A Assembly Diagram throughout to identify units. For Unit 5, see page 23 for instructions on four-triangle squares.

Strip Set 1—Make 3.

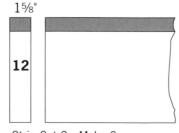

Strip Set 2—Make 2.

**1.** For Strip Set 1, join 1½"-wide strip of Fabric I and 1¼"-wide strip of Fabric II as shown. Make three strip sets. From these, cut fifty-two 2⅜"-wide segments for Unit 4.

**2.** For Strip Set 2, join 5½"-wide strip of Fabric I and 1¼"-wide strip of Fabric II as shown. Make two strip sets. From these, cut fifty-two 1⅝" segments for Unit 12.

**3.** Use diagonal-corner technique to make one of Unit 1. Make two each of units 3, 8, 10, and 11, making one unit a mirror image of the other.

**4.** Use diagonal-corner technique to join 6a to Unit 6. Use diagonal-end technique to add 6b. Make a mirror-image Unit 6 in same manner. Repeat to make two of Unit 7.

**5.** For Unit 5 triangle-squares, draw a 2 x 7-square grid of 2¾" squares on wrong side of each 7½" x 21¼" piece of Fabric V.

**6.** With right sides facing, pair one marked piece with matching piece of Fabric III. Pair second marked piece with matching piece of Fabric IV. Stitch grids as directed for triangle-squares on page 22.

**7.** Cut 28 triangle-squares from each grid. Discard two triangle-squares from each grid, leaving 26 triangle-squares of each fabric combination.

**8.** Draw a diagonal line on wrong side of each IV/V triangle-square.
**9.** With right sides facing and seams aligned, match a marked triangle-square with a III/V triangle-square so that each Fabric V triangle faces a different fabric. Stitch each pair as directed on page 23. Make 52 four-triangle squares for Unit 5.

## Block A Assembly

Assemble this block in four sections—X, Y, and two of Section Z. Refer to Block A Assembly Diagram throughout.

### Section X

**1.** Join units 1 and 2 in a row as shown.
**2.** Sew units 3 and 4 in a row as shown.
**3.** Join rows to complete Section X.

### Section Y

**1.** Join one pair of Unit 5 triangle-squares, positioning fabrics as shown.
**2.** Join units 6 and 7 in a row as shown.
**3.** Join mirror-image Unit 8s.
**4.** Join three rows. Add Unit 9 to bottom of section.

### Section Z

**1.** Join units 10 and 11. Add Unit 12 to side of combined units.
**2.** Use mirror-image units to make second Section Z.

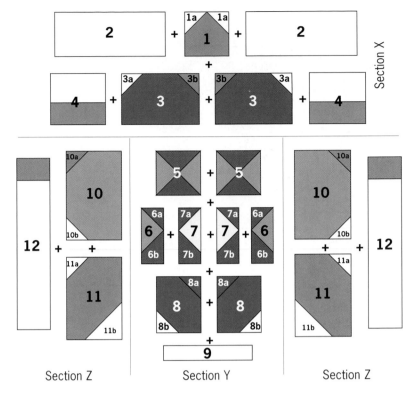

Block A Assembly Diagram

### Assembly

**1.** Sew sections Y and Z in a row as shown.
**2.** Join Section X to top of combined sections.
**3.** Make 26 of Block A.

## Block B Assembly

Refer to strip set diagrams and Block B Assembly Diagram.
**1.** For Strip Set 3, join 4"-wide and 4½"-wide strips of Fabric I to 2"-wide strip of Fabric II as shown. Make four strip sets. Press seam allowances toward Fabric II. From these strip sets, cut sixty-four 2"-wide segments for Unit 1.
**2.** For Strip Set 4, join 5½"-wide and 3"-wide strips of Fabric I to 2"-wide strip of Fabric II as shown. Make six strip sets. Press seam allowances toward Fabric II. From these strip sets, cut thirty-two 6½"-wide segments for Unit 2.
**3.** Join two of Unit 1 to sides of Unit 2 as shown, matching seam lines carefully.
**4.** Make 32 of Block B.

*(continued)*

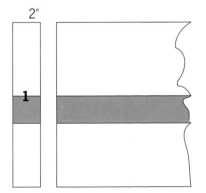

Strip Set 3—Make 4.

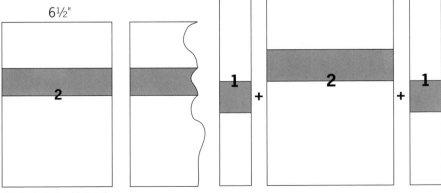

Strip Set 4—Make 6.

Block B Assembly Diagram

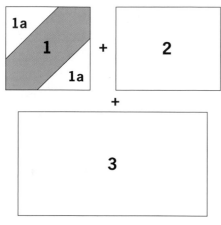

Block C Assembly Diagram

## Block C Assembly

**1.** Use diagonal-corner technique to make one of Unit 1.

**2.** Join units 1 and 2. Add Unit 3 to bottom of combined units.

**3.** Make 16 of Block C.

## Quilt Assembly

Refer to photo and Row Assembly Diagram for placement of blocks.

**1.** Lay out blocks for one each of rows 1, 2, 3, and 4 as shown. Note direction of each block.

**2.** For next row, lay out another Row 3, turning A and C blocks upside-down.

**3.** When satisfied with placement, join blocks in rows 1, 2, 3, 4, and 3. Join rows to make half of quilt.

**4.** Repeat steps 1–3 to make second half of quilt. Lay out both halves, turning one half upside-down for bottom of quilt.

**5.** Between two halves, lay out remaining blocks as shown for Row 5. When satisfied with placement, join blocks in Row 5.

**6.** Sew assembled quilt halves to both sides of Row 5.

## Borders

**1.** For inner border, join three 2"-wide Fabric III strips end-to-end for each side border. For top and bottom borders, join two strips each.

Row Assembly Diagram

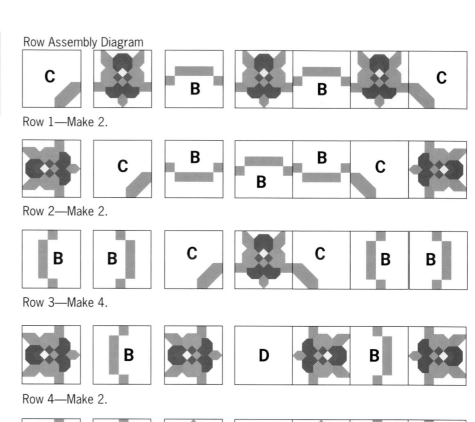

Row 1—Make 2.

Row 2—Make 2.

Row 3—Make 4.

Row 4—Make 2.

Row 5—Make 1.

**2.** Referring to instructions on page 25, measure quilt from side to side. Measuring outward from center of strips, trim top and bottom borders to match quilt width. Matching centers, sew borders to top and bottom edges of quilt.

**3.** Measure quilt from top to bottom; then trim remaining borders to match quilt length. Sew borders to quilt sides. Press seam allowances toward border.

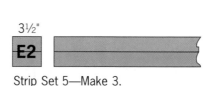

Strip Set 5—Make 3.

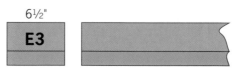

Strip Set 6—Make 3.

**4.** For middle border, repeat steps 1–3 with strips of Fabric V, eliminating top border (see photo).

### Scallop Border

Refer to Border Assembly Diagram throughout.

**1.** For Strip Set 5, join 2"-wide strips of fabrics II and V as shown. Make three strip sets. From these, cut thirty-two 3½"-wide segments for Unit E2.

**2.** For Strip Set 6, join 3½"-wide strip of Fabric V and 2"-wide strip of Fabric II as shown. Make three strip sets. From these, cut fifteen 6½"-wide segments for Unit E3.

**3.** For bottom border, select two E1, eight E2, three E3, and four E4. Join units in a row as shown. Be sure top edge of row is even. Sew border to bottom edge of quilt.

**4.** For left side border, select 12 E2, six E3, and six E4. Join units in a row, keeping top of row even. Sew border to left side of quilt.

**5.** Sew E5 across E3/E1 scallop at bottom corner.

**6.** The right side border is a mirror image of the left. Join units as shown. Sew border to right side of quilt and complete bottom corner as before.

## Quilting and Finishing

**1.** Mark quilting designs on quilt top as desired. On quilt shown, patchwork is outline-quilted. Use purchased stencils to mark swags, shells, and feathered wreaths in open areas.

**2.** Divide backing fabric into two 3¼-yard lengths. Cut one piece in half lengthwise. Join one narrow panel to each side of wide piece to assemble backing.

**3.** Layer backing, batting, and quilt top. Baste. Quilt as marked or as desired.

**4.** For bias binding, cut 34" square of Fabric II in half diagonally. Measuring from cut edges, cut 2"-wide diagonal strips. Join strips to make one strip 13 yards long.

**5.** See page 30 for directions on pressing and applying binding. Take special care to miter corners of scalloped border.

Border Assembly Diagram

Bottom Border

Left Side Border

Right Side Border

# Keep On Truckin'

*Complete with highways and road signs, this quilt has 15 pickups and panel trucks for aspiring little drivers to dream about. Scrap fabrics and two quick-piecing techniques make it easy to put together.*

## Finished Size

Quilt: 62" x 91"
Blocks: 15 truck blocks, 11" x 14"
      20 yield sign blocks, 3½" x 6½"
      8 stop sign blocks, 3½" square

## Quick-Piecing Techniques

Strip Piecing (see page 20)
Diagonal Corners (see page 20)

## Materials

| | | |
|---|---|---|
| | Fabric I (black solid) | 2½ yards |
| | Fabric II (white solid) | 2 yards |
| | Fabric III (red solid) | ½ yard |
| | Fabric IV (green solid) | ⅜ yard |
| | Fabric V (yellow solid) | ⅞ yard |
| | Fabric VI (blue solid) | 2 yards |
|  | Fabric VII (assorted red, purple, green, yellow, and black) | Scraps |
| | Backing fabric | 5½ yards |
| | Precut batting | 81" x 96" |
| | Black fine-point fabric marker | |

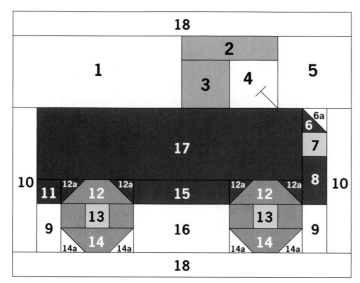

Block A—Make 6.

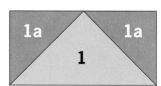

Block B—Make 4.

## Cutting

Cut all strips crossgrain, from selvage to selvage. For best use of yardage, cut pieces in order listed. Save scraps of fabrics I–V to cut truck pieces. Refer to diagrams to identify units.

### From Fabric I (black), cut:

✳ Six 3½"-wide strips. From these, cut:
  • Forty 3½" squares (E1a).
  • Sixty 1½" x 3½" (ABCD12, ABCD14).

✳ Eight 3"-wide strips for binding.
✳ Four 2½"-wide strips. From these, cut:
  • Forty-four 2½" x 3½" (H).
  • Four 2½" squares for outer border corners.
✳ Seventeen 1½"-wide strips. Set aside eight strips for side road sign borders. From remaining strips, cut:
  • Eight 1½" x 25" for top and bottom road sign borders.
  • Six 1½" x 17" for Strip Set 1.
  • Thirty-two 1½" squares (F1a).

Block E—Make 20.

Block F—Make 8.

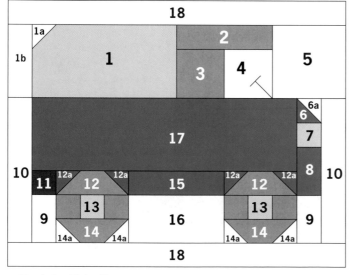

Block C—Make 3.

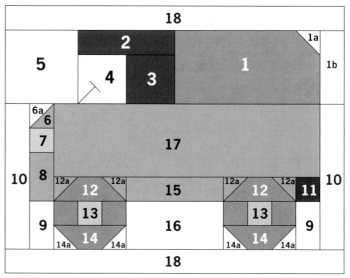

Block D—Make 2.

**From Fabric II (white), cut:**

✱ One 4½"-wide strip. From this, cut:
  • Fifteen 2½" x 4½" (ABCD16).
✱ Four 3½"-wide strips. From these and scrap from previous step, cut:
  • Ten 3½" x 7½" (A1, B1).
  • Twenty-seven 3½" squares (ABCD5, G).
✱ One 2½"-wide strip. From this, cut:
  • Fifteen 2½" squares (ABCD4).
✱ Twenty-seven 1½"-wide strips. Set aside six strips for Strip Set 2. From remaining strips, cut:
  • Thirty 1½" x 14½" (ABCD18).
  • Thirty 1½" x 6½" (ABCD10).
  • Five 1½" x 3½" (C1b, D1b).
  • Thirty 1½" x 2½" (ABCD9).
  • Eighty-two 1½" squares (ABCD6a, A7, ABCD14a, C1a, C7, D1a).

**From Fabric III (red), cut:**

✱ One 3½"-wide strip. From this, cut:
  • Eight 3½" squares (F1).
✱ Two 2½"-wide strips for Strip Set 3.

**From Fabric IV (green), cut:**

✱ Two 2½"-wide strips for Strip Set 3.

**From Fabric V (yellow), cut:**

✱ Four 3½"-wide strips. From these, cut:
  • Twenty 3½" x 6½" (E1).
✱ Two 2½"-wide strips for Strip Set 3.
✱ Two 1½"-wide strips. From these, cut:
  • Three 1½" x 17" for Strip Set 1.
  • Thirteen 1½" squares (ABCD7).

**From Fabric VI (blue), cut:**

✱ Seven 3½"-wide strips. From these, cut:
  • Seventy-four 3½" squares for highway sashing.
✱ Eight 2½"-wide strips for outer border.
✱ Twelve 1½" strips for Strip Set 2.

**From Fabric VII (scraps), cut:**

*Note:* Pieces are listed for 15 truck blocks. You might find it easiest to cut pieces for one block at a time.

✱ Fifteen 3½" x 11½" (ABCD17).
✱ Five 3½" x 6½" (C1, D1).
✱ Fifteen 2½" squares (ABCD3).
✱ Thirty 1½" x 4½" (ABCD2, ABCD15).
✱ Fifteen 1½" x 2½" (ABCD8).
✱ Ninety 1½" squares (ABCD6, ABCD11, ABCD12a).

## Units for Block A

Refer to Block Assembly Diagram to identify units.

**1.** For Strip Set 1, join 1½" x 17" strips of fabrics I and V as shown (Strip Set 1 Diagram). Make three strip sets. From these, cut thirty 1½"-wide segments for Unit 13.

**2.** Use diagonal-corner technique to make two each of units 12 and 14.

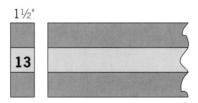

Strip Set 1—Make 3.

**3.** For Unit 6, place two squares (units 6 and 6a) with right sides facing. Stitching through both layers, sew a diagonal line from corner to corner. Trim seam allowance and press.

## Block A Assembly

Assemble this block in sections X, Y, and Z. Refer to Block Assembly Diagram throughout.

**1.** For Section X, join units 3 and 4. Add Unit 2 to top of 3/4 unit. Join units 1 and 5 to sides of row as shown.

**2.** For Section Y, join units 6, 7, 8, and 9 in a row. Add Unit 10 to side as shown.

**3.** For Section Z, begin by joining units 12, 13, and 14 as shown to make two wheels.

**4.** Join units 9 and 11 as shown; then join units 15 and 16 as shown.

**5.** Sew 9/11, 15/16, and both wheel units in a row as shown. Sew Unit 17 to top of row.

**6.** Sew Unit 10 to left side to complete Section Z.

**7.** Join sections Y and Z; then add Section X to top.  *(continued)*

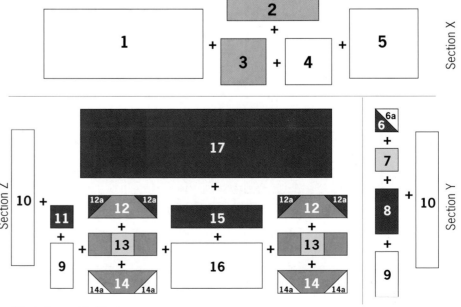

Block Assembly Diagram

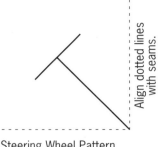

Align dotted lines with seams.

Steering Wheel Pattern

Unit C1 Diagram          Unit D1 Diagram

**8.** Sew Unit 18 to top and bottom of block.

**9.** Make six of Block A, using various fabric combinations.

**10.** Using a fine-tipped fabric pen, trace Steering Wheel Pattern onto Unit 4. For windshield, draw a line in the seam between units 4 and 5. (If you prefer, you can embroider windshield and steering wheel.)

## Block B Assembly

Block B is a mirror image of Block A. Make units in the same manner. Referring to Block B Diagram, make four of Block B.

## Blocks C and D Assembly

Blocks C and D are the same as blocks A and B, except for Unit 1. See Unit C1 Diagram and Unit D1 Diagram. Refer to Block Assembly Diagram throughout.

**1.** Use diagonal-corner technique to sew 1a to one corner of Unit 1. Add Unit 1b to side of unit.

**2.** Assemble remaining units as described for Block A.

**3.** Assemble blocks as for blocks A and B.

**4.** Make three of Block C and two of Block D.

## Highway Sashing Assembly

**1.** Join 1½"-wide strips of fabric II and VI as shown (Strip Set 2 Diagram). Make six strip sets. From these, cut sixty-six 3½"-wide segments for sashing.

**2.** For horizontal sashing, join eight Fabric VI sashing squares and seven Strip Set 2 segments as shown (Sashing Diagram). Make six sashing strips.

**3.** For side borders, join 13 sashing squares and 12 segments of Strip Set 2 in same manner. Make two side borders.

**4.** Use a pin to mark center of each sashing strip and border.

## Quilt Assembly

**1.** Referring to photo, sort truck blocks into five rows, with two pickups and one panel truck in each row. Trucks in each row should face same direction to avoid head-on collision!

**2.** When satisfied with placement, join blocks in each row.

**3.** Lay out rows as desired, placing a highway sashing strip between rows and at top and bottom as shown.

**4.** Match center of each sashing strip to center of adjacent row. Join rows and sashing. Trim ends of sashing strips to match ends of block rows.

**5.** Matching centers, sew highway borders to quilt sides. Trim ends of borders to match top and bottom edges of quilt.

## Road Sign Border Assembly

**1.** Use diagonal-corner technique to make 20 Block E yield signs (Block E Diagram) and eight Block F stop signs (Block F Diagram).

**2.** For top border, select eight Unit H, four of Block E, two Unit G (speed limit sign), and one Block F. Join units in a row as shown (Border Diagram).

**3.** Join two 1½" x 25" strips of Fabric I. Matching center seam with center of Block F, sew strip to top edge of border. Repeat for bottom edge of border.

**4.** Repeat steps 2 and 3 to make bottom border.

**5.** Sew borders to top and bottom edges of quilt.

**6.** For each side border, select 14 Unit H, six Block E, four Unit G, and three Block F. Assemble borders in same manner (Border Diagram), alternating E blocks with G/H units. End row with F blocks. Make two borders.

**7.** Sew borders to quilt sides.

2½

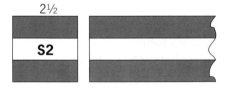

Strip Set 2—Make 6.

Sashing Diagram

Border Diagram

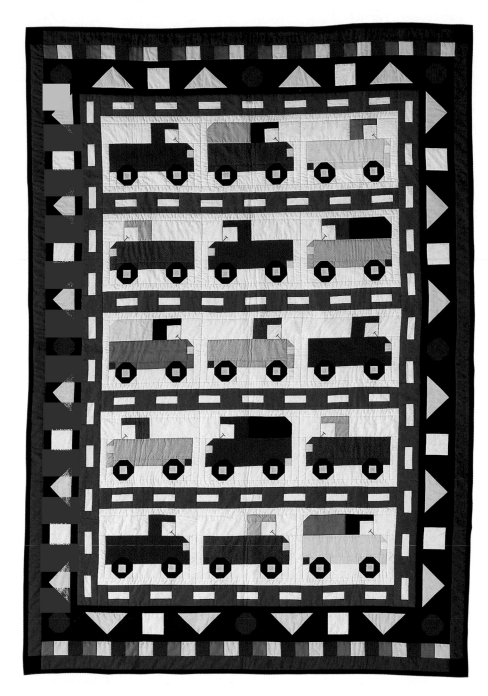

**3.** Pin borders to top edge, placing green square at left corner. Remove last red square on border if necessary. Sew border to top edge of quilt. Repeat for bottom border.

## Outer Border

**1.** For each side border, join two 2½"-wide strips of Fabric VI to ends of one 10"-long strip. For top and bottom borders, join two 32"-long strips end-to-end.

**2.** Referring to instructions on page 25, measure quilt from top to bottom. Trim long borders to match length.

**3.** Measure quilt from side to side. Trim top and bottom borders to match quilt width.

**4.** Sew longer borders to quilt sides. Press seam allowances toward borders.

**5.** Sew Fabric I border corners to ends of remaining borders. Press seam allowances away from corners.

**6.** Sew pieced borders to top and bottom edges of quilt.

## Quilting and Finishing

**1.** Mark quilting design on quilt top as desired. On quilt shown, patchwork is outline-quilted.

**2.** Divide backing into two 2¾-yard lengths. Cut one piece in half lengthwise. Join one narrow panel to each side of wide piece to assemble backing.

**3.** Layer backing, batting, and quilt top. Baste. Quilt as marked or as desired.

**4.** From Fabric I strips, make 9 yards of straight-grain binding. See page 30 for instructions on making and applying binding.

## Traffic Light Border Assembly

**1.** For Strip Set 3, join 2½"-wide strips of fabrics III, IV, and V as shown (Strip Set 3 Diagram). Make two strip sets. From these, cut twenty 2½"-wide segments.

**2.** Referring to photo, join 10 segments end-to-end, sewing red to green. Make two borders.

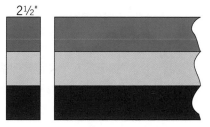

2½"

Strip Set 3—Make 2.

# Sunflowers

*A sawtooth border puts the finishing touch on a quilt that celebrates the warmth and joy of summer. Strip piecing and diagonal corners help make quick work of block construction. Sashing pulls it all together for a quilt that's a pleasure to make and own.*

## Finished Size

Quilt: 74" x 94"

Blocks: 24 flower blocks, 9" square
        12 flower and stem blocks, 9" x 19"

## Quick-Piecing Techniques

Strip Piecing (see page 20)
Diagonal Corners (see page 20)
Triangle-Squares (see page 22)

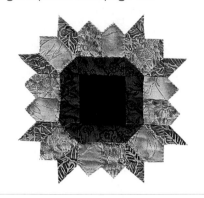

## Materials

| | | |
|---|---|---|
| | Fabric I (black solid) | 3½ yards |
| | Fabric II (ivory print) | 2⅝ yards |
| | Fabric III (light yellow print) | 1 yard |
| | Fabric IV (gold print) | 1 yard |
| | Fabric V (green print) | 1⅝ yards |
| | Fabric VI (rust print) | 2¾ yards |
| | Fabric VII (dark brown solid) | ⅜ yard |
| | Backing fabric | 5¾ yards |
| | Precut batting | 81" x 96" |

## Cutting

Cut all strips crossgrain, from selvage to selvage. For best use of yardage, cut pieces in order listed. Refer to diagrams to identify pieces.

**From Fabric I (black), cut:**

✳ Eleven 3" wide strips. Set aside nine strips for binding. From remaining strips, cut:
  • Eighty ⅞" x 3" (A5).

✳ Four 2¾"-wide strips for Strip Set 1.

✳ Eighteen 2½"-wide strips for borders.

✳ Ten 1½"-wide strips. Set aside four strips for Strip Set 2. From remaining strips, cut:
  • 160 1½" squares (A1a, A2a).

✳ Nine 1⅛"-wide strips. From these, cut:
  • 320 1⅛" squares (A6a, A7a).

**From Fabric II (ivory print), cut:**

✳ One 8¾"-wide strip. From this, cut:
  • One 8¾" x 12⅛" for E triangle-squares.
  • Two 4⅜" x 30" strips. From these, cut:
    • Twelve 4⅜" x 5" (C15).

✳ Three 2¾"-wide strips for Strip Set 3.    *(continued)*

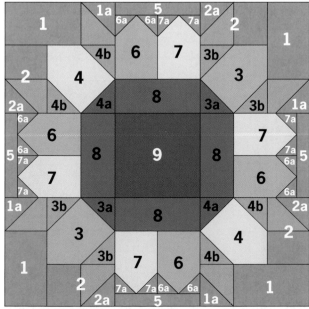

Block A—Make 20.

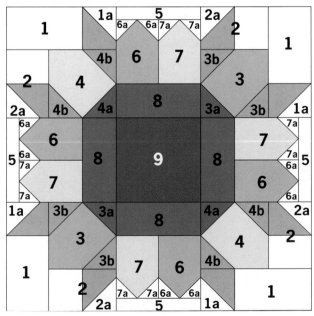

Block B—Make 4.

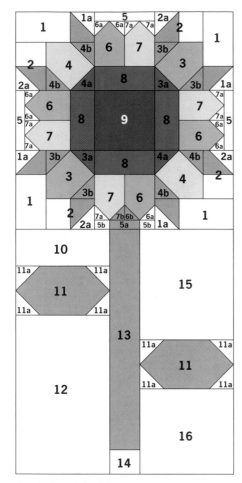

Block C—Make 12.

* Four 4⅜"-wide strips. From these, cut:
  * Twelve 4⅜" x 7" (C12).
  * Twelve 4" x 4⅜" (C16).
  * Twelve 2" x 4⅜" (C10).
  * Twelve 1½" x 1¾" (C14).
* Nine 3"-wide strips. From these and scraps from previous steps, cut:
  * 112 3" squares (D1a).
  * Fifty-two ⅞" x 3" (B5, C5).
* Eleven 1½"-wide strips. Set aside three strips for Strip Set 4. From remaining strips, cut:
  * 224 1½" squares (B1a, B2a, C1a, C2a, C11a).
* Seven 1⅛"-wide strips. From these, cut:
  * 232 1⅛" squares (B6a, B7a, C6a, C7a).
  * Twenty-four ⅞" x 1⅛" (C5b).

**From Fabric III (yellow print), cut:**
* Five 2½"-wide strips. From these, cut:
  * Seventy-two 2½" squares (A4, B4, C4).
* Six 2⅜"-wide strips. From these, cut:
  * 144 1¾" x 2⅜" (A7, B7, C7).
* Three 1½"-wide strips. From these, cut:
  * Sixty-three 1½" squares (sashing squares).

**From Fabric IV (gold print), cut:**
* Five 2½"-wide strips. From these, cut:
  * Seventy-two 2½" squares (A3, B3, C3).
* Six 2⅜"-wide strips. From these, cut:
  * 144 1¾" x 2⅜" (A6, B6, C6).

**From Fabric V (green print), cut:**
* Three 2½"-wide strips. From these, cut:
  * Twenty-four 2½" x 4⅜" (C11).
* Three 1¾"-wide strips. From these, cut:
  * Twelve 1¾" x 9½" (C13).
  * Twelve ⅞" x 1¾" (C5a).
* Twenty-five 1½"-wide strips. Set aside 14 strips for strip sets 1, 2, 3, 4. From remaining strips, cut:
  * 288 1½" squares (A3b, A4b, B3b, B4b, C3b, C4b).
* One 1⅛"-wide strip. From this, cut:
  * Twenty-four 1⅛" squares (C6b, C7b).

**From Fabric VI (rust print), cut:**
* Four 5½"-wide strips. From these, cut:
  * Fifty-six 3" x 5½" (D1).
* Thirty-nine 1½"-wide strips. From these, cut:
  * Ninety-eight 1½" x 9½" (sashing strips).
  * 144 1½" x 3" (A8, B8, C8).
  * 144 1½" squares (A3a, A4a, B3a, B4a, C3a, C4a).
* One 8¾" x 12⅛" for E triangle-squares.

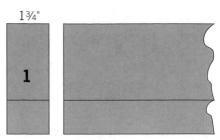

Strip Set 1—Make 4.

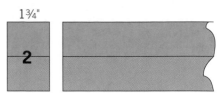

Strip Set 2—Make 4.

**From Fabric VII (brown solid), cut:**
* Three 3"-wide strips. From these, cut:
  * Thirty-six 3" squares (A9, B9, C9).

## Units for Block A

Refer to strip set diagrams and Blocks A & B Assembly Diagram to identify units.

**1.** For Strip Set 1, join 2¾" strip of Fabric I and 1½" strip of Fabric V as shown. Make four of Strip Set 1. From these, cut eighty 1¾"-wide segments for Unit 1.

**2.** For Strip Set 2, join 1½" strips of fabrics I and V. Make four of Strip Set 2. From these, cut eighty 1¾"-wide segments for Unit 2.

Unit 1 Diagram

**3.** Use diagonal-corner technique to add corner 1a to strip-set segments as shown (Unit 1 Diagram). In this manner, make four each of units 1 and 2.

**4.** Use diagonal-corner technique to make two each of units 3 and 4. Make four each of units 6 and 7.

## Block A Assembly

Assemble this block in vertical sections X, Y, and Z. Each completed section should measure 9½" in height. Refer to Blocks A & B Assembly Diagram throughout.

### Section X

**1.** Join units 2 and 4. Add Unit 1 to top of 2/4 unit.
**2.** Join units 6 and 7. Sew units 5 and 8 to sides of 6/7 as shown.
**3.** Join units 2 and 3. Add Unit 1 to left side of 2/3 unit.
**4.** Join units 1/2/4, 5/6/7/8, and 1/2/3 in a row as shown.

### Section Y

**1.** Join two pair of units 6 and 7, one for top and one for bottom of section.
**2.** Join Unit 5 to top of first 6/7 unit as shown.
**3.** Join units 8 and 9 in a row as shown.
**4.** Add second 6/7 unit and Unit 5 to complete section.

### Section Z

**1.** Join units 2 and 3. Add Unit 1 to right side of 2/3 unit.
**2.** Join units 6 and 7. Sew units 5 and 8 to sides of 6/7 as shown.
**3.** Join units 2 and 4. Add Unit 1 to bottom of 2/4 unit.
**4.** Join units 1/2/3, 5/6/7/8, and 1/2/4 in a row as shown.

### Assembly

Join sections X, Y, and Z to complete one block. Make 20 of Block A.

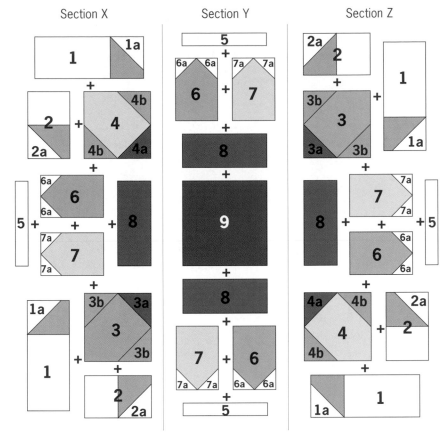

Blocks A & B Assembly Diagram

## Block B Assembly

Block B is made in the same manner as Block A, using Fabric II for background pieces. See Blocks A & B Assembly Diagram throughout.

**1.** For Strip Set 3, join 2¾" strip of Fabric II and 1½" strip of Fabric V as shown. Make three of Strip Set 3. From these, cut sixty-four 1¾"-wide segments for Unit 1. Set aside 48 segments for Block C.

**2.** For Strip Set 4, join 1½" strips of fabrics II and V as shown. Make three of Strip Set 4. From these, cut sixty-four 1¾"-wide segments for Unit 2. Set aside 48 segments for Block C.

**3.** Follow instructions for Block A Units to assemble remaining units for Block B.

**4.** Assemble Block B in same manner as for Block A. Make four of Block B. *(continued)*

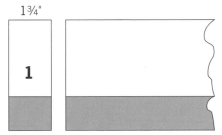

Strip Set 3—Make 3.

Strip Set 4—Make 3.

## Block C Assembly

The flower of Block C is almost the same as Block B. Refer to Blocks A & B Assembly Diagram and Block C Assembly Diagram.

**1.** Assemble flower units as described for Block B. For one pair of units 6 and 7, include diagonal corners 6b and 7b (Block C Assembly Diagram). Replace one Unit 5 with a pieced unit, joining 5b to both sides of 5a as shown.

**2.** Use diagonal-corner technique to make two of Unit 11 for stem section.

**3.** Follow instructions for Block A to assemble sections X and Z. In Section Y, substitute units 5, 6, and 7 (Block C Assembly Diagram). Join flower sections as before.

**4.** For stem section, join units 10, 11, and 12 in a row as shown. Join units 13 and 14. Make another row of units 15, 11, and 16 as shown. Join rows to complete section.

**5.** Join flower to stem section to complete Block C.

**6.** Make 12 of Block C.

## Quilt Assembly

Refer to Row Assembly Diagram for placement of blocks and sashing in vertical rows.

**1.** For Row 1, join nine sashing squares and eight sashing strips as shown. Make seven of Row 1. Press seam allowances toward sashing.

**2.** For Row 2, join four A blocks, two B Blocks, and one C block, sewing sashing strips between blocks as shown. Make two of Row 2.

**3.** For Row 3, join four A blocks and two C blocks with sashing strips between blocks as shown. Make two of Row 3.

**4.** For Row 4, join two A blocks and three C blocks with sashing strips between blocks as shown. Make two of Row 4.

**5.** Referring to photo, lay out rows 2, 3, 4, 4, 3, 2 side by side. Place a Row 1 between rows and at both sides. When satisfied with placement, join rows.

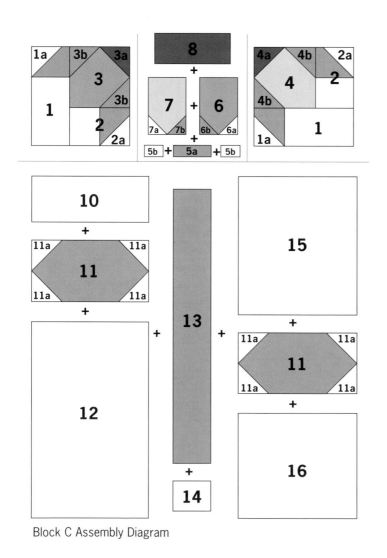

Block C Assembly Diagram

Row Assembly Diagram

Row 1—Make 7.

Row 2—Make 2.

Row 3—Make 2.

Row 4—Make 2.

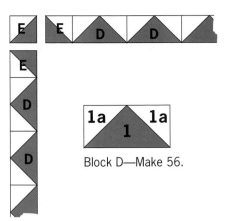

Block D—Make 56.

Sawtooth Border Diagram

## Borders

The inner and outer borders are plain strips of Fabric I. The middle border is a pieced sawtooth border.

### Inner Border

**1.** For each border, join two 2½"-wide strips end-to-end.

**2.** Referring to instructions on page 25, measure quilt from top to bottom. Centering seam, trim two borders to match length. Sew borders to quilt sides.

**3.** Measure quilt from side to side. Trim remaining borders to match quilt width. Sew borders to top and bottom edges of quilt. Press seam allowances toward borders.

### Sawtooth Border

**1.** Use diagonal-corner technique to make 56 of Block D.

**2.** Referring to triangle-square instructions on page 22, draw a 2 x 3-square grid of 3⅜" squares on wrong side of 8¾" x 12⅛" piece of Fabric II. Pair marked fabric with matching piece of Fabric VI, with right sides facing. Stitch grid as directed on page 22. Cut and press 12 triangle-squares.

**3.** For each side border, join 16 D blocks end-to-end (Sawtooth Border Diagram). Referring to photo, add an E block to both ends of each border. Sew borders to quilt sides. Press seam allowances toward inner border.

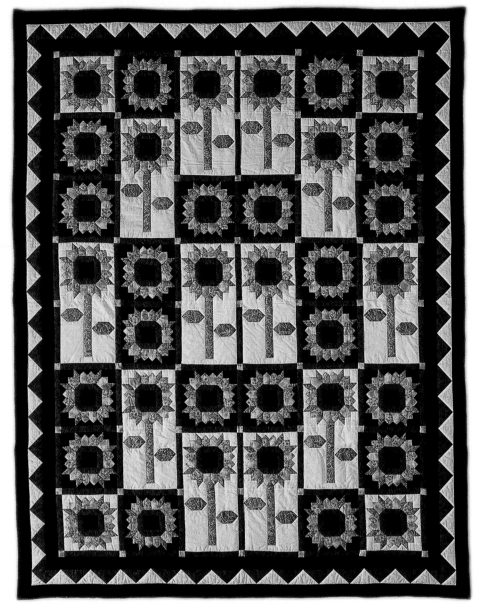

**4.** For top border, join 12 D blocks end-to-end. Add two E blocks to ends of row, checking photo to position Es correctly. Sew border to top edge of quilt. Repeat for bottom border.

### Outer Border

**1.** For each side border, join three Fabric I strips end-to-end. For top and bottom borders, join two strips.

**2.** Repeat steps 2 and 3 for inner border to sew outer borders to quilt.

## Quilting and Finishing

**1.** Mark quilting design on quilt top as desired. On quilt shown, patchwork is outline-quilted.

**2.** Divide backing into two 2⅞-yard lengths. Cut one piece in half lengthwise. Join one narrow panel to each side of wide piece to assemble backing.

**3.** Layer backing, batting, and quilt top. Baste. Quilt as marked or as desired.

**4.** From Fabric I strips, make 9¾ yards of straight-grain binding. See page 30 for instructions on making and applying binding.

# Tea for Two

*Tea with a friend is twice as nice with this little tablecloth or wall hanging. Choose fabrics to complement your china, and you'll set a pretty table. Quilt rows of "steam" over the cups or use a fabric marker to draw the lines.*

## Finished Size

Tablecloth: 49½" x 51½"
Blocks: 3 teapot blocks, 11" square
        6 teacup blocks, 11" square

## Quick-Piecing Techniques

Diagonal Corners (see page 20)
Diagonal Ends (see page 21)

## Materials

| | | |
|---|---|---|
| | Fabric I (white-on-white print) | 1⅛ yards |
| | Fabric II (pink print) | 1⅛ yards |
| | Fabric III (pink solid) | 1 yard |
| | Fabric IV (blue print) | ¼ yard |
| | Fabric V (blue solid) | ½ yard |
| | Backing fabric | 3 yards |
| | Precut lightweight batting (optional) | 72" x 90" |
| | Embroidery floss | |

## Cutting

Cut all strips crossgrain, from selvage to selvage. For best use of yardage, cut pieces in order listed. Refer to diagrams to identify pieces.

### From Fabric I (white), cut:

* Two 5½"-wide strips. From these, cut:
  * Six 5½" x 11½" (B1).
* One 4½"-wide strip. From this and scrap from previous step, cut:
  * Three 4½" x 11½" (A1).
  * Six 2½" x 4½" (A10a).
* One 3½"-wide strip. From this, cut:
  * Six 3½" squares (B2).

* Two 2½"-wide strips. From these, cut:
  * Nine 2½" squares (A2, A4a, A4b).
  * Thirty-nine 1½" x 2½" (A9, B3, B6, B9a).
* Five 1½"-wide strips. From these, cut:
  * Two 1½" x 35" for side sashing.
  * Nine 1½" x 11½" (A11, B10).
  * Twenty-one 1½" squares (A3a, A7a, B7).

### From Fabric II (pink print), cut:

* One 2½"-wide strip. From this, cut:
  * Four 2½" x 7½" (A4, A10).
  * Four 2½" squares (A3, A4b).

* Five 5"-wide strips for outer border.
* One 3½"-wide strip. From this, cut:
  * Four 3½" x 5½" (B5).
* One 1½"-wide strip. From this and scrap, cut:
  * Two 1½" x 7½" (A6).
  * Fourteen 1½" x 2½" (A7, A8, B6a).
  * Six 1½" squares (A2a, B8).

### From Fabric III (pink solid), cut:

* Five 3"-wide strips for binding.
* Four 2"-wide strips for middle border.
* Three 1½"-wide strips. From these, cut:
  * Four 1½" x 9½" (B9).
  * Four 1½" x 5½" (B4).
  * Eight 1½" x 2½" (B3a).
  * Ten 1½" squares (A1a, B5a).
  * Four 1" x 7½" (A5).

### From Fabric IV (blue print), cut:

* One 3½"-wide strip. From this, cut:
  * Two 3½" x 5½" (B5).
  * Two 2½" x 7½" (A4, A10).
  * Two 2½" squares (A3, A4b).

*(continued)*

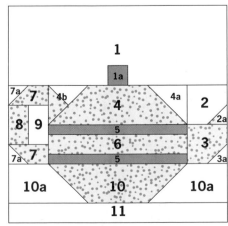

Block A—Make 2 with fabrics II/III.
       Make 1 with fabrics IV/V.

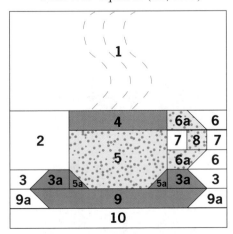

Block B—Make 4 with fabrics II/III.
       Make 2 with fabrics IV/V.

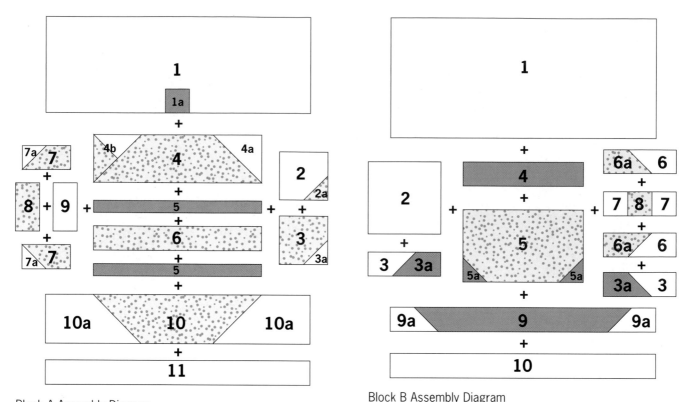

Block A Assembly Diagram

Block B Assembly Diagram

✳ One 1½"-wide strip. From this, cut:
- One 1½" x 7½" (A6).
- Seven 1½" x 2½" (A7, A8, B6a).
- Three 1½" squares (A2a, B8).

**From Fabric V (blue solid), cut:**

✳ Four 2½"-wide strips for first border.

✳ Two 1½"-wide strips. From these, cut:
- Two 1½" x 9½" (B9).
- Two 1½" x 5½" (B4).
- Four 1½" x 2½" (B3a).
- Five 1½" squares (A1a, B5a).
- Two 1" x 7½" (A5).

## Units for Block A

Refer to Block A Assembly Diagram throughout to identify units.

**1.** Use diagonal-corner technique to make two of Unit 7 and one each of units 2 and 3.

**2.** To make Unit 4b, draw a diagonal line on wrong side of 2½" square of Fabric I. Match marked square with 2½" square of Fabric II, with right sides facing. Stitch on

drawn line. Trim seam allowances to ¼" and press.

**3.** Use diagonal-corner technique to make one of Unit 4, using triangle-square for 4b.

**4.** Use diagonal-end technique to make one Unit 10.

**5.** Press under ¼" on three sides of square 1a. Matching raw edges, center square at bottom of Unit 1 and appliqué.

## Block A Assembly

Refer to Block A Assembly Diagram throughout.

**1.** Join units 4, 5, and 6 in a row as shown.

**2.** Join units 2 and 3. Sew 2/3 to right side of 4/5/6 unit.

**3.** Join units 8 and 9. Add Unit 7s to top and bottom of 8/9 as shown. Sew 7/8/9 to left side of 4/5/6 unit.

**4.** Sew Unit 1 to top of block.

**5.** Sew units 10 and 11 to bottom of block.

**6.** Make two blocks with fabrics I, II, and III. Make one block with fabrics I, IV, and V.

## Units for Block B

Refer to Block B Assembly Diagram throughout to identify units.

**1.** Use diagonal-corner technique to make one Unit 5.

**2.** Use diagonal-end technique to make one of Unit 9 and two each of units 3 and 6 (note that second unit is a mirror image of the first, so be sure to angle diagonal ends appropriately).

## Block B Assembly

Refer to Block B Assembly Diagram throughout.

**1.** Join units 2 and 3.

**2.** Join units 4 and 5 as shown. Sew 4/5 to right side of 2/3.

**3.** Sew Unit 7s to opposite sides of Unit 8.

**4.** Join units 6, 7/8, and 3 in a row as shown. Sew combined units to right side of 4/5.

**5.** Sew Unit 1 to top of block.

**6.** Join units 9 and 10 to bottom of block.

**7.** Make four of Block B with fabrics I, II, and III. Make two blocks with fabrics I, IV, and V.

## Tablecloth Assembly

**1.** Referring to photo, arrange blocks in three horizontal rows with one teapot and two cups in each row.

**2.** When satisfied with block placement, join blocks in rows.

**3.** Join rows.

## Borders

**1.** Join Fabric I sashing strips to sides of tablecloth.

**2.** Referring to instructions on page 25, measure quilt from side to side. Trim two Fabric VI border strips to match width. Sew borders to top and bottom edges of quilt.

**3.** Measure quilt from top to bottom; then trim remaining Fabric VI strips to match quilt length. Sew borders to quilt sides. Press seam allowances toward borders.

**4.** Sew Fabric III border strips to tablecloth in same manner.

**5.** For outer border, repeat Step 2 to sew Fabric II strips to top and bottom of tablecloth. For side borders, cut four 10"-long pieces from one remaining strip; then sew a short piece to each end of remaining two strips. Repeat Step 3 to sew side borders to tablecloth.

## Quilting and Finishing

**1.** Mark quilting design on tablecloth as desired. Quilt shown is outline-quilted. Lightly draw wavy lines of steam over cups.

**2.** Divide backing into two 1½-yard lengths. Cut one panel in half lengthwise, discarding one half. Join remaining half panel to full piece to make backing with an off-center seam.

**3.** Layer backing, batting (if desired), and tablecloth. Quilt as marked or as desired. Use two strands of embroidery floss to quilt steam lines.

**4.** From reserved strips, make 5⅞ yards of binding. See page 30 for instructions on making and applying straight-grain binding.

# Sweet Dreams

*This quilt is the next best thing to sleeping under the stars.
The sawtooth border encloses a galaxy of
golden stars and smiling moons. Select a navy or black
background fabric with white dots or
tiny stars, and the heavens are at your fingertips.*

## Finished Size
Quilt: 82" x 102"
Blocks: 2 moon blocks, 18" x 22"
12 star blocks, 11" x 14"

## Quick-Piecing Techniques
Diagonal Corners (see page 20)
Diagonal Ends (see page 21)
Triangle-Squares (see page 22)

## Materials

| | | |
|---|---|---|
| ■ | Fabric I (navy dot) | 4 yards |
| □ | Fabric II (white with gold print) | 1⅛ yards |
| ▨ | Fabric III (gold print) | 1¾ yards |
| ▧ | Fabric IV (yellow solid) | ¼ yard |
| ■ | Fabric V (grape print) | 3 yards |
| | Fabric VI (green print) | ¾ yard |
| | 90"-wide backing fabric | 3⅛ yards |
| | Precut batting | 90" x 108" |
| | Embroidery floss | |

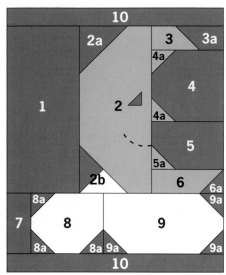

Block A—Make 1.

## Cutting

Cut all strips crossgrain, from selvage to selvage. For best use of yardage, cut pieces in order listed. Refer to block diagrams to identify pieces.

### From Fabric I (navy dot), cut:

✱ Four 14½"-wide strips. From these, cut:
  • Twelve 11½" x 14½" (D).
  • Two 6½" x 14½" (A1, B1).
  • One 7" square for triangle-square A2b, B2b.
  • Two 6½" squares (A4, B4).
✱ One 8"-wide strip. From this, cut:
  • One 8" x 19" for C6 triangle-squares.
  • Four 2" x 18½" (A10, B10).

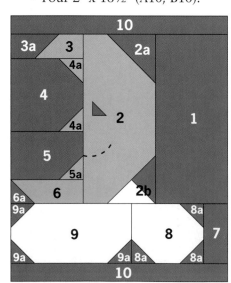

Block B—Make 1.

✱ Five 4½"-wide strips. From these, cut:
  • Four 4½" x 30" for sashing.
  • Two 4½" x 6½" (A5, B5).
  • Fourteen 4½" squares (A2a, B2a, C3).
✱ Four 4"-wide strips for inner border.
✱ Twelve 2½"-wide strips. From these, cut:
  • Thirty-six 2½" x 6½" (C1a, C11b).
  • Two 2½" x 5½" (A7, B7).
  • Fourteen 2½" x 4½" (A3a, B3a, C10).
  • Seventy-four 2½" squares (A6a, A8a, A9a, B6a, B8a, B9a, C2a, C7, C11a).

### From Fabric II (white print), cut:

✱ One 8"-wide strip. From this, cut:
  • One 8" x 19" for C5 triangle-squares.
  • One 7" square for triangle-square A2b, B2b.
✱ Three 5½"-wide strips. From these, cut:
  • Two 5½" x 10½" (A9, B9).
  • Two 5½" x 6½" (A8, B8).
  • Twelve 4½" x 5½" (C2).
  • Twelve 2½" x 5½" (C11).
✱ One 4½"-wide strip. From this, cut:
  • Twelve 3½" x 4½" (C8).
✱ Four 2½"-wide strips. From these, cut:
  • Twelve 2½" x 6½" (C1).
  • Twenty-four 2½" x 3½" (C4).

### From Fabric III (gold print), cut:

✱ One 8"-wide strip. From this, cut:
  • Two 8" x 19" for C5 and C6 triangle-squares.
✱ One 6½"-wide strip. From this, cut:
  • Two 6½" x 14½" (A2, B2).
  • Two 2½" x 6½" (A6, B6).
✱ Six 4½"-wide strips. From these and scraps, cut:
  • Twelve 4½" squares (C9).
  • Eighty 2½" x 4½" (A3, B3, E1).

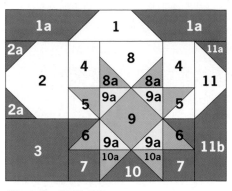

Block C—Make 12.

✱ Three 2½"-wide strips. From these and scraps, cut:
  • Fifty-four 2½" squares (A4a, A5a, B4a, B5a, C8a, C10a).

### From Fabric IV (yellow solid), cut:

✱ Three 2½"-wide strips. From these, cut:
  • Forty-eight 2½" squares (C9a).

### From Fabric V (grape print), cut:

✱ Nine 5½"-wide strips for outer border.
✱ Nine 3"-wide strips for binding.
✱ Ten 2½"-wide strips. From these, cut:
  • 160 2½" squares (E1a, saw-tooth border corners).
✱ From scraps, cut two moon eyes (see pattern, page 125).

### From Fabric VI (green print), cut:

✱ Eight 2½"-wide strips for middle border.

## Units for Block A

Refer to Block A Assembly Diagram throughout to identify units.

**1.** Use diagonal-corner technique to make one each of units 4, 5, 6, 8, and 9 as shown.

**2.** Sew diagonal corner 2a to Unit 2.

**3.** For Unit 2b, see page 22 for instructions on making triangle-squares. On wrong side of 7" square of Fabric II, draw one 4⅞" square. Draw one diagonal line from corner

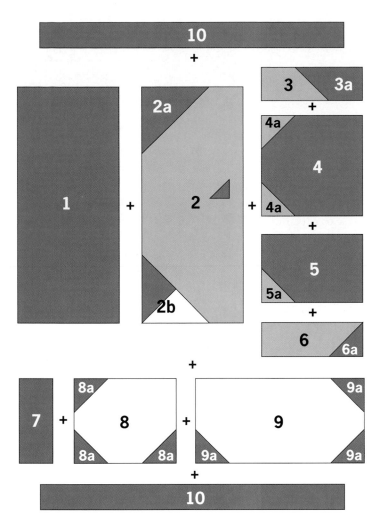

Block A Assembly Diagram

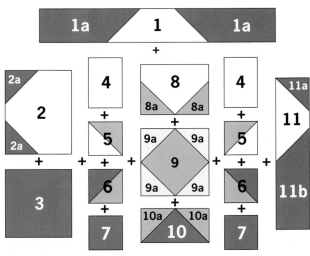

Block C Assembly Diagram

## Units for Block C

Refer to Block C Assembly Diagram throughout to identify units.

**1.** See page 22 for instructions on triangle-squares. On wrong side of 8" x 19" Fabric II piece, draw a 2 x 6-square grid of $2\frac{7}{8}$" squares. With right sides facing, match marked fabric with 8" x 19" piece of Fabric III. Stitch grid as directed on page 22. Cut 24 triangle-squares from grid for Unit 5.

**2.** Using 8" x 19" pieces of fabrics I and III, repeat Step 1 to get 24 triangle-squares for Unit 6.

**3.** Use diagonal-corner technique to make one each of units 2, 8, 9, and 10.

**4.** Use diagonal-end technique to make one of Unit 1.

**5.** Use diagonal-corner and diagonal-end techniques to make one of Unit 11. *(continued)*

to corner. With right sides facing, match marked fabric square with 7" square of Fabric I. Stitch on both sides of diagonal line. Cut on all drawn lines to get two triangle-squares. Set aside one for Block B.

**4.** With right sides facing, position triangle-square at bottom corner of Unit 2. Use diagonal-corner technique to sew diagonal corner 2b as shown.

**5.** Use diagonal-end technique to make one of Unit 3.

## Block A Assembly

Refer to Block A Assembly Diagram throughout.

**1.** Join units 3, 4, 5, and 6 in a vertical row as shown.

**2.** Join units 1, 2, and 3/4/5/6 in a row.

**3.** Join units 7, 8, and 9 as shown.

**4.** Sew moon section to top edge of cloud section.

**5.** Sew a Unit 10 to top and bottom edges of block.

**6.** For eye, turn under ¼" on all raw edges. Position triangle on Unit 2 a little above the "nose" (Unit 4a) and 1" from seam. Appliqué eye in place.

**7.** Starting at 5a seam, lightly draw a curve on Unit 2 for smile. Use two strands of floss to backstitch smile.

## Block B Assembly

Block B is a mirror image of Block A. Make units in the same manner, but reverse angle of diagonal end and positions of diagonal corners. Referring to block diagram, make one Block B.

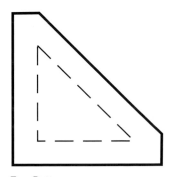

Eye Pattern

## Block C Assembly

Assemble this block in vertical rows, adding Unit 1 to top of joined rows. Refer to Block C Assembly Diagram throughout.

**1.** Join units 2 and 3.

**2.** Join units 4, 5, 6, and 7 in a row as shown.

**3.** Join units 8, 9, and 10.

**4.** Join units 4, 5, 6, and 7 in a row as shown, making a mirror image of row in Step 2.

**5.** Join rows as shown. Add Unit 11 to right edge of block.

**6.** Sew Unit 1 to top of block.

**7.** Make 12 of Block C.

## Quilt Assembly

Refer to Row Assembly Diagram for placement of blocks in rows. Assemble rows from top to bottom as shown. Press seam allowances toward D blocks throughout.

**1.** For sashing, join two 4½" x 30" strips of Fabric I end-to-end. Make two sashing strips.

**2.** For Row 1, join C blocks and Ds as shown. Sew sashing strip to left side of row; press seam allowances toward sashing and trim sashing even with blocks as necessary. Add Block A to top of row.

**3.** For rows 2 and 3, join C blocks and Ds as shown.

**4.** For Row 4, join C blocks and Ds as shown. Sew remaining sashing strip to right side of row; press seam allowances toward sashing and trim sashing even with blocks. Join Block B to bottom of row.

**5.** Join rows.

## Borders

**1.** For inner border, join two 4"-wide Fabric I strips end-to-end. Aligning centers, sew border to top of quilt. Repeat for bottom border. Trim borders even with quilt sides.

**2.** For middle border, join two Fabric VI strips end-to-end for each border. Referring to instructions on

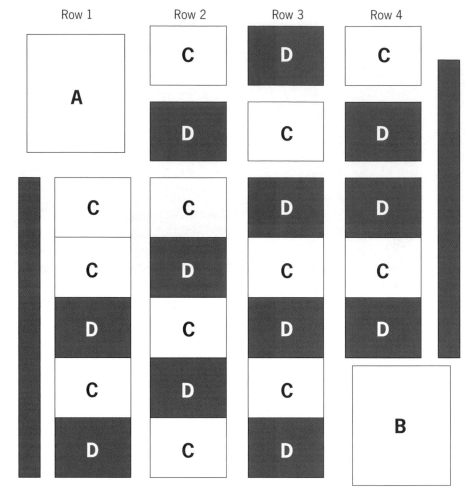

Row Assembly Diagram

page 25, measure quilt from top to bottom. Trim two borders to match length. Sew borders to quilt sides. Measure quilt width; then trim and sew remaining borders to top and bottom edges of quilt.

**3.** Use diagonal-corner technique to make 78 of Block E.

**4.** For each side sawtooth border, join 22 of Block E (Sawtooth Border Diagram). Referring to photo, sew borders to quilt sides, easing to fit as necessary.

**5.** For top sawtooth border, join 17 of Block E. Then join a 2½" square of Fabric V to each end of row. Join border to top edge of quilt, easing to fit as necessary. Repeat for bottom border.

**6.** Use 5½"-wide strips of Fabric V for outer border. Cut one strip in half.

**7.** For each side outer border, join a strip to both ends of one half-strip. Measure quilt from top to bottom; then trim borders to match quilt length. Sew borders to quilt sides.

**8.** Sew two remaining strips end-to-end. Measure quilt width; then trim and sew borders to top edge of quilt. Repeat for bottom border.

Block E—Make 78.

Sawtooth Border Diagram

## Quilting and Finishing

**1.** Mark quilting design on quilt top as desired. Quilt shown is outline-quilted, with hand-drawn stars and clouds randomly quilted in D blocks and outer border.

**2.** Layer backing, batting, and quilt top. Baste. Quilt as desired.

**3.** From reserved strips, make 10½ yards of binding. See page 30 for instructions on making and applying straight-grain binding.

# Field of Flowers

*Combine appliqué with quick-piecing techniques to showcase your quiltmaking talents. Use scrap fabrics to piece the blossoms; then appliqué stems and leaves onto the assembled quilt. If you like, appliqué flowers on the fence and over the border. See page 133 for instructions on freezer-paper appliqué and how to make bias stems quickly and easily. Turn to page 134 for another version of this lovely garden.*

## Finished Size
Quilt: 80½" x 104¼"
Blocks: 30 flower blocks, 7½" square
         36 nine-patch blocks, 7½" square
         14 fence blocks, 2½" x 16¼"
         7 appliqué flowers

## Quick-Piecing Techniques
Strip Piecing (see page 20)
Diagonal Corners (see page 20)

## Materials

| | | |
|---|---|---|
| | Fabric I (mint green print) | 6¼ yards |
| | Fabric II (dark green solid) | 2⅜ yards |
| | Fabric III (white-on-white print) | ⅞ yard |
| | Fabric IV (assorted yellows and golds) | Scraps |
| | Fabric V (assorted pastel prints) | Scraps |
| | Fabric VI (leaf green solid) | 1¼ yards |
| | Backing fabric | 6¼ yards |
| | Precut batting | 90" x 108" |
| | Freezer paper for appliqué | |

## Cutting
Cut all strips crossgrain, from selvage to selvage. For best use of yardage, cut pieces in order listed. Refer to diagrams to identify pieces. Appliqué patterns are on page 138. See page 133 for tips on cutting appliqué pieces with freezer paper.

**From Fabric I (mint green print), cut:**
* Three 8"-wide strips. From these, cut:
  * Six 8" squares (spacer square).
  * Twelve 3" x 8" (E).

* Eleven 5½"-wide strips. Set aside five strips for Strip Set 3 and outer borders. From remaining strips, cut:
  * Six 5½" x 34" for outer borders.
  * Five 5½" x 8" (I).
  * One 3" x 5½" (D).
* One 4¼"-wide strip for Strip Set 3.
* Eighteen 3"-wide strips. Set aside 14 strips for strip sets 1, 2, and 3. From remaining strips, cut:
  * Four 3" x 13" (H).
  * Four 3" squares (F).
  * Thirty 1¾" x 3" (A8).
  * Thirty 1⅛" x 3" (A9).

* Eight 1¾"-wide strips. From these, cut:
  * Thirty 1¾" x 3⅝" (A6).
  * Sixty 1¾" x 2⅜" (A5).
  * Twenty-eight 1¾" squares (C1a).
* Twenty-six 1⅛"-wide strips. From these, cut:
  * Thirty 1⅛" x 3⅝" (A7).
  * 120 1⅛" x 2⅜" (A4).
  * 600 1⅛" squares (A1a, A2a).
* Nine 3"-wide strips for binding.
*(continued)*

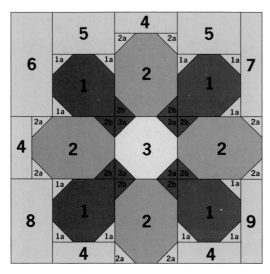

Block A—Make 30.

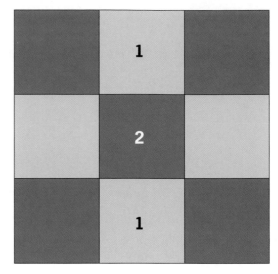

Block B—Make 36.

## From Fabric II (dark green), cut:

✽ Eighteen 3"-wide strips. Set aside 17 strips for strip sets 1 and 2. From remaining strip, cut:
  • Seven 3" squares (G).
✽ Ten 2"-wide strips for inner border.

## From Fabric III (white), cut:

✽ One 16¾"-wide strip. From this, cut:
  • Fourteen 3" x 16¾" (C1).
✽ Two 3"-wide strips for Strip Set 3.

## From Fabric IV (assorted yellows), cut:

✽ Thirty 2⅜" squares (A3).
✽ Seven appliqué flower centers (Pattern 3).

## From Fabric V (assorted pastels), cut:

✽ Four 2⅜" squares (A1) for each of 30 blocks.
✽ Four 2⅜" x 3" (A2) for each of 30 blocks.
✽ Twelve 1⅛" squares (A2b, A3a) for each of 30 blocks.
✽ Four of Pattern 1 for each of seven appliquéd flowers.
✽ Four of Pattern 2 for each of seven appliquéd flowers.

## From Fabric VI (leaf green), cut:

✽ One 34" square for bias stems.
✽ Forty leaves for appliqué (Pattern 2).

## Units for Block A

Refer to Block A Assembly Diagram throughout to identify units.
**1.** Use diagonal-corner technique to make four each of units 1 and 2.
**2.** Use diagonal-corner technique to make one of Unit 3.

## Block A Assembly

Assemble this block in sections X, Y, and Z. Each completed section should measure approximately 8" wide. Refer to Block A Assembly Diagram throughout.

### Section X

**1.** Sew Unit 5 to top edges of two Unit 1s. Be sure each Unit 1 is turned to position fabrics as shown.
**2.** Sew Unit 4 to top edge of Unit 2.
**3.** Join a 1/5 unit to sides of 2/4 unit.
**4.** Sew units 6 and 7 to sides of row.

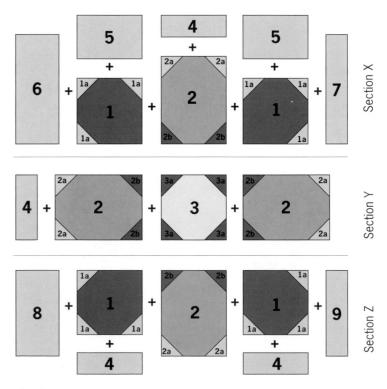

Block A Assembly Diagram

### Section Y

Join units 2, 3, and 4 in a row as shown.

### Section Z

**1.** Sew Unit 4 to bottom edges of two Unit 1s. Be sure each Unit 1 is turned to position fabrics as shown.
**2.** Join a 1/4 unit to sides of Unit 2.
**3.** Sew units 8 and 9 to sides of row.

### Assembly

Join sections to assemble block. Make 30 blocks, using as many fabric combinations as desired.

## Block B Assembly

Refer to strip set diagrams and Block B Assembly Diagram to identify units.

**1.** For Strip Set 1, join 3"-wide strips of fabrics I and II. Press seam allowances toward Fabric II. Make seven strip sets. From these, cut seventy-two 3"-wide segments for Unit 1. Cut another 17 units and set aside for quilt assembly.

**2.** For Strip Set 2, join 3"-wide strips of fabrics I and II as shown. Press seam allowances toward Fabric II. Make three strip sets. From these, cut thirty-six 3"-wide segments for Unit 2. Cut another four units and set aside for quilt assembly.

**3.** To assemble block, join two Unit 1s and one Unit 2 as shown.

**4.** Make 36 of Block B.

*(continued)*

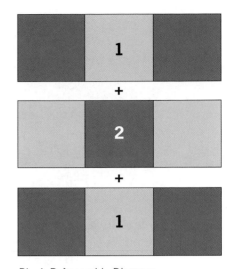

Block B Assembly Diagram

Strip Set 1—Make 7.

Strip Set 2—Make 3.

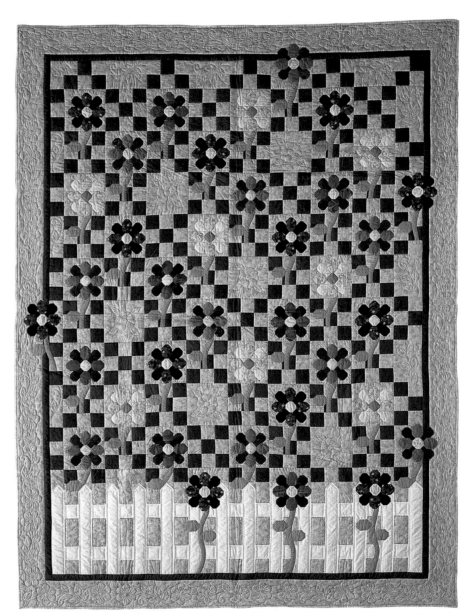

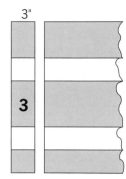

3"

**3**

Strip Set 3—Make 1.

## Fence Row Assembly

**1.** Use diagonal-corner technique to make 14 of Block C.

**2.** For Strip Set 3, join 3"-wide strips of Fabric III and 4¼"-wide strip, 5½"-wide strip, and 3"-wide strip of Fabric I as shown (Strip Set 3 Diagram). Press seam allowances toward Fabric I. From this strip set, cut thirteen 3"-wide segments.

**3.** Join C blocks and strip-set segments in a row, alternating blocks and segments as shown for Fence Row (Row Assembly Diagram).

## Row Assembly

Refer to photo and Row Assembly Diagram for placement of blocks and sashing units in rows.

**1.** For Sashing Row 1, join one D, five G, and four H as shown to make one row. Press seam allowances toward G squares.

**2.** For Sashing Row 2, join four Strip Set 1 segments, four E, two F, and one G as shown. Press seam allowances toward Fabric II. Make two of Sashing Row 2. Sew one row to bottom of Sashing Row 1. Sew second row to top of Fence Row.

**3.** Select four A blocks and four B blocks for each block row. Following Row Assembly Diagram, arrange blocks on the floor, moving blocks around to find a nice balance of scrap fabrics and color. Sprinkle in the six spacer squares in place of some A blocks, referring to photo. Alternate five of Block Row 1 and four of Block Row 2, adding sashing pieces and strip-set segments to row ends as shown.

**4.** When satisfied with arrangement of blocks, join blocks and sashing pieces in each row.

**5.** Lay out joined rows (including Fence Row) on floor to recheck position of blocks and sashing pieces. Do not join rows yet—there's some appliqué to do first!

## Appliqué

**1.** Cut 34" square of Fabric VI in half diagonally. Starting from cut edges, cut 1¾"-wide diagonal strips (Diagram 1). From these, cut thirty 7½"-long strips, three 15"-long strips, and four 4"-long strips.

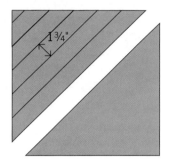

1¾"

Diagram 1

**2.** With wrong sides facing and edges aligned, fold each bias strip in half lengthwise. Machine-stitch ¼" from raw edge, making a narrow tube. On ironing board, flatten tube, rolling seam allowance to center. Press tube, pressing seam allowances open (Diagram 2).

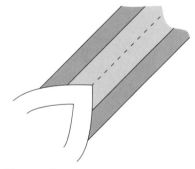

Diagram 2

**3.** Pin a 4"-long stem to each A block in last block row, centering end of stem over Unit 2 at bottom edge of flower and matching right sides and raw edges.

**4.** Pin 7½"-long stems to bottom of remaining A blocks in same manner. Set aside seven stems for appliquéd flowers.

**5.** Sew block rows together, securing stem ends in seams. Gently twist each stem into a gentle curve and pin in place on B blocks.

Row Assembly Diagram

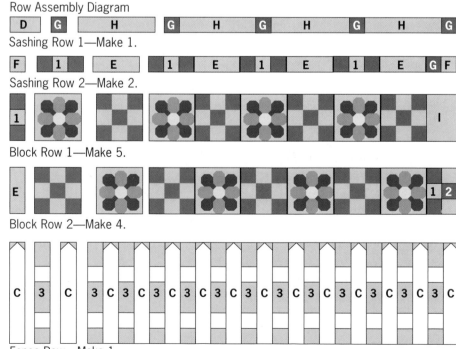

| D | G | H | G | H | G | H | G | H | G |

Sashing Row 1—Make 1.

| F | 1 | E | 1 | E | 1 | E | 1 | E | G | F |

Sashing Row 2—Make 2.

| 1 | | | | | | I |

Block Row 1—Make 5.

| E | | | | | | 1 | 2 |

Block Row 2—Make 4.

| C | 3 | C | 3 | C | 3 | C | 3 | C | 3 | C | 3 | C | 3 | C | 3 | C | 3 | C | 3 | C | 3 | C | 3 | C | 3 | C |

Fence Row—Make 1.

# Freezer-Paper Appliqué

Freezer paper makes appliqué so easy, you may wonder what you did without it. Freezer paper lets you turn the edges of each piece smoothly without a lot of fuss.

**1.** Trace pattern onto uncoated (dull) side of a piece of freezer paper. Cut a template for each appliqué piece. For example, this quilt has 37 leaves, so you'll need 37 freezer-paper templates of Pattern 2.

**2.** Position template on wrong side of appliqué fabric, with coated side against fabric. Using a warm iron, press for about five seconds until the coating melts just enough for the paper to stick to the fabric.

**3.** Using the paper edge as a guide, cut out the appliqué shape, adding a ¼" seam allowance around the template (Photo A).

**4.** Press seam allowances over edge of template (Photo B). If desired, use glue stick to put a bit of glue around template edges to hold seam allowances in place.

**5.** Pin appliqués in place on quilt. Hand-sew pieces in place with a blindstitch. If you prefer, use your sewing machine's blindhem stitch and nylon ("invisible") thread.

**6.** When appliqué is complete, trim background fabric under appliqué and remove freezer paper (Photo C).

**7.** Press appliqué facedown on a towel. Use a light spray of water if desired.

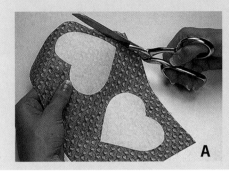 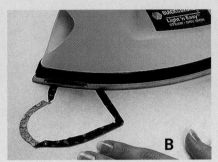 

**6.** Following instructions for freezer-paper appliqué, prepare 30 leaves. Pin a leaf in place adjacent to each stem. Appliqué stems and leaves.

**7.** Finish bottom of each stem one of two ways, as desired. You can turn under end of stem and appliqué in place. Or use a seam ripper to open seam in center of Block B so you can insert end of stem; then machine-stitch opening closed through all layers. Trim stem to seam allowance.

**8.** Prepare appliqué pieces for three flowers. Position flowers on fence as shown. Pin or glue back petals first (Pattern 1); then front petals (Pattern 2) and center (Pattern 3) last. Pin end of 15"-long stem under each flower. Curve stem, aligning bottom of stem with bottom of Fence Row. Position leaves as shown. Appliqué flowers, stems, and leaves on Fence Row.

## Borders

**1.** For inner border, join three 2"-wide strips of Fabric II end-to-end for each side border. Join two strips for top and bottom borders.

**2.** Referring to instructions on page 25, measure quilt from top to bottom. Trim side borders to match length. Matching centers, sew borders to quilt sides.

**3.** Measure quilt from side to side; then trim remaining borders to match quilt width. Sew borders to top and bottom edges of quilt.

**4.** For outer border, join three 5½" x 34" strips of Fabric I end-to-end for side borders. Join two full-length strips end-to-end for top and bottom borders. Repeat steps 2 and 3 to sew borders to quilt.

**5.** Prepare appliqué pieces for four flowers. Referring to photo, position flowers, stems, and leaves on border (two on right border, one at top, one on left border). Appliqué.

## Quilting and Finishing

**1.** Mark quilting design on quilt top as desired. On quilt shown, patchwork is outline-quilted. Border vine is a purchased stencil—look for a similar stencil at your local quilt shop.

**2.** Divide backing into two 3⅛-yard lengths. Cut one piece in half lengthwise. Join one narrow panel to each side of wide piece to assemble backing.

**3.** Layer backing, batting, and quilt top. Baste. Quilt as marked or as desired.

**4.** From Fabric I strips, make 10½ yards of straight-grain binding. See page 30 for instructions on making and applying binding.

# Field *of* Flowers Wall Hanging

*A white picket fence against a blue sky calls out for pretty pastel flowers.*
*Scaled down from the full-size quilt on page 128, this wall hanging*
*suggests another color scheme for a quick-pieced meadow.*

## Finished Size

Quilt: 55" x 61"
Blocks: 7 flower blocks, 7½" square
       10 nine-patch blocks, 7½" square
       9 fence blocks, 2½" x 16¼"
       3 appliqué flowers

## Quick-Piecing Techniques

Strip Piecing (see page 20)
Diagonal Corners (see page 20)
Diagonal Ends (see page 21)

## Materials

| | | |
|---|---|---|
| | Fabric I (medium blue print) | 3 yards |
| | Fabric II (dark blue print) | ¾ yard |
| | Fabric III (white-on-white print) | ¾ yard |
| | Fabric IV (assorted pastel prints) | Scraps |
| | Fabric V (green print) | ⅝ yard |
| | Backing fabric | 3⅝ yards |
| | Precut batting | 72" x 90" |

## Cutting

Cut all strips crossgrain, from selvage to selvage, except as noted. For best use of yardage, cut pieces in order listed. Refer to block diagrams to identify pieces. Appliqué patterns are on page 138.

### From Fabric I (medium blue), cut:

* One 5½"-wide strip for Strip Set 3.
* One 4¼"-wide strip for Strip Set 3.
* Six 3"-wide strips for strip sets 1, 2, and 3.
* One 8" x 65" lengthwise strip. From this, cut:
  * Three 8" squares (spacer square).
  * Two 5½" x 8" (D).
  * Three 3" x 8" (E).

* Two 5½" x 48" lengthwise strips and two 5½" x 65" strips for outer border.
* Four 3" x 65" lengthwise strips for binding.
* Three 1¾"-wide strips. From these, cut:
  * Seven 1¾" x 3⅝" (A6).
  * Seven 1¾" x 3" (A8).
  * Fourteen 1¾" x 2⅜" (A5).
  * Eighteen 1¾" squares (C1a).
* One 1⅛"-wide strip. From this and scraps, cut:
  * Seven 1⅛" x 3⅝" (A7).
  * Seven 1⅛" x 3" (A9).
  * Twenty-eight 1⅛" x 2⅜" (A4).
  * 140 1⅛" squares (A1a, A2a).

### From Fabric II (dark blue), cut:

* Five 3"-wide strips for strips sets 1 and 2.
* Five 1¾"-wide strips for inner border.

### From Fabric III (white), cut:

* One 16¾"-wide strip. From this, cut:
  * Nine 3" x 16¾" (C1).
* Two 3"-wide strips for Strip Set 3.

*(continued)*

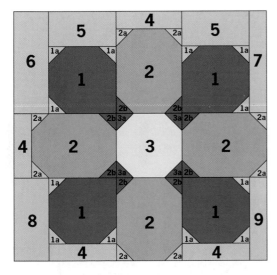

Block A—Make 7.

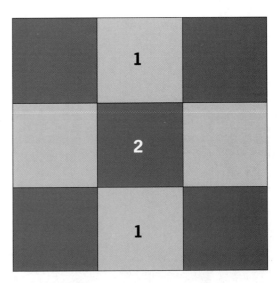

Block B—Make 10.

**From Fabric IV (assorted pastels), cut:**

* Five 2⅜" squares (A1, A3) for each of seven blocks.
* Four 2⅜" x 3" (A2) for each of seven blocks.
* Twelve 1⅛" squares (A2b, A3a) for each of seven blocks.
* Four of Pattern 1 for each of three appliqué flowers.
* Four of Pattern 2 for each of three appliqué flowers.
* One of Pattern 3 for each of three appliqué flowers.

**From Fabric V (green), cut:**

* One 18" square for bias stems.
* Eleven leaves for appliqué (Pattern 2).

## Block A Assembly

Refer to Block A Assembly Diagram throughout to identify units.

**1.** Use diagonal-corner technique to make four each of units 1 and 2.

**2.** Use diagonal-corner technique to make one of Unit 3.

**3.** Follow instructions for Block A Assembly on page 130. Make seven of Block A.

## Block B Assembly

Refer to strip set diagrams and Block B Assembly Diagram to identify units.

**1.** For Strip Set 1, join 3"-wide strips of fabrics I and II as shown. Make two strip sets. Press seam allowances toward Fabric II. From these, cut twenty-four 3"-wide segments for Unit 1. Set aside four segments for quilt assembly.

**2.** For Strip Set 2, join 3"-wide strips of fabrics I and II as shown. Press seam allowances toward Fabric II. From this strip set, cut thirteen 3"-wide segments. Set aside three segments for quilt assembly.

**3.** To assemble block, join two Units 1s and one Unit 2 as shown.

**4.** Make 10 of Block B.

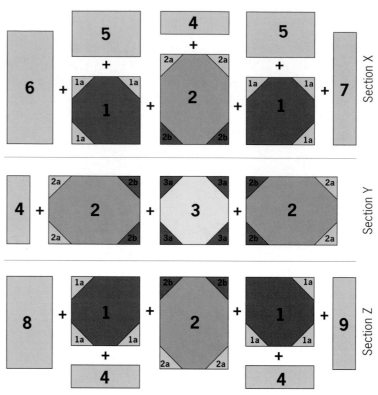

Block A Assembly Diagram

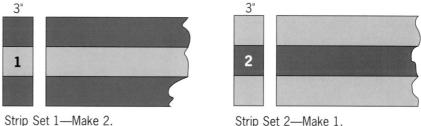

Strip Set 1—Make 2.   Strip Set 2—Make 1.

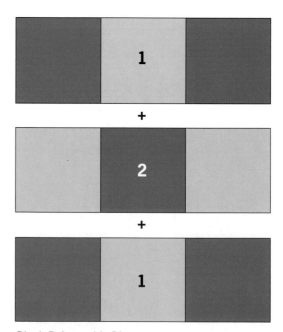

Block B Assembly Diagram

## Fence Row Assembly

**1.** Use diagonal-corner technique to make nine of Block C (Block C Diagram).
**2.** For Strip Set 3, join 3"-wide strips of Fabric III and 4¼"-wide, 5½"-wide strip, and 3"-wide strip of Fabric I as shown. Press seam allowances toward Fabric I. From this strip set, cut eight 3"-wide segments for Fence Row.

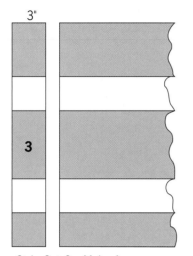

Strip Set 3—Make 1.

**3.** Join C blocks and strip-set segments in a row, alternating blocks and segments as shown (Row Assembly Diagram).

## Row Assembly

Refer to photo and Row Assembly Diagram for placement of blocks and sashing units in rows.

**1.** Select blocks, spacer squares, and strip-set segments for each row as shown. Arrange blocks on the floor, moving blocks around to find a nice balance of scrap fabrics and color. Sprinkle in the three spacer squares in place of A blocks in some rows. Lay out two of Row 1 and two of Row 2 as shown, alternating rows.
**2.** When satisfied with arrangement of blocks, join blocks and sashing pieces in each row. Lay out rows on floor to recheck position of blocks and sashing pieces. Do not join rows yet; wait until appliqué is done.

**3.** For Row 3, join three E strips and two Strip Set 1 segments as shown. Remove one Fabric I square from remaining Strip Set 2 segment; then sew segment to end of row as shown.
**4.** Sew Row 3 to top of Fence Row.

## Appliqué

**1.** Cut 18" square of Fabric VI in half diagonally. Starting from cut edges, cut 1¾"-wide diagonal strips (see Diagram 1, page 130). From these strips, cut six 7½"-long strips, two 4"-long strips, and two 15"-long strips for stems.
**2.** Follow steps 2–8 on pages 132 and 133 to prepare and appliqué stems and leaves for pieced blocks.
**3.** Prepare appliqué pieces for two flowers. Position flowers on fence as shown. Curve 15"-long stem from bottom of flower to bottom of Fence Row. Position leaves as shown. Appliqué stem, leaves, and flowers on Fence Row.

## Borders

**1.** Referring to instructions on page 25, measure quilt from side to side. Trim two 1¾"-wide strips of Fabric II to match quilt width. Sew borders to top and bottom edges of quilt.
**2.** Cut one remaining Fabric II strip into four 10" pieces. Sew one piece onto each end of remaining border strips to make side borders.
**3.** Measure quilt from top to bottom; then trim side borders to match quilt length. Matching centers, sew borders to quilt sides.
**4.** For outer border, repeat steps 1 and 3 to sew 5½"-wide strips of Fabric I to quilt.
**5.** Prepare appliqué pieces for remaining flower. Referring to photo, place flower and stem on right border. Appliqué. *(continued)*

Row Assembly Diagram

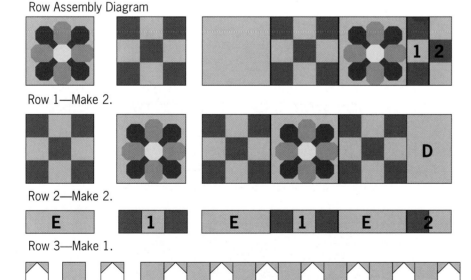

Row 1—Make 2.

Row 2—Make 2.

Row 3—Make 1.

Fence Row—Make 1.

## Quilting and Finishing

**1.** Mark quilting design on quilt top as desired. On quilt shown, patchwork is outline-quilted. The cable quilted in border is a purchased stencil. Look for a similar one at your local quilt shop.

**2.** Divide backing into two equal lengths. Cut one piece in half lengthwise. Discard one narrow panel. Join remaining narrow panel to one side of wide piece to assemble backing with off-center seam.

**3.** Layer backing, batting, and quilt top. Backing seam will parallel top and bottom edges of quilt. Baste. Quilt as marked or as desired.

**4.** From Fabric I strips, make 6¾ yards of straight-grain binding. See page 30 for instructions on making and applying binding.

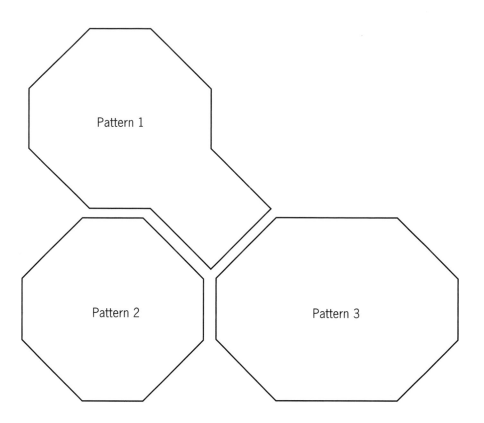

Pattern 1

Pattern 2

Pattern 3

# Hanging It Up

Hanging a quilt on the wall adds color and excitement to any decor. But it is important to protect a quilt while showing it off. Only a sturdy, lightweight quilt should be hung. If a quilt is in delicate condition, hanging will only hasten its deterioration.

## Making a Hanging Sleeve

The method most often used to hang a quilt is to sew a sleeve on the back so a dowel can be slipped through it. This method distributes the weight evenly across the width of the quilt.

**1.** From leftover backing fabric, cut or piece an 8"-wide strip that is the same length as the quilt edge.

**2.** On each end, turn under ½"; then turn under another ½". Topstitch to hem both ends.

**3.** With wrong sides facing, fold the fabric in half lengthwise and stitch the long edges together. Press seam allowances open and to the middle of the sleeve (Diagram 1).

**4.** Center the sleeve on the back of the quilt about 1" below the binding with the seam against the backing. Hand-sew the sleeve to the quilt through backing and batting along both long edges.

**5.** For large quilts, make two or three sleeve sections (Diagram 2) so you can use more nails or brackets to support the dowel to better distribute the quilt's weight.

Diagram 1

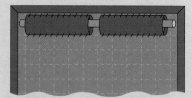

Diagram 2

# Santa Claus *Tree Skirt*

*It's easy to put some ho-ho-ho under your tree with this jolly tree skirt. If you have no patience for cutting and sewing lots of little triangles, relax! Quick-piecing takes the trial out of triangles. Stitch, snip, and presto—triangle-squares are ready to go.*

## Finished Size

Tree Skirt: 53" square

Blocks: 4 santa blocks, 8" x 20"
4 tree blocks, 20" square

## Materials

| | | |
|---|---|---|
| | Fabric I (green print) | 2½ yards |
| | Fabric II (parchment solid) | 2⅛ yards |
| | Fabric III (burgundy print) | ¾ yard |
| | Fabric IV (red-green-gold plaid) | ½ yard |
| | Fabric V (white-on-muslin print) | ½ yard |
| | Fabric VI (black solid) | ⅛ yard |
| | Fabric VII (brown solid) | ¾ yard |
| | Backing fabric | 3⅜ yards |
| | Batting | 72" x 90" |

Black fine-tipped fabric marker or two ½" buttons (optional)

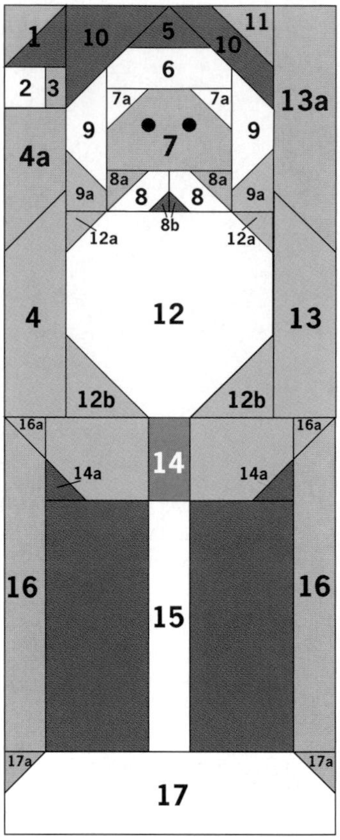

## Quick-Piecing Techniques

Strip Piecing (see page 20)
Diagonal Corners (see page 20)
Diagonal Ends (see page 21)
Triangle-Squares (see page 22)

Block A—Make 4.

## Cutting

Cut all strips crossgrain, from selvage to selvage. For best use of yardage, cut pieces in order listed. Refer to diagrams to identify pieces.

### From Fabric I (green), cut:

* One 27"-wide strip. From this, cut:
  • One 27" square for bias binding.
  • Eight 2" x 27" strips for outer border.
* Three 9⅛"-wide strips. From these, cut:
  • Five 9⅛" x 18⅝" for B1 triangle-squares.
  • One 8½" square for tree skirt center.
  • Four 3½" squares (B6).
* Two 3½"-wide strips for Strip Set 3.
* Eight 1½"-wide strips. From these, cut:
  • Sixteen 1½" x 21" (B9).

### From Fabric II (parchment), cut:

* Three 9⅛"-wide strips. From these, cut:
  • Five 9⅛" x 18⅝" for B1 triangle-squares.
  • Four 4½" squares (B7).
  • One 4⅜" x 6¾" for A1 triangle-squares.
  • Four 2½" x 3½" (A7).
* Two 7½"-wide strips for Strip Set 3.
* One 6½"-wide strip. From this, cut:
  • Eight 4" x 6½" (B3).
  • Four 2" x 6½" (A13a).
* Two 2"-wide strips. From these, cut:
  • Four 2" x 4" (A4a).
  • Twenty 2" squares (A11, B2).
* Eight 1½"-wide strips. From these and scrap, cut:
  • Eight 1½" x 26" for inner border.
  • Eight 1½" x 8½" (A16).
  • Sixteen 1½" squares (A8a, A17a).
  • Four 1" x 1½" (A3).

### From Fabric III (burgundy), cut:

* One 6¾"-wide strip. From this, cut:
  • One 4⅜" x 6¾" for A1 triangle-squares.
  • Two 3" x 37½" strips. From these, cut:
    • Eight 3" squares (A10).
    • Four 1½" x 3½" (A5).
    • Eight 1½" squares (A14a).
* Two 3"-wide strips for Strip Set 2.
* Eight 1"-wide strips. From these, cut:
  • Sixteen 1" x 19" (B8).
  • Eight 1" squares (A8b).

### From Fabric IV (plaid), cut:

* Two 3"-wide strips for Strip Set 1.
* One 2½"-wide strip. From this, cut:
  • Eight 2½" squares (A12b).
* One 2"-wide strip. From this and scrap from previous step, cut:
  • Eight 2" x 6" (A4, A13).
* One 1½"-wide strip. From this, cut:
  • Eight 1½" x 2" (A9a).
  • Sixteen 1½" squares (A12a, A16a).

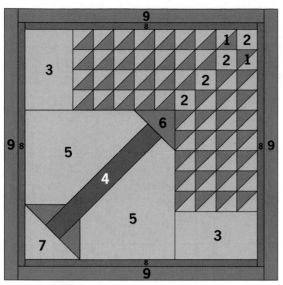

Block B—Make 4.

2½"

Strip Set 1—Make 1.

6½"

Strip Set 2—Make 1.

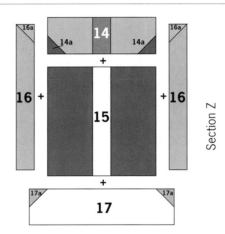

Section X

Section Y

Block A Assembly Diagram

Section Z

## From Fabric V (white), cut:

* One 5½"-wide strip. From this, cut:
  * Four 5½" squares (A12).
  * Four 2½" x 8½" (A17).
* Three 1½"-wide strips. Set aside one strip for Strip Set 2. From remaining strips, cut:
  * Twelve 1½" x 3½" (A6, A9).
  * Eight 1½" x 2" (A8).
  * Twelve 1½" squares (A2, A7a).

## From Fabric VI (black solid), cut:

* One 1½"-wide strip for Strip Set 1.

## From Fabric VII (brown solid), cut:

* Four 11½" squares (B4).

## Units for Block A

Refer to strip set diagrams and Block A Assembly Diagram throughout to identify units.

**1.** To make Unit 1, see page 14 for instructions on making triangle-squares. On wrong side of 4⅜" x 6¾" piece of Fabric II, draw a 1 x 2-square grid of 2⅜" squares. With right sides facing, align marked fabric with matching piece of Fabric III. Stitch grid as directed on page 22. Cut four triangle-squares from grid, one for each A block.

**2.** For Strip Set 1, join two 3"-wide strips of Fabric IV and one 1½"-wide strip of Fabric VI as shown. Press seam allowances toward Fabric VI. From this strip set, cut four 2½"-wide segments, one for each A block.

**3.** For Strip Set 2, join two 3"-wide strips of Fabric III and one 1½"-wide strip of Fabric V as shown. Press seam allowances toward Fabric III. From this strip set, cut four 6½"-wide segments, one for each A block.

**4.** Use diagonal-corner technique to make two each of units 8 and 16, making mirror-image units as shown. Make one each of units 7, 12, 14, and 17.

**5.** Use diagonal-end technique to make one each of units 4 and 13. Make two of Unit 9, making one unit a mirror image of the first.

## Block A Assembly

Assemble this block in sections X, Y, and Z. Refer to Block A Assembly Diagram throughout.

### Section X

**1.** Join units 2 and 3.

**2.** Sew Unit 1 to top of 2/3 unit.

**3.** Sew Unit 4 to bottom to of 2/3 unit as shown. *(continued)*

## Section Y

**1.** Join two of Unit 8 as shown.

**2.** Join units 5, 6, 7, and 8.

**3.** Sew Unit 9 to both sides of row, positioning mirror-image units as shown.

**4.** Use diagonal-corner technique to sew Unit 10 to both top corners of section.

**5.** Sew diagonal-corner Unit 11 to top right corner.

**6.** Sew Unit 12 to bottom of section; then add Unit 13 to right side.

## Section Z

**1.** Join units 14 and 15 as shown.

**2.** Sew Unit 16 to both sides of 14/15 unit, positioning mirror-image units as shown.

**3.** Join Unit 17 to bottom of section.

## Assembly

Join sections X, Y, and Z to complete block. Make four of Block A.

## Block B Assembly

Assemble this block in sections X, Y, and Z. Refer to Block B Assembly Diagram to identify units.

## Triangle-Squares

For Unit 1, see page 22 for instructions on making triangle-squares. On wrong side of each 9⅛" x 18⅝" piece of Fabric II, draw a 3 x 7-square grid of 2⅜" squares. With right sides facing, pair each marked fabric with a matching piece of Fabric I. Stitch grids as directed on page 22. Cut 42 triangle-squares from each grid, for a total of 210 (52 for each B block). Discard two.

## Section X

**1.** Select 12 of Unit 1 and four of Unit 2.

**2.** Join units in four rows, with three of Unit 1 and one Unit 2 in each row. Stagger position of Unit 2 in each row as shown.

**3.** Join four rows.

## Section Y

**1.** Select 20 of Unit 1 and one Unit 3 for each Section Y.

**2.** Make four rows of Unit 1, joining five triangle-squares in each row as shown. Join rows.

**3.** Sew Unit 3 to one end of combined rows as shown.

**4.** Make two of Section Y.

## Section Z

**1.** For Strip Set 3, join 7½"-wide strip of Fabric II and 3½"-wide strip of Fabric I as shown (Strip Set 3 Diagram). Make two of Strip Set 3. From these strip sets, cut eight 10½"-wide segments for Unit 5.

**2.** With right sides facing, position one Unit 5 on top of Unit 4 as shown, matching top left corners (Section Z Diagram, Figure A). Using diagonal-corner technique, stitch from corner to corner of Unit 5.

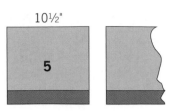

Strip Set 3—Make 2.

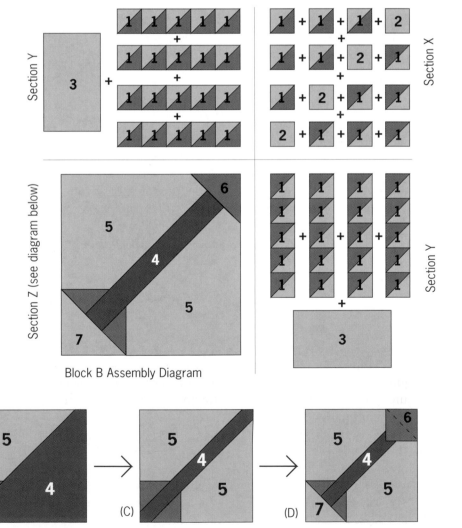

Block B Assembly Diagram

Section Z Diagram

Press Unit 5 to right side (Figure B) and trim excess fabric from seam allowances.

**3.** Use another strip-set segment to sew another diagonal corner to Unit 4 as shown (Figure C).

**4.** Use diagonal-corner technique to sew units 6 and 7 to opposite corners as shown (Figure D).

### Assembly

**1.** Join Section Y to left side of Section X as shown.

**2.** Sew second Section Y to right side of Section Z as shown.

**3.** Join X/Y section to Y/Z section.

**4.** Sew a Unit 8 to top and bottom edges of block. Trim ends even with block sides. Then sew a Unit 8 to each side of block. Press seam allowances toward Unit 8.

**5.** Add Unit 9 to block edges in same manner.

**6.** Make four of Block B.

## Tree Skirt Assembly

**1.** Referring to photo, sew B blocks to sides of two A blocks.

**2.** Join two remaining A blocks to sides of 8½" center square.

**3.** Sew two A/B rows to opposite sides of center row.

## Borders

**1.** For each inner border, join two 1½" x 26" strips of Fabric II.

**2.** Referring to instructions on page 25, measure quilt from top to bottom. Measuring from center seam, trim two borders to match length. Matching centers, sew borders to quilt sides.

**3.** Measure quilt from side to side; then trim remaining borders to match quilt width. Sew borders to top and bottom edges. Press seam allowances toward border.

**4.** For each outer border, join two 2" x 27" strips of Fabric I end-to-end. Follow steps 2 and 3 to sew borders to tree skirt.

## Quilting and Finishing

**1.** Mark quilting design on tree skirt as desired. Tree skirt shown is outline-quilted.

**2.** Divide backing into two equal lengths. Cut one piece in half lengthwise. Discard one narrow panel. Join remaining narrow panel to one side of wide piece.

**3.** Layer backing, batting, and quilt top. Baste. Quilt as desired.

**4.** Draw a 6" circle in center square. Cut out circle. Referring to photo, cut from circle to one corner of center square. Then cut straight down to edge of tree skirt, cutting through border of Block B.

**5.** For bias binding, cut 27" square of Fabric I in half diagonally. Starting from cut edges, cut 2"-wide diagonal strips. Join strips end-to-end to make a continuous strip 7 yards long.

**6.** With wrong sides facing, press binding strip in half. See page 30 for instructions on applying binding. Bias binding should curve nicely around circle.

**7.** Add eyes to Santas if desired. Use permanent marker to draw eyes or sew on ½"-diameter buttons.

# Breezing By

*Use scrap fabrics to create a rainbow of hot-air balloons afloat against a sky-blue background. Tassels, braid, and other trims add to the fun of making every block different.*

## Finished Size

Quilt: 64" x 104"

Blocks: 12 balloon blocks, 14" x 21½"

## Materials

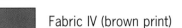

Fabric I (light blue solid)  4⅝ yards

Fabric II (yellow solid)  2⅜ yards

Fabric III (assorted scrap fabrics)  scraps

Fabric IV (brown print)  ⅛ yard

Backing fabric  6 yards

Batting  90" x 108"

Assorted ribbon, braid, and tassels  scraps

Brown embroidery floss

## Quick-Piecing Techniques

Strip Piecing (see page 20)

Diagonal Corners (see page 20)

Triangle-Squares (see page 22)

Four-Triangle Squares (see page 23)

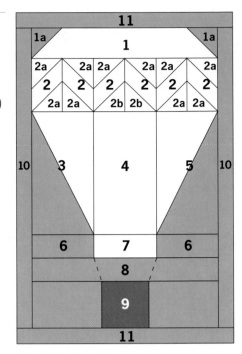

Block A—Make 7.

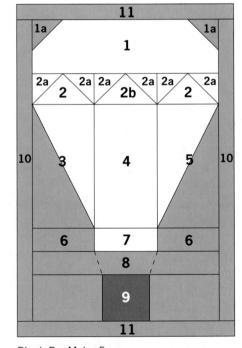

Block B—Make 5.

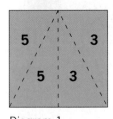

Diagram 1

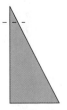

Diagram 2

## Cutting

Cut all strips crossgrain, from selvage to selvage. For best use of yardage, cut pieces in order listed. Refer to diagrams to identify pieces.

### From Fabric I (light blue), cut:

✱ Four 14½"-wide strips. From these, cut:
  - Twelve 11" x 14½" (spacer blocks).
  - Twenty-four 1½" x 14½" (A11, B11).

✱ Four 12½"-wide strips. From these, cut:
  - Four 12½" x 28¼" for C2 four-triangle squares.
  - Twelve 2" x 12½" (A8, B8).
  - One 7" x 11¾" for C1 triangle-squares.
  - Twenty-four 2½" squares (A1a, B1a).

✱ Two 9⅜"-wide strips. From these, cut:
  - Six 9⅜" squares. Cut squares as shown (Diagram 1) to get 12 triangles (A3, B3) and 12 mirror-image triangles (A5, B5). Trim ¾" from triangle tips (Diagram 2). Store triangles in separate bags.
  - Four 2" x 23" strips. From these and scrap, cut:
    - Twenty-four 2" x 4½" (A6, B6).

✱ Two 5"-wide strips for Strip Set 1.

✱ Twelve 1½" strips. From these, cut:
  - Twenty-four 1½" x 20" (A10, B10).

### From Fabric II (yellow), cut:

✱ Four 12½"-wide strips. From these, cut:
  - Four 12½" x 28¼" for C2 four-triangle squares.
  - One 7" x 11¾" for C1 triangle-squares.

✱ Nine 3"-wide strips for binding.

*(continued)*

### From Fabric III (scraps), cut:

*Note: Requirements are listed for one block. Referring to photo, make blocks with as many fabrics as desired.*

* One 2½" x 12½" (A1).
* Six 2½" x 4" (A2).
* Ten 2½" squares (A2a).
* Two 2½" squares (A2b).
* One 9⅜" square. Cut as shown in Diagram 1 to get one each of triangles 3 and 5. Discard extra triangles or use for another block. Trim ¾" from triangle tips (Diagram 2).
* One 4½" x 8½" (A4, B4).
* One 2" x 4½" (A7, B7).
* One 4" x 12½" (B1).
* Two 2½" x 4½" (B2).
* Six 2½" squares (B2a).
* One 2½" x 4½" (B2b).

### From Fabric IV (brown), cut:

* One 3½"-wide strip for Strip Set 1.

### Units for Block A

Refer to Block A Assembly Diagram to identify units. Use scrap fabrics to make one block at a time.

**1.** Use diagonal-corner technique to make one of Unit 1.

**2.** For Strip Set 1, join 5"-wide strips of Fabric I and 3½"-wide strip of Fabric IV to make one strip set as shown (Strip Set 1 Diagram). From this, cut twelve 3½"-wide segments for Unit 9. Set aside five units for Block B.

**3.** For units 3 and 5, join triangles of fabrics I and III as shown.

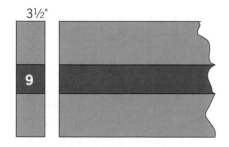

Strip Set 1—Make 1.

**4.** For Unit 2, use diagonal-corner technique to make two with 2a corners. Make two mirror-image 2/2a units in same manner but reverse angles of corners. Make one Unit 2 with one 2a corner and one 2b corner as shown. Make one mirror-image 2/2a/2b unit.

### Block A Assembly

Assemble this block in sections X and Y. Each completed section should measure approximately 12½" wide. Refer to Block A Assembly Diagram throughout.

**1.** For Section X, join six of Unit 2 in a row as shown, turning units to get correct fabric placement. Sew Unit 1 to top of row.

**2.** Join units 3, 4, and 5 in a row.

**3.** Join units 6 and 7 as shown. Sew this to bottom of 3/4/5 unit.

**4.** Add units 8 and 9 to bottom of section as shown.

**5.** Join sections X and Y.

**6.** Sew Unit 10 to sides of block.

**7.** Join Unit 11 to top and bottom of block.

**8.** Make seven of Block A.

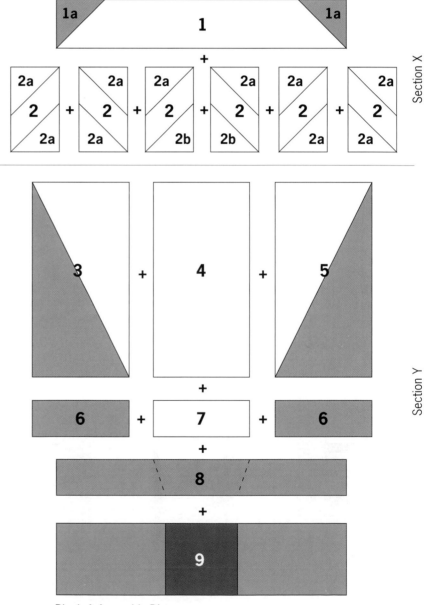

Block A Assembly Diagram

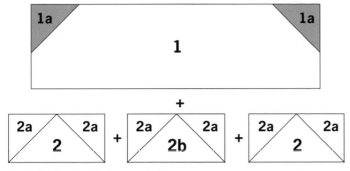

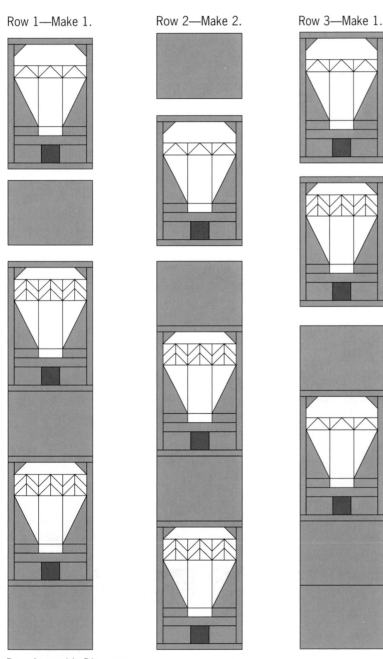

Block B, Section X Assembly Diagram

Row 1—Make 1.  Row 2—Make 2.  Row 3—Make 1.

Row Assembly Diagram

## Block B Assembly

**1.** Make units 1, 3, and 5 as for Block A.

**2.** Use diagonal-corner technique to make two of Unit 2/2a as shown. Make one of Unit 2b/2a.

**3.** Join three of Unit 2 in a row (Block B, Section X Assembly Diagram). Sew Unit 1 to top of row to complete Section X.

**4.** Follow Block A assembly instructions to complete Block B.

**5.** Make five of Block B.

## Quilt Assembly

**1.** Referring to photo on page 148 and Row Assembly Diagram, arrange blocks and spacer blocks in rows as shown. Make one each of rows 1 and 3 and two of Row 2. Arrange rows in 1-2-3-2 sequence. Move blocks around to get a pleasing balance of fabrics and color.

**2.** When satisfied with placement, join blocks in each row.

**3.** Join rows.

## Border

See page 22 for instructions for triangle-squares and four-triangle squares.

**1.** On wrong side of each 12½" x 28¼" piece of Fabric II, draw a 2 x 5-square grid of 5¼" squares. With right sides facing, pair marked fabric with matching piece of Fabric I. Stitch grids. Cut 20 triangle-squares from each grid to get 76 triangle-squares (and four extra). Press seam allowances toward Fabric I.

**2.** Draw a diagonal line on wrong side of 38 triangle-squares. With right sides together, match marked triangle-squares with unmarked triangle-squares with opposite fabrics facing. Stitch on both sides of drawn line as directed on page 23. Cut and press to get 76 C2 four-triangle squares. *(continued)*

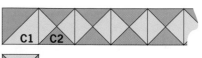

Border Diagram

**3.** On wrong side of 7" x 11¾" piece of Fabric II, draw a 1 x 2-square grid of 4⅞" squares. With right sides facing, pair marked fabric with matching piece of Fabric I. Stitch grid. Cut four C1 triangle-squares for border corners.

**4.** For each side border, join 24 C2 four-triangle squares (Border Diagram). Sew borders to quilt sides, easing as necessary.

**5.** For top border, join 14 C2 four-triangle squares. Join a C1 square to both ends of border, matching Fabric II edges. Sew border to top edge of quilt. Repeat for bottom border.

## Quilting and Finishing

**1.** Mark quilting design on quilt top as desired. On quilt shown, patchwork is outline-quilted and free-form clouds are quilted in spacer blocks.

**2.** Divide backing into three 2-yard lengths. Join three panels side-by-side to assemble backing 72" wide.

**3.** Layer backing, batting, and quilt top. Backing seams will be parallel to top and bottom edges of quilt top. Baste. Quilt as desired.

**4.** Use two strands of embroidery floss to backstitch lines between balloons and baskets.

**5.** From Fabric II strips, make 9⅝ yards of straight-grain binding. See page 30 for instructions on making and applying binding.

**6.** Hand-stitch trims and tassels to balloons as desired.

# Cabin in the **Stars**

*Set Log Cabin blocks inside a Variable Star, and you get
a new twist on an old favorite. The three blocks within the block
go together easily with a little piecing secret called a partial seam.*

## Finished Size
Quilt: 52" square
Blocks: 4 blocks, 17½" square

## Quick-Piecing Techniques
Strip Piecing (see page 20)
Diagonal Corners (see page 20)

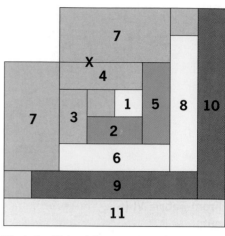

Block A—Make 16.

## Materials

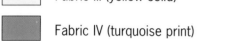
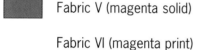

| | | |
|---|---|---|
| Fabric I (black dot) | | 2 yards |
| Fabric II (gray solid) | | ½ yard |
| Fabric III (yellow solid) | | ½ yard |
| Fabric IV (turquoise print) | | 1 yard |
| Fabric V (magenta solid) | | ¾ yard |
| Fabric VI (magenta print) | | ½ yard |
| Backing fabric | | 3¼ yards |
| Batting | | 72" x 90" |

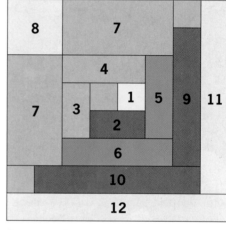

Block B—Make 16.

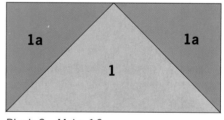

Block C—Make 16.

## Cutting
Cut all strips crossgrain, from selvage to selvage, except as noted. For best use of yardage, cut pieces in order listed. Refer to block diagrams to identify pieces.

### From Fabric I (black), cut:
* Four 1½"-wide strips for Strip Set 5.
* Five 1⅛"-wide strips. Set aside two strips for strip sets 1 and 2. From remaining strips, cut:
  * Two 1⅛" x 20" for strip sets 3 and 4.
  * Thirty-two 1⅛" x 1¾" (A3, B3).
* Six 3" x 56" lengthwise strips. Set aside four strips for binding. From remaining strips, cut:
  * Sixty-four 1¾" x 3" (A7, B7).
* Four 2½" x 56" lengthwise strips for outer border.
* Three 4¼" x 56" lengthwise strips. From these, cut:
  * Sixteen 4¼" x 8" (C1).
  * Four 2" squares (inner border corners).
  * Thirty-two 1⅛" x 2⅜" (A4, B4).

### From Fabric II (gray), cut:
* Two 2½"-wide strips for Strip Set 5.
* One 1¾"-wide strip. From this, cut:
  * Sixteen 1¾" squares (B8).
* Seven 1⅛"-wide strips. From these, cut:
  * Thirty-two 1⅛" x 5½" (A11, B12).
  * Sixteen 1⅛" x 4⅞" (B11).

### From Fabric III (yellow), cut:
* One 3⅝"-wide strip. From this, cut:
  * One 3⅝" x 20" for Strip Set 3.
  * Sixteen 1⅛" x 3" (A6).
* Five 1½"-wide strips for second border.
* One 1⅛"-wide strip for Strip Set 1.

### From Fabric IV (turquoise), cut:
* Four 4¼"-wide strips. From these, cut:
  * Thirty-two 4¼" squares (C1a).
  * Sixteen 1⅛" x 3" (B6).
* Eight 1½"-wide strips. From these, cut:
  * Eight 1½" x 24" for third border.
  * Thirty-two 1⅛" x 2⅜" (A5, B5).
  * Sixteen 1⅛" x 1¾" (A2).

**From Fabric V (magenta solid), cut:**

✳ One 4¼"-wide strip for Strip Set 2.

✳ One 3⅝" x 20" for Strip Set 4.

✳ Eight 1½"-wide strips. From these, cut:
  - Eight 1½" x 25" for fourth border.
  - Sixteen 1⅛" x 4⅞" (A10).
  - Sixteen 1⅛" x 1¾" (B2).

**From Fabric VI (magenta print), cut:**

✳ Four 2"-wide strips for inner border.

✳ One 4½" square (center).

## Block A Assembly

**1.** For one Strip Set 1, join 1⅛" strips of fabrics I and III as shown (Strip Set 1 Diagram). From this, cut thirty-two 1⅛"-wide segments for Unit 1. Set aside 16 units for Block B.

**2.** For one Strip Set 2, join 4¼"-wide strip of Fabric V and 1⅛"-wide strip of Fabric I as shown (Strip Set 2 Diagram). From this, cut thirty-two 1⅛"-wide segments, 16 for A9 and 16 for B10.

**3.** For Strip Set 3, join 3⅝" x 20" strip of Fabric III and 1⅛" x 20" strip of Fabric I as shown (Strip Set 3 Diagram). From this, cut sixteen 1⅛"-wide segments for Unit 8.

**4.** Join units 1 and 2 (Diagram 1). Sew Unit 3 to left side of combined units as shown.

**5.** Working clockwise around block, add units 4, 5, and 6 in numerical order (Diagram 2). As strips are added, press seam allowances away from newest strip.

**6.** Sew one Unit 7 to left side of block (Diagram 3). With right sides facing, align second Unit 7 with top right corner of block (Unit 5). Stitch seam, stopping about ¾" from end of Unit 4, as shown by X on diagram. Leaving this seam partially open enables you to join blocks A and B without having to sew a set-in seam.

**7.** Add Unit 8 to right side of block; then sew Unit 9 to bottom edge (Diagram 4). Add units 10 and 11 to complete block.

**8.** Make 16 of Block A.

## Block B Assembly

**1.** For Strip Set 4, join 3⅝" x 20" strip of Fabric V and 1⅛" x 20" strip of Fabric I as shown (Strip Set 4 Diagram). From this, cut sixteen 1⅛"-wide segments for Unit 9.

*(continued)*

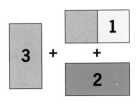

Diagram 1

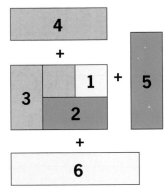

Diagram 2

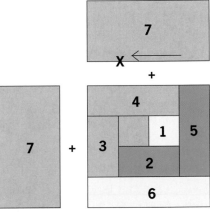

Diagram 3

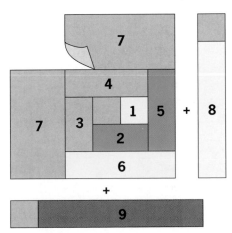

Diagram 4

1⅛"

Strip Set 1—Make 1.

1⅛" 1⅛"

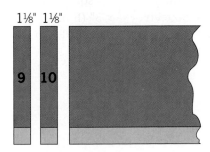

Strip Set 2—Make 1.

1⅛"

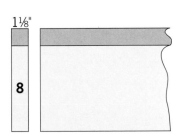

Strip Set 3—Make 1.

1⅛"

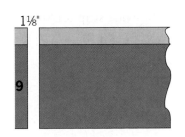

Strip Set 4—Make 1.

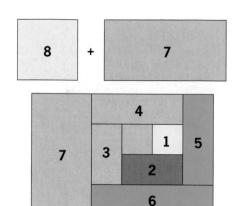

Diagram 5

**2.** Join units 1–6 in numerical order as for Block A, working clockwise from center and following diagrams for color placement. Add Unit 7 to left side of block. Join Unit 8 to second Unit 7 as shown (Diagram 5); then sew 7/8 unit to top edge of block.

**3.** Add units 9–12 in same manner as for Block A.

**4.** Make 16 of Block B.

## Block C Assembly

Use diagonal-corner technique to make 16 of Block C.

## Star Block Assembly

**1.** For each star block, select four each of blocks A, B, and C.

**2.** Join A blocks as shown (Diagram 6), turning blocks to place open corners to outside edges.

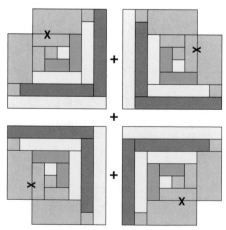

Diagram 6

**3.** Sew C blocks to edges of joined A blocks as shown (Diagram 7).

**4.** At one corner of star block, sew a B block to edge indicated by arrow (Diagram 7). Be sure B block is positioned with corner square to inside corner of star block.

**5.** Starting where partial seam ended, stitch to edge to complete adding Block B.

**6.** Repeat steps 4 and 5 to join B blocks at remaining corners.

**7.** Make four star blocks.

## Quilt Assembly

**1.** For Strip Set 5, join two 1½"-wide strips of Fabric I and one

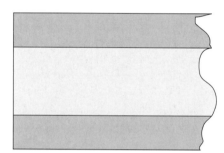

Strip Set 5—Make 2.

2½"-wide strip of Fabric II. Make two strip sets. From these, cut four 18"-long segments for sashing.

**2.** Referring to photo, join two star blocks with a sashing strip between them. Repeat for second pair of blocks. Press seam allowances toward sashing.

**3.** For center sashing row, join remaining sashing strips to sides of center square. Press seam allowances toward sashing.

**4.** Join rows.

## Borders

Press seam allowances toward outside edge of quilt throughout.

**1.** Referring to instructions on page 25, measure quilt from top to bottom and from side to side. Trim Fabric VI border strips to match length.

**2.** Sew two borders to quilt sides.

**3.** Add Fabric I squares to ends of remaining borders. Sew borders to top and bottom edges of quilt.

Diagram 7

**4.** Measure quilt length and piece Fabric III strips as necessary to make two borders. Sew borders to quilt sides. Repeat for top and bottom edges.

**5.** For third border, join two Fabric IV strips for each border. Measure quilt and sew borders to quilt as before. Repeat for fourth border, using Fabric V border strips.

**6.** Measure length of quilt again and trim two Fabric I borders to match length. Sew borders to quilt sides. Repeat for top and bottom edges.

## Quilting and Finishing

**1.** Mark quilting design on quilt as desired. Quilt shown is outline-quilted.

**2.** Divide backing fabric into two equal lengths. Cut one piece in half lengthwise. Join one narrow panel to wide piece. Discard remaining narrow panel.

**3.** Layer backing, batting, and quilt top. Baste. Quilt as desired.

**4.** From Fabric I strips, make 6 yards of straight-grain binding. See page 30 for instructions on making and applying binding.

**5.** See page 138 for tips on making a hanging sleeve.

# Nine Lives

*Because a cat is a cat, he'll purr at you for hours, and then abruptly turn and show you his south side. Scrap fabrics accentuate the many faces of these quick-pieced kitties. Four little mice prowl the checkerboard borders to make this cat-and-mouse game meowy cute.*

## Finished Size
Quilt: 80" x 100"
Blocks: 9 cat blocks, 16" x 22"
       4 mouse blocks, 4" x 8"

## Materials

| | | |
|---|---|---|
| ▪ | Fabric I (dark blue solid) | 3⅛ yards |
| ▪ | Fabric II (light green solid) | 1¼ yards |
| ▪ | Fabric III (medium blue solid) | 2¼ yards |
| ▪ | Fabric IV (rose solid) | 1⅜ yards |
| ▫ | Fabric V (muslin) | ¼ yard |
| ▫ | Fabric VI (assorted green, blue, and rose prints) | scraps |
| | Fabric VII (blue-on-white stripe) | 2¼ yards |
| | Backing fabric | 6 yards |
| | Batting | 90" x 108" |
| | Blue, rose, green, and red yarn | scraps |
| | Eight ¾"-diameter buttons for cats' eyes | |
| | Four ½"-diameter buttons for mouse eyes | |

## Quick-Piecing Techniques
Strip Piecing (see page 20)
Diagonal Corners (see page 20)
Diagonal Ends (see page 21)

## Cutting
Cut all strips crossgrain, from selvage to selvage, except as noted. For best use of yardage, cut pieces in order listed.

For scrap fabrics, select three each of blue, green, and rose. In addition to scrap fabrics, use fabrics II, III, and IV for some pieces in blocks A, B, and C. Refer to block diagrams to identify pieces.

### From Fabric I (dark blue), cut:
✳ Six 5½"-wide strips. From these, cut:
- Eighteen 5½" x 12½" (A1, B1).

✳ Sixteen 2½"-wide strips. From these and scrap, cut:
- Eighteen 2½" x 16½" (A11, B10).
- Twenty-seven 2½" x 6½" (A3, A4, B3, B4).
- Eighty-four 2½" squares (A2a, A5a, A6a, A7a, B2a, B5a, B6a, C1a, C5).

✳ One 1½"-wide strip. From this, cut:
- Four 1½" x 6½" (C3).
- Eight 1½" squares (B11, C2a).

✳ Nine 3"-wide strips for binding.

### From Fabric II (green), cut:
✳ One 6½"-wide strip. From this, cut:
- One 5½" x 6½" (A5).
- Six 3½" x 6½" (A2, B2).
- One 4½" x 5½" (A7).
- Two 4½" squares (A8, Unit D).

✳ Six 4½"-wide strips for strip sets 2 and 3.

✳ One 2½"-wide strip. From this, cut:
- One 2½" x 7½" (A6).
- Two 2½" x 5½" (B9).
- Six 2½" squares (A4a, A6c, A10, C4). *(continued)*

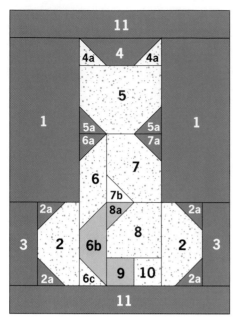

Block A—Make 5.

## From Fabric III (medium blue), cut:

* One 6½"-wide strip. From this, cut:
  * One 5½" x 6½" (A5).
  * Two 3½" x 6½" (A2).
  * Two 2½" x 6½" (A6b).
  * One 4½" x 5½" (A7).
  * One 4½" square (A8).
  * One 2½" x 7½" (A6).
  * Eight 2½" squares (A4a, A6c, A8a, A9, A10).
* Fourteen 4½"-wide strips for strip sets 1, 2, and 3.

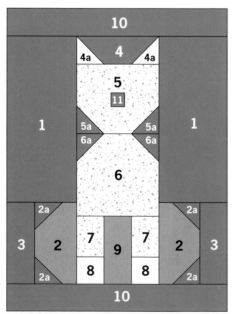

Block B—Make 4.

## From Fabric IV (rose), cut:

* One 6½"-wide strip. From this, cut:
  * One 5½" x 6½" (A5).
  * Six 3½" x 6½" (A2, B2).
  * One 4½" x 5½" (A7).
  * One 4½" square (A8).
* Seven 4½"-wide strips for strip sets 1 and 2.
* One 2½"-wide strip. From this, cut:
  * One 2½" x 7½" (A6).
  * Two 2½" x 5½" (B9).
  * Six 2½" squares (A4a, A6c, A10, C4).

## From Fabric V (muslin), cut:

* Three 2½"-wide strips. From these, cut:
  * Four 2½" x 8½" (C1).
  * Twenty-one 2½" squares (A7b, B4a, B8).
  * Four 1½" x 6½" (C2).

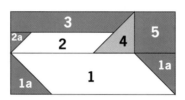

Block C—Make 4.

## From Fabric VI (scraps), cut:

* Block A tail pieces from one fabric of each color:
  * One 2½" x 6½" (A6b).
  * Two 2½" squares (A8a, A9).
* Block A body pieces from each of two blue prints:
  * One 5½" x 6½" (A5).
  * One 4½" x 5½" (A7).
  * One 4½" square (A8).
  * Two 3½" x 6½" (A2).
  * One 2½" x 7½" (A6).
  * Four 2½" squares (A4a, A6c, A10).
* Block B body pieces from each of two green and two rose prints:
  * One 6½" square (B6).
  * One 5½" x 6½" (B5).
  * Two 2½" x 3½" (B7).

## From Fabric VII (stripe), cut:

* Four 2½" x 77" lengthwise strips for sashing.
* Twelve 3" x 16½" crosswise strips for sashing.

Section X          Section Y          Section Z

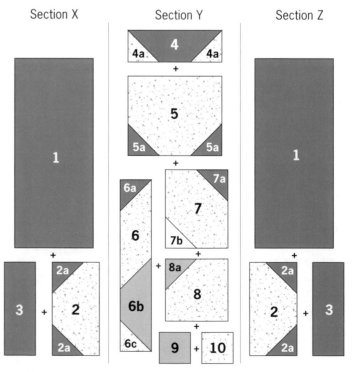

Block A Assembly Diagram

## Units for Block A

Refer to Block A Assembly Diagram to identify units.

**1.** Use diagonal-corner technique to make two of Unit 2 and one each of units 4, 5, 7, and 8.

**2.** For Unit 6, use diagonal-end technique to join pieces 6 and 6b. Then add diagonal corners to both ends of unit as shown.

## Block A Assembly

Assemble this block in sections X, Y, and Z. Each completed section should measure approximately 22½" long. Refer to Block A Assembly Diagram throughout.

### Sections X and Z

**1.** For each section, join units 2 and 3, turning Unit 2s as shown.

**2.** Add Unit 1 to top of 2/3 units.

### Section Y

**1.** Join units 9 and 10. Sew 9/10 unit to bottom of Unit 8.

**2.** Sew Unit 7 to top of Unit 8.

**3.** Join Unit 6 to side of combined unit 7/8/9/10.

**4.** Sew units 4 and 5 to top of section.

### Assembly

**1.** Sew sections X and Z to sides of Section Y.

**2.** Join Unit 11 to top and bottom of block.

**3.** Make five of Block A, using scrap fabrics as shown.

## Block B Assembly

Assemble this block in sections X, Y, and Z. Each completed section should measure approximately 22½" long. Refer to Block B Assembly Diagram throughout.

**1.** Use diagonal-corner technique to make two of Unit 2 and one each of units 4, 5, and 6.

**2.** For Section X, join units 2 and 3 as shown; then add Unit 1 to top of 2/3 unit.

**3.** Make Section Z in same manner, turning Unit 2 as shown.

**4.** For Section Y, join units 7 and 8 in pairs as shown. Sew these to sides of Unit 9. Join units 4, 5, 6, and 7/8/9 in a row as shown.

**5.** Sew sections X and Z to sides of Section Y.

**6.** Join Unit 10 to top and bottom of block.

**7.** Turn under ¼" on all edges of Unit 11. Appliqué square in center of Unit 5.

**8.** Make four of Block B, using scrap fabrics as shown.

**9.** Lightly trace smile pattern under each appliquéd nose.

## Block C Assembly

Refer to Block C Assembly Diagram to identify units.

**1.** Use diagonal-corner technique to make one each of units 1 and 2.

**2.** Join units 2 and 3. Use diagonal-corner technique to add Unit 4 on right side of 2/3 unit as shown.

**3.** Sew Unit 5 to end of 2/3/4 unit.

**4.** Sew Unit 1 to bottom of combined unit to complete block.

**5.** Make four of Block C, making two blocks with Fabric II ears and two blocks with Fabric IV ears.

*(continued)*

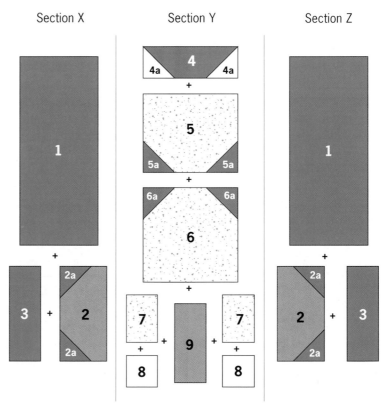

Block B Assembly Diagram

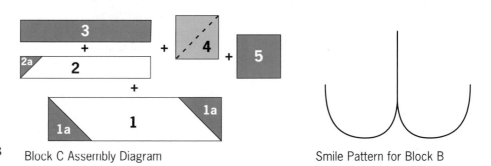

Block C Assembly Diagram

Smile Pattern for Block B

## Quilt Assembly

**1.** Referring to photo, lay out cat blocks in three vertical rows, alternating A and B blocks. Note that blue, rose, and green blocks are set in diagonal lines across the quilt. Place 16½"-long sashing strips between blocks and at top and bottom of each row. When satisified with block positions, join blocks and sashing strips in each row.

**2.** Lay out rows again to check position. Place long sashing strips between rows and at both sides. Join rows and sashing.

## Border

Refer to quilt photo throughout to check position of units.

**1.** For Strip Set 1, join two 4½"-wide strips of Fabric III and one strip of Fabric IV as shown (Strip Set 1 Diagram). Press seam allowances toward Fabric III. Make three strip sets. From these, cut twenty-three 4½"-wide segments for Unit 1.

**2.** For Strip Set 2, join one 4½"-wide strips of Fabrics II, III, and IV as shown (Strip Set 2 Diagram). Press seam allowances toward Fabric III. Make four strip sets. From these, cut thirty-six 4½"-wide segments for Unit 2.

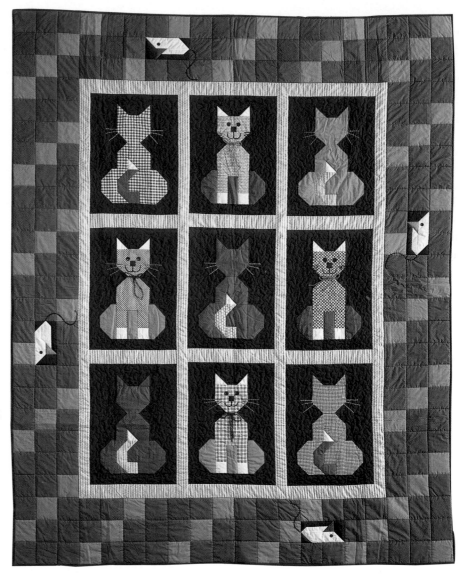

4½"

Strip Set 1—Make 3.

4½"

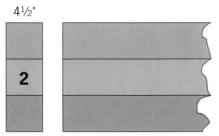

Strip Set 2—Make 4.

**3.** For Strip Set 3, join two 4½"-wide strips of Fabric III and one strip of Fabric II as shown. Press seam allowances toward Fabric III. Make two strip sets. From these, cut eighteen 4½"-wide segments for Unit 3.

**4.** For Unit D, select one Strip Set 2 segment and two Strip Set 3

4½"

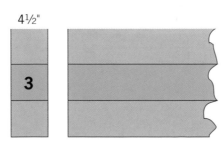

Strip Set 3—Make 2.

segments. Use a seam ripper to remove one square from each unit, leaving squares of fabrics II and III. Join one discarded square of Fabric III and 4½" square of Fabric II to make a fourth Unit D.

**5.** For Unit E, remove one Fabric III square from four Strip Set 1 segments.

**6.** For left side border, select five Unit 1, nine Unit 2, three Unit 3, and one each of Block C, Unit D, and Unit E. Join D and E units to Block C as shown (Left Side Border Diagram). Lay out units in a row, being careful to alternate position of Unit 2 as shown. Join units in row. Sew border to left edge of quilt, positioning bottom of mouse toward outside edge of quilt.

**7.** For right side border, select five Unit 1, eight Unit 2, four Unit 3, and one each of Block C, Unit D, and Unit E. Join D and E units to Block C as shown (Right Side Border Diagram). Lay out units in a row, being careful to alternate position of Unit 2 as shown. Join units in row. Sew border to right edge of quilt, with bottom of mouse toward outside edge of quilt.

**8.** For top border, select five Unit 1, nine Unit 2, four Unit 3, and one each of Block C, Unit D, and Unit E. Join D and E units to Block C as shown (Top Border Diagram). Join units in a row as shown. Sew

border to top edge of quilt, with bottom of mouse toward outside edge of quilt.

**9.** For bottom border, select four Unit 1, nine Unit 2, five Unit 3, and one each of Block C, Unit D, and Unit E. Join D and E units to Block C as shown (Bottom Border Diagram). Join units in a row as shown. Sew border to bottom edge of quilt, with bottom of mouse toward outside edge of quilt.

## Quilting and Finishing

**1.** Mark quilting design on quilt top as desired. On quilt shown, patchwork is outline-quilted. The background of each block is machine stipple-quilted.

**2.** Divide backing into two 3-yard lengths. Cut one piece in half lengthwise. Join one narrow panel to each side of wide piece to assemble backing.

**3.** Layer backing, batting, and quilt top. Baste. Quilt as marked or as desired.

**4.** From Fabric I strips, make 10½ yards of straight-grain binding. See page 30 for instructions on making and applying binding.

**5.** Sew two ¾" buttons on each B block for cats' eyes. Sew a ½" button in place on each C block.

**6.** Use yarn scraps to backstitch mouths and whiskers on cats and a tail for each mouse. On B blocks, tack a long length of yarn on each side of cat's neck and tie a bow.

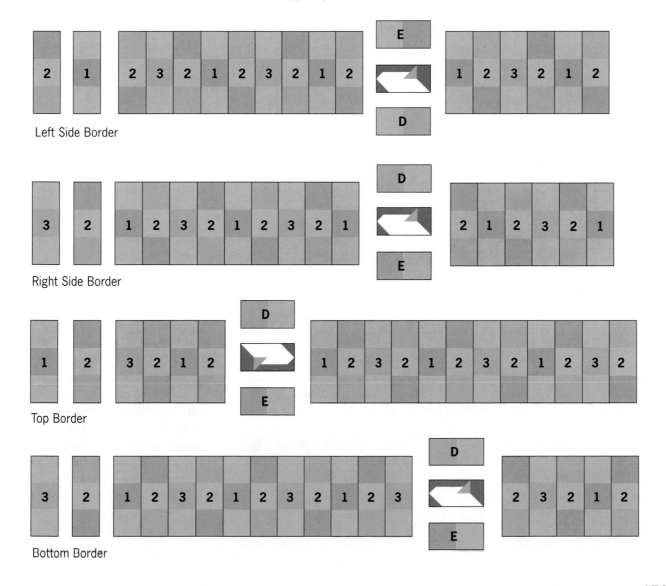

Left Side Border

Right Side Border

Top Border

Bottom Border

# Don't Sit Under the **Apple Tree**

*You'll be humming the familiar tune as you stitch this orchard of apple trees. The cheery picnic cloth also features falling apples and an army of happy ants ready for the feast to begin. Strip piecing makes the trees and checkerboard border extra quick.*

## Finished Size

Picnic Cloth: 60" x 60"
Blocks: 8 tree blocks, 13¾" square
12 ant blocks, 2½" x 13¾"

## Quick-Piecing Techniques

Strip Piecing (see page 20)
Diagonal Corners (see page 20)

## Materials

| | | |
|---|---|---|
| ■ | Fabric I (red print) | 1⅝ yards |
| □ | Fabric II (white-on-white print) | 2 yards |
| ▨ | Fabric III (lime green print) | ¼ yard |
| ▨ | Fabric IV (dark green print) | ⅞ yard |
| ■ | Fabric V (brown print) | ⅝ yard |
| ▨ | Fabric VI (bright blue solid) | ⅝ yard |
| | Backing fabric | 3⅞ yards |
| | Batting | 72" x 90" |
| | Brown fine-tipped fabric marker | |

## Cutting

Cut all strips crossgrain, from selvage to selvage, except as noted. For best use of yardage, cut pieces in order listed. Refer to block diagrams to identify pieces. See page 133 for tips on cutting appliqué pieces with freezer paper.

### From Fabric I (red), cut:

✳ Eighteen 1¾"-wide strips. Set aside 16 strips for strip sets 1 and 2. From two strips, cut:
  • Thirty-two 1¾" squares (A6, sashing squares).
✳ Eight apples for appliqué.
✳ Six 3"-wide strips for binding.

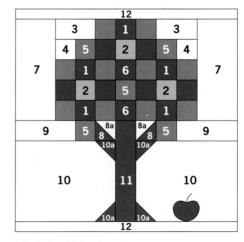

Block A—Make 8.

Apple Pattern

### From Fabric II (white), cut:

✳ One 14¼"-wide strip. From this, cut:
  • One 14¼" square (center square).
  • Sixteen 1⅛" x 14¼" (A12).
✳ Two 6¾"-wide strips. From these and scrap, cut:
  • Sixteen 5½" x 6¾" (A10).
✳ Three 3"-wide strips. From these, cut:
  • Sixteen 3" x 6¾" (A7).
  • Four 3" squares (Corner C).
✳ Four 1¾"-wide strips. From these and scrap, cut:
  • Sixteen 1¾" x 4¼" (A9).
  • Sixteen 1¾" x 3" (A3).
  • Thirty-two 1¾" squares (A4, A8a).
✳ Five 1½"-wide strips. From these, cut:
  • Twelve 1½" x 14¼" (B6).
  • Twelve 1¼" x 1½" (B4).
  • Twenty-four 1" x 1½" (B3).
✳ Eleven 1"-wide strips. From these, cut:
  • Twelve 1" x 14¼" (B5).
  • 288 1" squares (B1a, B2a).

### From Fabric III (lime green), cut:

✳ Five 1¾"-wide strips for Strip Set 2.  *(continued)*

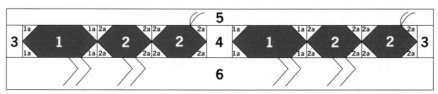

Block B—Make 12.

**From Fabric IV (dark green), cut:**

✳ Fourteen 1¾"-wide strips. Set aside 12 strips for Strip Set 1. From two strips, cut:
  • Forty 1¾" squares (A5).

**From Fabric V (brown), cut:**

✳ Four 1¾"-wide strips. From these, cut:
  • Eight 1¾" x 6¾" (A11).
  • Forty-eight 1¾" squares (A8, A10a).

✳ Five 1½"-wide strips. From these, cut:
  • Twenty-four 1½" x 3" (B1).
  • Forty-eight 1½" x 2¼" (B2).

**From Fabric VI (blue), cut:**

✳ Ten 1¾"-wide strips. From these, cut:
  • Twenty-four 1¾" x 14¼" (E sashing).
  • Sixteen 1¾" x 3" (D sashing).

## Units for Block A

Refer to strip set diagrams and Block A Assembly Diagram to identify units.

**1.** For Strip Set 1, join 1¾"-wide strips of fabrics I and IV as shown. Make six strip sets. Press seam allowances toward Fabric IV. From these strip sets, cut 128 1¾"-wide segments for Unit 1. Set aside 88 units for border.

**2.** For Strip Set 2, join 1¾"-wide strips of fabrics I and III as shown. Make five strip sets. Press seam allowances toward Fabric III. From these strip sets, cut 112 1¾"-wide segments for Unit 2. Set aside 88 units for border.

**3.** Use diagonal-corner technique to make two of Unit 10.

**4.** For Unit 8, match 1¾" squares of fabrics II and V, with right sides facing. On wrong side of Fabric II square, draw one diagonal line from corner to corner. Stitch on diagonal line. Trim seam allowance to ¼" and press. Make 16 of Unit 8, two for each block.

## Block A Assembly

Assemble block in sections X and Y. Completed sections should be 14¼" wide. Refer to Block A Assembly Diagram throughout.

### Section X

Main part of section consists of five horizontal rows as shown.

**1.** Join a Unit 3 to sides of Unit 1.
**2.** Join units 4 and 5 to sides of Unit 2.
**3.** Sew Unit 1s to sides of Unit 6. Repeat to make Row 5.
**4.** Join Unit 2s to opposite sides of one Unit 5.
**5.** Join rows 1–5.
**6.** Sew Unit 7s to sides of combined rows.

### Section Y

**1.** Join units 5, 8, and 9, making two mirror-image rows as shown.
**2.** Sew each 5/8/9 row to top of one Unit 10.
**3.** Sew combined units to sides of Unit 11.

### Assembly

**1.** Join sections X and Y.
**2.** Stitch Unit 12 to top and bottom of block.
**3.** Make 8 of Block A.
**4.** Appliqué apples at Unit 12 seam line. Use fabric pen to draw stems.

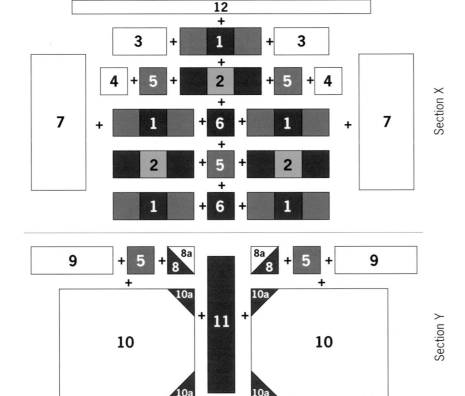

Block A Assembly Diagram

Strip Set 1—Make 6.

Strip Set 2—Make 5.

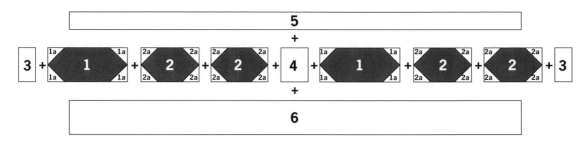

Block B Assembly Diagram

## Block B Assembly

Each completed block should measure 14¼" wide. Refer to Block B Assembly Diagram throughout.

**1.** Use diagonal-corner technique to make two of Unit 1 and four of Unit 2.

**2.** Join units in a row with units 3 and 4 as shown.

**3.** Sew Unit 5 to top of block and Unit 6 to bottom.

**4.** Use fabric pen to draw legs and antenna.

## Picnic Cloth Assembly

Assemble borders and blocks in horizontal rows. Refer to photo and Row Assembly Diagram throughout.

**1.** For Border Row, alternate 24 Strip Set 1 units and 23 Strip Set 2 units. Make two Border Rows.

**2.** For Row 1, join two pair of strip-set units as shown for ends of row. Join these with corner C, four D sashing strips, three B blocks, and another C square as shown. Make two of Row 1.

**3.** For Row 2, join two Strip Set 2 units, two D sashing strips, three E sashing strips, and four sashing squares. Make four of Row 2.

**4.** For Row 3, join three A blocks, four E sashing strips, and two B blocks as shown. For both ends of row, join six Strip Set 1 units and five Strip Set 2 units as shown; then sew these to row. Make two of Row 3.

**5.** For Row 4, join two A blocks, center square, two B blocks, and four E sashing strips as shown. For both ends of row, join six Strip Set 1 units and five Strip Set 2 units; then sew these to row. Make one of Row 4.

**6.** Lay out rows 1-3-4-3-1. Then put a Row 2 between each row. Lay out border rows at top and bottom. When satisfied with position of all rows, join rows.

## Quilting and Finishing

**1.** Mark quilting design on cloth as desired. Cloth shown is outline-quilted.

**2.** Divide backing into two equal lengths. Cut one panel in half lengthwise and discard one narrow panel. Sew remaining narrow panel to wide panel to assemble backing.

**3.** Layer backing, batting, and cloth. Baste. Quilt as desired.

**4.** From Fabric I strips, make 7 yards of binding. See page 30 for directions on making and applying straight-grain binding.

Row Assembly Diagram

Border Row—Make 2.

Row 1—Make 2.

Row 2—Make 4.

Row 3—Make 2.

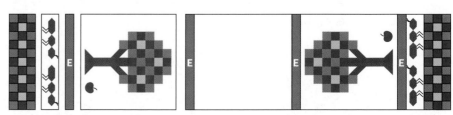

Row 4—Make 1.

# Flowerpot *Wall Hanging*

*Looking for a pretty way to store tools? Make this little wall hanging
for your sewing room, potting shed, or kitchen. Four handy pockets hold
quilting supplies, small gardening tools, note cards, or just stuff.*

## Finished Size

Quilt: 22½" x 29½"

Blocks: 4 flowerpot blocks, 5" x 11"
4 heart pocket blocks, 2½" x 6"

## Materials

| | | |
|---|---|---|
| | Fabric I (blue print) | ⅜ yard |
| | Fabric II (dark blue solid) | ¼ yard |
| | Fabric III (navy solid) | ⅝ yard |
| | Fabric IV (green solid) | ¼ yard |
| | Fabric V (terra-cotta solid) | ⅛ yard |
| | Fabric VI (rust print) | ⅛ yard |
| | Fabric VII (printed muslin) | ½ yard |
| | Backing fabric | ⅞ yard |
| | Batting | 29" x 36" |

Four ⅞"-diameter white buttons

## Quick-Piecing Techniques

Diagonal Corners (see page 20)
Four-Triangle Squares (see page 23)

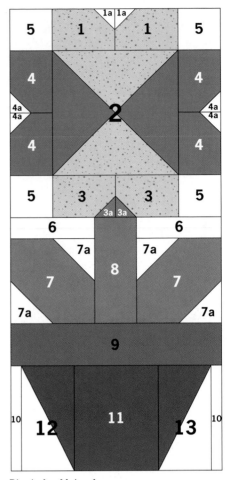

Block A—Make 4.

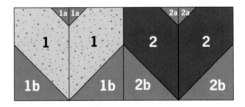

Block B—Make 4.

## Cutting

Cut all strips crossgrain, from selvage to selvage. For best use of yardage, cut pieces in order listed. Refer to diagrams to identify pieces.

### From Fabric I (blue), cut:

✷ One 6¼"-wide strip. From this, cut:
- One 6¼" x 10½" for A2 triangle-squares.
- Two 2" x 31" strips. From these, cut:
  - Sixteen 1½" x 2" (A1, A3).
  - Eight 2" x 3" (B1).

✷ Three 1¼"-wide strips for inner border.

### From Fabric II (dark blue), cut:

✷ One 6¼"-wide strip. From this, cut:
- One 6¼" x 10½" for A2 triangle-squares.
- Sixteen 1½" x 2" (A4).

### From Fabric III (navy), cut:

✷ Four 2"-wide strips. From these, cut:
- Two 2" x 27" and two 2" x 23" for outer borders.
- Eight 2" x 3" (B2).

✷ Three 3"-wide strips for binding.

### From Fabric IV (green), cut:

✷ One 2½"-wide strip. From this, cut:
- Eight 2½" squares (A7).
- Four 1½" x 3" (A8).

✷ One 2¼" x 24½" (16).

✷ One 2"-wide strip. From this and scrap, cut:
- Sixteen 2" squares (B1b, B2b).
- Twenty-four 1" squares (A3a, B1a, B2a).

### From Fabric V (terra-cotta), cut:

✷ Four 1½" x 5½" (A9).

### From Fabric VI (rust), cut:

✷ One 3⅞"-wide strip. From this, cut:
- One 3⅞" x 7¾". From this, cut four A12 triangles and four A13 triangles as shown (Diagram 1). Trim ¾" from tip of each triangle (Diagram 2). Store triangles separately.
- Four 2½" x 3" (A11).

*(continued)*

### From Fabric VII (muslin), cut:

✱ One 5½"-wide strip. From this, cut:
- One 5½" x 24½" (17).
- Two 1" x 5½" (18).
- One 3⅞" x 7¾". From this, cut four A12 triangles and four A13 triangles as shown (Diagram 1). Trim ¾" from tip of each triangle (Diagram 2). Store triangles separately.
- Eight ¾" x 3" (A10).

✱ Four 1½"-wide strips. From these, cut:
- Two 1½" x 25½" (15).
- Five 1½" x 11½" (14).
- Thirty-two 1½" squares (A5, A7a).

✱ One 1"-wide strip. From this and scrap, cut:
- Eight 1" x 2½" (A6).
- Twenty-four 1" squares (A1a, A4a).

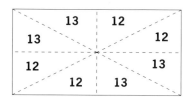

Diagram 1

Diagram 2

## Units for Block A

Refer to Block A Assembly Diagram throughout to identify units.

**1.** On wrong side of 6¼" x 10½" piece of Fabric I, draw a 1 x 2-square grid of 4¼" squares.

**2.** With right sides facing, match marked piece with corresponding piece of Fabric II. Stitch grid as described for triangle-squares on page 22. Cut four triangle-squares from grid. Press seam allowances toward Fabric II.

**3.** See page 23 for instructions on four-triangle squares. Draw a diagonal line on wrong side of two triangle-squares. With right sides facing and seams aligned, match a marked triangle-square with unmarked unit so that each triangle faces a different fabric. Stitch each pair as directed on page 23. Make four four-triangle squares for Unit 2, one for each block.

**4.** Join triangles of fabrics VI and VII to make one each of units 12 and 13.

**5.** Use diagonal-corner technique to make two each of units 1, 3, and 7 as shown. Note that second unit is mirror image of the first. Make units in same manner, but reverse angles of diagonal corners. Make four of Unit 4 in same manner.

## Block A Assembly

Assemble this block in sections X, Y, and Z. Each completed section should measure approximately 5½" wide. Refer to Block A Assembly Diagram throughout.

### Section X

**1.** Join units 1 and 3 in pairs as shown.

**2.** Sew combined units to top and bottom of Unit 2 as shown.

**3.** Join two pair of Unit 4, matching mirror-image units as shown. Sew Unit 5 to ends of each pair.

**4.** Join 4/5 units to sides of 1/2/3 unit.

### Section Y

**1.** Sew Unit 6 to top of each Unit 7.

**2.** Join 6/7 units to sides of Unit 8.

**3.** Sew Unit 9 to bottom of section.

### Section Z

Join units 10, 11, 12, and 13 in a row as shown.

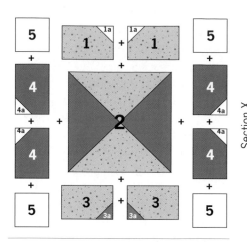

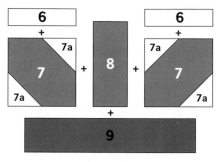

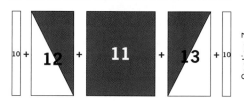

Block A Assembly Diagram

### Assembly

**1.** Join sections X, Y, and Z as shown.

**2.** Make four of Block A.

## Block B Assembly

Refer to Block B Assembly Diagram throughout.

**1.** Use diagonal-corner technique to make one each of units 1 and 2. Second unit is a mirror image of the first.

**2.** Join units in a row as shown.

**3.** Make four of Block B.

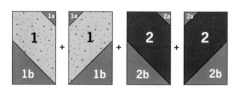

Block B Assembly Diagram

## Quilt Assembly

Refer to Quilt Assembly Diagram for placement of blocks and setting pieces in rows.

**1.** Join A blocks in a row with a Unit 14 strip between blocks and at row ends as shown.

**2.** Sew Unit 15 to top of row.

**3.** Join B blocks in a row. Sew Unit 16 to top of row.

**4.** Turn under ¼" on top edge of Unit 16. Then turn under another ¼" and press. Topstitch fold to make hem for pocket. Pin B/16 to Unit 17, matching sides and bottom edge.

**5.** Stitch Unit 18 to sides of pocket section, sewing through all layers. Sew Unit 15 to bottom edge in same manner.

**6.** Join sections.

## Borders

**1.** Referring to instructions on page 25, measure quilt from side to side. Cut two 1¼"-wide Fabric I strips to match width. Sew borders to top and bottom edges of quilt.

**2.** Measure quilt from top to bottom; then cut two borders from remaining strip to match quilt length. Sew borders to quilt sides.

**3.** For outer border, measure quilt and trim Fabric III strips to fit. Sew borders to quilt as before.

## Quilting and Finishing

**1.** Mark quilting design on quilt top as desired. On wall hanging shown, patchwork is outline-quilted.

**2.** Cut a 29" x 36" piece of backing fabric. Layer backing, batting, and quilt top. Baste. Quilt as marked or as desired. Topstitch through all layers between B blocks to top of Unit 16 to make four pockets.

**3.** Sew buttons to flower centers.

**4.** From Fabric III strips, make 3¼ yards of straight-grain binding. See page 30 for instructions on making and applying binding.

**5.** See page 138 for directions on making a hanging sleeve.

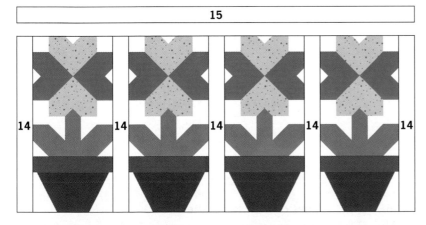

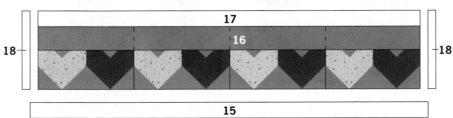

Quilt Assembly Diagram

# *T*uxedo Cats

*All of the twenty spiffy felines, posed in a garden of hearts and flowers, are made using the same fabrics and techniques, but half are mirror image. To create the interwoven pattern, follow assembly diagrams carefully to position blocks correctly. Make extra blocks to create decorative throw pillows.*

## Finished Size
Blocks: 20 cat blocks, 15" square
       49 flower blocks, 5" x 15"
       30 heart blocks, 5" square
Quilt: 85" x 105"

## Quick-Piecing Techniques
Diagonal Corners (see page 20)
Diagonal Ends (see page 21)
Triangle-Squares (see page 22)

## Materials

| | | |
|---|---|---|
| Fabric I (gray-on-black print) | | 3½ yards |
| Fabric II (gray print) | | 3½ yards |
| Fabric III (white-on-white print) | | 2 yards |
| Fabric IV (peach mini-print) | | 4 yards |
| Fabric V (dark green print) | | 2 yards |
| Fabric VI (medium green solid) | | ¾ yard |
| Fabric VII (burgundy solid) | | ½ yard |
| Fabric VIII (barn red print) | | ½ yard |
| Backing fabric | | 8 yards |

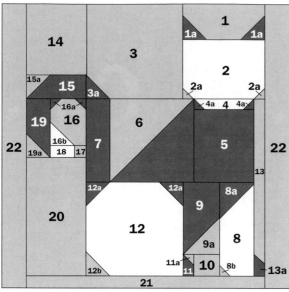

Block A—Make 10.

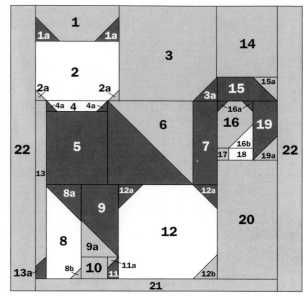

Block B—Make 10.

## Cutting

### From Fabric I (gray-on-black print), cut:
* Ten 3" x 42" strips for binding.
* Seven 2⅜" x 42" strips.
  From these, cut:
  * Eighty 2⅜" squares (A-8a, B-8a, H-1b).
  * Twenty 2⅜" x 4¼" (A-9, B-9).
* Four 4¼" x 42" strips.
  From these, cut:
  * Twenty 3⅝" x 4¼" (A-5, B-5).
  * Sixty 1⅜" x 4¼" (H-2).
* Twelve 1¾" x 42" strips.
  From these, cut:
  * 100 1¾" squares (A-1a, A-3a, A-12a, B-1a, B-3a, B-12a).
  * Forty 1¾" x 3⅝" (A-15, A-19, B-15, B-19).
  * Twenty 1¾" x 4⅞" (A-7, B-7).
  * Forty 1⅛" x 1¾" (A-11, A-13a, B-11, B-13a).
* Fourteen 1⅛" x 42" strips.
  From these, cut:
  * Sixty 1⅛" x 5½" (H-3).
  * 200 1⅛" squares (A-4a, A-16a, B-4a, B-16a, H-1a).
* One 12" x 28" for triangle-squares (A-6, B-6).

### From Fabric II (gray print), cut:
* Five 2⅜" x 42" strips.
  From these, cut:
  * Twenty 2⅜" x 4⅞" (A-1, B-1).
  * Twenty 2⅜" x 3" (A-16, B-16).
  * Twenty 2⅜" squares (A-9a, B-9a).

* Twenty 1¾" x 42" strips.
  From these, cut:
  * Forty 1¾" x 15½" (A-22, B-22).
  * Eighty 1¾" squares (A-10, A-12b, A-15a, A-19a, B-10, B-12b, B-15a, B-19a).
* Six 3⅝" x 42" strips.
  From these, cut:
  * Twenty 3⅝" x 6¾" (A-20, B-20).
  * Twenty 3⅝" x 4¼" (A-14, B-14).
* Fourteen 1⅛" x 42" strips.
  From these, cut:
  * Twenty 1⅛" x 9¼" (A-13, B-13).
  * Twenty 1⅛" x 13" (A-21, B-21).
  * 100 1⅛" squares (A-2a, A-8b, A-11a, A-17, B-2a, B-8b, B-11a, B-17).
* Three 5½" x 42" strips.
  From these, cut:
  * Twenty 5½" squares (A-3, B-3).
* One 12" x 28" for triangle-squares (A-6, B-6).

### From Fabric III (white-on-white print), cut:
* Seven 3⅝" x 42" strips.
  From these, cut:
  * Twenty 3⅝" x 4⅞" (A-2, B-2).
  * Sixty 2⅜" x 3⅝" (H-1).
  * Twenty 1⅛" x 3⅝" (A-4, B-4).
* Four 5½" x 42" strips.
  From these, cut:
  * Twenty 5½" squares (A-12, B-12).
  * Twenty 2⅜" x 5½" (A-8, B-8).

* Two 1¾" x 42" strips.
  From these, cut:
  * Twenty 1¾" squares (A-16b, B-16b).
  * Twenty 1⅛" x 1¾" (A-18, B-18).

### From Fabric IV (peach mini-print), cut:
* Fourteen 2⅜" x 42" strips.
  From these, cut:
  * Forty-nine 2⅜" squares (F-5).
  * Ninety-eight 1¾" x 2⅜" (F-3, F-8).
  * Ninety-eight 2⅜" x 3" (F-12, F-14).
* Twelve 1¾" x 42" strips.
  From these, cut:
  * Forty-nine 1¾" x 3" (F-6).
  * 196 1¾" squares (F-9a, F-17a).
* Seventy-one 1⅛" x 42" strips.
  From these, cut:
  * Ninety-eight 1⅛" x 15½" (F-19).
  * Ninety-eight 1⅛" x 3" (F-11, F-15).
  * Ninety-eight 1⅛" x 4¼" (F-18).
  * 539 1⅛" squares (F-1a, F-2a).

### From Fabric V (dark green print), cut:
* Six 3" x 42" strips.
  From these, cut:
  * Ninety-eight 1⅛" x 3" (F-10, F-16).
  * Forty-nine 2⅜" x 3" (F-13).
* Four 2⅜" x 42" strips.
  From these, cut:
  * Forty-nine 1⅛" x 2⅜" (F-4).
  * Forty-nine 1¾" x 2⅜" (F-7).

* Two 1⅛" x 42" strips.
  From these, cut:
  • Forty-nine 1⅛" squares (F-2b).
* One 26" square for triangle-squares
  (F-9, F-17).

**From Fabric VI (medium green solid), cut:**
* One 26" square for triangle-squares
  (F-9, F-17).

**From Fabric VII (burgundy solid), cut:**
* Six 2⅜" x 42" strips.
  From these, cut:
  • Ninety-eight 2⅜" squares (F-1).

**From Fabric VIII (barn red print), cut:**
* Six 2⅜" x 42" strips.
  From these, cut:
  • Ninety-eight 2⅜" squares (F-1,
  F-2).

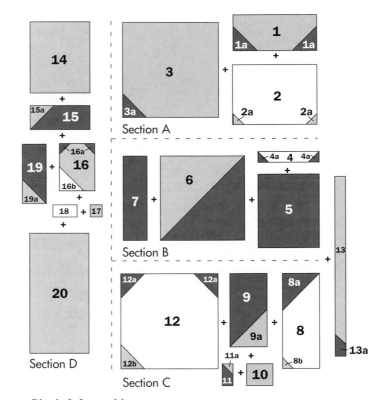

**Block A Assembly**

## Piecing the Cat Blocks

Refer to Block A Assembly Diagram
throughout to identify units.

**1.** Use diagonal-corner technique to
make one each of units 1, 2, 3, 4, 8,
9, 11, 12, 15, 16, and 19. Use
diagonal-end technique to make one
of Unit 13.

**2.** For Unit 6, see page 22 for instructions
on half-square triangles. On
wrong side of 12" x 28" piece of Fabric II, draw a 2 x 5-square grid of 5¼"
squares. With right sides facing,
match marked fabric with 12" x 28"
Fabric I piece. Stitch grid as directed
on page 22. Cut 20 triangle-squares
from the grid, one for each cat block.

**3.** To assemble Section A, join units 1
and 2; then add Unit 3 as shown.

**4.** To assemble Section B, begin by
joining units 4 and 5. Add Unit 6 and
then Unit 7 as shown.

**5.** To assemble Section C, begin by
joining units 10 and 11. Join this
combined unit to bottom of Unit 9;
then add Unit 8 and Unit 12 to each
side as shown.

**6.** Join sections B and C. Join Unit 13
to side of combined sections as shown.

**7.** To assemble Section D, begin by
joining units 17 and 18. Add Unit 16

to top edge of combined unit; then
join Unit 19 to side as shown. Join
units 14 and 15; then join both combined units. Complete Section D by
joining Unit 20 at bottom.

**8.** Join Section A to top of combined
BC unit. Join Section D to side of ABC.

**9.** Join Unit 21 at bottom of block;
then join one of Unit 22 to each side
as shown in Block A diagram.

**10.** Block B is made in the same
manner as Block A, but it is a mirror
image. Most units are made exactly
the same as for Block B, but some
require opposite positioning of fabric
colors and angles. Be sure to consult
Block B diagram carefully when making units 8, 9, 11, 12, 13, 16, and 19.

## Piecing the Heart Block

**1.** Use diagonal-corner technique to
make two of Unit 1. *Note that these
are mirror images, so be careful to position
each 1b piece as shown.*

**2.** Join the two halves of Unit 1 as
shown. Add a Unit 2 strip to top and
bottom edges of Unit 1. Join one of
Unit 3 to each side as shown.

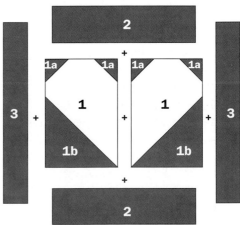

**Heart Block—Make 30.**

**Heart Block Assembly**

*(continued)*

## Piecing the Flower Block

**1.** Use diagonal-corner technique to make two of Unit 1 with Fabric VII centers and one of Unit 1 with Fabric VIII center (Flower Block Assembly Diagram). Make one of Unit 2. Join these units as shown to complete flower section.

**2.** The combined 6-7-8 unit is made using diagonal-end technique as shown below. Begin by joining pieces 6 and 7; trim excess fabric from seam allowance and press seam. Add piece 8 to end of combined unit in the same manner. Trim and press.

**3.** Make combined 12-13-14 unit in the same manner.

**4.** To make units 9 and 17, see page 22 for instructions on half-square triangles. On wrong side of 26" square of Fabric VI, draw a 7 x 7-square grid of 3⅜" squares. With right sides facing, match marked fabric with square of Fabric V. Stitch grid as directed on page 22. Cut 98 triangle-squares from the grid. Add diagonal corners (9a, 17a) to each triangle-square as shown below. When completed, designate 49 squares as Unit 9 and 49 squares as Unit 17.

**5.** Join units 3, 4, and 5 in a row; then join assembled 6-7-8 unit to bottom edge of this row. Join this combined unit to bottom of flower section.

**6.** Join units 9, 10, and 11 in a row; then assemble another row of units 15, 16, and 17 as shown. Join remaining assembled units to flower block as shown.

**7.** Join one of Unit 18 at top and bottom of block; then join a Unit 19 strip to each side as shown (Flower Block Diagram).

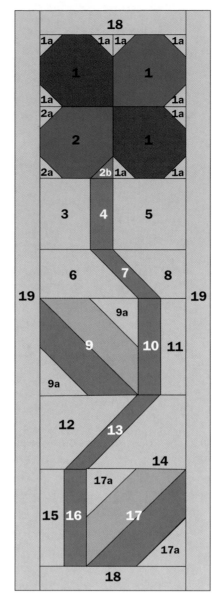

**Flower Block—Make 49.**

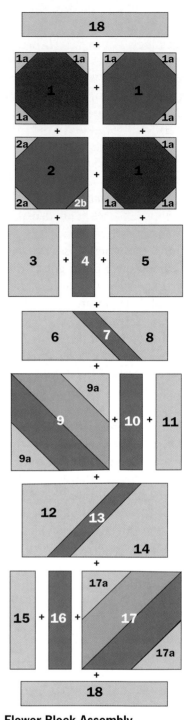

**Flower Block Assembly**

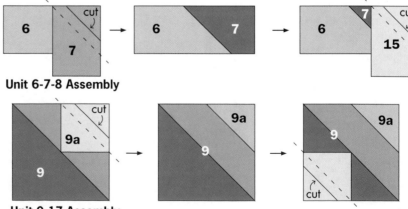

**Unit 6-7-8 Assembly**

**Unit 9-17 Assembly**

**172** Tuxedo Cats

## Quilt Assembly

**1.** Join blocks in rows as shown (Row Assembly Diagram). Make three of Row 1 and two of Row 2. Join remaining flower and heart blocks in a horizontal row as shown at top of Row 2.

**2.** Starting with a Row 1, join all rows, alternating row types in a 1-2-1-2-1 sequence.

**3.** Join remaining sashing row to bottom of last row. *Note:* The positions of the flowers follow a regular pattern when assembled as shown in the Row diagrams. But when this quilt was made, one flower block got turned the wrong way. Can you find the one that breaks the pattern? Hint: It's at one of the corners.

## Quilting and Finishing

**1.** Divide backing into two 4-yard lengths and assemble backing.

**2.** Layer backing, batting, and quilt top. Baste.

**3.** Mark quilting design on quilt top as desired. Outline-quilt patchwork and borders or quilt as desired.

**4.** Make 10½ yards of binding. See page 30 for directions on making and applying straight-grain binding.

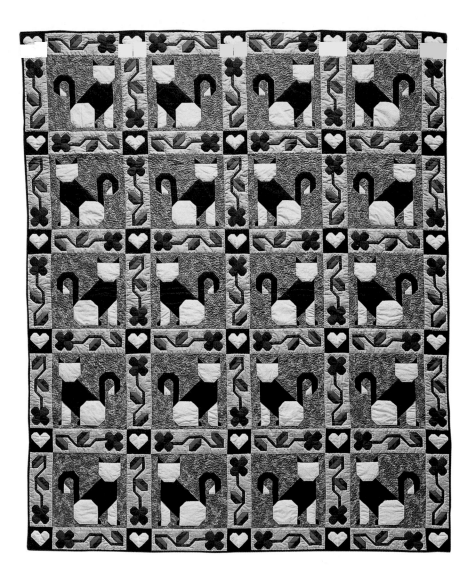

Row 1

Row 2

**Row Assembly**

# High Summer

*A meadow of luxurious green surrounds bright summer flowers, interpreted in an easy-to-piece geometric design. The optical illusion of circles within the different-colored blocks creates the sense of separate beds of pretty posies. The blocks are random combinations of light, medium, and dark values. As you sew, vary the placement of values within the blocks any way you like to create a garden uniquely yours.*

**Quick-Piecing Techniques:** Strip Piecing (see page 20)
Diagonal Corners (see page 20)
Triangle-Squares (see page 22)

## Finished Size
Blocks: 15 blocks, 20" square
Quilt: 68" x 112"

## Materials

| | | |
|---|---|---|
| | Fabric I (15 assorted light solids) | ⅛ yard each |
| | Fabric II (15 assorted light-medium solids) | ⅛ yard each |
| | Fabric III (15 assorted medium solids) | ⅛ yard each |
| | Fabric IV (15 assorted dark solids) | ⅛ yard each |
| | Fabric V (light green solid) | 2¾ yards |
| | Fabric VI (medium green solid) | 2 yards |
| | Fabric VII (dark green solid) | 5¼ yards |
| | Backing fabric | 6¾ yards |

## Cutting
Refer to diagrams on page 176 to identify blocks and units designated in cutting list.

**From each Fabric I (light solids), cut:**
* One 2" x 42" strip.
  From this, cut:
  • One 2" x 4" (4).
  • Two 2" squares (5a).
  • One 2" x 8" (8).

**From each Fabric II (light-medium solids), cut:**
* One 2" x 42" strip.
  From this, cut:
  • Two 2" squares (11a).
  • One 2" x 4" (12).
  • One 2" x 8" (13).

**From each Fabric III (medium solids), cut:**
* One 3⅞" x 42" strip.
  From this, cut:
  • One 3⅞" square (10).
  • Two 2" x 8" (8, 13).
  • Four 2" squares (9a).

**From each Fabric IV (dark solids), cut:**
* One 2½" x 42" strip.
  From this, cut:
  • One 2½" square (15).
  • Two 2" x 4" (4, 12).
  • Four 2" squares (6a).

**From Fabric V (light green), cut:**
* Twenty 1¼" x 42" strips for mitered borders.
* Fifty-two 1¼" x 42" strips (14, sashing).

**From Fabric VI (medium green), cut:**
* Three 14⅝" x 42" strips.
  From these, cut:
  • Fifteen 7⅜" x 14⅝" (2, 3). Cut these rectangles as shown in Cutting diagram to get eight triangles from each piece for a total of 120 triangles.*
* Two 18" squares for triangle-squares (1).

**From Fabric VII, (dark green) cut:**
* Ten 3" x 42" strips for binding.
* Ten 1" x 42" strips for mitered borders.

* Three 14⅝" x 42" strips.
  From these, cut:
  • Fifteen 7⅜" x 14⅝" (2, 3).
    Cut these rectangles as shown in
    Cutting diagram to get eight trian-
    gles from each piece for a total of
    120 triangles.*

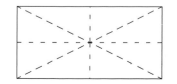

**Cutting**

* Two 2½" x 42" strips.
  From these, cut:
  • Thirty 2½" squares for sashing.
* Twenty-six 1" x 42" strips
  (14, sashing).
* One 18" x 42" strip.
  From this, cut:
  • Two 18" squares for triangle-
    squares (1).
* Fifteen 2" x 42" strips.
  From these, cut:
  • 180 2" x 3½" (5, 6, 9, 11).

* Three 3½" x 42" strips.
  From these, cut:
  • Thirty 3½" squares (7).
* Two 3⅞" x 42" strips.
  From these, cut:
  • Fifteen 3⅞" squares (10).

* *Note:* Each rectangle yields eight
triangles, four of which point to the left
and four to the right. Designate "lefties"
for Unit 2 and "righties" for Unit 3.
Trim ⅞" from tip of all these triangles.

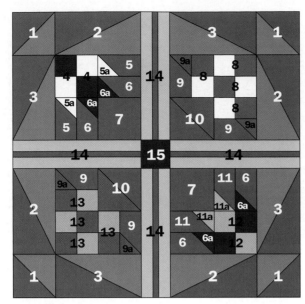

*High Summer Block—Make 15.*

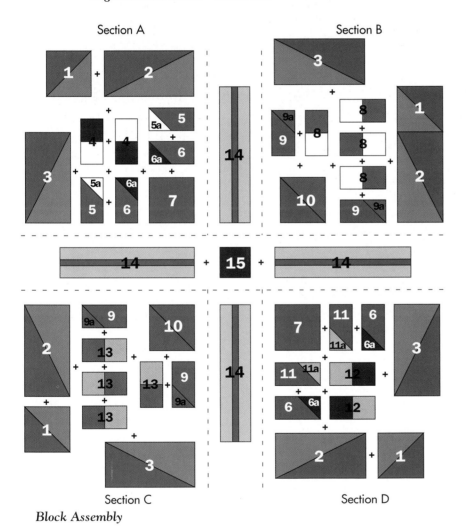

Section A

Section B

Section C

Section D

*Block Assembly*

## Piecing the Blocks

**1.** See page 22 for instructions on half-square triangles. On wrong side of each 18" square of Fabric VI, draw a 4 x 4-square grid of 3⅞" squares. With right sides facing, match each marked fabric with an 18" square of Fabric VII. Stitch each grid as directed on page 22. Cut 32 triangle-squares from each grid (60 for Unit 1 and four extra).

**2.** Referring to Block diagram, join lefty triangles of fabrics VI and VII to make Unit 2. The resulting rectangle will measure 3½" x 6½". Make 60 of Unit 2. Using righties, make 60 of Unit 3 in the same manner.

**3.** For each block, join one 2" x 4" piece of Fabric I and one 2" x 4" piece of Fabric IV to make a strip set. From this, cut two 2"-wide segments for Unit 4. Repeat, using 2" x 4" pieces of fabrics II and IV, to make two of Unit 12.

**4.** For each block, join one 2" x 8" strip of Fabric I and one 2" x 8" strip of Fabric III to make a strip set. From this, cut four 2"-wide segments for Unit 8. Repeat, using 2" x 8" strips of fabrics II and III, to make four of Unit 13.

**5.** For each block, use diagonal-corner technique to make two each of units 5 and 11 and four each of units 6 and 9.

**6.** For Unit 10, draw a diagonal line on wrong side of each 3⅞" square of Fabric III. With wrong sides facing, match each marked square with a square of Fabric VII. Stitch a ¼" seam on both sides of drawn line. Cut on drawn line to get two triangle-squares. Make two of Unit 10 for each block.

**7.** Referring to Unit 14 as shown in Block Assembly diagram, join long strips of fabrics V and VII. Make 26 of this strip set. Cut four 9½"-wide segments from each strip set (104 total). Set aside 60 segments for Unit 14 and 44 segments for quilt sashing.

**8.** To assemble Section A, begin by joining two of Unit 4 as shown in Block Assembly diagram, turning one unit upside down. Join one Unit 5 and one Unit 6; then add this to bottom of Unit 4 pair. To assemble right half of flower, join remaining units 5 and 6 to Unit 7 in a vertical row as shown. Join halves to complete flower. Join Unit 3 to left side of flower; press seam allowances toward Unit 3. Join units 1 and 2 as shown; press seam allowances toward Unit 2. Join 1-2 unit to top of flower to complete Section A.

**9.** To assemble Section B, join three of Unit 8 in a vertical row, turning units as shown in Block Assembly diagram. Join one of Unit 9 to bottom of this row. Join remaining Unit 8 to remaining Unit 9; then add this to top of Unit 10, positioning triangle-square as shown. Join both rows to complete flower. Join Unit 3 to top of flower; then press seam allowances toward Unit 3. Join units 1 and 2 as shown; press seam allowances toward Unit 2. Join 1-2 unit to right side of flower section to complete Section B.

**10.** To assemble Section C, join three of Unit 13 in a vertical row, turning units as shown in Block Assembly diagram. Join one of Unit 9 to top of this row. Join remaining Unit 13 to remaining Unit 9; then add this to bottom of Unit 10, positioning triangle-square as shown. Join both rows to complete flower. Join Unit 3 to bottom of flower; then press seam allowances toward Unit 3. Join units 1 and 2 as shown; press seam allowances toward Unit 2. Join 1-2 unit to left side of flower to complete Section C.

**11.** To assemble Section D, begin by joining two of Unit 12 as shown. Join one Unit 11 and one Unit 6; then add this combined unit to left side of Unit 12 pair. To assemble top of flower, join remaining units 6 and 11 to Unit 7 in a row as shown. Join halves to complete flower. Join Unit 3 to right side of flower; press seam allowances toward Unit 3. Join units 1 and 2 as shown; press seam allowances toward Unit 2. Join 1-2 unit to bottom of flower section to complete Section D.

**12.** Referring to Block Assembly diagram, join sections A and B with one Unit 14 between them. Press seam allowances toward Unit 14. Join sections C and D in the same manner.

**13.** Join Unit 15 between two of Unit 14 as shown. Stitch top and bottom halves of block to opposite sides of 14-15 unit as shown in Block Assembly diagram. Press seam allowances toward Unit 14. Make 15 High Summer blocks.

## Quilt Assembly

**1.** Referring to Sashing Unit diagram, join all remaining sashing strips in pairs with a Fabric VII sashing square between each pair. You will have eight sashing squares left over.

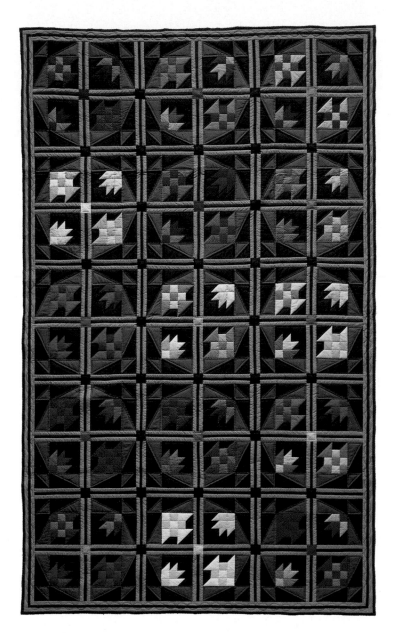

**2.** Referring to photograph above, arrange blocks as desired in five horizontal rows of three blocks each. Position a sashing unit between blocks in each row as shown. Join blocks in rows.

**3.** Referring to photograph, assemble remaining sashing units in four horizontal rows of three units each, adding sashing squares between units.

**4.** Assemble block rows and sashing rows, alternating row types as shown in photograph.

**5.** To assemble borders, join border strip of fabrics V and VII in strip sets in the same manner as for sashing. Join three strip sets end-to-end for each side border and two strips sets each for top and bottom borders.

**6.** Matching centers of each quilt side and border strip, join borders to assembled quilt top. Miter border corners.

## Quilting and Finishing

Outline-quilt patchwork and borders or quilt as desired.

Make 10½ yards of binding. See page 30 for directions on making and applying straight-grain binding.

*Sashing Unit*

# Country Hearts

*Lavish fringe decorates the edges of this linen throw. When made with cotton fabrics, it can be bound traditionally to make a cozy lap quilt. The combination of two solids and one print makes the fabric selection easy in any color scheme.*

**Quick-Piecing Techniques:**    Diagonal Corners (see page 20)
Diagonal Ends (see page 21)

## Finished Size
Blocks: 24 blocks, 11" square
Throw: 48" x 70", plus fringe

## Materials*

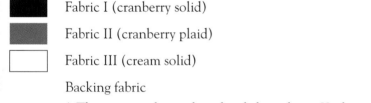

| | | |
|---|---|---|
| Fabric I (cranberry solid) | 2¼ yards |
| Fabric II (cranberry plaid) | 1⅜ yards |
| Fabric III (cream solid) | 2½ yards |
| Backing fabric | 2⅛ yards |

*\* Throw pictured is made with upholstery linen. Yardages given are for 54"-wide linen. To make the same size throw with 44"-wide cotton fabric, add ¾ yard to each fabric.*

## Cutting
Refer to diagrams on page 180 to identify blocks and units designated in cutting list.

When using 44"-wide fabric, cut additional strips as necessary to cut number of pieces specified.

### From Fabric I, (cranberry solid) cut:
✳ Two 2½" x 72" lengthwise strips and two 2½" x 46" crossgrain strips for borders.

✳ Six 1" x 48" strips.
   From these, cut:
     • 288 1" squares (1d, 6a, 9a).
✳ Three 1¼" x 48" strips.
   From these, cut:
     • Ninety-six 1¼" squares (5).
✳ Twenty-four 1½" x 48" strips.
   From these, cut:
     • 192 1½" x 2¼" (6b, 9b).
     • 192 1½" x 3½" (7, 11).
✳ Two 8" x 48" for fringe. (If using cotton fabric, use these pieces to make binding.)

### From Fabric II (cranberry plaid), cut:
✳ Nine 2" x 54" strips.
   From these, cut:
     • Ninety-six 2" x 3" (1).
     • Ninety-six 2" squares (2).
✳ Six 1½" x 54" strips.
   From these, cut:
     • 192 1½" squares (1c, 13).
✳ Five 1" x 54" strips.
   From these, cut:
     • Ninety-six 1" squares (8a).
     • Ninety-six 1" x 1½" (17a).
✳ Eight 1¼" x 54" strips.
   From these, cut:
     • Ninety-six 1¼" x 1¾" (14).
     • Ninety-six 1¼" x 2½" (16).

### From Fabric III (cream solid), cut:
✳ Thirty-four 1" x 54" strips.
   From these, cut:
     • 672 1" squares (1a, 2a, 7a, 11a).
     • Ninety-six 1" x 3½" (8).
     • Ninety-six 1" x 1½" (10).
     • Ninety-six 1" x 4" (12).
     • Ninety-six 1" x 2" (17).
✳ Five 2" x 54" strips.
   From these, cut:
     • Ninety-six 2" x 2½" (1b).
✳ Six 1¼" x 54" strips.
   From these, cut:
     • Ninety-six 1¼" x 2" (3).
     • Ninety-six 1¼" squares (4).
✳ Seventeen 1½" x 54" strips.
   From these, cut:
     • 192 1½" x 2¾" (6, 9).
     • Ninety-six 1½" squares (7b).
     • Ninety-six 1½" x 2" (11b).
✳ Four 1¾" x 42" strips.
   From these, cut:
     • Ninety-six 1¾" squares (15).

*Country Hearts Block—Make 24.*

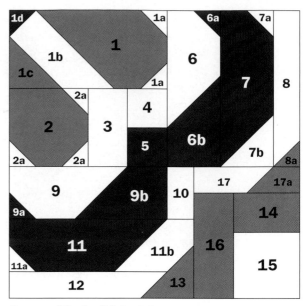

*Quarter Block—Make 96.*

## Piecing the Blocks

**1.** Referring to Section A of Quarter Block Assembly diagram, use diagonal-corner technique to add 1a pieces to two adjacent corners of piece 1 as shown. Use diagonal-end technique to add 1b to opposite side of piece 1. Join pieces 1c and 1d as diagonal corners. Make four of Unit 1 for each block.

**2.** Using diagonal-corner technique, make units 2, 7, and 8 as shown. Use diagonal-end technique to make Unit 17.

**3.** Units 6, 9, and 11 are made with both diagonal-corner and diagonal-end techniques. Make each unit as shown.

**4.** To assemble Section A, begin by joining units 2 and 3. Join units 4 and 5 and then join it to Unit 3 as shown. Complete Section A by joining Unit 1 to top of assembled section.

**5.** To make Section B, join units 6, 7, and 8 as shown.

**6.** To make Section C, begin by joining units 9 and 10 as shown. Next, join Unit 12 to the bottom of Unit 11. Add Unit 13 to the combined 11-12 piece as a diagonal corner. Complete Section C by joining assembled units.

**7.** To make Section D, begin by joining units 14 and 15. Add Unit 16 to one

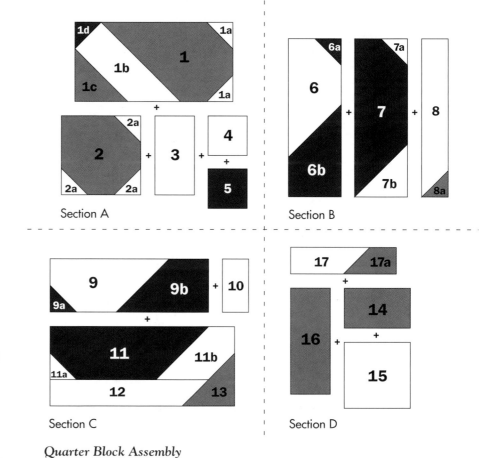

*Quarter Block Assembly*

side as shown. Complete Section D by adding Unit 17 to top of assembled section.

**8.** Join sections A and B; then join sections C and D. Complete quarter block by joining top and bottom halves.

**9.** Make four quarter blocks for each block. Join quarter blocks in pairs, rotating as necessary to position 1d triangles at center. Join pairs to complete each block.

## Quilt Assembly

**1.** Referring to photograph, join completed blocks in six horizontal rows of four blocks each. Join rows.

**2.** Join short border strips to top and bottom edges of throw. Press seam allowances and trim excess border length. Add side borders in the same manner.

## Finishing

**1.** With right sides facing, center one linen fringe piece at top edge of throw, matching long raw edges. (Throw should extend at least ¼" beyond fringe piece on each side.) Topstitch edge. Repeat at bottom edge of throw. *Note:* If using cotton fabric, omit fringe and set aside this fabric to make binding.

**2.** With right sides facing, join backing to throw, stitching a ¼" seam around all edges. (Be sure to keep sides of fringe piece out of seam.) Leave a 10" opening in one side for turning. Trim excess backing fabric from seam allowances.

**3.** Turn throw right side out. Press. Slipstitch opening closed.

**4.** Fray fringe pieces by pulling out horizontal threads up to the edge of the throw. Separate vertical threads into equal sections as desired. Knot each section close to throw edge.

**5.** Tie throw with cream-colored pearl cotton if desired.

**6.** If using cotton fabric, quilt throw as desired. Make 6⅞ yards of binding. See page 30 for directions on making and applying straight-grain binding.

# Paw of the Bear

Traditional Bear's Paw blocks alternate with pieced polar bears in this contemporary version of a favorite classic. The blocks are set on the diagonal, framed with borders of green and strip-pieced patchwork made to look like stacked bricks. We recommend this project for experienced quiltmakers.

**Quick-Piecing Techniques:**   Strip Piecing (see page 20)
Diagonal Corners (see page 20)
Triangle-Squares (see page 22)

## Finished Size

Blocks: 10 Bear blocks, 12" square       Quilt: 66" x 100"
12 Bear's Paw blocks, 12" square

## Materials

|  |  |  |
|---|---|---|
| Fabric I (white marbled-look print) | 1⅜ yards |
| Fabric II (cranberry print) | 2 yards* |
| Fabric III (green-on-green print) | 3¼ yards* |
| Fabric IV (navy print) | 2 yards |
| Fabric V (light gray mini-print) | 2⅝ yards |
| Backing fabric | 6⅛ yards |
| ¼"-diameter cording for optional pillow | 2⅛ yards |

*Add ½ yard of these two fabrics for each optional pillow. Other fabrics should have enough scraps left over to make two more bear blocks.*

## Cutting

Refer to diagrams on page 184 to identify blocks and units designated in cutting list.

**From Fabric I (white), cut:**
* Three 4" x 42" strips.
  From these, cut:
  • Ten 4" x 9⅜" (1).

* Two 2" x 42" strips.
  From these, cut:
  • Twenty 2" x 3¾" (2).
* One 2¼" x 42" strip.
  From this, cut:
  • Ten 2¼" squares (3b).
* One 2⅝" x 42" strip.
  From this, cut:
  • Ten 2⅝" squares (4a).

* One 1½" x 42" strip.
  From this, cut:
  • Ten 1½" squares (3a).
  • Twenty 1¼" squares (3c, 4b).
* Two 7" x 42" strips for pieced borders.

**From Fabric II (cranberry), cut:**
* Ten 1" x 42" strips.
  From these, cut:
  • Twenty 1" x 9½" (9).
  • Twenty 1" x 10½" (10).
* One 6⅞" x 42" strip.
  From this, cut:
  • Three 6⅞" squares.
    Cut these in quarters diagonally to get four triangles (7) from each square (includes two extra).
  • Three 6⅛" squares.
    Cut these in quarters diagonally to get four triangles (6) from each square (includes two extra).
* One 9½" x 42" strip.
  From this, cut:
  • Three 9½" squares.
    Cut these in quarters diagonally to get four triangles (22) from each square (includes two extra).
  • Three 1½" x 12" and one 1¼" x 12".
    From these, cut:
    • Eighteen 1½" squares (18).
    • Ten 1¼" squares (2a).
* Two 3¾" x 42" strips.
  From these and scraps, cut:
  • Ten 3¾" x 3⅞" (3).
  • Ten 3" x 3¾" squares (4).

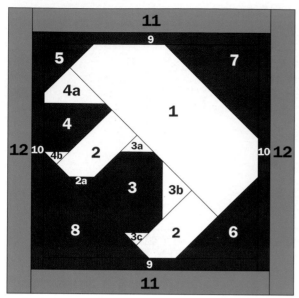

Block A—Make 10.

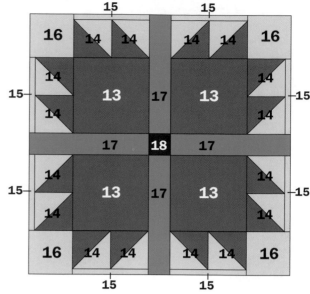

Block B—Make 12.

* One 7⅝" x 42" strip.
  From this, cut:
  * Three 7⅝" squares.
    Cut these in quarters diagonally to
    get four triangles (8) from each
    square (includes two extra).
  * Three 4⅛" squares.
    Cut these in quarters diagonally to
    get four triangles (5) from each
    square (includes two extra).
* Two 7" x 42" strips for pieced
  borders.

### From Fabric III (green), cut:

* Eight 3" x 42" strips for binding.
* Eight 2" x 42" strips for inner border.
  From six of these, cut:
  * Six 2" x 29½".
  * Four 2" x 7½".
* Eight 3" x 42" strips for outer border.
  From two of these, cut:
  * Six 3" x 14".
* One 2½" x 42" strip.
  From this, cut:
  * Eight 2½" squares for pieced
    border corners.
* Twenty-six 1½" x 42" strips.
  From these, cut:
  * Twenty 1½" x 10½" (11).
  * Twenty 1½" x 12½" (12).
  * Ten 1½" x 12" (25).
  * Ten 1½" x 13" (26).
  * Forty-eight 1½" x 6" (17).

### From Fabric IV (navy), cut:

* Six 4" x 42" strips.
  From these, cut:
  * Fifty-four 4" squares (13).
* One 25½" x 42" strip.
  From this, cut:
  * Four 10" x 25½" for triangle-
    squares (14).
* Two 7" x 42" strips for pieced borders.

### From Fabric V (light gray), cut:

* One 25½" x 42" strip.
  From this, cut:
  * Four 10" x 25½" for triangle-
    squares (14).
* Two 4" x 42" strips.
  From these, cut:
  * Ninety-six ¾" x 4" (15).
* Nine 2½" x 42" strips.
  From these, cut:
  * Forty-eight 2½" squares (16).
  * Ten 2½" x 8¾" (23).
  * Ten 2½" x 10¾" (24).
  * Six 2¼" squares (19).
* One 8" x 42" strip.
  From this, cut:
  * Three 8" squares.
    Cut these in quarters diagonally to
    get four triangles (20) from each
    square.
* Four 1½" x 42" strips.
  From these, cut:
  * Twelve 1½" x 12" (21).
* Two 7" x 42" strips for pieced borders.

## Piecing the Bear Blocks

**1.** Referring to Diagram 1, trim two
corners of Unit 1 as shown.

**2.** Using diagonal-corner technique,
make one Unit 2 for bear's front leg,
joining pieces 2 and 2a as shown in
Block A Assembly diagram. Referring
to Diagram 2, trim one corner from
another 2 piece for back leg.

**3.** Using diagonal-corner technique,
make one of Unit 3.

**4.** Using diagonal-corner technique,
make one of Unit 4 as shown in Diagram 3. Trim bottom left corner as
shown.

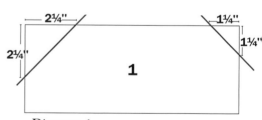

Diagram 1

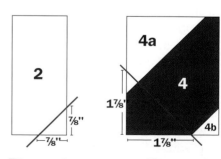

Diagram 2          Diagram 3

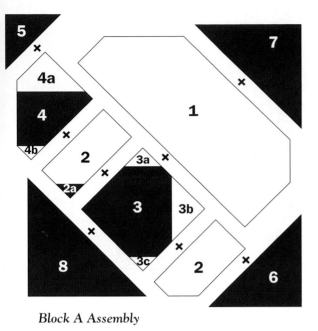

*Block A Assembly*

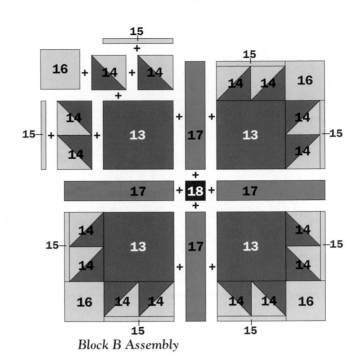

*Block B Assembly*

**5.** Join both of Unit 2 to sides of Unit 3 as shown in assembly diagram. Add Unit 4 to end of row as shown.

**6.** Join Unit 1 to top of combined units. Press seam allowances toward Unit 1.

**7.** Join triangles 5, 6, 7, and 8 to center unit in numerical order, centering each one carefully. Press seam allowances toward triangles. Bear block should now be 9½" square.

**8.** Join a Unit 9 to top and bottom edges of block; then add a Unit 10 to each side. Press seam allowances toward edge of block. Join units 11 and 12 in the same manner to complete block. Make 10 of Block A.

## Piecing the Bear's Paw Blocks

**1.** See page 17 for instructions on half-square triangles. On wrong side of each 10" x 25½" pieces of Fabric V, make a 3 x 9-square grid of 2⅝" squares. With right sides facing, match each marked fabric with 10" x 25½" piece of Fabric IV. Stitch each grid as directed on page 17. Cut 54 triangle-squares from each grid (216 total) for Unit 14.

**2.** Referring to Block B Assembly diagram, join two pairs of Unit 14. (Be careful to position fabrics as shown for each pair.) Add a Unit 15 to top edge of both pairs.

**3.** Join one 14-15 unit to left side of Unit 13 as shown. Press seam allowances toward Unit 13. Join Unit 16 to left side of remaining 14-15 unit; press seam allowances toward Unit 16. Combine units to complete one paw section.

**4.** Make four paw sections for each block.

**5.** Positioning paw sections as shown in assembly diagram, join two blocks in a horizontal row with one Unit 17 between sections. Press seam allowances toward Unit 17.

**6.** To make center strip, join a Unit 17 to opposite sides of one Unit 18. Press seam allowances toward Unit 18.

**7.** Combine three sections to complete block. Make 12 of Block B.

## Piecing the Setting Triangles

**1.** Referring to Setting Triangle X Assembly diagram, make six paw sections as you did for Bear's Paw blocks, omitting Unit 15 and substituting Unit 19 for Unit 16.

**2.** To prevent stretching, stay-stitch diagonal edges of Unit 20 as described on page 13.

**3.** Positioning paw section as shown in assembly diagram, join Unit 20 to top and left side of each

paw section. Triangles are slightly smaller than paw section, so align corners as shown in assembly diagram. Press seam allowances toward Unit 20.

**4.** Join one Unit 21 to right side of triangle as shown. Press seam allowances toward Unit 21. Add Unit 18 to another Unit 21; press seam allowance toward Unit 21. Join 18-21 strip to bottom of triangle. Unit 21 will extend past triangles.

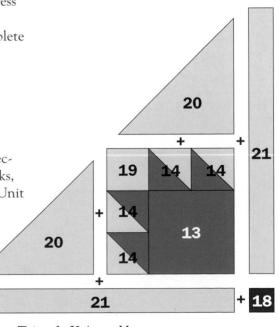

*Setting Triangle X Assembly*

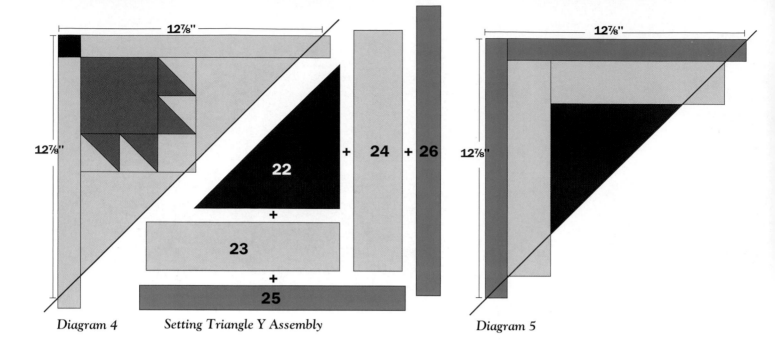

**Diagram 4**   **Setting Triangle Y Assembly**   **Diagram 5**

**5.** Referring to Diagram 4, align a long ruler with diagonal edges of Unit 20 triangles. With a rotary cutter, trim tip of Unit 19 and ends of each Unit 21 as shown. Legs of trimmed setting triangle should measure approximately 12⅞". Make six of Setting Triangle X.

**6.** Stay-stitch diagonal edges of Unit 22 triangles.

**7.** To assemble Setting Triangle Y, join units in numerical order as shown in Setting Triangle Y Assembly diagram.

**8.** Referring to Diagram 5, align a long ruler with diagonal edge of Unit 22. With a rotary cutter, trim ends of units 23, 24, 25, and 26 as shown. Legs of trimmed setting triangle should measure approximately 12⅞". Make 10 of Setting Triangle Y.

## Quilt Assembly

**1.** Referring to Quilt Assembly diagram and photograph, join blocks and setting triangles in diagonal rows as indicated. Join rows.

**2.** Join three 2" x 29½" strips of Fabric III end-to-end to make an 87½"-long inner border for each side. Join 2" x 7½" strips to both ends of each 42"-long border strip to make top and bottom borders.

**3.** Measure quilt top length, measuring through middle rather than along sides. Measuring from center, trim long borders to this length. Sew borders to quilt sides, matching centers and easing as necessary. (See page 15 for tips on easing.) Press seam allowances toward borders.

**4.** Measure quilt width through middle of quilt top. Trim short borders accordingly; then join borders to top and bottom edges of quilt.

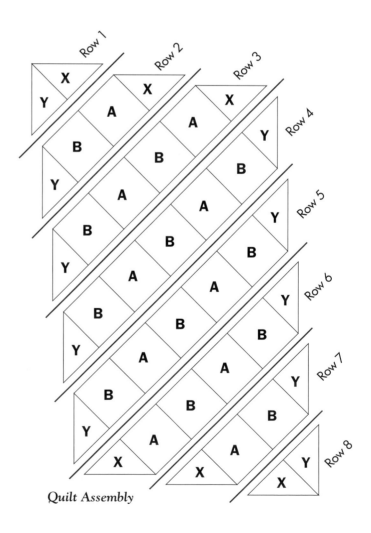

*Quilt Assembly*

## Making the Strip-Pieced Borders

1. Referring to diagram of Strip Set 1, join 7" x 42" strips of fabrics I, IV, V, and II as shown. Make two strip sets. From these, cut twenty-four 2½"-wide segments. (Because this strip set is so wide, you will have to fold it to accommodate your longest ruler.)

2. Join three segments end-to-end, keeping fabrics in the same sequence. Join this strip to top of quilt. Trim pieced strip even with quilt sides.

3. Join two more strip-set segments to end of piece left over from top border. Join this strip to bottom edge in the same manner.

4. Starting with leftover piece, join three more segments end-to-end. Trim bottom of combined strip to match length of quilt side. Join Fabric III border squares to both ends of side border; then join border to one side of quilt. Repeat for opposite quilt side.

5. Repeat steps 2, 3, and 4 to make second row of pieced borders. Join borders to each edge in the same sequence, staggering fabrics so combined borders resemble stacked bricks.

6. Join 3" x 42" strips of Fabric III to both ends of a 14"-long strip to make a 97"-long outer border for each side. Join 3" x 14" strips to both ends of a 42"-long strip to make top and bottom borders.

7. Measure quilt top length as before; then trim side borders to match. Sew borders to quilt sides, matching centers and easing as necessary. Press seam allowances toward borders.

8. Measure quilt width and trim short borders accordingly. Join borders to top and bottom edges of quilt.

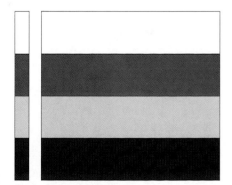

*Strip Set 1—Make 2.*

## Quilting and Finishing

The quilt shown is outline-quilted around patchwork, with haunches and an ear added to each bear. The same bear outline is quilted in Setting Triangle Y. A pawprint is quilted in each paw section. Concentric triangles fill the sides of each Setting Triangle X. The three outer borders are quilted with parallel lines, spaced 2" apart, that are perpendicular to the quilt edges. Make stencils and mark quilt before layering and basting. Quilt as desired.

Make 9½ yards of binding. See page 30 for directions on making and applying straight-grain binding.

# Oriental Desire

*This quilt mixes prints in rich blues, blushing pinks, and vibrant rose to create the exotic look of oriental porcelain. Many quilt shops now carry blue-and-white fabrics with traditional Far Eastern motifs like the fan print used here.*

**Quick-Piecing Techniques:** Diagonal Corners (see page 20)
Triangle-Squares (see page 22)

## Finished Size
Blocks: 20 blocks, 20" square
Quilt: 87" x 107"

## Materials

| | | |
|---|---|---|
| | Fabric I (medium blue print) | 3¼ yards |
| | Fabric II (dark blue print) | 1¼ yards |
| | Fabric III (dark blue print) | 2 yards |
| | Fabric IV (medium blue print) | ¾ yard |
| | Fabric V (medium rose print) | ⅞ yard |
| | Fabric VI (light rose print) | 1¾ yards |
| | Fabric VII (bright blue print) | ¼ yard |
| | Fabric VIII (dark blue print) | 1¾ yards |
| | Fabric IX (dark blue print) | ¼ yard |
| | Fabric X (medium blue print) | 1½ yards |
| | Fabric XI (medium rose print) | 1½ yards |
| | Fabric XII (dark rose print) | 1 yard |
| | Fabric·XIII (navy solid) | 1¼ yards |
| | Backing fabric | 8 yards |

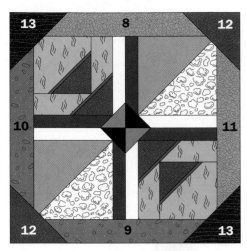

Oriental Desire Block—Make 20.

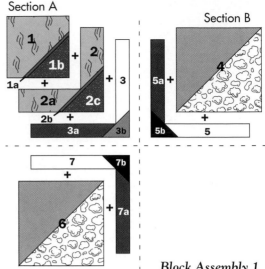

Section A

Section B

Section C

Block Assembly 1

## Cutting

### From Fabric I (medium blue), cut:
* Ten 3" x 42" strips for binding.
* Ten 1" x 42" strips for middle border.
  From four of these, cut:
  • Four 1" x 23".
  • Four 1" x 12".
* Nine 5½" x 42" strips.
  From these, cut:
  • Forty 5½" squares (1).
  • Forty 2½" x 5½" (2).
* Three 7½" x 42" strips.
  From these, cut:
  • Forty 2½" x 7½" (2a).

### From Fabric II (dark blue), cut:
* Nine 4½" x 42" strips.
  From these, cut:
  • Eighty 4½" squares (1a, 2b).

### From Fabric III (dark blue), cut:
* Eight 3¾" x 42" strips.
  From these, cut:
  • Eighty 3¾" squares (1b, 2c).
* Six 5½" x 42" strips.
  From these, cut:
  • Forty 5½" squares (12).

### From Fabric IV (medium blue), cut:
* Three 7½" x 42" strips.
  From these, cut:
  • Eighty 1½" x 7½" (3, 5, 7).

### From Fabric V (medium rose), cut:
* Three 8½" x 42" strips.
  From these, cut:
  • Eighty 1½" x 8½" (3a, 5a, 7a).

### From Fabric VI (light rose), cut:
* Three 18" x 42" strips.
  From these, cut:
  • Five 18" squares for triangle-squares (4, 6).

### From Fabric VII (bright blue), cut:
* Three 18" x 42" strips.
  From these, cut:
  • Five 18" squares for triangle-squares (4, 6).

### From Fabric VIII (dark blue), cut:
* Three 2½" x 42" strips.
  From these, cut:
  • Forty 2½" squares (3b).

### From Fabric IX (dark blue), cut:
* Three 2½" x 42" strips.
  From these, cut:
  • Forty 2½" squares (5b, 7b).

### From Fabric X (medium blue), cut:
* Twenty 2½" x 42" strips.
  From these, cut:
  • Twenty 2½" x 16½" (9).
  • Twenty 2½" x 20½" (10).

### From Fabric XI (medium rose), cut:
* Twenty 2½" x 42" strips.
  From these, cut:
  • Twenty 2½" x 16½" (8).
  • Twenty 2½" x 20½" (11).

### From Fabric XII (dark rose), cut:
* Six 5½" x 42" strips.
  From these, cut:
  • Forty 5½" squares (13).

### From Fabric XIII (navy solid), cut:
* Twenty-two 2" x 42" strips for inner and outer borders.
  From 10 of these, cut:
  • Six 2" x 25".
  • Four 2" x 22".
  • Two 2" x 19".

## Piecing the Blocks

1. To begin Section A, make a diagonal corner on piece 1 with 1a. Trim and press. Make another diagonal corner on the *same* corner with piece 1b to complete Unit 1. Add Unit 2 to right side of Unit 1 as shown in Section A Assembly diagram; then join Unit 2a to bottom of combined unit. Repeat

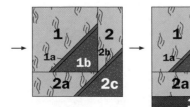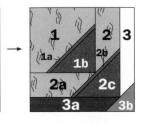

*Section A Assembly*

double diagonal corner with 2b and 2c as shown. To complete Section A, join units 3 and 3a; then add diagonal corner 3b. Make 40 of Section A.

**2.** See page 17 for instructions on half-square triangles. On wrong side of each 18" square of Fabric VI, draw a 2 x 2-square grid of 7⅞" squares. With right sides facing, match each marked fabric with an 18" square of Fabric VII. Stitch each grid as directed on page 17. Cut 8 triangle-squares from each grid (40 total—20 for Unit 4 and 20 for Unit 6).

**3.** Assemble Section B in the same manner as for Unit 3 of Section A. To begin, join Unit 5 to blue side of Unit 4. Join Unit 5a to rose side of Unit 4. To complete Section B, add diagonal corner 5b. Make 20 of Section B.

**4.** Section C is made in the same manner as Section B, but Unit 6 is turned around. Follow Block Assembly 1 diagram carefully. Make 20 of Section C.

**5.** Referring to Block Assembly 2 diagram, join sections A and B in pairs and sections C and A as shown. Turn blocks as shown in diagram for correct fabric placement. Join two halves as shown.

**6.** Join units 8 and 9 to top and bottom edges of block as shown in Block diagram; then join units 10 and 11 to sides.

**7.** Join diagonal corners 12 and 13 as shown to complete block.

## Quilt Assembly

**1.** Referring to photograph, join completed blocks in five horizontal rows of four blocks each. All blocks are positioned in the same manner, with Fabric XII corners at top left. Join rows.

**2.** To piece each inner side border, join a 19" strip of Fabric XIII between two 42" strips to make two 102"-long border strips. To piece inner top and bottom borders, join a 22"-long strip onto both ends of two 42" strips to make two 85"-long borders.

**3.** Matching centers of quilt side and border strip, join long borders to sides of quilt. Press seam allowances and trim excess border fabric at ends. Add borders at top and bottom edges in the same manner.

**4.** To piece each middle side border, join two 42" strips of Fabric I; then join a 12" strip onto both ends of each strip to make two 106"-long border strips. To piece top and bottom borders, join a 23" strip onto both ends of each remaining 42" strip to make two 87"-long strips.

**5.** Add middle side borders to quilt top; then add top and bottom borders.

**6.** To piece each outer side border, join a 25" strip of Fabric XIII between two 42" strips to make two 108"-long border strips. To piece outer top and bottom borders, join a 25" strip onto both ends of two 42"-long border strips to make two 91"-long borders. Join side borders to quilt top in the same manner as inner border; then join top and bottom borders.

## Quilting and Finishing

Outline-quilt patchwork or quilt as desired.

Make 11⅛ yards of binding. See page 30 for directions on making and applying straight-grain binding.

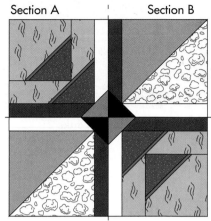

*Block Assembly 2*

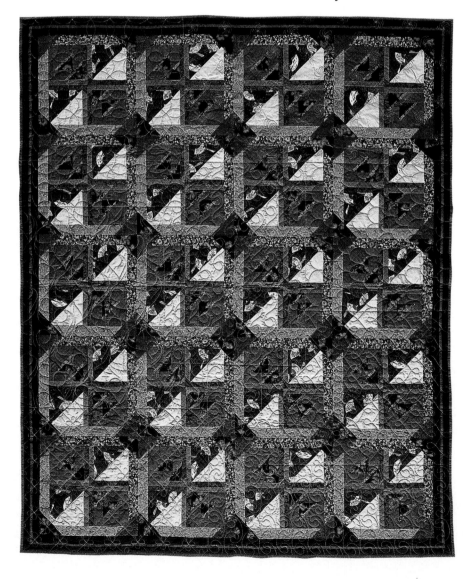

# Celtic *Rose*

*Strip piecing makes this garden bloom quickly and easily. For the roses, pick the color of your favorite flower; then surround it with garden greens and the background color of your choice.*

**Quick-Piecing Techniques:** Strip Piecing (see page 20)

## Finished Size

Blocks: 80 blocks, 8" square          Quilt: 90" x 110"

## Materials

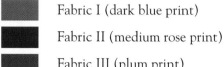

| | | |
|---|---|---|
| ▪ | Fabric I (dark blue print) | 3 yards |
| ▪ | Fabric II (medium rose print) | 1 yard |
| ▪ | Fabric III (plum print) | 1½ yards |
| ▪ | Fabric IV (medium green print) | 1¼ yards |
| ▪ | Fabric V (light green print) | 5¾ yards |
| | Backing fabric | 8¼ yards |

*Block X—Make 40.*

## Cutting

*Note:* Most of these strips are not cut down into smaller segments until after they are joined into strip sets. Then segments cut from each strip set become individual units. In this cutting list, strips are identified by unit, not strip set.

### From Fabric I (dark blue), cut:

* Ten 3" x 42" strips for binding.
* Twenty-one 2½" x 42" strips (1, 3, 5, 9, 11).
* Three 4½" x 42" strips (12).
* Two 2½" x 42½" strips.
  From these, cut:
  • Nineteen 2½" squares for sashing and borders.

### From Fabric II (medium rose), cut:

* Five 2½" x 42" strips (1).
* Three 4½" x 42" strips (11).

### From Fabric III (plum), cut:

* Five 2½" x 42" strips.
  From these, cut:
  • Forty 2½" x 4½" (2).
* Three 4½" x 42" strips (3).
* Three 6½" x 42" strips (12).

### From Fabric IV (medium green), cut:

* Six 4½" x 42" strips (4, 5).
* Seven 2½" x 42" strips (6, 10).

* Three 2½" x 42" strips.
  From these, cut:
  • Forty 2½" squares for sashing and borders.

### From Fabric V (light green), cut:

* Six 2½" x 42" strips (4, 5).
* Five 6½" x 42" strips (6).
* Eleven 8½" x 42" strips.
  From these, cut:
  • Forty 4½" x 8½" (7).
  • Ninety 2½" x 8½" (8).
* Six 8½" x 42" strips (9, 10).

## Piecing the Blocks

**1.** Referring to strip set diagrams at right, join 2½"-wide strips of fabrics I and II to assemble five of Strip Set A. Press seam allowances toward Fabric I. From these strip sets, cut eighty 2½"-wide segments for Unit 1.

**2.** Join 2½"-wide strips of Fabric I to 4½"-wide strips of Fabric III to make three of Strip Set B. Press seam allowances toward Fabric III. From these strip sets, cut forty 2½"-wide segments for Unit 3.

**3.** Join 2½"-wide strips of Fabric V to 4½"-wide strips of Fabric IV to make three of Strip Set C. From these strip sets, cut forty 2½"-wide segments for Unit 4.

*Strip Set A—Make 5.*

*Strip Set B—Make 3.*

*Strip Set C—Make 3.*

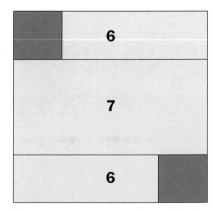

*Block Y—Make 40.*

**4.** Join 2½"-wide strips of fabrics I and V to 4½"-wide strips of Fabric IV as shown to make three of Strip Set D. From these strip sets, cut forty 2½"-wide segments for Unit 5.

**5.** Join 2½"-wide strips of Fabric IV to 6½"-wide strips of Fabric V to make five of Strip Set E. From these strip sets, cut eighty 2½"-wide segments for Unit 6.

**6.** Referring to Block X Assembly diagram, join two of Unit 1 to make a four-patch. Join Unit 2 to right side of joined Unit 1 as shown; press joining seam allowance toward Unit 2. Add Unit 3 to bottom of assembled units. Join Unit 4 to right side of center square as shown; press seam allowance toward Unit 4. Join Unit 5 to bottom of block as shown. Make 40 of Block X.

**7.** Referring to Block Y Assembly diagram, join two of Unit 6 to opposite sides of Unit 7. Make 40 of Block Y.

*Strip Set D—Make 3.*

*Strip Set E—Make 5.*

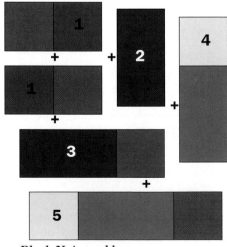

*Block X Assembly*

## Piecing the Sashing and Borders

**1.** Referring to diagrams at right, assemble strip sets F and G as shown. Press seam allowances toward Fabric V.

**2.** From Strip Set F, cut fifty-six 2½"-wide segments for Unit 9.

**3.** From Strip Set G, cut thirty-two 2½"-wide segments for Unit 10.

**4.** Assemble strip sets H and J as shown. Press seam allowances toward Fabric I.

**5.** From Strip Set H, cut thirty-six 2½"-wide segments for Unit 11.

**6.** From Strip Set J, cut thirty-six 2½"-wide segments for Unit 12. When these segments are cut, most of the third strip set will be left over. Pull out the stitching in this leftover segment to separate fabrics I and III. From the Fabric III piece, cut four 2½"-wide segments for outer borders.

## Quilt Assembly

**1.** Referring to Row Assembly diagram, join four of Block X and four of Block Y to make Block Row A, positioning blocks as shown and adding a Unit 8 sashing strip between blocks. Complete Row A with Unit 8 and Unit 11 sashing strips on each end of the row. Make six of Block Row A.

**2.** Referring to diagram to position blocks correctly, make four of Block Row B in the same manner.

**3.** To make Sashing Row 1, join eight of Unit 9 end-to-end as shown. At right end of assembled row, join one Fabric I square and then one Fabric IV square.

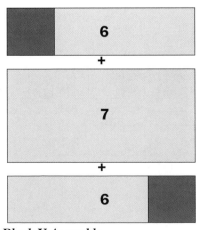

*Block Y Assembly*

*Strip Set F—Make 4.*

*Strip Set G—Make 2.*

*Strip Set H—Make 3.*

*Strip Set J—Make 3.*

Complete row by joining one Fabric IV square to left end as shown. Make two of Sashing Row 1.

**4.** To make Sashing Row 2, join four of Unit 9 and four of Unit 10 as shown. Add squares of fabrics I and IV to row ends. Make five of Sashing Row 2.

**5.** To make Sashing Row 3, join five of Unit 9 and three of Unit 10 as shown. Add squares of fabrics I and IV to row ends. Make four of Sashing Row 3.

**6.** To assemble top half of quilt, join sashing and block rows in the following sequence: 1, A, 2, B, 3, A, 2, B, 3, A. Repeat same sequence to make bottom half. Join top section to remaining

Sashing Row 2. Then turn bottom section upside down so that its Row 1 is at bottom and Block Row A is at top. Join this Block Row A to Sashing Row 2 at bottom of top section.

**7.** To make Border Row 1, join eight of Unit 12 end-to-end as shown. Press seam allowances toward Fabric I. Complete row by joining one 2½" x 6½" piece of Fabric III to right end as shown. Make two of Border Row 1.

**8.** To make Border Row 2, join eight of Unit 11 with Fabric IV squares between units. Press seam allowances toward Fabric IV. End row with squares of fabrics I and IV at both ends as shown. Make two of Border Row 2.

**9.** Join a Border Row 2 to top and bottom edges of assembled quilt top; then add Border Row 1 in the same manner.

**10.** To make side borders, repeat assembly of Border Row 1, using 10 of Unit 12 and one 2½" x 6½" piece of Fabric III. Complete row by adding a Fabric I square to both ends. Add one border strip to each side of quilt top.

## Quilting and Finishing

Mark a 6"-diameter quilting design in each Block Y and a 1½" x 7" design in each Fabric V sashing unit. Quilt marked designs and outline-quilt each Block X. Quilt borders as desired.

Make 11½ yards of binding. See page 30 for directions on making and applying straight-grain binding.

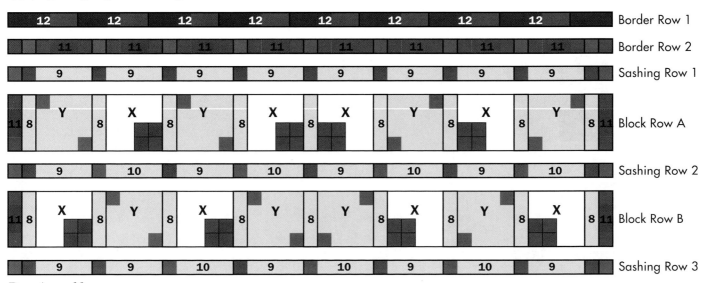

*Row Assembly*

# Baby Bunnies Crib Set

Quick cutting and piecing techniques make the little pieces in this bunny block a snap to cut and stitch. In less time than ever before, you can make this cute nursery ensemble using fabrics of sweet pastels or bright primaries. We've given separate yardage requirements for the wall hanging and the crib bumpers if you wish to make them without the crib quilt.

**Quick-Piecing Techniques:**  Strip Piecing (see page 20)
Diagonal Corners (see page 20)
Diagonal Ends (see page 21)
Triangle-Squares (see page 22)

## Finished Size

Blocks: 9 bunny blocks for quilt, 8" x 12"
      2 bunny blocks for wall hanging, 8" x 12"
      6 heart blocks for quilt, 6" square
      1 heart block for wall hanging, 6" square

Quilt: 50" x 50"
Wall Hanging: 24" x 34"

## Materials*

| | | |
|---|---|---|
| Fabric I (pink-on-blue print) | 1¾ yards |
| Fabric II (blue solid) | 1 yard |
| Fabric III (blue-and-ivory check) | 1 yard |
| Fabric IV (light pink print) | 1¼ yards |
| Fabric V (bright pink solid) | 1⅛ yards |
| Fabric VI (pink texture-look print) | ¾ yard |
| Backing fabric for crib quilt | 3 yards |

*Yardage includes enough fabric to make wall hanging from the same fabric. See instructions for making wall hanging separately and for additional yardage required for bumpers.*

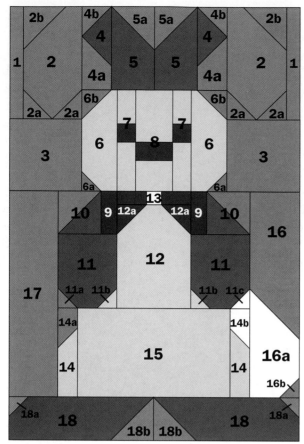

*Block A—Make 9.*

## Cutting for Crib Quilt

*Note:* Cutting list below is for crib quilt only. Separate instructions follow for wall hanging.

### From Fabric I (pink-on-blue print), cut:

✸ One 11" x 42" strip. From this, cut:
  • One 9" x 11" for triangle-squares (A-10).
  • Two 2" x 33" strips. From these, cut:
    • Eighteen 1¼" x 2" (A-4a).
    • Twelve 2" squares (B-1b).
    • Seven 1" x 33" strips. From these, cut:
      • Four 1" x 16½" (21).
      • Nine 1" x 1½" (A-14a).
      • Fifty-four 1" squares (A-6a, A-11a, A-16b, A-18a).
      • Eighteen 1" x 3½" (A-1).
✸ Two 1¼" x 42" strips. From these, cut:
  • Fifty-four 1¼" squares (A-2a, A-6b).
✸ One 5½" x 42" strip. From this, cut:
  • Four 5½" x 6½" (19).

✸ Six 1¾" x 42" strips. From these, cut:
  • Nine 1¾" x 6" (A-17).
  • Nine 1¾" x 4½" (A-16).
  • Fifty-four 1¾" squares (A-2b, A-5a, A-18b).
✸ Two 2½" x 42" strips. From these, cut:
  • Two 2½" x 8½" (20).
  • Eighteen 2½" x 2¾" (A-3).
✸ Three 3½" x 42" strips. From these, cut:
  • Twelve 3½" squares (B-1a).
  • Eight 3½" x 6½" (22).
✸ Five 1½" x 42" strips. From these, cut:
  • Twelve 1½" x 12½" (23).
  • Twelve 1½" squares (B-1c).

### From Fabric II (blue), cut:

✸ One 1" x 42" strip for Strip Set 1 (A-7, A-8).
✸ Two 1¼" x 42" strips for Strip Set 2 (A-13).
✸ One 1" x 42" strip. From this, cut:
  • Eighteen 1" x 1¾" (A-9).

✸ One 1¼" x 42" strip. From this, cut:
  • Eighteen 1¼" squares (A-12a).
✸ Three 2" x 42" strips for Strip Set 3 (B-1).
✸ Two 2½" x 42" strips for checkerboard borders.
✸ Three 3½" x 42" strips for checkerboard corner blocks.

### From Fabric III (blue-and-ivory check), cut:

✸ One 1" x 42" strip. From this, cut:
  • Nine 1" squares (A-11c).
  • Nine 1" x 1½" (A-14b).
✸ One 1" x 42" strip for Strip Set 2 (A-13).
✸ One 1¾" x 42" strip. From this, cut:
  • Nine 1¾" x 3¼" (A-16a).
✸ Three 2" x 42" strips for Strip Set 3 (B-1).
✸ Two 2½" x 42" strips for checkerboard borders.
✸ Three 3½" x 42" strips for checkerboard corner blocks.

### From Fabric IV (light pink print), cut:

✸ Twelve 1½" x 42" strips. From these, cut:
  • Twelve 1½" x 26" for quilt borders.
  • Eighteen 1½" x 3½" (A-6).
  • Eighteen 1" squares (A-11b).
  • Eighteen 1" x 2¼" (A-14).
✸ One 2" x 42" strip for Strip Set 1 (A-7, A-8).
✸ One 1½" x 42" strip for Strip Set 1 (A-7, A-8).
✸ One 2½" x 42" strip. From this, cut:
  • Nine 2½" x 3¼" (A-12).
✸ One 5" x 42" strip. From this, cut:
  • Nine 2¾" x 5" (A-15).

### From Fabric V (bright pink), cut:

✸ Five 3" x 42" strips for binding.
✸ Two 2" x 42" strips. From these, cut:
  • Eighteen 2" x 3½" (A-2).
✸ One 1¼" x 42" strip. From this, cut:
  • Eighteen 1¼" squares (A-4b).

**From Fabric VI (pink texture print), cut:**

* ✱ One 2" x 42" strip.
  From this, cut:
  • Eighteen 1¼" x 2" (A-4).
* ✱ One 2½" x 42" strip.
  From this, cut:
  • Eighteen 2¼" x 2½" (A-11).
* ✱ One 11" x 42" strip.
  From this, cut:
  • One 9" x 11" for triangle-squares (A-10).
  • Six 1¾" x 33" strips.
    From these, cut:
    • Eighteen 1¾" x 2¾" (A-5).
    • Eighteen 1¾" x 4½" (A-18).

## Piecing the Bunny Blocks

**1.** Using diagonal-corner technique, make one of Unit 12 and two each of units 2, 5, 6, and 18. Note that in each case, the second unit is a mirror image. Refer to Block A Assembly diagram carefully to position pieces correctly.

**2.** Using diagonal-corner technique, make one of Unit 11 with diagonal corners 11a and 11b as shown in Assembly diagram. Make another Unit 11, using diagonal corners 11b and 11c.

**3.** Using diagonal-end technique, make one of Unit 14 with diagonal end 14a. Then make a mirror-image unit, using diagonal end 14b as shown in Assembly diagram.

**4.** Use diagonal-end technique to add piece 4a to piece 4. Complete Unit 4 by adding diagonal corner 4b as shown in Assembly diagram. Make a mirror-image unit for second Unit 4.

**5.** To make Unit 16, use diagonal-end technique to add piece 16a to piece 16. Complete unit by adding diagonal corner 16b as shown.

**6.** Assemble strips designated for units 7 and 8 as shown in diagram for Strip Set 1, joining 1½" and 2" strips of Fabric IV to 1" strip of Fabric II. For Unit 7, cut eighteen 1"-wide segments. For Unit 8, cut nine 1½"-wide segments.

**7.** Assemble strips designated for Unit 13 as shown in diagram for Strip Set 2, joining 1¼" strips of Fabric II to both sides of 1" strip of Fabric III. Cut nine 1"-wide segments for Unit 13.

**8.** To make Unit 10, see page 22 for instructions on half-square triangles. On wrong side of 9" x 11" piece of Fabric I, draw a 3 x 4-square grid of 2⅛" squares. With right sides facing, match marked fabric with 9" x 11" piece of Fabric VI. Stitch grid as directed on page 22. Cut 24 triangle-squares from grid—this includes two for each block for both quilt and wall hanging, plus two extras.

**9.** To assemble Section A, begin by joining one of Unit 1 to one side of each Unit 2 as shown in Assembly diagram. Add Unit 3 to bottom of joined units. Join units 4 and 5 in a row as shown, being careful to position mirror-image units correctly on right and left sides of center. Join units 6, 7, and 8 in a row as shown. Join the two rows; then add combined 1-2-3 units to sides to

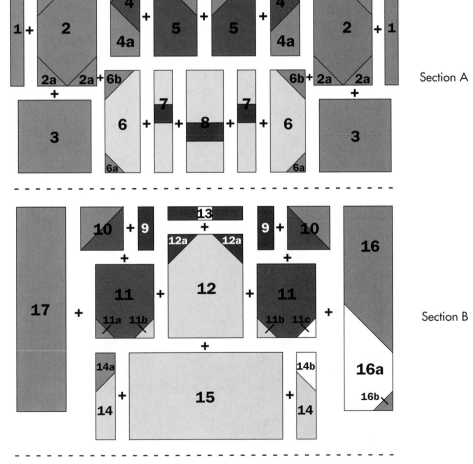

*Block A Assembly*

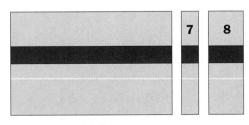

*Strip Set 1—Make 1.*

*Strip Set 2—Make 1.*

**10.** To assemble Section B, begin by joining one of Unit 9 to Fabric VI side of each Unit 10 as shown in Assembly diagram. Join combined 9-10 units to top of each Unit 11. Join Unit 13 to top of Unit 12; then join all combined units in a row as shown. Join one of Unit 14 to each side of Unit 15, referring to diagram to position mirror-image units correctly. Join combined 14-15 units to bottom of first combined unit. Join units 16 and 17 to sides as shown to complete Section B.

**11.** To assemble Section C, join two of Unit 18 as shown.

**12.** Join sections A, B, and C to complete one bunny block. Make nine bunny blocks for crib quilt.

## Piecing the Heart Blocks

**1.** Referring to diagram of Strip Set 3, join 2" strips of fabrics II and III. Make three strip sets. From these, cut fifty-six 2"-wide segments. Join segments in rows of four as shown in Heart Unit 1 diagram. Make 12 of Unit 1.

**2.** Positioning Unit 1 with a Fabric II square in the upper left corner, join diagonal corners 1a, 1b, and 1c to make left half of one block as shown in Block B Assembly diagram.

**3.** Positioning Unit 1 in the same manner, join diagonal corners as shown to make a mirror-image unit for right half of block.

**4.** Join halves to complete one block. Make six heart blocks.

## Piecing the Checkerboard Borders

Referring to diagram of Strip Set 3, join 2½" strips of fabrics II and III. Make two strip sets. From these, cut twenty-two 2½"-wide segments (set aside remainder for wall hanging). Referring to Quilt Assembly diagram, join segments in two rows of 11 segments each.

## Piecing the Corner Blocks

Referring to diagram of Strip Set 3, join 3½" strips of fabrics II and III. Make three strip sets. From these, cut thirty-two 3½"-wide segments. Join segments in eight rows of four segments each, in the same manner as for Heart Unit 1. Referring to Quilt Assembly diagram, join these rows in pairs to make each checkerboard corner block.

## Crib Quilt Assembly

**1.** Join a Unit 19 to top and bottom edges of two heart blocks. Join a Unit 20 to top and bottom edges of one bunny block. Referring to Quilt Assembly diagram, assemble center section by joining these units with four of Unit 21 as shown.

**2.** Join checkerboard borders to top and bottom of center section as shown.

**3.** Join Fabric IV border strips to sides of center section. Press seam allowances towards borders; then trim excess border fabric. Add borders to top and bottom edges in the same manner.

**4.** Join a Unit 22 to top and bottom edges of four heart blocks. Add bunny blocks to both sides of two of these heart units; then join a Unit 23 to bunny block sides to complete two outer sections.

**5.** Referring to Quilt Assembly diagram, join one completed outer section to top and bottom edges of center section.

**6.** Join a Unit 23 to both sides of two remaining heart units. Add bunny blocks and Unit 23 strips as shown to complete side sections.

**7.** Join corner blocks to both sides of each side section. Join these sections to quilt sides.

**8.** Join remaining Fabric IV strips in pairs end-to-end to make four borders.

**9.** Mark center of each quilt side. Matching centers, join border strips to sides of quilt. Press seam allowances toward borders; then trim excess fabric from both ends of borders. Add borders to top and bottom in the same manner.

## Quilting and Finishing

Outline-quilt patchwork in blocks and checkerboard borders. Quilt background as desired.

Make 5⅞ yards of straight-grain binding for crib quilt. See page 30 for directions on making and applying binding.

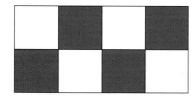

*Heart Unit 1*

*Strip Set 3*

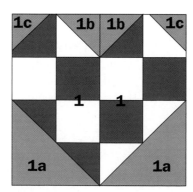

*Block B—Make 6.*

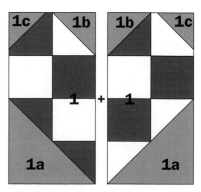

*Block B Assembly*

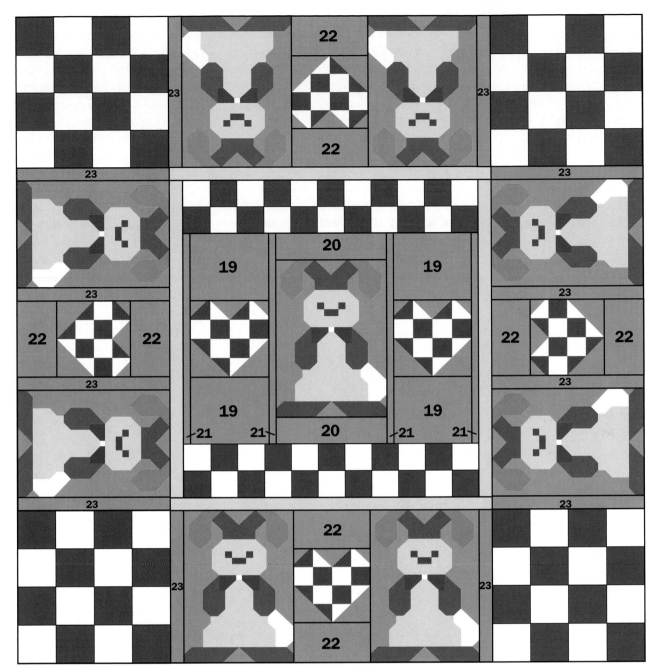

*Crib Quilt Assembly*

## Wall Hanging Cutting

To make wall hanging from same fabrics as crib quilt, the only additional yardage needed is ¾ yard for backing. Use fabrics left over from quilt to cut pieces listed below (except for Unit 10, which was sewn during preparation for crib quilt). To make wall hanging separately, you need ¼ yard each of fabrics I, II, III, and VI, ½ yard each of fabrics IV and V, and ¾ yard backing fabric.

**From Fabric I (pink-on-blue print), cut:**

✱ One 3½" x 42" strip.
   From this, cut:
   • Two 3½" x 6½" (22).
   • Four 1" x 3½" (A-1).
   • Two 3½" squares (B-1a).
   • One 3½" x 6½" for triangle-squares (A-10).
   • Four 2½" x 2¾" (A-3).

✱ One 2" x 42" strip.
   From this, cut:
   • Two 2" squares (B-1b).
   • Four 1¼" x 2" (A-4a).
   • Two 1½" squares (B-1c).
   • Twelve 1¼" squares (A-2a, A-6b).
   • Twelve 1" squares (A-6a, A-11a, A-16b, A-18a).
   • Two 1" x 1½" (A-14a).

✱ One 1¾" x 42" strip.
   From this, cut:
   • Twelve 1¾" squares (A-2b, A-5a, A-18b).
   • Two 1¾" x 4½" (A-16).
   • Two 1¾" x 6" (A-17).

**From Fabric II (blue), cut:**

✴ Three 2½" x 42" strips.
   From these, cut:
   • Two 2½" x 42" and one 2½" x 10" for checkerboard borders.
   • One 2" x 16" (B-1).
   • Two 1¼" x 2" (A-13).
   • Four 1¼" squares (A-12a).
   • One 1" x 7" (A-7, A-8).
   • Four 1" x 1¾" (A-9).

**From Fabric III (blue-and-ivory check), cut:**

✴ Three 2½" x 42" strips.
   From these, cut:
   • Two 2½" x 42" and one 2½" x 10" for checkerboard borders.
   • One 2" x 16" (B-1).
   • Two 1¾" x 3¼" (A-16a).
   • One 1" x 2" (A-13).
   • Two 1" x 1½" (A-14b).
   • Two 1" squares (A-11c).

**From Fabric IV (light pink print), cut:**

✴ Six 1½" x 42" strips.
   From these, cut:
   • Two 1½" x 33" and two 1½" x 24½" for outer border.
   • Two 1½" x 10½" and two 1½" x 14½" for inner border.
   • Four 1½" x 3½" (A-6).
   • Four 1" x 2¼" (A-14).
   • Four 1" squares (A-11b).

✴ One 2¾" x 42" strip. From this, cut:
   • Two 2¾" x 5" (A-15).
   • Two 2½" x 3¼" (A-12).
   • One 2" x 7" and one 1" x 7" (A-7, A-8).

**From Fabric V (bright pink), cut:**

✴ Three 3" x 42" strips for binding.
✴ One 4" x 42" strips.
   From this, cut:
   • Seven 4" x 6" for hanging loops.
✴ One 2" x 42" strip.
   From this, cut:
   • Four 2" x 3½" (A-2).
   • Four 1¼" squares (A-4b).

**From Fabric VI (pink texture print), cut:**

✴ One 4½" x 42" strip.
   From this, cut:
   • Four 4½" squares (24).
   • Four 1¾" x 4½" (A-18).
   • One 3½" x 6½" for triangle-squares (A-10).
   • Four 2¼" x 2½" (A-11).
✴ One 1¾" x 42" strip.
   From this, cut:
   • Four 1¾" x 2¾" (A-5).
   • Four 1¼" x 2" (A-4).

## Wall Hanging Assembly

**1.** To make two bunny blocks, begin by following steps 1-5 under Piecing the Bunny Blocks on page 199.

**2.** To make units 7 and 8, join designated strips of Fabric IV to 1" x 7" strip of Fabric II. For Unit 7, cut four 1"-wide segments. For Unit 8, cut two 1½"-wide segments.

**3.** To make Unit 13, join 1¼" x 2" pieces of Fabric II to both sides of 1" x 2" piece of Fabric III. Cut two 1"-wide segments for Unit 13.

**4.** If you've made the crib quilt, you already have eight triangle-squares left over for the wall hanging's Unit 10. If making the wall hanging separately, see page 22 for instructions on half-square triangles to make Unit 10. On wrong side of 3½" x 6½" piece of Fabric I, draw a 1 x 2-square grid of 2⅛" squares. With right sides facing, match marked fabric with 3½" x 6½" piece of Fabric VI. Stitch grid as directed on page 22. Cut four triangle-squares from grid, two for each block.

**5.** Follow steps 9-12 under Piecing the Bunny Blocks to complete two blocks.

**6.** Referring to diagram of Strip Set 3, join 2" x 16" strips of fabrics II and III. Cut eight 2"-wide segments. Join segments in rows of four as shown in Heart Unit 1 diagram. Make two of Unit 1. Follow steps 2-4 under Piecing the Heart Blocks to make one heart block.

**7.** Join a Unit 22 to top and bottom of remaining heart block. Join bunny blocks to both sides of heart unit.

**8.** Join 20½" strips of Fabric IV to top and bottom edges of center section; then join 14½" strips to side edges.

**9.** For checkerboard borders, join 2½" x 42" strips of fabrics II and III as shown in diagram of Strip Set 3. Join 2½" x 10" strips in the same manner. From these, cut thirty-eight 2½"-wide segments.

**10.** Referring to Wall Hanging Assembly diagram, join checkerboard segments to make two rows of 12 segments each. Join checkerboard borders to top and bottom edges of center section.

**11.** Join remaining segments to make two rows of seven segments each. Join Unit 24 corner squares to both ends of each row. Join rows to quilt sides.

**12.** Join 33" border strips to top and bottom edges of wall hanging; then join 24½" strips to quilt sides.

**13.** Outline-quilt patchwork or quilt as desired.

**14.** To make hanging loops, press under ¼" on short sides of each loop piece. With right sides facing, fold each piece in half lengthwise. Stitch ¼" from raw edge. Turn right side out and press seam to center back of each strip.

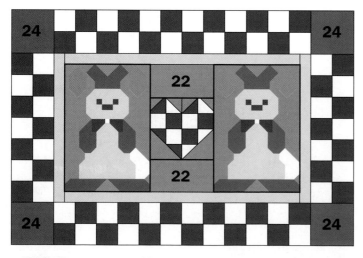

*Wall Hanging Assembly*

**15.** Fold each loop piece in half. Matching raw edges, pin a loop to backing at each top corner. Pin remaining loops to top edge in the same manner, spacing them approximately 3⅝" apart. Topstitch loop ends to backing.

**16.** Make 120" of straight-grain binding. See page 30 for directions on making and applying binding. Binding will cover raw ends of hanging loops.

## Crib Bumpers

These instructions are for two 6" x 26" bumpers and two 6" x 50" bumpers. Adjust yardage and instructions as necessary to make different sizes.

To make bumpers that coordinate with crib quilt, you will need an additional 1¾ yards of Fabric II (includes backing) and ⅝ yard of Fabric III. Additional materials needed are ¾ yard of muslin, 10⅛ yards of ⅛"-diameter pink cording, ⅝ yard of 60"-wide low-loft batting for quilting, and 1⅛ yards of 60"-wide high-loft batting for padding.

**1.** From Fabric II, cut and set aside four 6½" x 42" strips for backing and eight 1½" x 42" strips for ties.

**2.** Cut eight 2½" x 42" strips from each of fabrics II and III. Cut two strips of each fabric in half.

**3.** Referring to Strip Set 4 diagram, join full-length strips to make two strip sets and half-strips to make third strip set. Use remaining strips to assemble Strip Set 5 in the same manner. Cut thirty-eight 2½"-wide segments each from strip sets 4 and 5.

**4.** For each short bumper, join 13 segments in a row, alternating segments. For each long bumper, join 25 segments in the same manner.

**5.** For quilting, cut four 6½" x 42" strips of muslin. From two strips, cut 6½" x 28" pieces for short bumpers. Piece remaining muslin to make two 6½" x 55" backings for long bumpers. Cut and piece Fabric II backing in the same manner; then cut two matching pieces of batting for each bumper.

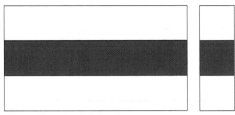

*Strip Set 4—Make 3.*

*Strip Set 5—Make 3.*

**6.** Sandwich a layer of low-loft batting between checkerboard (faceup) and muslin for each bumper. Outline-quilt patchwork. Trim batting and muslin to edge of patchwork.

**7.** Matching raw edges and beginning at center on one long side, pin cording around each bumper on right side. Clip corners and overlap cording ends. Using zipper or cording foot, stitch close to cording.

**8.** With right sides facing, place Fabric II backing on quilted bumper. Add two layers of high-loft batting; then pin. Turn bumper over, with batting on bottom. Stitch around bumper on top of cording stitches through all layers. Leave a 7" opening in one long side of each bumper. Clip corners and turn bumper right side out. Press lightly. Slipstitch opening closed.

**9.** From tie fabric, cut sixteen 1½" x 20" strips. Press under ¼" on short ends of each strip; then press under ¼" on each long edge. With wrong sides facing, press each strip in half lengthwise. Topstitch all pressed edges. Fold ties in half. Pin fold of one tie to back of each bumper corner and topstitch to secure.

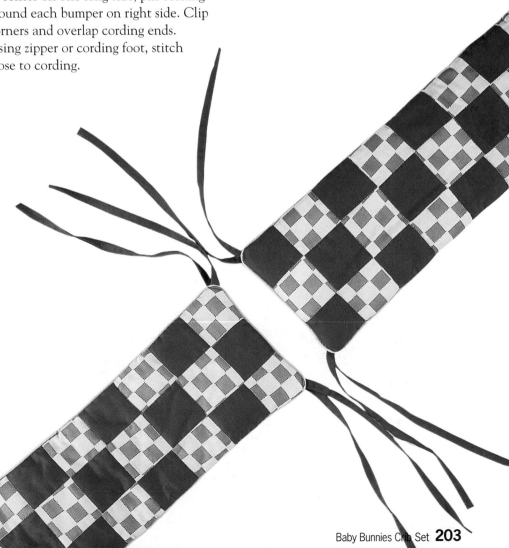

# Water *Lily*

*Strip piecing makes fast work of the corners in each of these pretty lily blocks. This quilt features light and dark lilies alternating in a lavender sea. What other color schemes might be effective? Try pink and white lilies framed in green, or use bright-colored scraps to make a variety of lilies set in a sea of dark blue. You'll find instructions for the coordinating pillow sham on page 209.*

**Quick-Piecing Techniques:**  Strip Piecing (see page 20)

**Finished Size**

Blocks: 42 blocks, 7¾" square          Quilt: 78¼" x 101"

## Materials

| | | |
|---|---|---|
| | Fabric I (dark purple print) | 4½ yards |
| | Fabric II (lavender print) | 3 yards |
| | Fabric III (purple solid) | 1¼ yards |
| | Fabric IV (purple print) | ⅜ yard |
| | Fabric V (purple print) | 1¾ yards |
| | Fabric VI (dark purple print) | ⅛ yard |
| | Fabric VII (lavender print) | ⅛ yard |
| | Backing fabric | 6¼ yards |

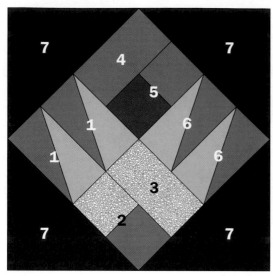

*Block A—Make 24.*

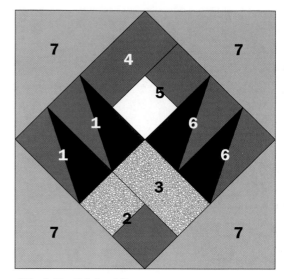

*Block B—Make 18.*

## Cutting

### From Fabric I (dark purple print), cut:
* Nine 3" x 42" strips for binding.
* Six 4¾" x 42" strips.
  From these, cut:
  * Forty-eight 4¾" squares.
    Cut each square in half diagonally to get 96 A-7.
* Twelve 5¼" x 42" strips.
  From these, cut:
  * Forty-five 5¼" x 10¼" (8, 9).
    Cut these rectangles as shown in Cutting diagram to get eight triangles from each piece for a total of 360 triangles.*
* Two 4" x 42" strips.
  From these, cut:
  * Nine 4" x 8" (B-1, B-6).
    Cut these rectangles as shown in Cutting diagram to get eight triangles from each piece for a total of 72 triangles.*
* Nine 3" x 42" strips for outer border.
  From three of these strips, cut:
  * Two 3" x 21".
  * Four 3" x 18".

### From Fabric II (lavender print), cut:
* Five 4¾" x 42" strips.
  From these, cut:
  * Thirty-six 4¾" squares.
    Cut each square in half diagonally to get 72 B-7.

* Twelve 5¼" x 42" strips.
  From these, cut:
  * Forty-five 5¼" x 10¼" (8, 9).
    Cut these rectangles as shown in Cutting diagram to get eight triangles from each piece for a total of 360 triangles.*
* Three 4" x 42" strips.
  From these, cut:
  * Twelve 4" x 8" (A-1, A-6).
    Cut these rectangles as shown in Cutting diagram to get eight triangles from each piece for a total of 96 triangles.*

### From Fabric III (purple), cut:
* Five 4" x 42" strips.
  From these, cut:
  * Twenty-one 4" x 8" (A-1, A-6, B-1, B-6).
    Cut these rectangles as shown in Cutting diagram to get eight triangles from each piece for a total of 168 triangles.*
* Two 3¼" x 42" strips.
  From these, cut:
  * Forty-two 1⅞" x 3¼" (A-4, B-4).
* Five 1⅞" x 42" strips (A-2, A-5, B-2, B-5).

### From Fabric IV (purple print), cut:
* Two 3¼" x 42" strips.
  From these, cut:
  * Forty-two 1⅞" x 3¼" (A-3, B-3).
* Two 1⅞" x 42" strips (A-2, B-2).

### From Fabric V (purple print), cut:
* Nine 4¼" x 42" strips.
  From these, cut:
  * Forty-two 4¼" x 8¼" (10).
* Nine 2" x 42" strips for inner border.
  From three of these strips, cut:
  * Six 2" x 16".

### From Fabric VI (dark purple print), cut:
* Two 1⅞" x 42" strips (A-5).

### From Fabric VII (lavender print), cut:
* One 1⅞" x 42" strip (B-5).

*Note: Each rectangle yields eight triangles, four of which point to the right and four to the left. Store "righties" and "lefties" separately. Trim ¾" from narrow tip of all these triangles.

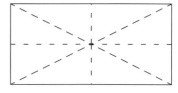

*Cutting*

## Piecing the Blocks

1. To make Unit A-1, join small triangles of fabrics II and III, using righties. The resulting rectangle will measure 1⅞" x 3¼". Make two of Unit 1. Make two of Unit A-6 in the same manner, using lefties.

2. Join 1⅞" strips of fabrics III and IV to make two of Strip Set 1. From these, cut forty-two 1⅞"-wide segments for units A-2 and B-2. (*Note:* Save all strip-set remnants for optional pillow sham.)

*Strip Set 1*

*Strip Set 2*

*Strip Set 3*

3. Join 1⅞" strips of fabrics III and VI to make two of Strip Set 2. From these strip sets, cut twenty-four 1⅞"-wide segments for Unit A-5.

4. Join 1⅞" strips of fabrics III and VII to make one of Strip Set 3. From this strip set, cut eighteen 1⅞"-wide segments for Unit B-5.

5. To assemble Block A, begin by joining two of Unit 1 as shown in Block Assembly diagram. Join units 2 and 3; then add this combined unit to Unit 1 pair. To assemble top half of block, join units 4 and 5 and two of Unit 6 in a row as shown. Join halves to complete lily section. Join A-7 triangles to opposite sides of lily section; press seam allowances toward triangles. Add A-7 triangles to remaining sides to complete block. Make 24 of Block A.

6. Make 18 of Block B in the same manner, referring to block diagram for color and placement of each unit.

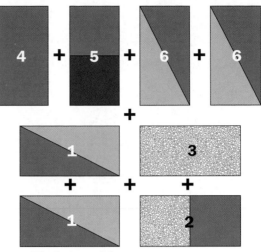

*Block Assembly*

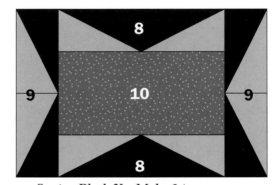

*Setting Block X—Make 24.*

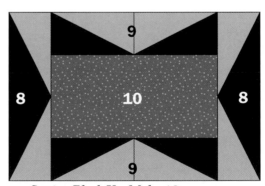

*Setting Block Y—Make 18.*

## Piecing Setting Blocks

1. Using a scant ¼" seam allowance, join 360 pairs of large triangles of fabrics I and II, making 180 lefty pairs and 180 righty pairs. Each resulting rectangle will be 2½" x 4⅜".

2. Paying careful attention to color placement as shown in setting block diagrams, join one lefty rectangle and one righty rectangle to form Unit 8.

Make 96 of Unit 8. Join remaining rectangles as shown to make 84 of Unit 9.

3. Positioning fabrics as shown in Setting Block X diagram, join one of Unit 8 to each long side of Unit 10. Add one of Unit 9 to each side as shown. Make 24 of Setting Block X.

4. Make 18 of Setting Block Y in the same manner, changing positions of units 8 and 9 as shown.

## Quilt Assembly

**1.** Join three of Block B and four of Setting Block X to make Row 1, alternating blocks as shown (Row Assembly diagram). Make six of Row 1.

**2.** Join four of Block A and three of Setting Block Y to make Row 2, positioning blocks as shown. Complete Row 2 with a Unit 8 on each end of the row, positioning fabrics as shown. Make six of Row 2.

**3.** Starting with a Row 1 and alternating row types, join all rows.

**4.** To piece inner border for top edge, join a 16" strip of Fabric V to both ends of a 42" strip to make a 73"-long border. Matching centers of quilt and border, join border to top edge of quilt top. Press seam allowances and trim border fabric at ends. Repeat for bottom edge.

**5.** To piece inner side borders, join a 42" strip of Fabric V to both ends of each remaining 16" strip to make a 99"-long border strip. Join borders to quilt sides in the same manner.

**6.** For top and bottom outer borders, join an 18" strip of Fabric I to both ends of a 42" strip to make two 77"-long borders. For sides, join a 42" strip to both ends of a 21" strip to make two 104"-long borders. Join outer borders to quilt in the same manner as inner borders.

## Quilting and Finishing

Quilt in-the-ditch around all patchwork. Quilt an X from corner to corner of all A and B blocks. Quilt a diagonal grid of 1" squares in all Unit 10 pieces.

Make $10\frac{5}{8}$ yards of binding. See page 30 for directions on making and applying straight-grain binding.

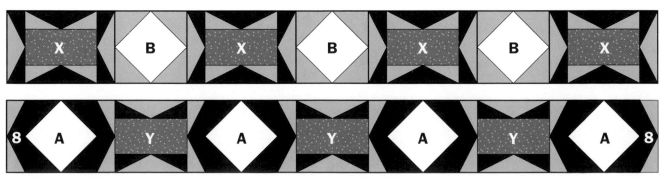

Row 1

Row 2

*Row Assembly*

# Water Lily Pillow Sham

## Finished Size

Blocks: 3 blocks, 7¾" square          Sham: 26¾" x 61¼" (Queen size)

*Use the same fabrics, instructions, and diagrams that you used to make the Water Lily quilt for this coordinating pillow sham. Unit numbers correspond to quilt units unless otherwise indicated.*

## Materials

| | | |
|---|---|---|
| ■ | Fabric I (dark purple print) | 2¼ yards |
| ▨ | Fabric II (lavender print) | ⅜ yard |
| ▨ | Fabric III (purple solid) | ⅜ yard |
| ▨ | Fabric IV (purple print) | ¼ yard |
| ▨ | Fabric V (purple print) | ¼ yard |
| | Muslin for quilting lining | 1¾ yards |
| | 4"-wide Battenberg lace | 4⅞ yards |

## Cutting

### From Fabric I (dark purple print), cut:

* Two 5¼" x 42" strips.
  From these, cut:
  * Three 5¼" x 10¼" (9).
    Cut these rectangles as shown in Cutting diagram on page 206 to get 24 triangles.*
  * Two 5¼" x 18" for outer border.
  * Four 2½" squares (Sham-1).
* One 2½" x 42" strip.
  From this, cut:
  * Four 2½" x 10" (Sham-2).
* Two 5¼" x 62" lengthwise strips for outer border.
* Two 27¼" x 33" for backing.
* Two 4" x 8" (B-1, B-6).
  Cut these rectangles as shown in Cutting diagram on page 206 to get 16 triangles. (Only 12 are needed; discard four extras.)*

### From Fabric II (lavender print), cut:

* One 5¼" x 42" strip.
  From this, cut:
  * Three 5¼" x 10¼" (9).
    Cut these rectangles as shown in Cutting diagram on page 206 to get 24 triangles.*
* One 4¾" x 42" strip.
  From this, cut:
  * Six 4¾" squares.
    Cut each square in half diagonally to get 12 triangles (B-7).

### From Fabric III (purple), cut:

* Four 2½" x 42" strips.
  From these, cut:
  * Four 2½" x 26" and two 2½" x 12½" for inner border.
  * Three 1⅞" squares (B-2).
* Three 1⅞" x 3¼" (B-4).

* Two 4" x 8" (B-1, B-6).
  Cut these rectangles as shown in Cutting diagram on page 206 to get 16 triangles. (Only 12 are needed; discard four extras.)*

### From Fabric IV (purple print), cut:

* One 1⅞" x 42" strip.
  From this, cut:
  * Three 1⅞" squares (B-2).
  * Three 1⅞" x 3¼" (B-3).
* Five 1¼" x 42" strips.
  From these, cut:
  * Four 1¼" x 27" and two 1¼" x 17" for middle border.

### From Fabric V (purple print), cut:

* Two 6" x 8¼" (Sham-3).

*Note: Each rectangle yields eight triangles, four of which point to the right and four to the left. Store "righties" and "lefties" separately. Trim ¾" from narrow tip of all these triangles.

## Piecing Blocks and Sashing

1. Referring to block diagrams and instructions for Water Lily blocks on pages 206 and 207, make three of Block B. Use three segments of Strip Set 3 left over from the quilt for Unit 5.
2. Referring to diagrams and instructions on page 207, make 12 of Unit 9.
3. Join one of Unit 9 to top and bottom edges of each Water Lily block.
4. Join one of Unit 9 to each long side of Sham Unit 3. Join Sham Unit 2 to top and bottom edges of assembled units.
5. Join Sham Unit 1 squares to ends of two remaining Unit 9.
6. Referring to Pillow Sham Assembly diagram, join assembled units in a row.

## Adding Borders

1. Join 12½" strips of Fabric III to short sides of sham top. Piece pairs of 26" strips end-to-end to make two 51½"-long border strips for top and bottom edges. Matching centers of sham and border strip, join borders to top and bottom edges. Press seam allowances toward borders and trim excess border fabric at ends.
2. Join middle borders to sham in the same manner, adding short strips to sides first and then piecing pairs of long strips to make borders for top and bottom edges.
3. Join outer borders to pillow sham.
4. Cut four pieces of lace to fit along seam lines between middle and outer borders. Pin or baste lace in place, butting ends of adjacent pieces at corners.

## Quilting and Finishing

1. Cut muslin and batting slightly larger than sham. Quilt in-the-ditch around patchwork. Quilt a diagonal grid of 1" squares in Unit 3 and inner border. Topstitch lace edges to secure them, quilting into sham at the same time.
2. Press under ¼" on one short end of each backing piece. Press under another ¼" and topstitch in place to hem.
3. With right sides facing and corners matching, place backing pieces on sham front, overlapping hemmed edges of backing pieces in center. Stitch ¼" around sham. Trim excess batting and lining from seam allowances and clip corners. Turn sham right side out.

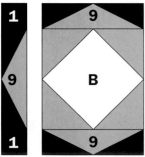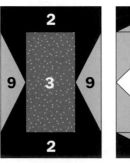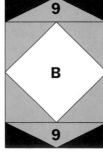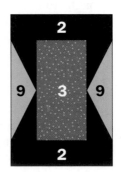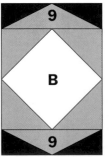

*Pillow Sham Assembly*

# Pillow Talk

*Add style to your decor with a batch of pretty pillows. The pillows and shams in this book have envelope-style backs that are fast to assemble and easy to remove for cleaning. Use the following instructions to finish any pillow top.*

## Materials

For each pillow back, you need two fabric rectangles. The *width* of each rectangle must be the same as the width of the front. The *height* of each rectangle should be half the height of the front plus 3". For example, if your pillow patchwork is 12½" square, then backing rectangles should be 12½" x 9½".

Make or purchase a pillow form that is the desired finished size of the pillow. If you want to buy a form but the patchwork is not a standard size, add borders around the block to make it big enough to accommodate an available form.

## Instructions

**1.** On one widthwise edge of each rectangle, turn under ¼" and then ⅝". Press fold. Topstitch ½" from folded edge and then edgestitch.

**2.** With wrong side up, lay one rectangle on table. Referring to diagram, position second rectangle (also wrong side up) so that hemmed edges overlap and both pieces form a square or rectangle that matches pillow front. Pin layers together at envelope opening. Machine-baste overlapped edges at sides.

**3.** With right sides facing and raw edges aligned, stitch back to front around all edges, taking a ½" seam. Backstitch at overlap points.

**4.** Remove pins. Clip corners; then turn pillow right side out through envelope opening. Insert pillow form.

## Adding a Ruffle

**1.** Measure around sides of pillow front and multiply the total by 2 to determine length of ruffle strip needed.

**2.** Cut or piece fabric strips that are twice as wide as the desired finished ruffle plus 1". (Example: Cut strips 7" wide to make a finished ruffle 3" wide.) Join strips end-to-end to make a continuous strip equal to needed length. Join ends.

**3.** With wrong sides facing and raw edges aligned, fold strip in half lengthwise and press. Measure four equal sections and mark each with a pin.

**4.** Stitch a line of loose basting ⅜" from raw edge of first ruffle section, leaving 2" of thread at each end. Repeat for remaining ruffle sections.

**5.** On pillow front, mark center of each side with a pin. With right sides facing, pin end of one ruffle section at one center point on pillow front. Gather ruffle, distributing fullness evenly, until section fits between pins. Aligning raw edges, pin gathered section to pillow front. Repeat for remaining sections.

**6.** Stitch back to pillow front as described above, with ruffle sandwiched in between.

# Stained Glass Floral

A beautiful scalloped border provides the finishing touch for this intricate design. The joined blocks create a fascinating pattern of interweaving lattice that carries through to the scallops. Make a complete bedroom ensemble with these instructions for a matching flanged pillow, table cover, and embellished linens. We recommend this project for experienced quiltmakers.

---

**Quick-Piecing Techniques:**   Diagonal Corners (see page 20)
Diagonal Ends (see page 21)
Four-Triangle Squares (see page 23)

**Finished Size**
Blocks: 30 blocks, 17" square        Quilt: 98" x 109½"
      17 scallops, 6½" x 17"

**Materials\***

| | | |
|---|---|---|
| ☐ Fabric I (tan-on-ivory print) | 5¼ yards |
| ▨ Fabric II (tan solid) | 1 yard |
| ▨ Fabric III (slate blue solid) | 5¾ yards |
| ▨ Fabric IV (dark blue print) | 3 yards |
| ▨ Fabric V (navy solid) | 3¼ yards |
| Backing fabric | 9 yards |

*\* See instructions for matching pillow, table topper, and embellished linens for additional yardage needed.*

---

## Cutting

*Note:* In the following cutting list and throughout these instructions where pieces are used in all four scallops (Blocks B, C, D, and E), designation is Scallops plus a unit number. Pieces designated as A-, B-, C-, D-, and E- are used only in individual blocks.

**From Fabric I (tan-on-ivory print), cut:**

✱ Twenty-seven 2" x 42" strips.
 From these, cut:
  • 120 2" x 4" (A-2).
  • 240 2" squares (A-11).
  • 120 1" x 2" (A-8).

✱ Fifty-four 1½" x 42" strips.
 From these, cut:
  • 1,148 1½" squares (A-1a, A-3, A-10a, A-14a, Scallops-3a, Scallops-10a).
  • 154 1½" x 2" (A-5, Scallops-4).
  • Thirty-four 1½" x 6" (Scallops-2).
  • Thirty-four 1" x 1½" (Scallops-8).

✱ Twelve 1" x 42" strips.
 From these, cut:
  • 480 1" squares (A-7a, A-9b, A-12a).

✱ Eight 2½" x 42" strips.
 From these, cut:
  • 120 2½" squares (A-6).

✱ Three 3½" x 42" strips.
 From these, cut:
  • Thirty 3½" squares (A-15).

**From Fabric II (tan), cut:**

✱ Two 15" x 42" strips.
 From these, cut:
  • Three 15" x 21" for triangle-squares (A-13, Scallops-11).

**From Fabric III (slate blue), cut:**

✱ Three 15" x 42" strips.
 From these, cut:
  • Six 15" x 21" for triangle-squares (A-13, Scallops-11).

✱ Twenty-three 2" x 42" strips.
 From these, cut:
  • 120 2" x 3" (A-1).
  • 120 1½" x 2" (A-4).
  • 120 2" squares (A-7).
  • 164 1" x 2" (A-18a, Scallops-4a, C-1a, D-1a, E-1a).

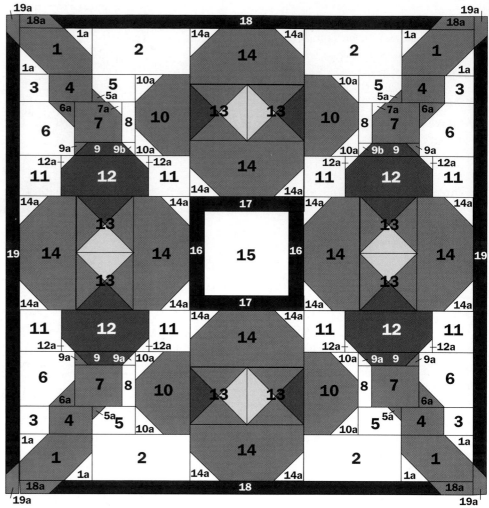

*Block A—Make 30.*

✱ Six 1" x 42" strips.
 From these, cut:
  • 240 1" squares (A-5a, A-9a).

✱ Nineteen 4½" x 42" strips.
 From these, cut:
  • 274 2½" x 4½" (A-14, Scallops-10).
  • Thirty-four 2" x 4½" (Scallops-3).

✱ Twelve 1½" x 42" strips.
 From these, cut:
  • Sixty-eight 1½" x 2½" (Scallops-2a, Scallops-5).
  • 120 1½" squares (A-6a).
  • 144 1" x 1½" (A-19a, B-1a).

✱ From scraps, cut:
  • One 2½" square.
   Cut this square in half diagonally to get two triangles (D-13, E-13).
  • One 2" square.
   Cut this square in half diagonally to get two triangles (D-12, E-12).

**From Fabric IV (dark blue print), cut:**

✱ Thirteen 2½" x 42" strips.
 From these, cut:
  • 120 1" x 2½" (A-9).
  • 120 2½" x 3½" (A-10).

✱ Six 1½" x 42" strips.
 From these, cut:
  • Sixty-eight 1½" squares (Scallops-4b, Scallops-6).
  • Thirty-four 1½" x 3½" (Scallops-9).

✱ Eleven 2" x 42" strips.
 From these, cut:
  • 120 2" x 3½" (A-12).
  • Seventeen 2" squares.
   Cut each square in half diagonally to get 34 triangles (Scallops-7).

✱ Two 15" x 42" strips.
 From these, cut:
  • Three 15" x 21" for triangle-squares (A-13, Scallops-11).

## From Fabric V (navy), cut:

✱ One 34" square for bias binding.

✱ Sixty-nine 1" x 42" strips.
   From these, cut:
   • Seventy-two 1" x 16½" (A-19, B-1).
   • Five 1" x 15½" (C-1, D-1, E-1).
   • Sixty 1" x 14½" (A-18).
   • Sixty 1" x 4½" (A-17).
   • Sixty 1" x 3½" (A-16).

✱ Three 1½" x 42" strips for top border.

## Piecing the Blocks

1. To make units A-13 and Scallops-11, see page 23 for instructions on *four-square* triangles. On wrong side of each 15" x 21" piece of Fabric III, draw a 4 x 6-square grid of 3¼" squares. With right sides facing, match three marked pieces with 15" x 21" pieces of Fabric II. Match remaining three marked pieces with 15" x 21" pieces of Fabric IV. Stitch each grid as directed for *half-square* triangles on page 22. Cut 48 triangle-squares from each grid (288 total). Press seam allowances on all triangle-squares toward Fabric III.

2. Referring to instructions on page 23, draw a diagonal line on wrong side of each Fabric II/III triangle-square. With right sides facing and seams aligned, match marked triangle-squares with Fabric III/IV triangle-squares so that Fabric III in each square is on top of different fabric in opposite square. Stitch these pairs as directed on page 23. Make 282 quarter-triangle squares. Designate 240 as Unit A-13, 34 as Scallops-11, and eight for matching pillow. Use six remaining triangle-squares for coordinating tablecloth or embellished linens or discard.

3. Using diagonal-corner technique, make one each of units 1, 5, 6, 7, 9, 10, and 12 as shown in Section A of Section Assembly diagram.

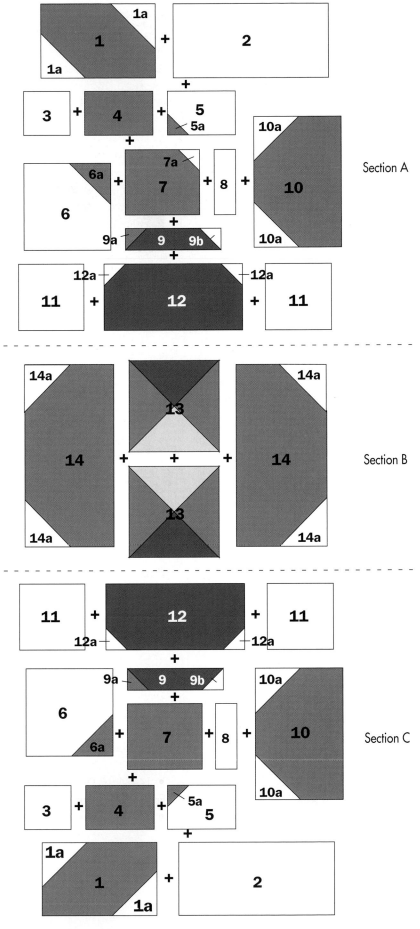

Section A

Section B

Section C

*Section Assembly*

**4.** To assemble Section A, begin by joining units 7 and 8. Add Unit 9 to bottom of combined units as shown. Join Unit 6 to left side of units 7 and 9. Join units 3, 4, and 5 in a row; then add row to top of combined 6-7-8-9 unit. Join Unit 10 to right side. Join units 1 and 2; then add this row to top. Join units 11 and 12 in a row as shown and add row to bottom of combined units to complete Section A. Make two of Section A for each block.

**5.** Using diagonal-corner technique, make two of Unit 14 for each Section B.

**6.** To assemble Section B, join two of Unit 13, positioning fabrics as shown in Section Assembly diagram. Join one of Unit 14 to each side of Unit 13 pair as shown to complete Section B. Make four of Section B for each block.

**7.** Section C is a mirror image of Section A. Using diagonal-corner technique, make one each of units 1, 5, 6, 7, 9, 10, and 12, being careful to position each corner as shown in Section Assembly diagram. Following diagram, assemble units for Section C in the same sequence as for Section A. Make two of Section C for each block.

**8.** Referring to color diagram of Block A to make center square, join a Unit 16 to opposite sides of Unit 15. Add Unit 17 to top and bottom to complete center square.

**9.** Referring to Block A Assembly diagram, join sections A, B, and C as shown for left side of block. Join one of each section in the same manner for

right side of block (this section is turned upside down when sections are joined). For middle section, join one of Section B to top and bottom of center square. Join three parts of block as shown in Assembly diagram.

**10.** Using diagonal-end technique, make two each of units 18 and 19, being careful to change angle of opposite ends on each unit as shown in Block A diagram. Add Unit 18 to top and bottom of block. Complete block by joining Unit 19 to sides. Make 30 Stained Glass Floral blocks.

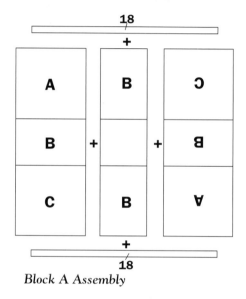

*Block A Assembly*

## Piecing the Scallops

**1.** To begin Block B, use diagonal-end technique to make one of Unit B-1 as shown in Scallop Assembly diagram.

**2.** Make one of Unit 2; then change angle of diagonal end to make a mirror image of Unit 2 as shown.

**3.** To prepare Unit 3, measure and mark a 1¾" square on wrong side of fabric at *bottom left corner* of half of the pieces. Draw a diagonal line through this square from lower right corner to upper left corner. On wrong side of remaining pieces, draw a 1¾" square at *bottom right corner*. Draw a diagonal line from lower left corner to upper right corner. Cut on these diagonal lines and discard trimmed triangle.

**4.** Using diagonal-corner technique, add 3a to each Unit 3 piece as shown in Scallop Assembly diagram, being careful to position corners correctly. For each Block B, make one of Unit 3 and one mirror image Unit 3.

**5.** To make Unit 4, join pieces 4 and 4a to make a square. Add diagonal corner 4b as shown, making two mirror-image units for each Block B.

**6.** Set two of Unit 5 aside for blocks D and E. On remaining Unit 5 pieces, mark a 1¼" square on one end. Draw diagonal lines through each square as described in Step 3. Trim Unit 5 pieces.

**7.** In the same manner, mark 1¼" squares on *two opposite corners* of 17 Unit 10 pieces as shown in Scallop Assembly diagram and trim. Add diagonal corners to remaining 17 Unit 10 pieces as shown.

**8.** Join a Unit 11 pair, positioning fabrics as shown. Add a trimmed Unit 10 to bottom of joined Unit 11 pair; then add a Unit 10 with corners to top.

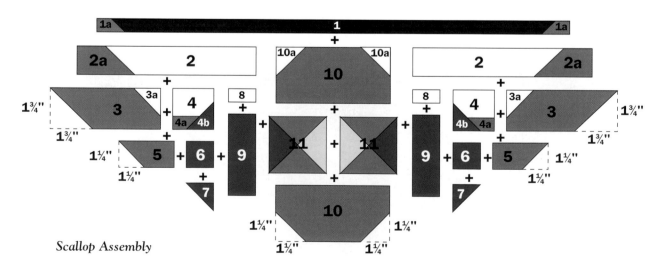

*Scallop Assembly*

**9.** To assemble left side of Block B, refer to Scallop Assembly diagram. Begin by joining square end of Unit 5 to Unit 6. Add Unit 7 to bottom of Unit 6. Join Unit 4 to square end of Unit 3 as shown; then join this to top of 5-6-7 unit as shown. Join Unit 8 to top of Unit 9 and add this to right side of combined units. Add Unit 2 to top.

**10.** Make right side of block in the same manner, using mirror-image units.

**11.** Join left and right sides of scallop to center section as shown. Add Unit B-1 to top to complete scallop. Make 12 of Block B.

**12.** For Block C, use diagonal-end technique to make Unit C-1 as shown. Repeat steps 2–11 to assemble Block C in the same manner as Block B, substituting Unit C-1. Make three of Block C.

**13.** To make one Block D scallop, assemble right side and center as for blocks B and C. For left side, add Unit 12 to an untrimmed Unit 5 as shown in Block D diagram; then continue to assemble left side as before. Join Unit 13 to left corner as shown to complete Block D.

**14.** Block E is a mirror image of Block D. Assemble center and left sections as for blocks B and C. For right side, add units 12 and 13 as described in Step 13. Make one Block E as shown.

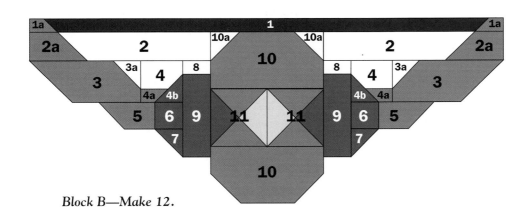

*Block B—Make 12.*

*Block C, Unit 1*

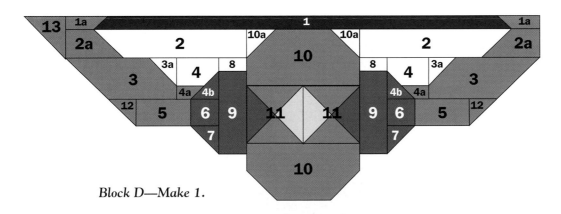

*Block D—Make 1.*

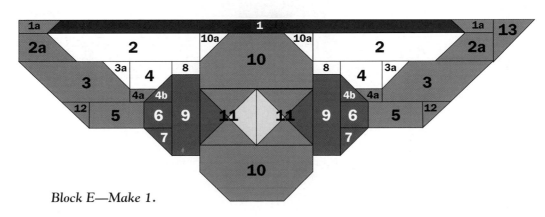

*Block E—Make 1.*

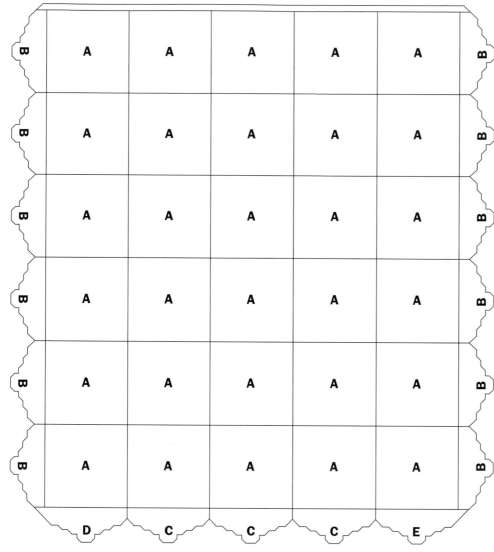

*Quilt Assembly*

## Quilt Assembly

**1.** Join A blocks in six horizontal rows of five blocks each. Join rows.

**2.** Referring to Quilt Assembly diagram, join six of Block B end-to-end to make a row for each quilt side. Join one row to each quilt side, matching corners at top and bottom.

**3.** Join three of Block C in the same manner for quilt bottom. Add Block D to left end of row and Block E to right end. Join row to bottom of quilt, matching corners.

**4.** Join three 1½"-wide strips of Fabric V end-to-end for top border. Trim 10" from each end. Matching centers of border and quilt top, join border to quilt. Referring to Quilt Assembly diagram, trim corners at same angle to match adjacent scallops.

## Quilting and Finishing

Outline-quilt patchwork or quilt as desired.

For bias binding, cut 34" square of Fabric V in half diagonally. Starting from cut edges, cut 2"-wide diagonal strips. Join strips end-to-end to make a continuous strip 14 yards long. Press strip in half with wrong sides facing, being careful not to stretch bias. Follow directions on page 30 for applying binding. Take special care to miter corners and angles around scalloped edge.

## Flanged Pillow

To make one pillow, you need additional yardage in the following quantities: ¼ yard of Fabric I, ⅛ yard each of fabrics III and IV, ¾ yard of Fabric V, and one 18" square each of muslin and batting.

**1.** From Fabric V, cut four 2¼" x 21" pieces for flange and two 12½" x 21" pieces for pillow back. Set these aside.

**2.** Cut pieces for one of Block A. Follow instructions given for quilt to assemble one block, using eight of Unit 13 left over from quilt top.

**3.** Sandwich batting between block (faceup) and muslin. Quilt pillow as desired; then trim batting and muslin even with block.

**4.** Join flange strips to top and bottom edges. Trim excess fabric even with sides of block. Join remaining strips to pillow sides.

**5.** See page 211 for instructions on making a lap-back finish with 12½" x 21" backing pieces. When backing is complete, topstitch in seam lines between block and flange strips through both layers.

**6.** Insert a custom-made or purchased 18"-square pillow form.

## Table Topper

To make one 38"-square table topper, you need additional yardage in the following quantities: ¾ yard each of fabrics I and III, ⅜ yard of Fabric IV, 2 yards of Fabric V (includes backing and binding), and a 42" square of batting.

**1.** For backing, cut a 42" square of Fabric V. For binding and borders, cut eight 2½" x 42" strips.

**2.** Cut two 15" x 21" pieces of Fabric III for quarter-square triangles. Using matching pieces of fabrics II and IV left over from quilt, mark and stitch grids as directed in Step 1 under Piecing the Blocks. Following instructions in Step 2, make 48 triangle-squares. Use 32 triangle-squares for table topper and set remaining squares aside for linens.

**3.** Cut pieces for four of Block A. Follow instructions given for quilt to assemble four blocks.

**4.** Join blocks in two rows of two blocks each; then join rows.

**5.** Add Fabric V border strips to opposite sides of assembled blocks. Press seam allowances toward borders and trim excess border fabric. Add borders to remaining sides in the same manner.

**6.** Quilt table topper as desired; then trim batting and backing even with block.

**7.** Join four remaining strips end-to-end to make 4⅜ yards of binding. See page 30 for directions on making and applying straight-grain binding.

## Embellished Linens

To embellish one queen-size sheet and two standard pillowcases, you need additional yardage in the following quantities: ¼ yard each of fabrics I and IV, ½ yard of Fabric III, ⅛ yard of Fabric V. If you have not already made quarter-square triangles as described in Table Topper Step 2, add ½ yard each of fabrics II, III, and IV.

**1.** If you have not already made the table topper, refer to Step 2 of those instructions to make quarter-square triangles. You need 16 triangle-squares.

**2.** For sheet, cut pieces for six of Block B. For each pillowcase, you will make one scallop that is a hybrid of blocks D and E—that is, the center section remains the same, but you will make the left side of Block D and the right side of Block E. Cut pieces for two of Block D/E hybrid for pillowcases.

**3.** For sheet, follow instructions given for quilt to assemble six B blocks.

**4.** Join blocks end-to-end in a row. Press under ¼" around scallop edge, clipping corners to seam line. Turn under ¼" along top edge and press.

**5.** Fold scallop border in half to find center. Find center of sheet in the same manner. Matching centers, pin border to top edge of sheet.

**6.** If border is longer than sheet, trim border to within ¼" of sheet sides. Press under ¼" on border ends and pin even with sheet sides.

**7.** Appliqué or topstitch border edges to sheet. Quilt in-the-ditch through border and sheet for extra stability.

**8.** For pillowcases, assemble left side and center of block, referring to diagram of Block D. For right side, refer to diagram of Block E. Make two blocks.

**9.** Turn and press raw edges of blocks as directed for sheet border. Appliqué or topstitch one block to side edge of each pillowcase. Quilt as above if desired.

# Which Came First?

*The chicken or the egg? Each gets equal credit in this charming picnic cloth, complete with napkins tucked into corner pockets. Strip-pieced borders frame eight whimsical hens and their eggs.*

---

**Quick-Piecing Techniques:**   Strip Piecing (see page 20)
Diagonal Corners (see page 20)
Diagonal Ends (see page 21)
Triangle-Squares (see page 22)

## Finished Size

Blocks:  8 chicken blocks, 9" x 18"
43 egg blocks, 2¼" x 3"

Cloth: 67½" x 68½" with
four 14"-square
napkins

## Materials

| | | |
|---|---|---|
| | Fabric I (blue solid) | 4⅜ yards |
| | Fabric II (gold-on-yellow print) | 2 yards |
| | Fabric III (black-on-red print) | 1¾ yards |
| | Fabric IV (white-on-white print) | 1⅜ yards |
| | Fabric V (brown-on-gold print) | ¼ yard |
| | Fabric VI (gold solid) | ⅛ yard |
| | Fabric VII (black solid) | ⅛ yard |
| | Backing fabric | 4¼ yards |

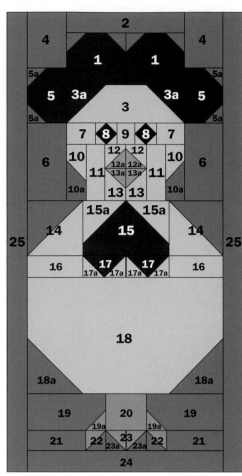

*Chicken Block—Make 8.*

## Cutting

### From Fabric I (blue), cut:
* One 15" x 42" strip.
  From this, cut:
  • One 15" x 29"; then cut this piece into twelve 1¼" x 29" strips (egg border sashing).
  • One 8" x 15" for triangle-squares (14).
  • One 5" x 8" for triangle-squares (22).
* Twenty-five 1¼" x 42" strips.
  From these, cut:
  • Eight 1¼" x 23" (egg border sashing).
  • Sixteen 1¼" x 18½" (25).
  • Eight 1¼" x 5" (2).
  • Eight 1¼" x 8" (24).
  • 252  1¼" squares (1a, 5a, 23a, 26a).
  • Sixteen 1¼" x 2" (10a).
  • Twenty-four 1¼" x 2¾" (21, 28).
* Three 2" x 42" strips.
  From these, cut:
  • Thirty-two 2" x 3½" (6, 19).

* Six 2¾" x 42" strips.
  From these, cut:
  • Sixteen 2" x 2¾" (4).
  • Sixteen 2¾" squares (18a).
  • Thirty-six 2¾" x 3½" (27).
  • Six 2⅜" x 2¾" (29).
* Eight 4½" x 35" strips for outer borders.
* Four 11" squares for corner pockets.
* Four 14" squares and four 9½" squares for napkins.

### From Fabric II (gold-on-yellow print), cut:
* Seven 4" x 42" strips for binding.
* Three 2¾" x 42" strips.
  From these, cut:
  • Forty 2¾" squares for sashing squares and napkin corners.
* Two 5" x 42" strips. From these, cut:
  • Eight 2" x 5" (3).
  • Eight 5" x 8" (18).
* Seven 1¼" x 42" strips.
  From these, cut:
  • Sixteen 1¼" x 1⅝" (7).
  • Forty 1¼" squares (9, 17a).
  • Sixteen 1¼" x 2" (10).
  • Thirty-two 1¼" x 2" (11, 16).
  • Sixteen 1¼" x 1½" (12).
  • Sixteen 1¼" x 1¾" (13).
* Two ⅞" x 42" strips.
  From these, cut:
  • Sixty-four ⅞" squares (8a).
* One 2" x 42" strip.
  From this, cut:
  • Sixteen 2" squares (15a).
* One 8" x 15" for triangle-squares (14).

### From Fabric III (black-on-red print), cut:
* Two 3" x 42" strips for pocket binding.
* Thirty-one 1¼" x 42" strips for strip-pieced sashing.
* Two 2¾" x 42" strips.
  From these, cut:
  • Sixteen 2¾" squares (1).
  • Eight 2¾" x 3½" (15).
* Three 2" x 42" strips.
  From these, cut:
  • Sixteen 2" squares (3a).
  • Sixteen 2" x 2¾" (5).
  • Sixteen 1¼" x 2" (17).

### From Fabric IV (white-on-white print), cut:
* Twenty-six 1¼" x 42" strips for strip-pieced sashing.
* Three 3½" x 42" strips.
  From these, cut:
  • Forty-three 2¾" x 3½" (26).

### From Fabric V (brown-on-gold print), cut:
* One 5" x 8" for triangle-squares (22).
* One 1¼" x 34" strip.
  From this, cut:
  • Sixteen 1¼" squares (19a).
* One 2" x 34" strip.
  From this, cut:
  • Eight 1¼" x 2" (23).
  • Eight 2" squares (20).

### From Fabric VI (gold), cut:
* One 1¼" x 42" strip.
  From this, cut:
  • Thirty-two 1¼" squares (12a, 13a).

### From Fabric VII (black), cut:
* One 1¼" x 42" strip.
  From this, cut:
  • Sixteen 1¼" squares (8).

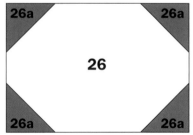

*Egg Block—Make 43.*

## Piecing the Blocks

**1.** Referring to Chicken Block Assembly diagram, use diagonal-corner technique to make two each of units 1, 5, 8, 12, 13, 17, and 19; then make one each of units 3, 15, 18, and 23. Use diagonal-end technique to make two of Unit 10.

**2.** To make Unit 14, see page 22 for instructions on triangle-squares. On wrong side of 8" x 15" piece of Fabric I, draw a 2 x 4-square grid of 3⅛" squares. With right sides facing, match marked fabric with 8" x 15" piece of Fabric II. Stitch grid as directed on page 22. Cut 16 triangle-squares from the grid, two for each block.

**3.** To make Unit 22, mark a 2 x 4-square grid of 1⅝" squares on wrong side of 5" x 8" piece of Fabric I. With right sides facing, match marked fabric with 5" x 8" piece of Fabric V. Stitch grid as directed on page 22. Cut 16 triangle-squares from the grid, two for each block.

**4.** To assemble Section A, begin by joining two of Unit 1 as shown in Block Assembly diagram. Join Unit 2 to top of Unit 1 as shown; then join Unit 3 to bottom. Join Unit 4 to Unit 5, positioning Unit 5 as shown, for each side of Section A. Join combined 4-5 units to sides to complete Section A.

**5.** To assemble Section B, begin by joining units 7, 8, and 9 in a row as shown. Join units 12 and 13; then add units 10 and 11 in a row. Join both rows. Complete Section B by adding one of Unit 6 to each side as shown.

**6.** To assemble Section C, join one of Unit 14 to each side of Unit 15. Join units 16 and 17 in a row as shown. Join rows to complete Section C.

**7.** To assemble Section E, join one of Unit 19 to each side of Unit 20 as shown. Join units 21, 22, and 23 in a row as shown. Join rows; then add Unit 24 at bottom.

**8.** Join sections A-E in order as shown in assembly diagram. Complete chicken block by adding a Unit 25 to each side.

**9.** Using diagonal-corner technique, make 43 egg blocks as shown.

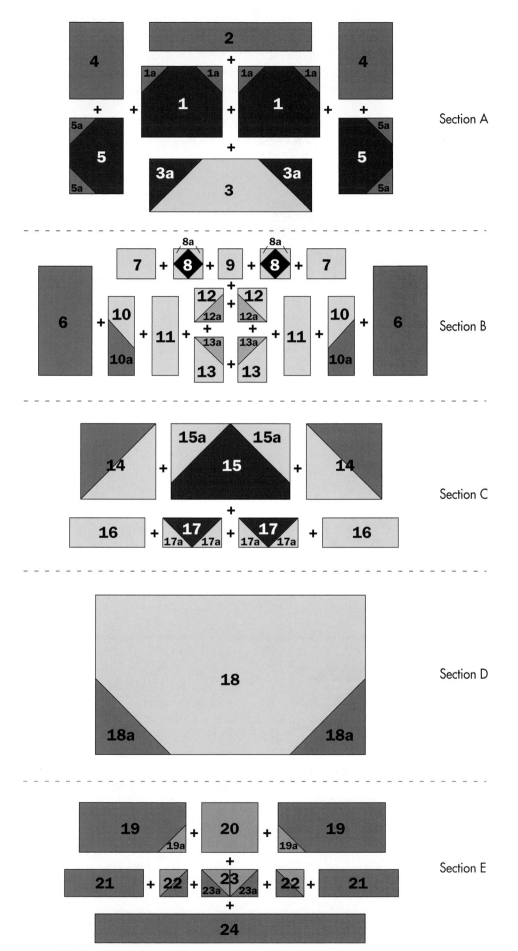

*Chicken Block Assembly*

## Strip-Pieced Sashing

See page 20 for general instructions on strip piecing. Save strip set remnants for napkin trim.

**1.** Referring to diagrams of strip sets A and B, join 1¼" x 42" strips of fabrics III and IV as shown. Press all seam allowances toward Fabric III.

**2.** Cut thirty-two 3½"-wide segments of Strip Set A and sixteen 3½"-wide segments of Strip Set B. Join segments as shown to make 16 of Sashing Unit 1.

**3.** Cut twenty 6½"-wide segments of Strip Set A and ten 6½"-wide segments of Strip Set B. Join segments as shown to make 10 of Unit 2, adding yellow sashing squares to both ends of each unit.

**4.** Stitch one of Sashing Unit 1 to top and bottom edges of each chicken block.

**5.** Referring to quilt photograph, join four chicken blocks in a row with Unit 2 sashing strips between them and at both ends of row. Repeat to make second row of chicken blocks.

**6.** Cut sixteen 4¼"-wide segments of Strip Set A and fourteen 4¼"-wide segments of Strip Set B. Join segments as shown to make two of Sashing Unit 3.

**7.** Cut ten 5" segments and two 5⅜" segments from each strip set. Join segments as shown to make two of Sashing Unit 4, adding yellow corner squares to ends of each unit. Set aside sashing units 3 and 4 until egg border is added.

## Egg Borders

**1.** Referring to border diagram, join four egg blocks and three of Unit 27 as shown. Add a Unit 28 at both ends of row. Make four rows. Press seam allowances away from egg blocks.

**2.** Add 1¼" x 23" Fabric I sashing strips to long sides of each egg row.

**3.** For long egg borders, join nine egg blocks and eight of Unit 27 in a row in the same manner. Add Unit 29 pieces to ends of each row. Assemble three rows. Piece two 29" Fabric I sashing strips end-to-end to make sashing for long sides of each row. Matching centers, join sashing strips to egg rows. Trim excess sashing fabric from ends.

**4.** Join shorter egg rows to ends of chicken rows. Adjust border seams as necessary to make border ends align with ends of chicken blocks.

**5.** Join a long egg border to top of each chicken row, aligning ends. Add remaining border to bottom of one row.

**6.** Position rows as shown in photograph and join.

## Quilt Assembly

**1.** Join Sashing Unit 3 to opposite sides of cloth. Then join Sashing Unit 4 to remaining edges.

**2.** Join pairs of outer border strips end-to-end to make four border strips.

**3.** Mark center of each quilt side. Matching centers, join borders to top and bottom edges of quilt. Press seam allowances toward borders; then trim excess fabric from both ends of borders. Add side borders in the same manner.

## Quilting

Outline-quilt patchwork and borders or quilt as desired. Trim batting and backing even with quilt top.

## Corner Pockets

**1.** With wrong sides facing, fold each 11" square in half diagonally. Baste raw edges together.

**2.** With wrong sides facing, press Fabric III binding strips in half lengthwise. Cut 17" of binding for each pocket.

**3.** With right sides facing and raw edges aligned, stitch binding to each triangle's diagonal edge. Turn binding over to wrong side of triangle and top-stitch. Trim excess binding at ends.

**4.** Matching raw edges at corners, baste triangles to quilt top.

## Finishing

Make 7⅞ yards of straight-grain binding. See page 30 for directions on making and applying binding.

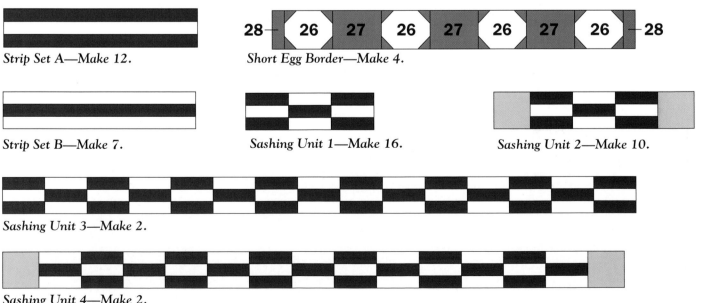

*Strip Set A—Make 12.*

*Short Egg Border—Make 4.*

*Strip Set B—Make 7.*

*Sashing Unit 1—Make 16.*

*Sashing Unit 2—Make 10.*

*Sashing Unit 3—Make 2.*

*Sashing Unit 4—Make 2.*

## Napkins

1. Cut thirty-two 2¾"-wide segments from remainder of Strip Set A and sixteen 2¾"-wide segments from Strip Set B.

2. Join segments in rows of three, placing one B segment between two A segments. Make 16 rows. Add a yellow corner square to both ends of eight rows.

3. With right sides facing, join short sashing rows to opposite sides of each 9½" napkin square. Add long sashing rows to remaining sides.

4. With right sides facing, match each pieced napkin to a 14" napkin square. Stitch around all sides, leaving a 4" opening in one side for turning. Turn napkin right side out; slipstitch opening closed.

5. By hand or machine, quilt in-the-ditch on patchwork seam lines.

*Napkin—Make 4.*

# Stars & Stripes

*Strip-pieced stripes and stars of half-square triangles create an All-American wall hanging or table cover. In red, white, and blue, it makes a patriotic statement, but this design works just as well in other color combinations.*

**Quick-Piecing Techniques:** Strip Piecing (see page 20)
Triangle-Squares (see page 22)

### Finished Size
Blocks: 40 blocks, 6" square          Wall Hanging: 60" x 60"

### Materials

| | | |
|---|---|---|
| | Fabric I (navy solid) | 1½ yards |
| | Fabric II (muslin) | 2⅛ yards |
| | Fabric III (barn red solid) | 1⅛ yards |
| | Fabric IV (black-on-red textured-look print) | 1¾ yards |
| | Backing fabric | 3¾ yards |

### Cutting
Refer to diagrams on page 228 to identify blocks and units designated in cutting list.

**From Fabric I (navy), cut:**
* Two 14" x 42" strips.
  From these, cut:
  • Four 14" x 21" for triangle-squares (1).
* Eight 2" x 42" strips. From these, cut:
  • 156  2" squares (3).
* One 2½" x 42" strip. From this, cut:
  • Four 2½" x 9½" (4).

**From Fabric II (muslin), cut:**
* Two 14" x 42" strips.
  From these, cut:
  • Four 14" x 21" for triangle-squares (1).
* Four 3½" x 42" strips.
  From these, cut:
  • Forty 3½" squares (2).
* Eighteen 1⅜" x 42" strips for strip sets.

**From Fabric III (barn red), cut:**
* Twenty-six 1⅜" x 42" strips for strip sets.

**From Fabric IV (black-on-red textured print), cut:**
* Eight 2½" x 42" strips for borders.
* Six 3" x 42" strips for binding.
* One 4½" x 42" strip.
  From this, cut:
  • Eight 4½" squares (7).
* Two 6½" x 42" strips.
  From these, cut:
  • Eight 6½" squares (8).
  • Two 2½" x 29" strips.
    From these, cut:
    • Four 2½" x 4" (6).
    • Four 2" x 2½" (5).
    • Four 2" squares (3a).

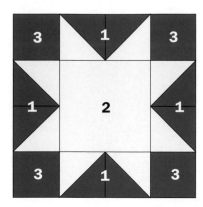

Block A—Make 36.

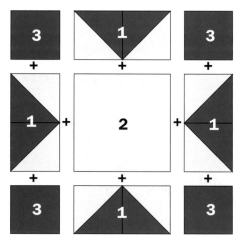

Block B—Make 4.

## Piecing the Star Blocks

**1.** See page 22 for instructions on triangle-squares. On wrong side of each 14" x 21" piece of Fabric II, draw a 5 x 8-square grid of 2⅜" squares. With right sides facing, match each marked fabric with 14" x 21" piece of Fabric I. Stitch each grid as directed on page 22. Cut 80 triangle-squares from each grid (320 total).

**2.** To make Unit 1, join all triangle-squares in pairs, positioning the dark triangles in the center of each pair.

**3.** Referring to Block A Assembly diagram, add a Unit 1 to opposite sides of Unit 2. Press seam allowances toward Unit 2.

**4.** Join a Unit 3 square to both ends of each remaining Unit 1. Press seam allowances toward Unit 3. Join units to top and bottom of center section.

**5.** Make Block B in the same manner as Block A, substituting a red Unit 3a in one corner as shown in Block B diagram.

## Center Section Assembly

**1.** Referring to Center Section Assembly diagram, join four of Block B, positioning red corners as shown.

**2.** Join a Unit 5 to each end of two Unit 4 strips. Press seam allowances toward Unit 4. Join units to top and bottom of 4-star center section.

**3.** Join Units 4 and 6 as shown. Press seam allowances toward Unit 4. Join units to sides of center section.

## Strip Piecing

Referring to strip set diagrams, join 1⅜"-wide strips of Fabrics II and IV as shown to make Strip Set 1 and Strip Set 2. Use a generous ¼" seam so that Strip Set 1 measures 4½" wide and Strip Set 2 measures 6½" wide. Adjust seams as necessary to achieve desired widths.

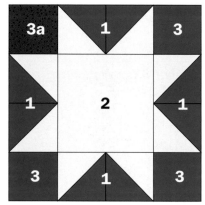

Block A Assembly

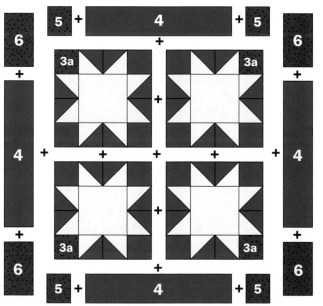

Center Section Assembly

Strip Set 1—Make 6.

Strip Set 2—Make 2.

*Quilt Assembly*

## Quilt Assembly

Refer to Quilt Assembly diagram throughout assembly.

**1.** Determine length of one side of center section. From two of Strip Set 1, cut four pieces equal to that length. If all four sides are not equal, cut these strip set pieces equal to the measurement of the *shortest* side.

**2.** Join trimmed strip sets to top and bottom edges of center section, referring to page 19 for tips on easing.

**3.** Join a Unit 7 to each end of two remaining trimmed strip-set pieces. Join these units to sides of center section.

**4.** Join remaining star blocks in rows, making four rows of four blocks each and four rows of five blocks each.

**5.** Join four-star rows to top and bottom edges of quilt.

**6.** Join a Unit 8 to each end of remaining four-star rows. Join these rows to quilt sides.

**7.** Measure quilt sides as in Step 1. From remaining Strip Set 1 units, cut four strips to needed length. Join trimmed strip sets to top and bottom edges of quilt. Add a Unit 7 to each end of remaining strips. Join these strips to quilt sides.

**8.** Cut each Strip Set 2 in half. Join each segment to one end of a five-star row. Compare rows to sides of quilt and trim strip-set end to match quilt. Join trimmed strips to top and bottom edges of quilt.

**9.** Add a Unit 8 to each end of remaining rows. Join rows to quilt sides.

**10.** Join border strips in pairs end-to-end. Measuring from center of each strip, cut two 2½" x 58" borders and two 2½" x 62" borders. Matching centers of borders and quilt, join shorter borders to top and bottom edges; then trim ends of border to match quilt sides. Add remaining borders to quilt sides in the same manner.

## Quilting and Finishing

Outline-quilt patchwork or quilt as desired. Purchased stencils were used to mark 4" stars in Units 7 and 8.

Make 7 yards of binding. See page 30 for directions on making and applying straight-grain binding.

# Friends

This charming quilt gives your little girl 23 dolls to sleep with, and she'll love naming each new friend. The diagonal-corner technique makes the dolls quick to sew. You'll enjoy creating individual outfits for each doll with scraps of fabric, ribbon, and lace. The hair is made from knotted strips of torn muslin—it's easy and it's fun! The quilt pictured has buttons for added whimsy, but parents should consider safety when choosing embellishments. To make one more friend, see page 236 for patterns and instructions for the Best Friend Doll.

**Quick-Piecing Techniques:** Diagonal Corners (see page 20)

## Finished Size
Blocks: 18 doll blocks, 12" x 18"          Quilt: 65" x 101"
         5 doll blocks, 12" x 24"
         4 heart blocks, 9½" square

## Materials

|   | | |
|---|---|---|
| Fabric I (muslin or other flesh color) | ¾ yard |
| Fabric II (pink-and-blue marbled-look print) | 2 yards |
| Fabric III (solid dark pink) | 1½ yards |
| Fabric IV (solid medium pink) | 1½ yards |
| Fabric V (burgundy print) | 2 yards |
| Fabric VI (scraps of 30 assorted pink and blue fabrics) | ¼ yard each |
| Heavy unbleached muslin for hair bows | ¾ yard |
| Backing fabric | 6 yards |
| Assorted buttons | |
| Assorted scraps of lace and ribbon trims | |
| Brown, red, and black fine-tipped fabric markers | |

## Cutting

### From Fabric I (muslin), cut:

✱ Three 5" x 42" strips.
 From these, cut:
 • Twenty-three 4½" x 5" (A-1, B-1, C-1).

✱ Two 1⅞" x 42" strips.
 From these, cut:
 • Forty-six 1⅝" x 1⅞" (A-7, B-7, C-7).

✱ One 2½" x 42" strip.
 From this, cut:
 • Twenty-three 1¾" x 2½" (A-12, B-12, C-12).
  *Note:* Leg color is optional. To make tights for some dolls, substitute ticking scraps for some of these pieces.

### From Fabric II (pink-and-blue print), cut:

✱ Eight 1" x 42" strips for middle borders.
 From four of these, cut:
 • Four 1" x 32¾".
 • Four 1" x 9".

✱ Two 13" x 42" strips.
 From these, cut:
 • Four 13" squares. Cut each square in half diagonally to get eight triangles for quilt corners.
 • Five 4⅞" squares. Cut each square in half diagonally to get 10 triangles (A-9).
 • Five 3⅞" squares. Cut each square in half diagonally to get 10 triangles (A-10).

✱ One 12½" x 42" strip.
 From this, cut:
 • Five 4¼" x 12½" (A-19).
 • Five 2¾" x 12½" (A-20).

✱ Two 1¾" x 42" strips.
 From these, cut:
 • Forty 1¾" squares (A-1a, A-11a).
 • Ten 1" x 1¾" (A-13).

✱ One 4½" x 42½" strip.
 From this, cut:
 • Ten 4¼" x 4½" (A-2).

✱ Three 2½" x 42" strips.
 From these, cut:
 • Ten 2½" x 9½" (A-18).
 • Ten 1½" x 2" (A-17).
 • Ten ⅞" x 1⅞" (A-8).

✱ From strip scraps, cut:
 • Ten 3" x 3¼" (A-15).
 • Thirty 1" squares (A-16a).

### From Fabric III (dark pink), cut:

✱ Three 1¾" x 42" strips.
 From these, cut:
 • Seventy-two 1¾" squares (B-1a, B-11a).

✱ Two 4⅞" x 42" strips.
 From these, cut:
 • Nine 4⅞" squares. Cut each square in half diagonally to get 18 triangles (B-9).
 • Nine 3⅞" squares. Cut each square in half diagonally to get 18 triangles (B-10).

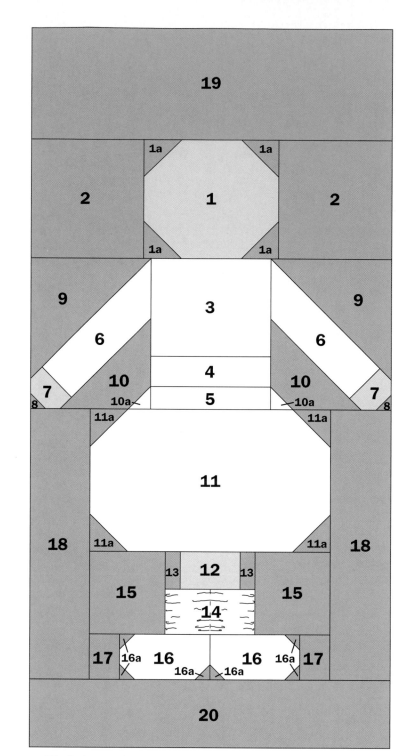

*Block A—Make 5.*

* Two 4½" x 42" strips.
  From these, cut:
  • Eighteen 4¼" x 4½" (B-2).
* Three 1" x 42" strips.
  From these, cut:
  • Eighteen 1" x 1¾" (B-13).
  • Eighteen 1" squares (B-16a).
  • Eighteen 1" x 1½" (B-17a).
* Two 3" x 42" strips.
  From these, cut:
  • Eighteen 3" x 3¼" (B-15).
  • Eighteen ⅞" x 1⅞" (B-8).
* Four 2½" x 42½" strips.
  From these, cut:
  • Eighteen 2½" x 8½" (B-18a).

**From Fabric IV (medium pink), cut:**

* Three 1¾" x 42" strips.
  From these, cut:
  • Seventy-two 1¾" squares (C-1a, C-11a).
* Two 4½" x 42" strips.
  From these, cut:
  • Eighteen 4¼" x 4½" (C-2).
* Two 4⅞" x 42" strips.
  From these, cut:
  • Nine 4⅞" squares. Cut each square in half diagonally to get 18 triangles (C-9).
  • Nine 3⅞" squares. Cut each square in half diagonally to get 18 triangles (C-10).
* Three 1" x 42" strips.
  From these, cut:
  • Eighteen 1" x 1¾" (C-13).
  • Eighteen 1" squares (C-16a).
  • Eighteen 1" x 1½" (C-17a).
* Two 3" x 42" strips.
  From these, cut:
  • Eighteen 3" x 3¼" (C-15).
  • Eighteen ⅞" x 1⅞" (C-8).
* Four 2½" x 42½" strips.
  From these, cut:
  • Eighteen 2½" x 8½" (C-18a).

**From Fabric V (burgundy print), cut:**

* Two 6¼" x 42" strips.
  From these, cut:
  • Four 6¼" squares (21).
  • Eight 4¼" x 6¼" (22).
* Eight 3" x 42" strips for binding.

* From strip scraps, cut:
  • Seventy-two 1" squares (B-16b, C-16b).
* Twenty 1½" x 42" strips.
  From 14 of these, cut:
  • Two 1½" x 27" and four 1½" x 31½" for inner border.
  • Two 1½" x 18" and four 1½" x 13½" for outer border.
  • Eight 1½" x 14½" for corner borders.
  • Thirty-six 1½" x 2½" (B-18b, C-18b).
  • Thirty-six 1½" squares (B-17b, C-17b).

**From assorted Fabric VI scraps, cut the following pieces for *each* doll block:**

* One 5¼" x 8½" (11-skirt).*
* One 1¼" x 4½" (5-skirt top).*
* Two 1¼" squares (10a-skirt top sides).*
* One 1½" x 4½" (4-belt).
* One 3¾" x 4½" (3-blouse).
* Two 1⅞" x 5½" (6-sleeves).
* One 3½" square (14-socks).
* Two 2" x 3½" (16-shoes).

*Note:* Cut units 5, 10a, and 11 from same fabric to give uniform appearance to skirt. Mix and match other fabrics as desired.

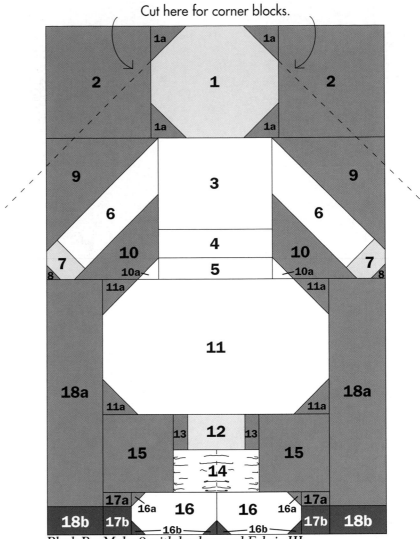

Block B—Make 9 with background Fabric III.
Block C—Make 9 with background Fabric IV.

## Piecing the Doll Blocks

**1.** Center face pieces (Unit 1) over full-size face pattern on page 238, leaving ¼" seam allowance extending on all sides. Using pen color indicated on pattern, trace face details onto each piece. Add red dots for freckles if desired. Let ink dry before piecing Unit 1.

**2.** Referring to Block A Assembly diagram, use diagonal-corner technique to make one each of units 1, 11, and 16.

**3.** For each arm, join units 6, 7, and 8 in a row as shown in Block A Assembly diagram.

**4.** Referring to Arm Assembly diagram, add Unit 9 to left side of one arm, placing triangle at top of arm so that tip overlaps arm top ¼" as shown. Press triangle open. Aligning ruler with top edge of triangle, trim arm top at a 45° angle as shown. Next, align ruler with left edge of triangle to trim bottom of unit. Join Unit 10 to right side of arm with tip overlapping arm top ¼" as before. Press triangle open; then align ruler with triangle edge to trim bottom of hand as shown. Trim triangle tips from seam allowances. Add diagonal corner 10a as shown in Block A Assembly diagram to complete arm unit.

**5.** Make right arm unit in the same manner, reversing triangle positions to make a mirror-image unit.

**6.** Run a gathering stitch down sides of each Unit 14 piece. Gather sides to reduce height to 2". Topstitch sides and center to secure gathers.

**7.** To assemble Section A, join one of Unit 2 to opposite sides of each Unit 1 as shown in Block A Assembly diagram.

**8.** To assemble Section B, begin by joining units 3, 4, and 5 in a row as shown. Join arm units to sides, making sure that arm tops match at blouse shoulders.

**9.** To assemble Section C, begin by joining one of Unit 13 to both sides of Unit 12. Add Unit 14 to bottom of this unit as shown. Join one of Unit 15 to each side of combined unit. Join two of Unit 16 as shown; then add one of Unit 17 to each end of row. Join this row to bottom of assembled units 14 and 15. Join Unit 11 to top; then add one of Unit 18 to each side as shown.

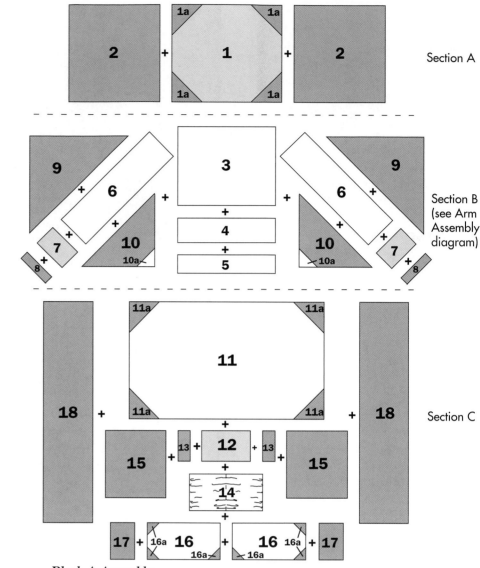

Section A

Section B (see Arm Assembly diagram)

Section C

*Block A Assembly*

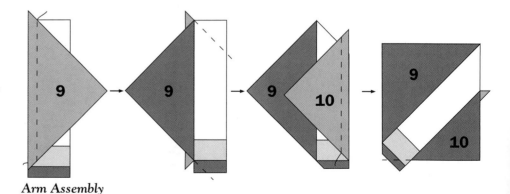

*Arm Assembly*

**10.** Join sections A, B, and C. Complete Block A by adding Unit 19 to top and Unit 20 to bottom. Make five of Block A.

**11.** To make blocks B and C, follow steps 1 through 8 above. Note that Unit 16 has two colors of diagonal corners in these blocks. For units 17 and 18, join a and b parts to make a complete unit; then follow Step 9 above to assemble Section C. Join sections. In this manner, make nine of Block B and nine of Block C.

## Piecing the Corner Heart Blocks

**1.** Referring to Block D diagram, join one of Unit 22 to adjacent sides of each Unit 21 as shown, stopping stitching ¼" from inner corner of heart.

**2.** On wrong side of each Unit 22 piece, measure and mark 2" on both sides of each corner. Draw a diagonal line connecting these points. Trim each corner on diagonal line as shown.

## Quilt Assembly

**1.** Referring to quilt photograph, join five A blocks in a row, turning blocks 2 and 4 upside down as shown. Match seams carefully so dolls' hands align.

**2.** Join two 1½" x 31½" strips of Fabric V end-to-end for each side border. Matching centers of block row and borders, sew border to each long side of center section. Press seam allowances toward borders. Join 1½" x 27" strips of Fabric V to each short side to complete center section.

**3.** Referring to photo, join six doll blocks for each long side of quilt, alternating B and C blocks and matching Fabric V at feet. Join three blocks for each short side in the same manner.

**4.** Blocks at both ends of each row must be mitered for corners. Referring to Block B/C diagram, pick out stitching to remove top 1a triangle from head on appropriate outside edge. Press exposed seam allowance flat; then align ruler with raw edge. Trim units 2 and 9 on that side as shown.

**5.** Join 1½" x 14½" strips of Fabric V to one straight leg of each 13" corner triangle of Fabric II. Strips are longer than triangle sides. Referring to Corner Assembly diagram, join one triangle to each mitered block, aligning Fabric V strip at bottom. Align ruler with mitered edge of block to trim triangle and Fabric V strip as shown.

**6.** Join three-block rows to short sides of quilt, beginning and ending stitching ¼" from row ends. Join six-block rows to long sides of quilt in the same manner.

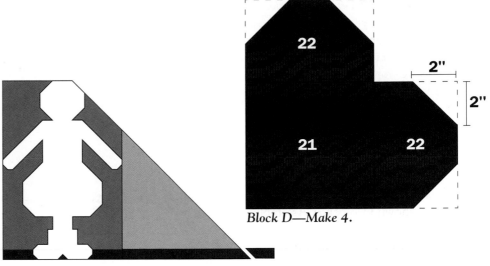

Block D—Make 4.

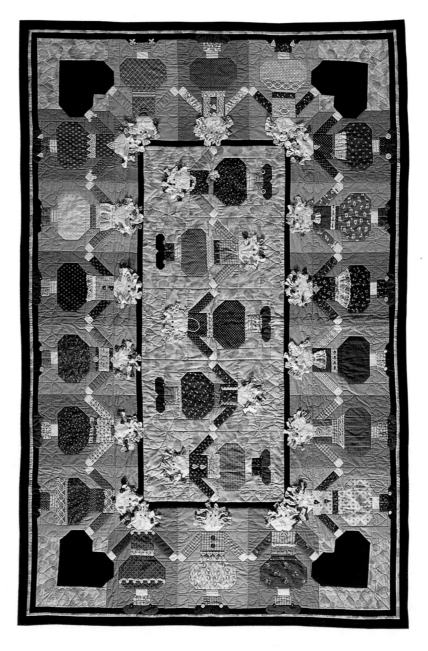

Corner Assembly

**7.** With right sides facing, pin corners together, matching triangles and borders. Beginning at corner of inner border, stitch each mitered seam. Press seam allowances to one side.

**8.** Turn under ¼" on all edges of each heart block and press. Center a heart on each corner so that top of heart meets dolls' hands. Heart cleft and bottom point should align with mitered seam. Hand-appliqué hearts in place.

**9.** For Fabric II borders, join two 42"-long strips end-to-end; then add a 9" strip to both ends to make a 101"-long border for each side. Join two 1" x 32¾" strips to make a 65" border for each end. Matching centers, join long borders to quilt sides. Press seam allowances toward border and trim excess border fabric. Join short borders to remaining sides in the same manner.

**10.** For outer border, join a 1½" x 42" strip of Fabric V to both ends of an 18"-long strip to make a 101" border for each quilt side. Join these to long sides of quilt as before. Next, join 13½" strips to both ends of a 42" strip to make a 68"-long border for each end. Join these to remaining quilt sides.

## Quilting and Finishing

**1.** Mark quilting designs on quilt top as desired, using homemade or purchased stencils. The quilt shown has small hearts quilted at block corners and large hearts quilted in heart blocks.

**2.** Quilt a line down center of legs and socks. Quilt marked designs. Outline-quilt patchwork and corner hearts.

**3.** Make 9¾ yards of binding. See page 30 for directions on making and applying straight-grain binding.

**4.** Tear heavy muslin into twenty-three 1" x 42" strips; then tear each strip into 4½" pieces. Tear 4½" pieces of scrap dress fabrics. Tie a tight knot in center of each piece. Trim excess threads. Scatter bows on each doll's head as desired and hand-tack securely in place.

**5.** Embellish dresses with scraps of ribbon and lace. Add buttons as desired. Buttons should not be used on quilts intended for very young children.

# Best Friend Doll

*This best friend will go everywhere with the little girl who loves her and chooses her special name. This easy-to-make doll is the finishing touch to the Friends quilt or an ideal gift for any occasion. You can make her from scrap fabrics, but you'll find yardage for purchased materials below.*

## Finished Size
Approximately 21" tall

## Materials

| | |
|---|---|
| Fabric I (muslin or other flesh color) | ⅜ yard |
| Fabric II (dark slate blue) | ⅛ yard |
| Fabric III (light cranberry print) | ⅜ yard |
| Fabric IV (slate blue mini-dot) | ¼ yard |
| Fabric V (blue-on-ivory stripe or ticking) | ⅛ yard |
| Fabric VI (white solid) | ¼ yard |
| ¼"-wide ecru lace trim | 2 yards |
| 2"-wide lace trim with fabric center strip | ⅜ yard |
| Two ⅞"-diameter decorative buttons | |
| One ⅝"-diameter ribbon rose | |
| Brown, red, and black fine-tipped fabric markers | |
| Template material | |
| Polyester filling | |

**4.** Clip curves and corners to seam line; then trim seam allowance to ⅛". Turn head/body right side out.

**5.** Turn under ¼" around each armhole and at bottom edge. Press hems and topstitch.

**6.** With right sides facing and straight edges aligned, join a hand to one end of each arm piece. With right sides facing, join two arms, leaving top open. Turn arm to right side; then stuff to within 2" of top. Baste arm top where stuffing stops to secure stuffing. Repeat to make second arm.

**7.** Slip arm seam allowances into body armholes. Topstitch arms in place.

**8.** Stuff head and body firmly to within ½" of bottom. Baste bottom edges together loosely to keep stuffing from falling out.

**9.** With right sides facing, join long edges of two leg pieces to make a tube. Repeat to make second leg. Do not turn tubes yet.

**10.** With right sides facing, join two shoe pieces, leaving top open. Turn shoe right side out. Repeat to make second shoe.

**11.** With right sides facing, fold one sock piece in half widthwise and join short edges to make a tube. Turn sock right side out. With wrong sides facing, fold sock in half so that raw edges align, making a tube of double thickness. Press folded edge. Repeat to make second sock.

**12.** Place a shoe inside one sock, with raw edges aligned and back seam of shoe matching sock seam. (Sock will be larger, so fold a few small pleats to make edges match.) With raw edges aligned and sock/shoe seam matching one leg seam, place sock/shoe inside one leg. Pin or baste all layers; then machine-stitch around raw edges. Turn leg right side out. Repeat to complete second leg.

**13.** Stuff legs to within 2" of top. Baste leg tops to secure stuffing.

**14.** Loosen body basting enough to insert legs. Pin or baste legs in place. Topstitch across body bottom through all layers, securing legs.

## Cutting

For head/body, hands, and shoes, make templates from patterns on page 238 and 239.

**From Fabric I (muslin or flesh), cut:**
✳ Two head/bodies.
✳ Four hands.
✳ Four 3" x 5" for arms.

**From Fabric II (dark slate blue), cut:**
✳ Four shoes.

**From Fabric III (cranberry print), cut:**
✳ One 6½" x 16" for skirt.
✳ Two 6" x 9" for blouse.
♦ Two 6" x 7½" for socks.

**From Fabric IV (blue mini-dot), cut:**
✳ Two 5¼" x 9" for sleeves.
✳ One 5" x 8" for apron.

**From Fabric V (stripe), cut:**
✳ Four 3" x 6" for tights.
(For natural-colored legs, cut these pieces from Fabric I.)

**From Fabric VI (white), cut:**
✳ One 7" x 16" for petticoat.

## Doll Body Assembly

**1.** Center one head piece over full-size pattern on page 238. Using pen color indicated on pattern, trace face details onto muslin. Let ink dry.

**2.** With right sides facing, join heads by stitching from dot to dot around shoulders and head. Backstitch.

**3.** On each side of body, begin stitching again 3" below shoulder dot and stitch to bottom edge. Backstitch at beginning and end of each seam.

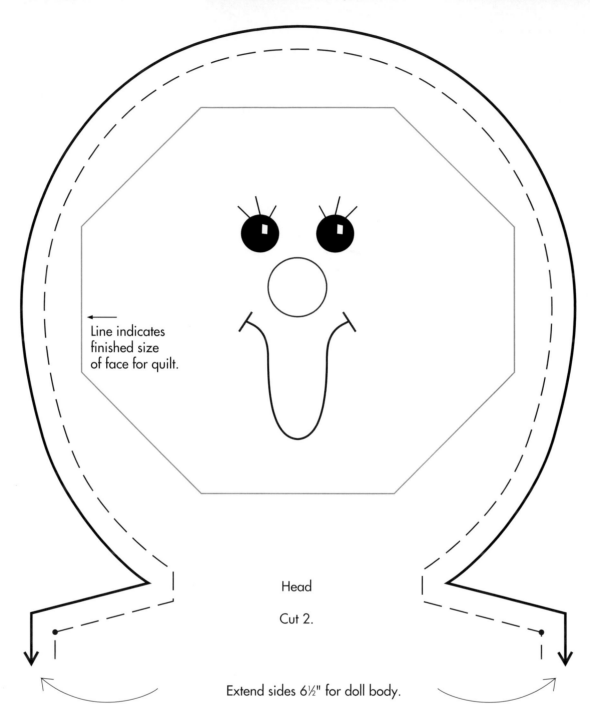

Line indicates finished size of face for quilt.

Head

Cut 2.

Extend sides 6½" for doll body.

**15.** Pull socks down a little to cover leg/shoe seam lines, giving socks a rumpled look. Sew buttons to top front of shoes. Remove any visible basting stitches.

## Making Doll Hair

Tear scraps of fabrics I, III, and IV into 1"-wide strips. Tear strips into 5"-long pieces. Tie knots in center of each piece. Clip raveled threads. Tack bows to doll's head, mixing colored bows with muslin bows evenly. Cover head back, top, and around face with bows.

## Doll Dress Assembly

**1.** With right sides facing, join short sides of petticoat. Turn right side out. To hem, turn under ¼" on one long edge; then turn under ¼" again and press. Position ¼" lace trim on top of hem and topstitch, securing hem.
**2.** Turn under ¼" hem at top edge of petticoat and gather. Slip petticoat onto doll and pull gathers to fit waist. Secure gathers and hand-tack petticoat to body.
**3.** To make neck and back opening, fold one blouse piece in half lengthwise and then crosswise, creasing to mark

center. On wrong side of fabric, align a ruler with crosswise crease and draw a 2¾"-long line (1⅜" on each side of center point) as shown in Blouse Facing diagram. Next, draw a line on lengthwise crease from center point to bottom edge as shown. Put both blouse pieces together with right sides facing and stitch ¼" from drawn lines. Cut through both layers on marked lines and clip corners as indicated in red.
**4.** Turn blouse right side out and press. Hand-sew ¼" lace trim around neck edge and down one side of back opening.

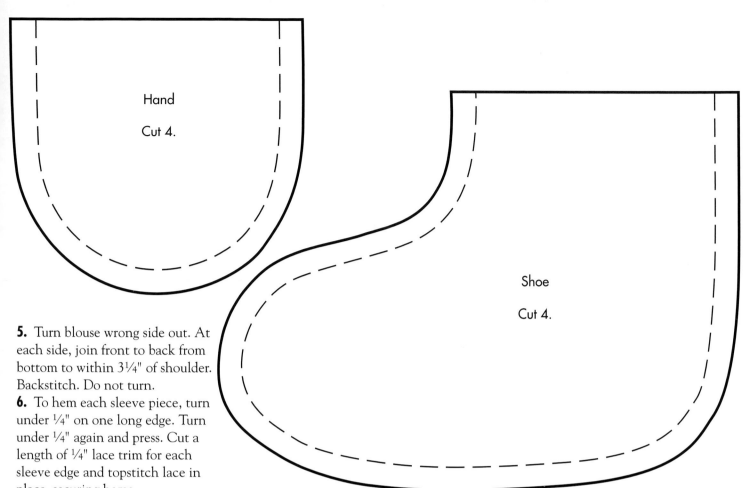

Hand

Cut 4.

Shoe

Cut 4.

**5.** Turn blouse wrong side out. At each side, join front to back from bottom to within 3¼" of shoulder. Backstitch. Do not turn.

**6.** To hem each sleeve piece, turn under ¼" on one long edge. Turn under ¼" again and press. Cut a length of ¼" lace trim for each sleeve edge and topstitch lace in place, securing hems.

**7.** With right sides facing, fold each sleeve in half and join short ends to make a tube. Turn right side out. Gather top edge to measure 6¼". With right sides facing, insert gathered end of each sleeve into blouse armhole, adjusting gathers to fit. Stitch sleeves to blouse.

**8.** Turn blouse right side out. Tack ribbon rose to center front at neckline.

**9.** To make skirt, join short sides of skirt piece with right sides facing, starting at one edge and stopping 3" from opposite edge. Backstitch. Press under seam allowance on both sides of 3" opening. Topstitch edges of opening.

**10.** Turn under ¼" at skirt bottom; then turn under ½" and press. Slipstitch hem. Gather skirt top to fit bottom of blouse. With right sides facing, join skirt to blouse, matching back openings.

**11.** Gather bottom of each sleeve ½" from top of lace trim. Put dress on doll. Pull sleeve gathers tight around arm and secure gathers. Slipstitch edges of dress back together, allowing back lace trim to cover stitches.

**12.** Turn under ¼" along one long edge of apron and both short sides. Press; then turn under another ¼" on all three sides. Topstitch side hems. Cut a length of ¼" lace trim to fit bottom edge, turning ends of lace over sides to back. Topstitch lace, securing bottom hem. Gather top edge of apron to 5½".

**13.** Cut a length of 2"-wide lace trim to fit around doll's waist, overlapping ½" in back. Center waistband on gathered apron top and topstitch. Turn under ¼" on one end of trim.

**14.** Put apron on doll, pinning waistband around waist.

**15.** To make apron shoulder straps, cut two 8" lengths of ¼" lace trim. Tack one end of each piece inside apron waistband at front about 2½" apart. Turn lace over shoulders and tack remaining ends inside waistband at back. Tack apron waistband to dress. Overlap waistband ends at back and tack to secure.

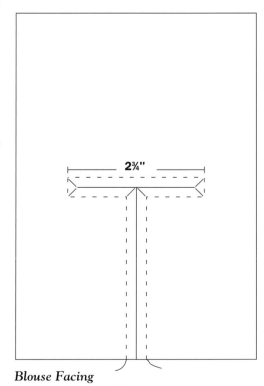

2¾"

*Blouse Facing*

# Black-Eyed Susan

*A humble flower becomes a masterpiece in this easy-to-sew design. The appliquéd leaves are an elegant touch to a quilt that assembles in no time with basic patchwork techniques and strip piecing. Use scraps to make accessory pillows for an ensemble that's bright as sunshine.*

**Quick-Piecing Techniques:** Strip Piecing (see page 20)
Diagonal Corners (see page 20)

## Finished Size
Blocks: 17 blocks, 12" square
4 corner blocks, 15½" square

Quilt: 83½" x 104½"

## Materials

| | | |
|---|---|---|
| | Fabric I (white-on-white print) | 4 yards |
| | Fabric II (yellow-on-black print) | 2¼ yards |
| | Fabric III (black mini-print) | 1 yard |
| | Fabric IV (yellow solid) | 3⅝ yards |
| | Fabric V (green mini-print) | 1 yard |
| | Backing fabric | 6 yards |
| | Tracing paper or template plastic | |

## Cutting
Refer to diagrams on pages 242 and 243 to identify blocks and units designated in cutting list.

### From Fabric I (white-on-white), cut:
* Four 14½" x 42" strips.
   From these, cut:
   • Thirty-four 4" x 14½" for pieced outer border.
* Ten 1½" x 42" strips.
   From these, cut:
   • Thirty-six 1½" x 5" (4).
   • 144 1½" squares (2a).
* Twelve 2⅞" x 42" strips for strip sets 1 and 2.
* Three 2½" x 42" strips.
   From these, cut:
   • Thirty-six 2½" squares (1).
* One 13" x 42" strip. From this, cut:
   • Three 13" squares.
   Cut squares in half diagonally to get six setting triangles.

### From Fabric II (yellow-on-black print), cut:
* One 30" square for bias binding.
* Eight 4" x 42½" strips.
   From these, cut:
   • Seventy-two 2½" x 4" (2).
   • Thirty-six 4" squares (3).
* Five 2½" x 42" for strip sets 3 and 4.

### From Fabric III (black mini-print), cut:
* Ten 1¼" x 42½" strips for inner border.
   From eight of these, cut:
   • Eight 1¼" x 26".
   • Four 1¼" x 16½".
* Three 1½" x 42" strips.
   From these, cut:
   • Fifty-four 1½" squares (3a, 5).
   • Nine 1½" x 3½" (6).
* One 2½" x 42" strip.
   From this, cut:
   • Four 2½" squares (9).
* Five 1¼" x 42" strips.
   From these and scraps from previous steps, cut:
   • Eight 1¼" x 14½" (10).
   • Eight 1¼" x 16" (11).

### From Fabric IV (yellow), cut:
* Thirteen 2⅞" x 42" strips for strip sets 1 and 2.
* Four 2½" x 42" strips for strip sets 3 and 4.
* One 2⅞" x 42" strip.
   From this, cut:
   • Eight 2⅞" squares (7).
* Four 16" x 42" strips.
   From these, cut:
   • Thirty-eight 4" x 16" for pieced outer border.

### From Fabric V (green mini-print), cut:
* One 6½" x 42" strip.
   From this, cut:
   • Sixteen 2½" x 6½" (8).
* Two 8" x 42" strips.
   From these, cut:
   • Twelve 5½" x 8" for leaves.
* Four 1¾" x 26" for inner border.

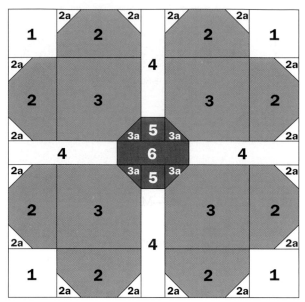

Block A—Make 9.

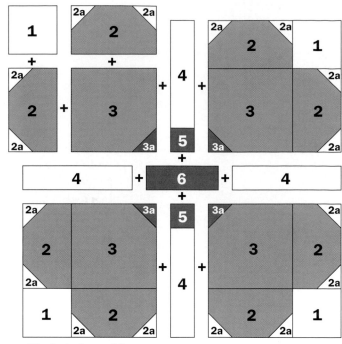

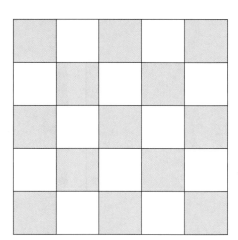

Block A Assembly

## Piecing the Blocks

**1.** Using diagonal-corner technique, make eight of Unit 2 and four of Unit 3 as shown in Block A Assembly diagram.

**2.** Referring to upper left corner of Block A Assembly diagram, join Unit 1 to side of one Unit 2; then join another Unit 2 to top of one Unit 3. Press both seam allowances toward Unit 2. Join these combined units as shown to complete one petal section. Make three more petal sections in the same manner.

**3.** Join one Unit 5 to one end of two of Unit 4 as shown.

**4.** Turning petal sections as shown, join two sections to opposite sides of each 4-5 unit.

**5.** To make center bar, join two of Unit 4 to opposite ends of Unit 6.

**6.** Join petal sections to both sides of center bar as shown to complete block. Make nine of Block A.

**7.** Referring to diagrams of strip sets 1 and 2, use a scant seam allowance to join strips of fabrics I and IV as shown. Each finished strip set should measure 12½" wide. Press seam allowances toward Fabric IV.

**8.** For Block B, cut twenty-four 2⅞"-wide segments from Strip Set 1 and sixteen segments from Strip Set 2. Each segment is a horizontal row of the block.

**9.** Referring to Block B Assembly diagram, arrange three Strip Set 1 segments and two Strip Set 2 segments in rows as shown. Join rows to complete block. Make eight of Block B.

**10.** For Block C, cut sixteen 2⅞"-wide segments of Strip Set 1 and eight segments of Strip Set 2.

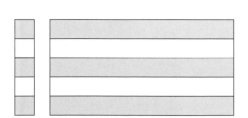

Strip Set 1—Make 3.

Strip Set 2—Make 2.

Block B—Make 8.

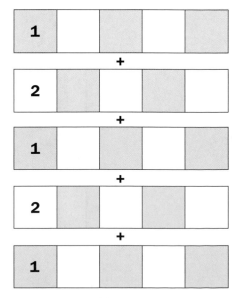

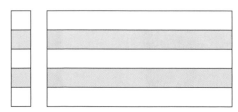

Block B Assembly

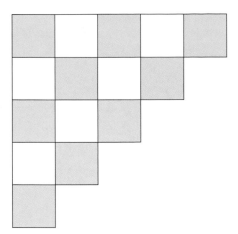

Block C—Make 8.

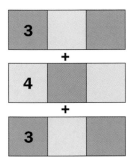

**3**
+
**4**
+
**3**

Nine-Patch Assembly

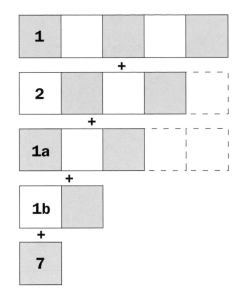

**1**
+
**2**
+
**1a**
+
**1b**
+
**7**

Block C Assembly

**11.** Arrange segments in horizontal rows as shown in Block C Assembly diagram. Row 1 is a segment from Strip Set 1. Row 2 is a Strip Set 2 segment with a Fabric I square removed. For next row, separate a Strip Set 1 segment between third and fourth squares as shown—the three-square unit becomes Row 1a and the two-square unit becomes Row 1b. The last row is a Unit 7 square. Join rows as shown to complete one block. Make eight of Block C.

**12.** Referring to diagrams of strip sets 3 and 4, join strips of fabrics II and IV as shown. Each finished strip set should measure 6½" wide. Press seam allowances toward Fabric II.

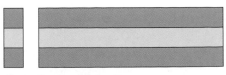

Strip Set 3—Make 2.

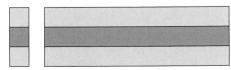

Strip Set 4—Make 1.

**13.** Cut thirty-two 2½"-wide segments from Strip Set 3 and 16 segments from Strip Set 4.

**14.** Referring to Nine-Patch Assembly diagram, arrange two Strip Set 3 segments and one Strip Set 4 segment in rows as shown. Join rows. Make four nine-patches for each Block D.

**15.** Referring to Block D Assembly diagram, join a nine-patch to opposite sides of two of Unit 8. Press seam allowances toward Unit 8.

**16.** To make Block D center bar, join a Unit 8 to opposite sides of each Unit 9. Press seam allowances toward Unit 8. Join nine-patch rows to opposite sides of center bar as shown.

**17.** Add a Unit 10 to top and bottom of block as shown in block diagram. Join Unit 11 to remaining sides to complete Block D. Make four of Block D.

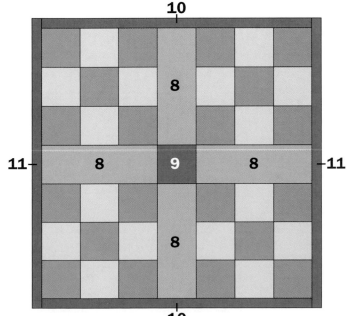

Block D—Make 4.

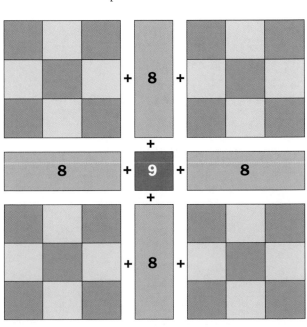

Block D Assembly

## Appliqué

Trace leaf pattern onto tracing paper or template plastic. Cut out leaf template; then mark one side of template as right side. Trace template onto six 5½" x 8" pieces of Fabric V with right side up; then trace template on remaining pieces with right side down. For machine appliqué, cut out each leaf on drawn line. For hand appliqué, add ¼" seam allowance when cutting.

Referring to photograph, position two leaves on each setting triangle as shown, keeping leaves clear of seam allowances on triangle edges. Using method of your choice, appliqué leaves in place on all six triangles.

## Quilt Assembly

**1.** Referring to Quilt Assembly diagram, join blocks A, B, C, and setting triangles in diagonal rows as shown. Then join rows.

**2.** Before adding borders, use a rotary cutter and acrylic ruler to trim excess fabric from edges of Block C.

**3.** For side borders, join a 15"-long strip of Fabric III to both ends of each 42½"-long strip. Matching centers of border and quilt side, join borders to quilt sides.

**4.** Join two 27½"-long strips of Fabric III to opposite sides of each 27½"-long strip of Fabric V, making four strip sets.

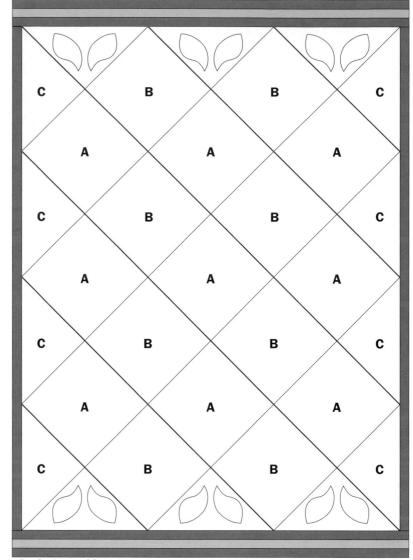

*Quilt Assembly*

Leaf

Cut 6.
Reverse and cut 6.

**5.** Referring to Quilt Assembly diagram, join two strip sets end-to-end for top border. Matching center seam of border with center of top edge, join border to quilt top. Repeat for bottom border.

**6.** For each side outer border, join eleven 4" x 16" pieces of Fabric IV and ten 4" x 14½" pieces of Fabric I in a row as shown in photograph. Join borders to quilt sides, easing to fit as necessary. (See page 19 for tips on easing.)

**7.** For top border, join eight 4" x 16" pieces of Fabric IV and seven 4" x 14½"

pieces of Fabric I in a row as shown. Add one of Block D to each end of the row. Join row to top of quilt. Repeat for bottom border.

## Quilting and Finishing

**1.** Outline-quilt blocks or quilt as desired. Quilt veins in leaves. Quilt straight lines in each piece of outer border, 1" from each seam line.

**2.** Before applying binding, decide whether to leave corners square on Fabric IV pieces in outer border or to trim

them as shown in photograph. To mark a curve at each corner, use bottom of a coffee mug or soda can as a template. Trim corners as desired.

**3.** Cut 30" square of Fabric II in half diagonally. Starting from each diagonal edge, cut 2"-wide strips. Join strips end-to-end to make a continuous strip of bias binding. With wrong sides facing, press strip in half, being careful not to stretch bias edges. See page 30 for directions on applying binding.

# Mountain Greenery

*Combine scraps with three quick-piecing techniques to create a wall hanging that celebrates our native land. The four blocks that comprise this design represent blue skies and purple-tinged mountains sheltering forests and wildlife. Strip piecing makes quick work of tree trunks and antlers. Dimensional ears and jute tails add charm to frolicking deer. The Christmas tree skirt on page 253 is made with the same blocks.*

**Quick-Piecing Techniques:**  Strip Piecing (see page 20)
Diagonal Corners (see page 20)
Diagonal Ends (see page 21)

## Finished Size

Blocks: 4 mountain blocks, 7" square
10 pine tree blocks, 7" square
4 deer blocks, 6¼" x 8¾"
32 tree blocks, 4" x 4⅞"

Wall Hanging: 44" x 60"

## Materials

| | | |
|---|---|---|
| | Fabric I (white solid) | ⅛ yard |
| | Fabric II (six assorted lavender prints and solids) | scraps or ⅛ yard each |
| | Fabric III (32 assorted green prints and solids) | scraps or ⅛ yard each |
| | Fabric IV (dark brown solid) | ¼ yard |
| | Fabric V (light tan print) | 1½ yards |
| | Fabric VI (tan print) | ¼ yard |
| | Fabric VII (pale blue solid) | ⅜ yard |
| | Fabric VIII (medium blue solid) | ⅜ yard |
| | Fabric IX (navy solid) | 1⅜ yards |
| | Backing fabric | 3¾ yards |
| | ⅛"-wide jute trim | ⅛ yard |
| | Template material or tracing paper | |

## Cutting

Before cutting, trace ear pattern onto template material or tracing paper.

**From Fabric I (white), cut:**

✱ Two 1½" x 42" strips.
  From these, cut:
  - Four 1½" x 7½" (A-9).
  - Four 1½" x 6½" (A-8).

**From Fabric II scraps, cut:**

✱ Four 3½" squares (A-1) from darkest lavender.

✱ Four 1½" x 3½" (A-2) from dark lavender.

✱ Eight 1½" x 4½" (A-3, A-4) from dark or medium lavenders.

✱ Four 1½" x 5½" (A-5) from light lavender.

✱ Four 1½" x 5½" (A-6) and four 1½" x 6½" (A-7) from lightest lavender.

**From Fabric III scraps, cut:**

✱ Thirty-two 4⅝" x 4⅞" (D-1).

✱ Forty 1½" x 3½" (B-3, B-6, B-9, B-12).

✱ Forty 1½" x 4½" (B-4, B-7, B-10, B-13).

**From Fabric IV (dark brown), cut:**

✱ Three 1" x 42" strips for strip sets 1 and 2.

✱ Three ⅝" x 42" strips for strip sets 3 and 4.

**From Fabric V (light tan print), cut:**

✱ Two 2¾" x 42" strips for Strip Set 1.

✱ Five 2¼" x 42" strips for strip sets 2 and 3.

✱ One 2½" x 42" strip for Strip Set 4.

✱ One 1½" x 42" strip for Strip Set 4.

✱ One 1⅜" x 42" strip for Strip Set 4.

✱ One 4¾" x 42" strip.
  From this, cut:
  - Four 2¼" x 4¾" (C-5).
  - Five 3⅞" squares. Cut each square in half diagonally to get 10 triangles (B-1).
  - Four 3" x 3¼" (C-1).

✱ One 1" x 42" strip.
  From this, cut:
  - One 1" x 31" (22).
  - Four 1" x 1¾" (C-9a).

✱ Five 1½" x 42" strips.
  From these, cut:
  - Twenty 1½" x 3½" (B-11).
  - Twenty 1½" x 2½" (B-8).
  - Twenty-four 1½" squares (B-5, C-13a).
  - Four 1½" x 3" (C-4).
  - Four 1½" x 2⅞" (C-14).
  - Four 1" x 1½" (C-7a).
  - Eight 1⅜" squares (C-15b, C-16b).
  - Four 1¼" squares (C-10b).
  - Four 1⅛" squares (C-12a).
  - Eight 1" squares (C-6a).

✱ One 7⅞" x 42" strip.
  From this, cut:
  - Three 7⅞" squares. Cut each square in half diagonally to get six triangles (20).
  - One 5⅞" square. Cut square in half diagonally to get two triangles (21).
  - Three 1¼" x 9¼" (24).
  - Two 1⅞" x 9¼" (23).

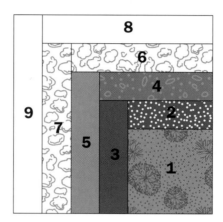

*Block A—*

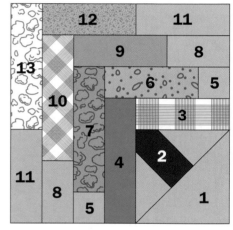

*Block B—Make 10.*

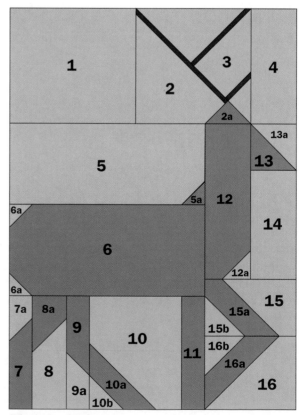

*Block C—Make 4.*

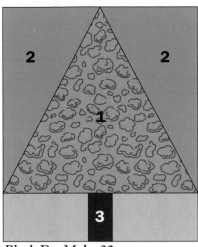

Block D—Make 32.

* One 2½" x 42" strip.
  From this, cut:
  • Four 2½" x 3" (C-10).
  • Four 2⅛" x 2½" (C-16).
  • Four 1¼" x 2½" (C-8).
  • Four 1¾" x 2⅛" (C-15).

## From Fabric VI (tan print), cut:

* One 2½" x 42" strip.
  From this, cut:
  • Four 2½" x 4¾" (C-6).
  • Four 1" x 2½" (C-7).
  • Four 2⅛" squares (C-16a).
  • Four 2" squares (C-10a).
* One 1¾" x 42" strip.
  From this, cut:
  • Four 1¾" x 2⅛" (C-15a).
  • Four 1¼" x 1¾" (C-8a).
  • Four 1½" squares (C-13).
  • Four 1½" x 3⅞" (C-12).
  • Two 1½" squares. Cut each square in half diagonally to get four triangles (C-2a).
* One 1" x 42" strip.
  From this, cut:
  • Four 1" x 3" (C-11).
  • Four 1" x 2¼" (C-9).
  • Four 1" squares (C-5a).
* From scraps, cut:
  • Eight ears, cutting four with template faceup and four more with template facedown.

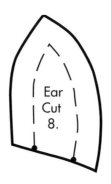

Ear
Cut
8.

## From Fabric VII (pale blue), cut:

* One 10⅞" x 42" strip.
  From this, cut:
  • One 10⅞" square. Cut square in half diagonally to get two triangles (19).
  • One 7⅞" square. Cut square in half diagonally to get two triangles (18). Discard one triangle.
  • One 7½" square (17).

## From Fabric VIII (medium blue), cut:

* Two 5½" x 42" strips.
  From these, cut:
  • Eight 5½" x 10½".
    Cut these as shown in Cutting diagram to get eight D-2 triangles from each piece, four of which point to the right and four to the left. Store "righties" and "lefties" separately. Trim ¾" from narrow tip of all 64 of these triangles.

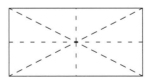

Cutting

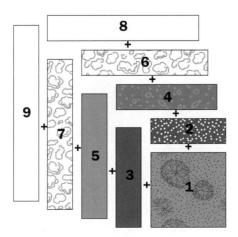

Block A Assembly

## From Fabric IX (navy), cut:

* Five 3" x 42" strips for binding.
* Six 2½" x 42" strips.
  From four of these, cut:
  • Four 2½" x 23" for outer border.
  • Two 2½" x 16" for outer border.
  • Three 1¼" x 19".
    From these, cut:
    • Fourteen 1¼" x 4½" (25).
* Six 1½" x 42" strips.
  From these, cut:
  • Two 1½" x 41" for inner border.
  • Four 1½" x 22¾" for inner border.
  • Four 1½" x 5⅜" (26).
* Two 1¾" x 42" strips.
  From these, cut:
  • Ten 1¾" x 5⅜" (27).

## Piecing the Mountain Blocks

Referring to Block A Assembly diagram, join units in numerical order as shown. As strips are added, press seam allowances away from newest strip. Make four of Block A.

## Piecing the Pine Tree Blocks

1. For Block B, refer to Strip Set 1 diagram and join two 2¾" x 42" strips of Fabric V to opposite sides of one 1" x 42" strip of Fabric IV. Cut strip set into ten 2¾"-wide segments.
2. Fold each segment in half to find center of long edge and mark. Referring to Diagram 1, cut from both bottom corners to center of top edge to make one tree trunk (Unit 2).

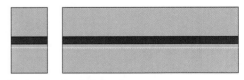

Strip Set 1—Make 1.

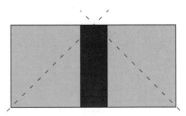

Diagram 1

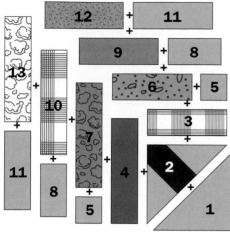

*Block B Assembly*

**3.** Join diagonal edges of units 1 and 2 as shown in Block B Assembly diagram, making a square. Press seam allowances toward Unit 1.

**4.** Join Unit 3 to top of square; then add Unit 4 to left side as shown.

**5.** Join Unit 5 to one end of Unit 6; then join 5-6 unit to top of block. Join another Unit 5 to one end of Unit 7; then join 5-7 unit to left side.

**6.** Join a Unit 8 to ends of units 9 and 10. Join a Unit 11 to ends of unit 12 and 13. Join combined units in order shown in Block B Assembly diagram. Make 10 of Block B.

*Strip Set 2—Make 2.*

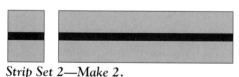

*Strip Set 3—Make 1.*

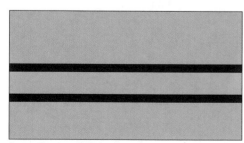

*Strip Set 4—Make 1.*

**7.** For border pine trees (Block D), begin by making two of Strip Set 2, joining two 2¼" x 42" strips of Fabric V to opposite sides of one 1" x 42" strip of Fabric IV for each strip set. Press seam allowances toward Fabric IV. From these strip sets, cut thirty-two 1½"-wide segments for tree trunks (Unit D-3).

**8.** With right sides facing, fold each 4⅝" x 4⅞" piece of Fabric III in half lengthwise as shown in Diagram 2. With fold at right, cut through both layers from bottom left to top right as shown. Discard trimmed corners. Trim ½" from tip of each remaining D-1 triangle.

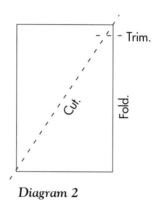

*Diagram 2*

**9.** Referring to Block D Assembly diagram, join a righty Unit 2 to left side of Unit 1, aligning trimmed tip of Unit 2 with bottom edge of Unit 1. Join a lefty Unit 2 to opposite side of Unit 1 in the same manner.

**10.** Join Unit 3 to bottom of tree top to complete pine tree block. Make 32 of Block D.

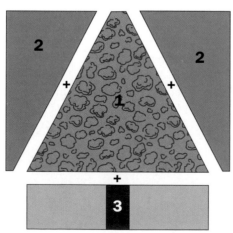

*Block D Assembly*

## Piecing the Deer Blocks

**1.** Referring to Strip Set 3 diagram, join 2¼" x 42" strip of Fabric V to ⅝" x 42" strip of Fabric IV. From this, cut four 4¾"-wide segments. Fold each segment in half to find center of one long edge and mark. Referring to Diagram 3, cut from both bottom corners of each segment to center of top edge to make one C-2 triangle. Next, trim 1" from left corner of triangle as shown in Diagram 4. Join triangle 2a to cut edge to complete Unit 2.

**2.** Referring to Strip Set 4 diagram, join three strips of Fabric V and two ⅝" x 42" strips of Fabric IV as shown, placing 2½"-wide strip on top, 1⅜"-wide strip in middle, and 1½"-wide strip at bottom. From this strip set, cut four 2⅜"-wide segments. Fold each segment in half to find center of one long edge and mark. Referring to Diagram 5, cut from both bottom corners of each segment to center of top edge to make one C-3 unit.

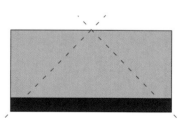

*Diagram 3*

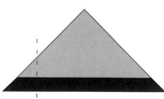

*Diagram 4*

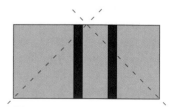

*Diagram 5*

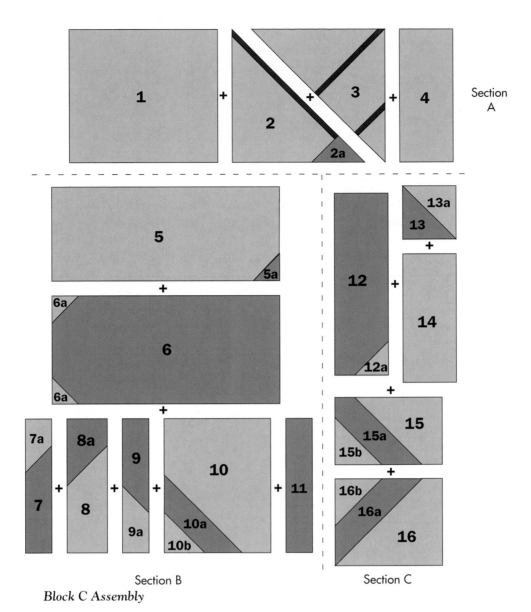

Section
A

Block C Assembly

Section B

Section C

**3.** Using diagonal-corner technique, make one each of units 5, 6, 12, and 13 as shown in Block C Assembly diagram.

**4.** Units 10 and 16 have double diagonal corners. For Unit 10, add 10a as a diagonal corner; then add 10b to the same corner in the same manner. Make Unit 16 in the same manner.

**5.** Using diagonal-end technique, make one each of units 7, 8, and 9.

**6.** Unit 15 is a combination of diagonal-end and diagonal-corner techniques. Add 15a to 15 as a diagonal end; then join diagonal corner 15b as shown.

**7.** To assemble Section A of block, join Unit 2 to Unit 3. Join units 1 and 4 to sides of 2-3 square as shown.

**8.** To assemble Section B, begin at bottom. Join units 7, 8, 9, 10, and 11 in a row as shown. Join Unit 6 to top of row. Cut a ¾"-long piece of jute for each block. Matching raw edges, pin one end of jute to top edge of Unit 6 where 6 and 6a meet. Join Unit 5 to top of Unit 6, catching jute in seam. Ravel jute end to fluff tail.

**9.** To assemble Section C, join units 13 and 14 as shown. Join Unit 12 to left side; then join units 15 and 16 to bottom.

**10.** With right sides facing, join two ear pieces, stitching from dot to dot and leaving straight edge open. Trim and clip seam allowance; then turn right side out. Fold bottom corners of ear in, overlapping at center as shown in Diagram 6. Matching raw edges and with fold faceup, pin ear to bottom of Unit 2 where 2 and 2a meet.

*Diagram 6*

**11.** To assemble block, join sections B and C. Join Section A to top, catching ear in seam. Make four of Block C.

## Quilt Assembly

**1.** Referring to Quilt Assembly diagram, join A and B blocks in diagonal rows as indicated by red lines. Add units 17, 18, 20, and 21 to row ends as shown. Join rows; then join Unit 19 triangles to top corners. Complete center section by joining Unit 22 to bottom.

**2.** Join four deer blocks in a row as shown, sewing a Unit 24 between blocks. Join a Unit 23 to each row end. Join deer row to bottom of center section.

**3.** Join two 1½" x 22¾" strips of Fabric IX end-to-end to make a 45"-long border for each side. Join borders to quilt sides. Press seam allowances toward border and trim border ends.

**4.** Assemble two side rows of eight D blocks each, sewing a Unit 25 between blocks. Join a row to each quilt side, easing as necessary. (See page 19 for tips on easing.)

**5.** Join 1½" x 41" strips of Fabric IX to top and bottom. Press seam allowances toward border and trim border ends.

**6.** For top and bottom rows, begin by joining six D blocks for each row, sewing a Unit 27 between blocks. Join a Unit 26 to both ends of each row; then add one more block at each end. Join rows to top and bottom of quilt, aligning each Unit 26 with inner side borders.

**7.** Join a 2½" x 16" strip of Fabric IX to end of a 42"-long strip for each outer side border. Join borders to quilt sides. Press seam allowances toward border and trim ends.

**8.** For each top and bottom outer border, join two 2½" x 23" strips of Fabric IX end-to-end. Join borders to top and bottom edges. Press and trim as before.

## Quilting and Finishing

Outline quilt patchwork or quilt as desired.

Make 5⅞ yards of binding. See page 30 for directions on making and applying straight-grain binding.

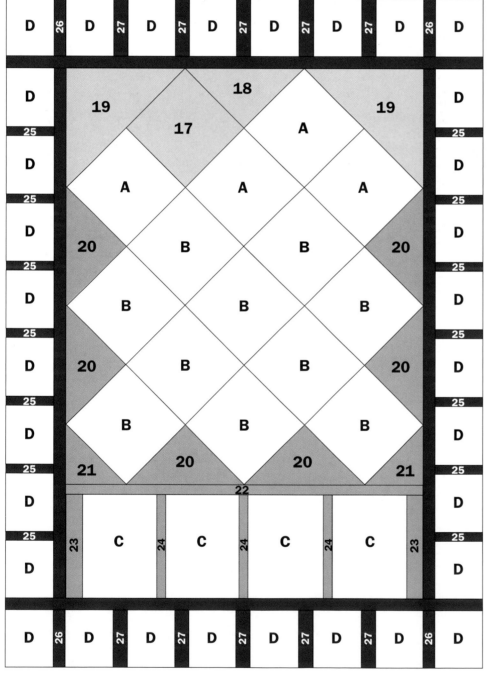

*Quilt Assembly*

# Mountain Greenery Tree Skirt

Dress your tree in homespun holiday style with patchwork pine trees, pinwheels, and prancing reindeer. This fast and easy project is an excellent introduction to four quick-piecing techniques, so it's ideal for beginners.

## Quick-Piecing Techniques:

Strip Piecing (see page 20)
Diagonal Corners (see page 20)
Diagonal Ends (see page 21)
Triangle-Squares (see page 22)

## Finished Size

Blocks: 8 pinwheel blocks, 7" square       Tree Skirt: 41" square
       8 pine tree blocks, 7" square
       4 deer blocks, 7" x 8¾"
       4 striped blocks, 5¼" x 7"

## Materials

| | | |
|---|---|---|
| | Fabric I (white-on-red pinstripe) | ⅝ yard |
| | Fabric II (brick red plaid) | ⅝ yard |
| | Fabric III (five assorted green prints and checks) | scraps or ⅛ yard each |
| | Fabric IV (dark brown print or solid) | scraps or ⅛ yard |
| | Fabric V (red-on-tan mini-print) | ⅜ yard |
| | Fabric VI (brown mini-dot) | ¼ yard |
| | Fabric VII (red-and-green homespun plaid) | ⅝ yard |
| | Fabric VIII (dark cranberry plaid) | 1⅛ yards |
| | Fabric IX (dark green check or print) | ⅜ yard |
| | Backing fabric | 1¼ yards |
| | ⅛"-wide jute trim | ⅛ yard |

## Cutting

Before cutting, make a template of ear pattern (page 249).

### From Fabric I (pinstripe), cut:

* One 20" square for triangle-squares (A-1).
* One 7½" square for skirt center.

### From Fabric II (brick red plaid), cut:

* One 20" square for triangle-squares (A-1).

### From Fabric III scraps, cut:

* Eight 1½" x 3½" (B-3) and eight 1½" x 4½" (B-4).

* Eight 1½" x 3½" (B-6) and eight 1½" x 4½" (B-7).
* Eight 1½" x 3½" (B-9) and eight 1½" x 4½" (B-10).
* Eight 1½" x 3½" (B-12) and eight 1½" x 4½" (B-13).
* Four 3⅞" squares. Cut each square in half diagonally to get eight triangles (B-1).

### From Fabric IV (dark brown), cut:

* One 1" x 42" strip for Strip Set 1.
* Three ⅝" x 42" strips for strip sets 3 and 4.

*Block A —Make 8.*

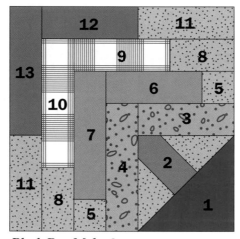

*Block B —Make 8.*

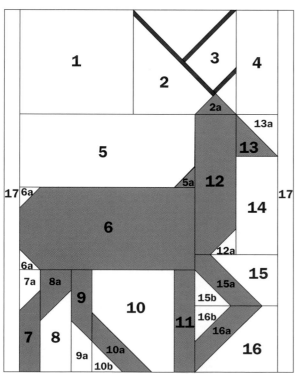

*Block C —Make 4.*

*Strip Set 5—Make 1.*

### From Fabric V (red/tan mini-print), cut:

* Two 2¾" x 42" strips for Strip Set 1.
* Three 1½" x 42" strips.
  From these, cut:
  * Sixteen 1½" x 3½" (B-11).
  * Sixteen 1½" x 2½" (B-8).
  * Sixteen 1½" squares (B-5).

### From Fabric VI (brown mini-dot), cut:

* One 2½" x 42" strip. From this, cut:
  * Four 2½" x 4¾" (C-6).
  * Four 1" x 2½" (C-7).
  * Four 2⅛" squares (C-16a).
  * Four 2" squares (C-10a).
* One 1¾" x 42" strip.
  From this, cut:
  * Four 1¾" x 2⅛" (C-15a).
  * Four 1¼" x 1¾" (C-8a).
  * Four 1½" squares (C-13).
  * Four 1½" x 3⅞" (C-12).
  * Two 1½" squares. Cut each square in half diagonally to get four triangles (C-2a).
* One 1" x 42" strip.
  From this, cut:
  * Four 1" x 3" (C-11).
  * Four 1" x 2¼" (C-9).
  * Four 1" squares (C-5a).
* From scraps, cut:
  * Eight ears, cutting four with template faceup and four more with template facedown.

### From Fabric VII (red-and-green plaid), cut:

* One 2¼" x 42" strip for Strip Set 3.
* One 2½" x 42" strip for Strip Set 4.
* One 1½" x 42" strip for Strip Set 4.
* One 1⅜" x 42" strip for Strip Set 4.
* One 1½" x 42" strip.
  From this, cut:
  * Four 1½" squares (C-13a).
  * Four 1" x 1½" (C-7a).
  * Eight 1⅜" squares (C-15b, C-16b).
  * Four 1¼" squares (C-10b).
  * Four 1⅛" squares (C-12a).
  * Eight 1" squares (C-6a).
* One 3" x 42" strip. From this, cut:
  * Four 3" x 3¼" (C-1).
  * Four 1½" x 3" (C-4).
  * Four 2½" x 3" (C-10).
  * Four 1½" x 2⅞" (C-14).
  * Four 1" x 1¾" (C-9a).

* One 2½" x 42" strip.
  From this, cut:
    • Four 1¼" x 2½" (C-8).
    • Four 2⅛" x 2½" (C-16).
    • Four 2¼" x 4¾" (C-5).
    • Four 1¾" x 2⅛" (C-15).
* Two ⅞" x 42" strips.
  From these, cut:
    • Eight ⅞" x 9¼" (C-17).

### From Fabric VIII (cranberry plaid), cut:

* One 18" square for bias binding.
* Four 1½" x 42" strips for Strip Set 5.
* Four 2½" x 42" strips for outer border.

### From Fabric IX (dark green), cut:

* Three 1½" x 42" strips for Strip Set 5.
* Four 1½" x 38" for inner border.

## Piecing the Blocks

**1.** See page 22 for instructions on triangle-squares. On wrong side of 20" square of Fabric I, draw a 4 x 4-square grid of 4⅜" squares. With right sides facing, match marked fabric with 20" square of Fabric II. Stitch grid as directed on page 22. Cut 32 triangle-squares from grid.

**2.** Referring to Block A Assembly diagram, join four triangle-squares in two rows of two squares each. Join rows to complete Block A. Make 8 of Block A.

**3.** For Block B, follow steps 1–6 of Piecing the Pine Tree Blocks for wall hanging (page 249). Referring to Block B diagram at left for fabric placement, make eight of Block B for tree skirt.

**4.** For Block C, follow Piecing the Deer Blocks instructions given for wall hanging (page 250). Referring to Block C diagram at left, make four of Block C. Complete blocks by joining one of Unit 17 to both sides as shown here.

**5.** For striped blocks, refer to Strip Set 5 diagram to join 1½" x 42" strips of fabrics VIII and IX as shown. Cut strip set into four 5¾" segments.

## Tree Skirt Assembly

**1.** Referring to Tree Skirt Assembly diagram, join two A blocks and two B blocks as shown to make each corner

section. Green triangles in diagram indicate position of each B-1 for correct placement of pine trees.

**2.** For center sections, join a striped block to top of each C block.

**3.** For top row, join two corner sections with a center section between them as shown in diagram. Repeat for bottom row, positioning fabrics as shown. Assemble middle row by joining center sections to opposite sides of 7½" square of Fabric I. Join rows.

*Block A Assembly*

**4.** Join Fabric IX border strips to top and bottom edges of tree skirt. Press seam allowances toward borders; then trim excess border fabric at ends. Join borders to remaining sides in the same manner.

**5.** Join Fabric VIII borders to tree skirt in the same manner as inner border.

## Quilting and Finishing

**1.** Mark a 1½"-wide cable in border. Outline-quilt patchwork or quilt as desired. Quilt border design.

**2.** Draw a 6" circle in center square. To make skirt opening, cut out circle and down one seam as indicated by dashed line in Tree Skirt Assembly diagram.

**3.** For bias binding, cut 18" square of Fabric VIII in half diagonally. Starting from cut edges, cut 2"-wide diagonal strips. Join strips end-to-end to make a continuous strip 5 yards long. Press strip in half with wrong sides facing, being careful not to stretch bias. Follow directions on page 30 for applying binding to skirt opening and around borders.

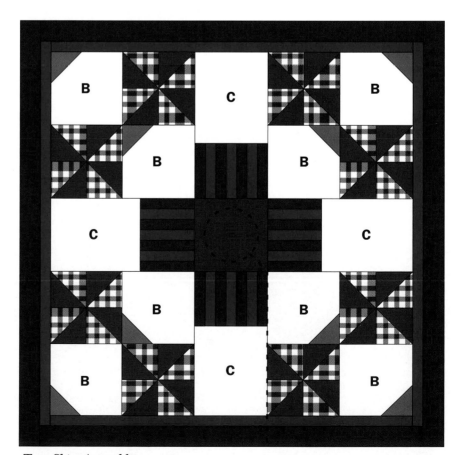

*Tree Skirt Assembly*

# Mountain Greenery Stockings

*There's nothing like plaid to evoke the cozy atmosphere of a country Christmas. Mix up scraps of plaids, checks, and little prints in tan, cranberry, and forest green to make this pair of holiday stockings. Hung by the mantel with care, they will delight and impress your family and guests—and only you will know how fun and easy they are to make!*

**Quick-Piecing Techniques:**  Strip Piecing (see page 20)
Diagonal Corners (see page 20)
Diagonal Ends (see page 21)

**Finished Size**
Blocks: 1 pine tree block, 7" square          Stockings: 9¾" x 18"
1 deer block, 6¾" x 8¾"

**Materials (for both stockings)**

| | |
|---|---|
| Fabric I (green-on-tan check) | ½ yard |
| Fabric II (red-on-tan plaid) | ¼ yard |
| Fabric III (four green plaids and checks) | scraps |
| Fabric IV (red-on-tan mini-print) | ½ yard |
| Fabric V (dark brown print) | ¼ yard |
| Fabric VI (dark brown print or solid) | scraps |
| Fabric VII (cranberry plaid) | 10" square |
| Lining fabric | ¾ yard |
| Fleece or low-loft batting | ¾ yard |
| ⅛"-wide jute trim | 1" |
| ⅛"-diameter cording | 2½ yards |
| Template material or tracing paper | |
| Tear-away stabilizer (optional for machine embroidery only) | |

**Cutting**
Before cutting, trace deer ear pattern (page 249) and stocking toe pattern (page 258) onto template material or tracing paper.

**From Fabric I (green-on-tan check), cut:**
✱ One 11" x 42" strip. From this, cut:
  • One 11" x 20" for deer stocking back.
  • One 8" x 11" for deer stocking toe (Stocking-1).
  • One 2½" x 7¼" (Stocking-2).
  • Two ¾" x 9¼" (C-17).
  • One 2¼" x 5" for Strip Set 3.
  • One 1" x 1½" (C-7a).
  • One 1" x 1¾" (C-9a).
  • Two 1" squares (C-6a).
✱ One 3" x 42" strip. From this, cut:
  • One 3" x 3¼" (C-1).
  • One 2½" x 3" for Strip Set 4.
  • One 1½" x 3" for Strip Set 4.
  • One 1⅜" x 3" for Strip Set 4.
  • One 1½" x 3" (C-4).
  • One 2½" x 3" (C-10).
  • One 1½" x 2⅞" (C-14).
  • One 1¼" x 2½" (C-8).
  • One 2⅛" x 2½" (C-16).
  • One 2¼" x 4¾" (C-5).
  • One 1¾" x 2⅛" (C-15).
  • One 1½" square (C-13a).
  • One 1¼" square (C-10b).
  • Two 1⅜" squares (C-15b, C-16b).
  • One 1⅛" square (C-12a).

**From Fabric II (red-on-tan plaid), cut:**

✱ Two 7" x 14½" for cuffs.

✱ Two 1¼" x 4" for hangers.

**From Fabric III (assorted greens), cut:**

✱ One 1½" x 3½" (B-3) and one 1½" x 4½" (B-4).

✱ One 1½" x 3½" (B-6) and one 1½" x 4½" (B-7).

✱ One 1½" x 3½" (B-9) and one 1½" x 4½" (B-10).

✱ One 1½" x 3½" (B-12) and one 1½" x 4½"(B-13).

**From Fabric IV (red-on-tan mini-print), cut:**

✱ One 11" x 42" strip. From this, cut:
  • One 11" x 20" for tree stocking back.
  • One 8" x 11" for tree stocking toe (Stocking-1).
  • One 3½" x 11". From this, cut:
    • Two 1½" x 3½" (B-11).
    • Two 1½" x 2½" (B-8).
    • Two 1½" squares (B-5).
    • One 3½" x 7¼" (Stocking-5).
    • Two 2⅜" x 2¾" for Strip Set 1.
    • One 4¼" square. Cut this square in half diagonally to get two triangles (Stocking-4).
    • One 2⅛" square. Cut this square in half diagonally to get two triangles (Stocking-3).

**From Fabric V (dark brown print), cut:**

✱ One 2½" x 42" strip. From this, cut:
  • One 2½" x 4¾" (C-6).
  • One 1" x 2½" (C-7).
  • One 2⅛" square (C-16a).
  • One 1¾" x 2⅛" (C-15a).
  • One 1" x 2¼" (C-9).
  • One 2" square (C-10a).
  • One 1½" square (C-13).
  • One 1½" x 3⅞" (C-12).
  • One 1½" square. Cut square in half diagonally to get two triangles (C-2a). Discard one triangle.
  • One 1¼" x 1¾" (C-8a).
  • One 1" x 3" (C-11).
  • One 1" square (C-5a).

✱ From scraps, cut:
  • Two ears, cutting one with template faceup and one with template facedown.

**From Fabric VI (dark brown), cut:**

✱ One 1" x 2⅜" for Strip Set 1.

✱ Three ⅝" x 5" for strip sets 3 and 4.

**From Fabric VII (cranberry plaid), cut:**

✱ One 10" square for piping.

**From each of lining and fleece, cut:**

✱ Two 11" x 20" pieces for each stocking.

## Piecing the Blocks

**1.** To make pine tree (Block B), begin with Step 1 of Piecing the Pine Tree Blocks instructions given for wall hanging (page 249). To make Strip Set 1, join designated pieces of fabrics V and VI to make a miniature strip set that is 2¾" wide. Follow steps 2–6 to make one Block B, omitting piece B-1.

**2.** To make deer (Block C), follow Piecing the Deer Blocks instructions given for wall hanging (page 250). Use designated strips to make strip sets 3 and 4. Make one of Block C. Complete block by joining one of Unit 17 to both sides.

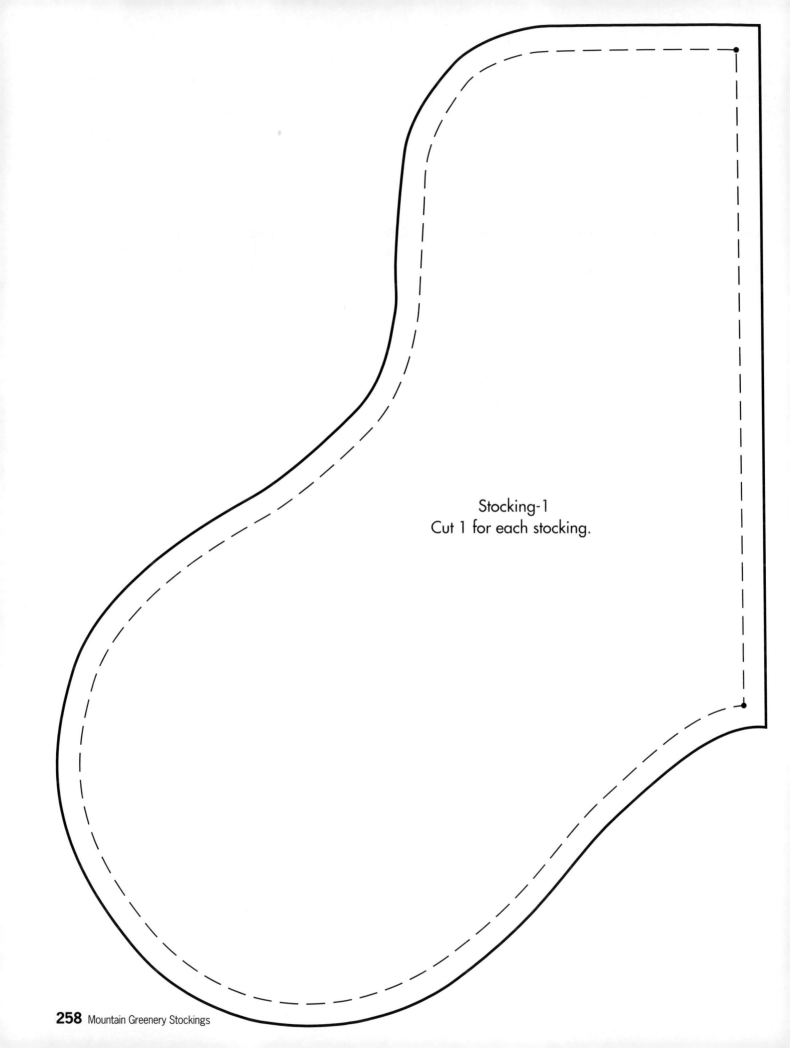

Stocking-1
Cut 1 for each stocking.

**5.** Layer back, fleece, and lining. Machine-quilt backs with randomly curving lines or as desired.

**6.** Cut 10" square of Fabric VII in half diagonally. Starting from cut edges, cut 1"-wide diagonal strips. Join strips end-to-end to make a continuous bias strip approximately 45" long for each stocking. Use bias to cover cording to make piping. Use a zipper foot on your sewing machine to stitch piping to each stocking front. (It's all right if piping doesn't reach top of stocking since cuff will cover top.)

**7.** With right sides facing, join backs to fronts, leaving tops open. Trim and clip seam allowances. Turn stockings right side out.

**8.** Press under ¼" on both long sides of each hanger strip. With wrong sides facing, fold each pressed strip in half lengthwise, bringing folded edges together. Topstitch through all layers close to edge. Matching raw edges, stitch hanger ends to lining back at seam on left side of stocking.

**9.** With wrong sides facing, fold each cuff piece in half lengthwise and press to crease. Unfold cuff. By hand or by machine, satin-stitch a name or initials in center of strip, positioning bottom of letters ³⁄₈" from crease. Letters should be approximately 1½" high.

**10.** With right sides facing, join ends of each cuff. Press seam allowances open. Turn tubes right side out. Press under ¼" at bottom edge of each cuff (edge farthest from embroidery).

**11.** Use pins to mark center back on each stocking. With raw edges aligned, place one unfolded cuff inside each stocking top, with right side of cuff against lining. Align cuff seam with center back of stocking. Stitch cuff to stocking top, catching hanger end in stitching.

**12.** Pull each cuff out. With wrong sides facing, refold cuff on crease (embroidery will be upside down and facing in). Pin hemmed edge over seam allowance at stocking top and topstitch or slipstitch by hand. Fold each cuff down over stocking top and pull each hanger up.

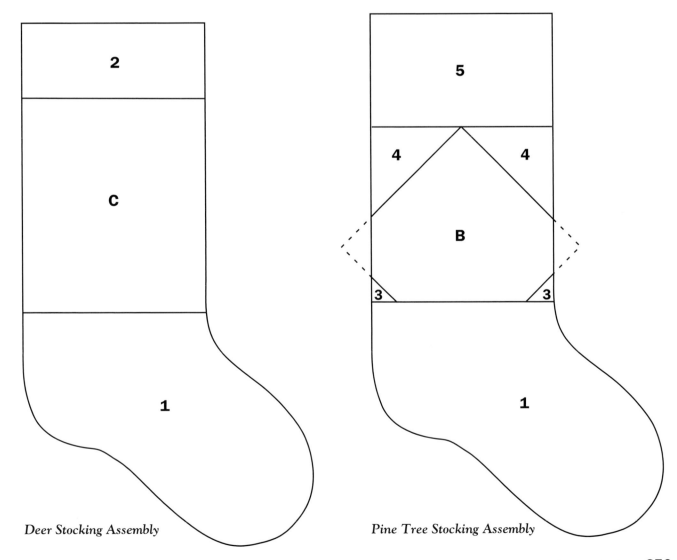

*Deer Stocking Assembly*          *Pine Tree Stocking Assembly*

# Trellis

A variety of quick-piecing techniques creates blossoms of luscious grape and teal climbing a patchwork trellis. When the flower blocks and leaf blocks are joined, the block outlines seem to disappear amid a garden of pretty posies. Even the flowers at the border corners blend so well into the design that they seem to have grown there. We recommend this quilt for experienced quiltmakers.

**Quick-Piecing Techniques:**

Strip Piecing (see page 20)
Diagonal Corners (see page 20)
Diagonal Ends (see page 21)
Triangle-Squares (see page 22)

## Finished Size

Blocks: 10 leaf blocks, 18" square          Quilt: 90" x 106"
     10 flower blocks, 18" square
      4 corner flower blocks, 20" triangle

## Materials

| | | |
|---|---|---|
| | Fabric I (light mauve-and-teal mottled-look print) | 4¼ yards |
| | Fabric II (white-on-white print) | 2⅜ yards |
| | Fabric III (dark teal solid) | ½ yard |
| | Fabric IV (dark teal texture-look print) | ⅝ yard |
| | Fabric V (dark mauve solid) | ⅝ yard |
| | Fabric VI (burgundy print) | ½ yard |
| | Fabric VII (dark mauve-and-teal texture-look print) | 2¼ yards |
| | Fabric VIII (light mauve solid) | ¾ yard |
| | Fabric IX (dark teal print) | 2 yards |

## Cutting

Refer to diagrams on pages 262 and 266 to identify blocks and units designated in cutting list.

**From Fabric I (light mauve-and-teal mottled print), cut:**

✷ One 9⅞" x 42" strip. From this, cut:
  • Two 9⅞" squares. Cut both squares in half diagonally to get four triangles (17).
  • Ten 1¼" x 9" (A-7).
✷ Ten 9¼" x 42" strips.
  From these, cut:
  • Thirty-eight 9¼" squares. Cut each square in quarters diagonally to get 152 triangles (15).
  • Five 4⅞" squares. Cut each square in half diagonally to get 10 triangles (B-9).
✷ Five 1¼" x 42" strips.
  From these, cut:
  • Ninety 1¼" squares (A-2a, A-3a, A-8b).
  • Ten 1¼" x 8⅜" (A-6).
✷ Five 2" x 42" strips.
  From these, cut:
  • Forty 2" x 4" (A-4).
  • Ten 2" x 3½" (B-8).

* Five 1¼" x 42" strips for Strip Set 1 (A-8).
* Three 5¼" x 42" strips.
  From these, cut:
  * Twenty 5¼" squares. Cut each square in half diagonally to get 40 triangles (B-1).
  * Ten 2" x 5" (B-6).
* One 4" x 42" strip.
  From this, cut:
  * One 4" x 12½" for triangle-squares (B-5a).
  * Five 3⅞" squares. Cut each square in half diagonally to get 10 triangles (B-3).
* From scraps, cut:
  * Five 1⅞" squares. Cut each square in half diagonally to get 10 triangles (B-5b).
  * Ten 1½" squares (B-4a).

**From Fabric II (white-on-white), cut:**
* Thirty-four 1⅞" x 42" strips.
  From these, cut:
  * Twenty 1⅞" x 10½" (B-12).
  * Thirty 1⅞" x 13¼" (A-9, B-14).
  * Ten 1⅞" x 11⅞" (B-13).
  * Seventy-six 1⅞" x 7" (16).
  * Ten 1⅞" x 5½" (B-10).
  * Ten 1⅞" x 5" (B-2).
  * Ten 1⅞" x 2" (B-7).
  * Ten 1⅞" squares (B-13b).
* One 4" x 42" strip. From this, cut:
  * One 4" x 12½" for triangle-squares (B-5a).
  * Five 2¼" squares. Cut each square in half diagonally to get 10 triangles (B-9a).
  * Four 2" squares (C-5).
* Five 1⅞" x 42" strips for Strip Set 1 (A-8).

**From Fabric III (dark teal), cut:**
* Two 1⅞" x 42" strips.
  From these, cut:
  * Ten 1⅞" squares (A-9a).
  * Ten 1¼" x 1⅞" (A-6a).
  * Ten 1⅞" x 3¼" (B-13a).
* Five 1½" x 42" strips.
  From these, cut:
  * Ten 1½" x 15" (B-11).
  * Ten 1¼" squares (A-8c).
* One 2⅝" x 42" strips.
  From this, cut:
  * Ten 2⅝" squares (A-8a).

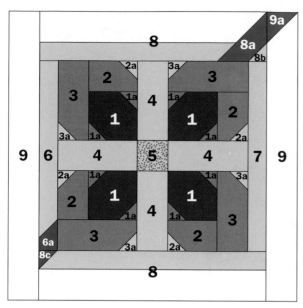

*Block A—Make 10.*

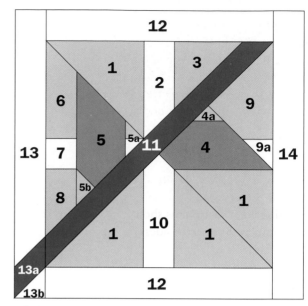

*Block B—Make 10.*

**From Fabric IV (dark teal print), cut:**

✱ Two 4⅞" x 42" strips.
  From these, cut:
  • Ten 4⅞" squares. Cut each square in half diagonally to get 20 triangles (B-4, B-5).
  • Two 1½" x 28½" for Border 1.
✱ Six 1½" x 42" strips for Border 1.

**From Fabric V (dark mauve), cut:**

✱ Three 1¼" x 42" strips.
  From these, cut:
  • Eighty 1¼" squares (A-1a).
✱ Four 1⅞" x 42" strips.
  From these, cut:
  • Forty 1⅞" x 4" (A-3).
✱ Three 2⅝" x 42" strips.
  From these, cut:
  • Sixteen 2⅝" squares (C-1).
  • Forty 1⅞" x 2⅝" (A-2).

**From Fabric VI (burgundy print), cut:**

✱ Three 2⅝" x 42" strips.
  From these, cut:
  • Forty 2⅝" squares (A-1).
✱ One 1¼" x 42" strip.
  From this, cut:
  • Thirty-two 1¼" squares (C-1a).
✱ Two 1⅞" x 42" strips.
  From these, cut:
  • Sixteen 1⅞" x 4" (C-3).
✱ From scraps, cut:
  • Sixteen 1⅞" x 2⅝" (C-2).

**From Fabric VII (dark mauve-and-teal texture print), cut:**

✱ Eight 6½" x 42" strips for Border 4.
  From four of these, cut:
  • Four 6½" x 36".
✱ One 9⅜" x 42" strip. From this, cut:
  • Four 9⅜" squares. Cut each square in half diagonally to get eight triangles (C-7).
✱ One 6⅞" x 42" strip.
  From this, cut:
  • Two 6⅞" squares. Cut each square in half diagonally to get four triangles (C-8).
  • Three 2" x 28" strips.
  From these, cut:
  • Twelve 2" x 4" (C-4).
  • Ten 2" squares (A-5).
✱ Four 1½" x 42" strips.
  From these, cut:
  • Four 1½" x 20" (C-9).
  • Four 1½" x 21" (C-10).
✱ From scraps, cut:
  • Twenty-four 1¼" squares (C-2a, C-3a).

**From Fabric VIII (light mauve), cut:**

✱ Ten 2½" x 42" strips for Border 2.
  From these, cut:
  • Six 2½" x 29".
  • Four 2½" x 36".
✱ From scraps, cut:
  • Four 2" x 4" (C-6).
  • Eight 1¼" squares (C-2b, C-3b).

**From Fabric IX (dark teal print), cut:**

✱ Ten 3" x 42" strips for binding.
✱ Eight 2½" x 42" strips for Border 3.
  From four of these, cut:
  • Four 2½" x 36" for Border 3.
  • Eight 2" squares (C-7a).
✱ Ten 1½" x 42" strips for Border 5.
  From two of these, cut:
  • Two 1½" x 25".
  • Two 1½" x 10".

## Piecing the Flower Blocks

**1.** Referring to Block A Assembly diagram, use diagonal-corner technique to make one of Unit 9 and four each of units 1, 2, and 3.

**2.** Using diagonal-end technique, make one of Unit 6.

**3.** Referring to Strip Set 1 diagram, join designated strips of fabrics I and II as shown. Make five strip sets. Cut four 10½"-wide segments from each strip set to get 20 of Unit 8.

**4.** Referring to top of Block A Assembly diagram, use diagonal-corner technique to add 8a to one of Unit 8. Press 8a; then add 8b in the same manner.

**5.** Referring to bottom of Block A Assembly diagram, use diagonal-corner technique to add 8c to one of Unit 8.

*Strip Set 1—Make 5.*

**6.** Referring to upper left corner of assembly diagram, join Unit 2 to top of Unit 1 as shown. Join Unit 3 to left side of 1-2 unit. Make three more 1-2-3 units in the same manner for petal sections.

**7.** Join two petal sections with one of Unit 4 between them. Press seam allowances toward Unit 4. Repeat with second pair of petal sections.

**8.** Join one of Unit 4 to opposite sides of Unit 5.

**9.** Positioning petal sections as shown, join both sections to opposite sides of combined 4-5-4 unit.

**10.** Join Unit 6 to left side of block as shown; then add Unit 7 to right side.

**11.** Positioning 8a and 8c as shown, join Unit 8 strips to top and bottom.

**12.** Positioning 9a as shown, join a Unit 9 to each side to complete block. Make 10 of Block A in this manner.

## Piecing the Leaf Blocks

*Note:* Before constructing blocks, see page 17 for tips on stabilizing triangles to prevent stretching bias edges.

This block is made by assembling the units into four large triangles, which are then joined into pairs and sewn to opposite sides of the center stem piece.

**1.** To make triangle 1-2-3, begin by joining Unit 1 to Unit 2 as shown in Block B Assembly diagram, aligning short leg of triangle with side and end of Unit 2. Join Unit 3 to opposite side of Unit 2 in the same manner. Referring to Diagram 1, align ruler with triangle edges and trim Unit 2 as shown.

**2.** To make Unit 5a, see page 22 for instructions on triangle-squares. On wrong side of 4" x 12½" piece of Fabric II, draw a 1 x 5-square grid of 1⅞" squares. With right sides facing, match

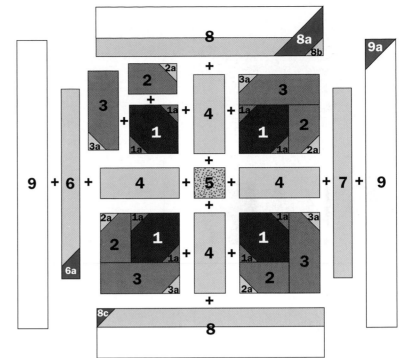

*Block A Assembly*

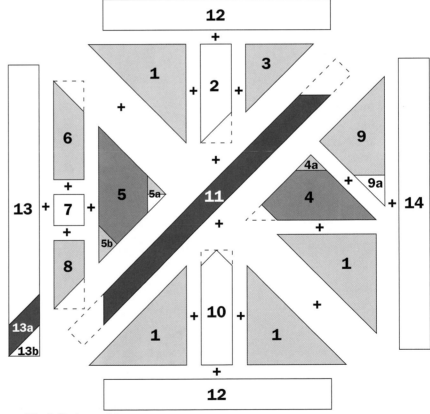

*Block B Assembly*

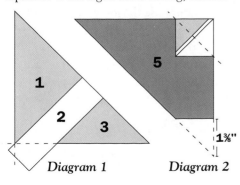

*Diagram 1*          *Diagram 2*

marked fabric with 4" x 12½" piece of Fabric I. Stitch grid as directed on page 22. Cut 10 triangle-squares from grid.

**3.** With right sides facing, place one triangle-square at corner of one Unit 5 triangle, positioning triangle-square

fabrics and seam as shown in Diagram 2. Using diagonal-corner technique, stitch diagonally across square, perpendicular to triangle-square seam. Trim and press diagonal corner.

**4.** Trim 1⅜" from tip of Unit 5 as shown in Diagram 2. Join 5b to Unit 5 at cut edge.

**5.** To make triangle 5-6-7-8, begin by joining units 6, 7, and 8 in a row as shown in Block B Assembly diagram. Press seam allowances away from Unit 7. With right sides facing, join this to Unit 5, carefully aligning 5b seam line with 7-8 seam line. Press joining seam allowance away from Unit 5. Referring to Diagram 3, align ruler with triangle edges and trim units 6 and 8 as shown.

**6.** On one end of each Unit 9 triangle, measure a right angle with 2½"-long legs as shown in Diagram 4. Draw a diagonal line from right-angle corner to triangle edge as shown in red. Cut off triangle tip on drawn line. Join 9a to Unit 9 at cut edge.

**7.** Using diagonal-corner technique, make one of Unit 4.

**8.** To make triangle 1-4-9, join units 4 and 9, matching edges as shown in Block B Assembly diagram. Join Unit 1 to long edge of Unit 4, aligning edges of units 1 and 9. Referring to Diagram 5, align ruler with edge of Unit 1 and trim tip of Unit 4 as shown.

**9.** To make triangle 1-10-1, join a Unit 1 to long sides of Unit 10 as shown in Block B Assembly diagram, aligning bottom edges of all three pieces. Referring to Diagram 6, align ruler with triangle edges and trim Unit 10 as shown.

**10.** Referring to assembly diagram, join triangle 1-2-3 to triangle 5-6-7-8. In the same manner, join triangle 1-4-9 to triangle 1-10-1.

**11.** Join block halves to opposite sides of stem (Unit 11), matching seam lines carefully. Trim ends of Unit 11 even with triangle edges.

**12.** Join one of Unit 12 to top and bottom of block.

**13.** Using diagonal-end technique, join 13a to Unit 13. Then add diagonal corner 13b. Join assembled Unit 13 to left edge of block. Join Unit 14 to right edge to complete block. Make 10 of Block B in this manner.

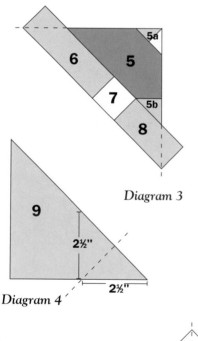

Diagram 3

Diagram 4

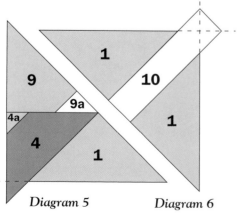

Diagram 5     Diagram 6

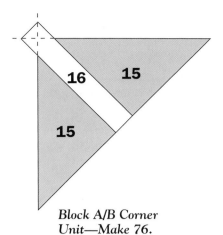

*Block A/B Corner Unit—Make 76.*

## Adding Block Corners

Each block is set on point and squared off with triangular corners. All corners are the same except the four that fall at the corners of the assembled quilt.

**1.** Referring to Block A/B Corner Unit diagram, join Unit 15 triangles to sides of Unit 16. Align ruler with triangle edges and trim Unit 16 as shown. Make 76 corner units.

**2.** With right sides facing, align a corner unit on one side of a flower block so that Unit 16 is centered over one Unit 4 of the block. Join corner to block. Referring to diagram of Block A1, add corner units to remaining sides. Make eight of Block A1 in this manner.

**3.** Referring to diagram of Block A2, add one Unit 17 triangle to top right corner of one flower block. Join corner units to remaining sides to complete Block A2.

**4.** Referring to diagram of Block A3, add one Unit 17 triangle to bottom right corner of remaining flower block. Join corner units to remaining sides to complete Block A3.

**5.** Using leaf blocks, repeat step 2 to make eight of Block B1. To make blocks B2 and B3, position Unit 17 triangles as shown in diagrams; then add corner units to remaining sides.

*Block A1—Make 8.*

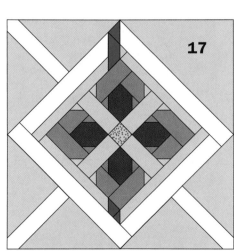

*Block A2—Make 1.*

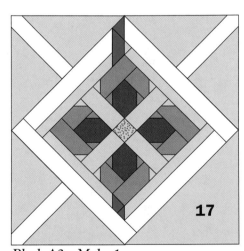

*Block A3—Make 1.*

*Block B1—Make 8.*

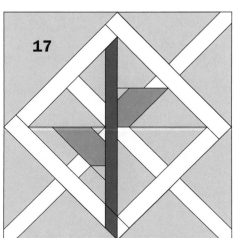

*Block B2—Make 1.*

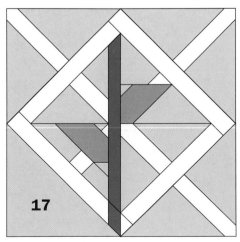

*Block B3—Make 1.*

## Piecing the Corner Flower Blocks

**1.** Referring to Block C diagram, assemble units 1-6 in the same manner as for Block A. Be careful to note position of contrasting fabrics in units 2b, 3b, and 6.

**2.** Using diagonal-corner technique, join C-7a to corners of C-7 triangles.

**3.** Referring to Block C diagram, join one of Unit 7 to opposite sides of each Block C. Add Unit 8 as shown, making combined units into a large triangle.

**4.** Join Unit 9 and then Unit 10 as shown. Align ruler with Unit 7 triangles and trim ends of units 9 and 10.

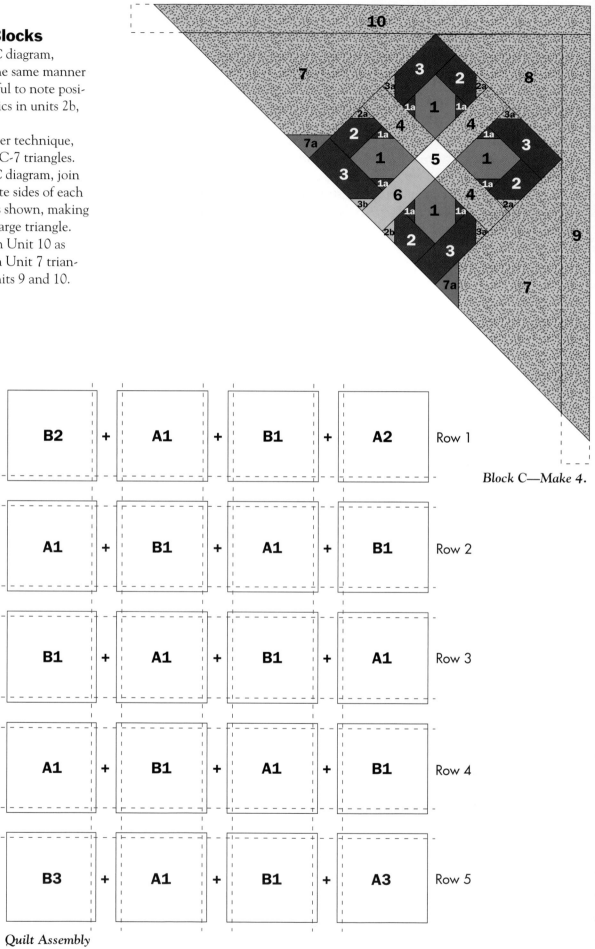

*Block C—Make 4.*

| | | | | | | | |
|---|---|---|---|---|---|---|---|
| **B2** | + | **A1** | + | **B1** | + | **A2** | Row 1 |
| **A1** | + | **B1** | + | **A1** | + | **B1** | Row 2 |
| **B1** | + | **A1** | + | **B1** | + | **A1** | Row 3 |
| **A1** | + | **B1** | + | **A1** | + | **B1** | Row 4 |
| **B3** | + | **A1** | + | **B1** | + | **A3** | Row 5 |

*Quilt Assembly*

## Quilt Assembly

Each block must be trimmed on two or more edges before it can be joined to its neighbor. Only the edges on the outside of the assembled quilt are not trimmed. Lay out blocks in rows as shown in Quilt Assembly diagram before you begin.

**1.** To make Row 1, trim 1" from bottom and both sides of one Block A1 and one Block B1. Trim 1" from bottom and right side of Block B2. Trim 1" from bottom and left side of Block A2. Join trimmed blocks in a row as shown.

**2.** Continue trimming and joining blocks in this manner to assemble rows 2-5, carefully noting block positions and trim lines indicated in Quilt Assembly diagram. Join rows.

**3.** For Border 1, join two 1½" x 42" strips of Fabric IV end-to-end for each side. Join a 28½"-long strip and a 42" strip for top and bottom borders.

**4.** Measure length of quilt top, measuring through middle rather than along sides. Trim Border 1 side borders to this length, cutting equal amounts from both ends of border strip. Sew borders to quilt sides, easing as necessary.

**5.** Measure quilt width through middle of quilt top. Trim remaining borders accordingly; then join borders to top and bottom edges of quilt.

**6.** For Border 2, join three 2½" x 29" strips of Fabric VIII end-to-end for each side. Matching centers of border strips and quilt, join borders to quilt sides. Join two 36"-long strips for top and bottom borders and join to quilt in the same manner.

**7.** For Border 3, join two 2½" x 42" strips of Fabric IX for each side and two 36"-long strips for top and bottom borders. For Border 4, join 6½"-wide strips of Fabric VII in the same manner. Aligning center seams, join matching strips of borders 3 and 4. Matching centers of combined border strips to center of each quilt side, join borders to quilt as before. Note that these borders do not meet at corners, but the ends will be covered by corner blocks.

**8.** Referring to Border Assembly diagram, baste corner flower blocks to quilt, aligning seams of borders and corners. Straight edges of corner blocks should align with edge of Border 4. Stitch corners in place and check for seam alignment. Trim borders underneath corners to ¼" seam allowance.

**9.** For Border 5, join a 1½" x 42" strip of Fabric IX to both ends of a 25"-long strip for each side. Join borders to quilt sides. Press seam allowances toward borders and trim excess fabric from ends. Join a 42" strip to both ends of a 10"-long strip for bottom and top borders and join to quilt.

## Quilting and Finishing

Mark a 3"-wide cable or feather quilting design over borders 2 and 3 and widely spaced cross-hatching in Border 4. Outline-quilt patchwork; then stitch meandering lines of stipple quilting in background fabric to enhance trellis. Quilt border motifs.

Make 11⅛ yards of binding. See page 30 for directions on making and applying straight-grain binding.

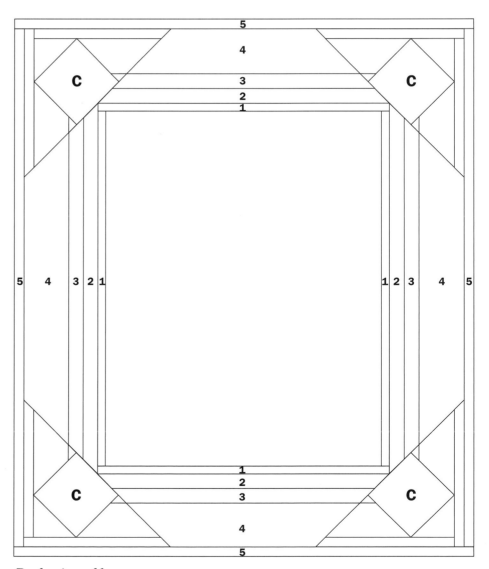

*Border Assembly*

# Till the Cows Come Home

*Round and round the cattle go, through patchwork fields and forests that surround the homes at the heart of this whimsical quilt. You can make all 36 bovine beauties from the same fabrics or with scraps for a more diverse herd. Strip piecing makes quick work of all the fences, tree trunks, and checkerboard borders. Because there is so much piecing in this quilt, we recommend it for experienced quiltmakers.*

**Quick-Piecing Techniques:** Strip Piecing (see page 20)
Diagonal Corners (see page 20)

### Finished Size
Blocks: 36 cow blocks, 6" x 10"      Quilt: 90½" x 110½"
12 large tree blocks, 4" x 6"
80 small tree blocks, 2½" x 3½"
8 long-stemmed tree blocks, 2½" x 5"
4 corner tree blocks, 7½" square
2 house blocks, 8" x 16"

### Materials

| | | |
|---|---|---|
| ■ | Fabric I (black-on-burgundy check) | 1 yard |
| ▨ | Fabric II (brick red print) | ⅛ yard or scraps |
| ▨ | Fabric III (dark salmon print) | ⅛ yard or scraps |
| ▨ | Fabric IV (salmon-pink solid) | 1⅞ yards |
| ■ | Fabric V (brown solid or print) | 1 yard |
| ▨ | Fabric VI (light green solid) | 1⅜ yards |
| ■ | Fabric VII (green print) | 1⅜ yards or scraps |
| □ | Fabric VIII (ivory miniprint) | 4 yards |
| ■ | Fabric IX (dark brown or black print) | ⅜ yard or scraps |
| ▨ | Fabric X (black-on-brown print) | 1 yard or scraps |
| ■ | Fabric XI (burgundy solid) | 3⅛ yards |
| | Backing fabric | 8⅜ yards |
| | Black or brown embroidery floss | 1 skein or scraps |

### Cutting
Refer to diagrams on page 270 to identify blocks and units designated in cutting list.

**From Fabric I (black-on-burgundy check), cut:**
✴ Ten 3" x 42" strips for binding.
✴ One 2½" x 42" strip. From this, cut:
  • Four 2½" squares (A-1a, A-2a).
  • Two 1½" squares (A-4).

**From Fabric II (brick red print), cut:**
✴ Two 2½" x 8½" (A-2).

**From Fabric III (dark salmon print), cut:**
✴ One 1¾" x 42" strip. From this, cut:
  • Four 1¾" x 6" (A-15).
  • Two 1½" x 2" (A-14).
  • Four 1¼" x 2" (A-12).

**From Fabric IV (salmon-pink), cut:**
✴ One 14¾" x 42" strip.
  From this, cut:
  • One 7¼" x 14¾" (G-1).
    Cut this rectangle as shown in Cutting diagram to get eight G-1 triangles. Trim ¾" from narrow tip of each triangle.
  • Two 4½" x 34".
    From these, cut:
    • Twelve 4½" squares (19).
    • Two 2¼" x 6" for Strip Set 3a (G-3).

* Fifteen 3" x 42" strips for strip sets 5 and 6 (checkerboard borders).
* From scraps, cut:
  * Two 1½" x 3½" (A-11).
  * Four 1¼" x 3½" (A-9).

## From Fabric V (brown), cut:

* Eighteen ⅞" x 42" strips for Strip Set 1.
* Three 1" x 42" for strip sets 2 and 3 (B-3, C-3, D-3).
* Four 2½" x 42" strips.
  From these, cut:
  * 116 1¼" x 2½" (A-7, 21).
  * One 1" x 6" for Strip Set 3a (G-3).

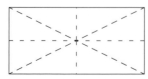

*Cutting*

## From Fabric VI (light green), cut:

* Sixteen 1½" x 42" strips for sashing.
* Eighteen 1" x 42" strips for tree/fence sashing.
* One 3" x 42" strip.
  From this, cut:
  * Eight 1¼" x 3" (C-4).
  * Two 2⅞" squares. Cut each square in half diagonally to get four G-4 triangles.
  * Two 1½" x 16½" (A-18).

## From Fabric VII (green print*), cut:

* Nine 3¼" x 42" strips.
  From these, cut:
  * Eighty-eight 3¼" x 3⅞" (B-2, C-2).

*Note: You can use a different green scrap for each tree or cut yardage as stated.

* One 4⅞" x 42" strip.
  From this, cut:
  * Four 4⅞" x 7⅜" (G-2).
* Two 4¾" x 42" strips.
  From these, cut:
  * Twelve 4¾" x 6¼" (D-2).

## From Fabric VIII (ivory mini-print), cut:

* Eighteen ⅞" x 42" strips for Strip Set 1 (fences).
* Nine 1" x 42" strips for Strip Set 1 (fences).
* Four 1½" x 42" strips for Strip Set 2 (B-3).
* Two 2¼" x 42" strips for Strip Set 3 (C-3, D-3).
* Two 3¼" x 42" strips for Strip Set 4 (E-2, F-2).

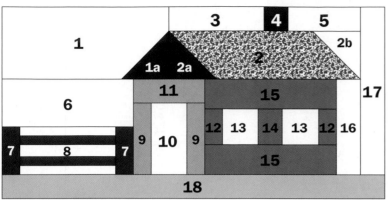

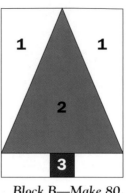

**Block B—Make 80.**
**Block D—Make 12.**

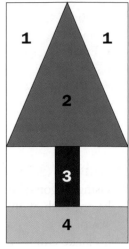

**Block C—Make 8.**

**Block A—Make 2.**

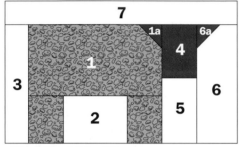

**Block E—Make 18.**

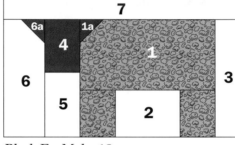

**Block F—Make 18.**

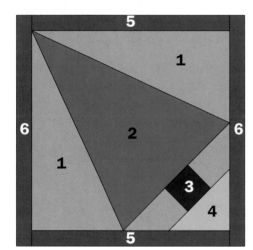

**Block G—Make 4.**

✱ Fourteen 2" x 42" strips.
From these, cut:
- Two 2" x 25" (27).
- Four 2" x 15½" (26).
- Sixteen 2" x 9¼" (25).
- Eight 2" x 12" (23).
- Four 2" x 11½" (22).
- Two 2" x 3½" (A-10).
- Four 2" squares (A-13).
- Thirty-six 2" x 3¼" (E-5, F-5).

✱ One 2½" x 42" strip.
From this, cut:
- Two 2½" squares (A-2b).
- Two 2½" x 6" (A-6).
- Four 2¼" x 4" (28).

✱ Seventeen 1½" x 42" strips.
From these, cut:
- Thirty-six 1½" x 10½" (E-7, F-7).
- Thirty-six 1½" x 5½" (E-3, F-3).
- Two 1½" x 3½" (A-5).
- Four 1½" x 4½" (A-3, A-16).
- Two 1½" x 7½" (A-17).
- Eight 1½" x 6½" (24).

✱ Two 8⅞" x 42" strips.
From these, cut:
- Twenty-two 3¾" x 8⅞" (B-1, C-1).
Cut these as shown in Cutting diagram to get eight triangles from each piece (a total of 176). Trim ⅞" from narrow tip of each triangle. Each rectangle yields four triangles that point to the right and four that point left. Store righties and lefties separately.

✱ One 5¼" x 42½" strip.
From this, cut:
- Three 5¼" x 13¾" (D-1).
Cut these as shown in Cutting diagram to get eight triangles from each piece (a total of 24). Trim 1⅛" from narrow tip of each triangle. Each rectangle yields four triangles that point to the right and four that point left. Store righties and lefties separately.

✱ Two 5½" x 42" strips.
From these, cut:
- Thirty-six 2¼" x 5½" (E-6, F-6).
✱ From scraps, cut:
- Two 3½" x 7½" (A-1).

**From Fabric IX (dark brown or black), cut:**

✱ Two 2¾" x 42" strips.
From these, cut:
- Thirty-six 2" x 2¾" (E-4, F-4).
✱ Three 1½" x 42" strips.
From these, cut:
- Seventy-two 1½" squares (E-1a, E-6a, F-1a, F-6a).

**From Fabric X (black-on-brown print), cut:**

✱ Three 6¼" x 42" strips.
From these, cut:
- Thirty-six 3½" x 6¼" (E-1, F-1).
✱ Four 2" x 42" strips for Strip Set 4 (E-2, F-2). *Note:* If you want scrap cows in your herd, cut shorter strips from fabrics to match E-1 and F-1 pieces.

**From Fabric XI (burgundy), cut:**

✱ Fifteen 3" x 42" strips for strip sets 5 and 6 (checkerboard borders).
✱ Four 1¾" x 42" strips for top and bottom inner borders.
✱ Six 2¾" x 42" strips. From these, cut:
- Six 2¾" x 32" for side inner borders.
- Two 2" x 10½" for top and bottom outer borders.
✱ Ten 2" x 42" strips for outer borders.

✷ Two 6½" x 42" strips.
From these, cut:
• Eight 6½" squares (20).
• Eight 1¼" x 6½" (G-5).
• Four 1¼" x 16".
From these, cut:
• Eight 1¼" x 8" (G-6).

## Piecing the House Blocks

**1.** Using diagonal-corner technique, make one each of units 1 and 2 as shown in Block A Assembly diagram.
**2.** To make Unit 8, refer to diagram of Strip Set 1. Join ⅞" x 42" strips of Fabric V to sides of one 1" x 42" strip of Fabric VIII. Complete strip set with ⅞"-wide strips of Fabric VIII on outside edges. Make one strip set. From this, cut two 4½"-wide segments for Unit 8; set aside remainder of strip set for other fence units.
**3.** Join units 3, 4, and 5 in a row as shown. Join this combined unit to top of Unit 2.
**4.** Join Unit 1 to left side of 2-3-4-5 unit to complete roof section.
**5.** Join one of Unit 7 to both short sides of one Unit 8; then add Unit 6 to top of fence section.
**6.** Join a Unit 9 to both long sides of Unit 10. Add Unit 11 to top of 9-10 unit.
**7.** Join units 12, 13, and 14 in a row as shown in assembly diagram. Join a Unit 15 to top and bottom edges of combined unit; then add Unit 16 to right side.
**8.** Join three combined units in a row as shown to complete fence/house middle section.
**9.** Join roof to top of fence/house section. Join Unit 17 to right side of block; then add Unit 18 to bottom edge to complete block. Make two of Block A.

*Strip Set 1—Make 9.*

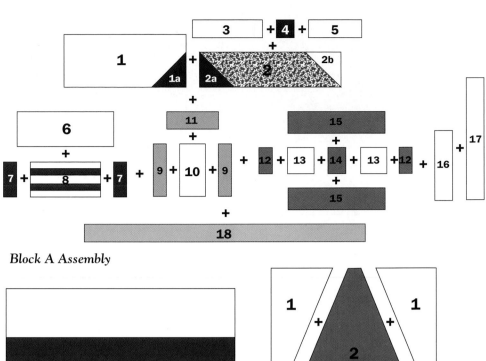

*Block A Assembly*

*Strip Set 2—Make 2.*

*Strip Set 3—Make 1.*

*Block B/C/D Assembly*

*Diagram 1*    *Diagram 2*

## Piecing the Tree Blocks

**1.** Referring to diagrams of strip sets 2 and 3, join strips of Fabrics V and VIII as shown. Make two of Strip Set 2 and one of Strip Set 3. From Strip Set 2, cut eighty 1"-wide segments for B-3. From Strip Set 3, cut twelve 1¼"-wide segments for D-3. From remainder of Strip Set 3, trim ¾" from *each* long edge; then cut eight 1¾"-wide segments for Unit C-3.
**2.** With right sides facing, fold each 3¼" x 3⅞" piece of Fabric VII in half lengthwise as shown in Diagram 1. With fold at right, cut through both layers

from bottom left to top right as shown. Discard trimmed corners. Trim ⅜" from tops of remaining B-2/C-2 triangles.
**3.** For Block B, join Unit 1 triangles to both sides of each Unit 2, positioning righty and lefty triangles as shown. To sew each seam, align raw edges at top as shown in Diagram 2. Press seam allowances toward Unit 1. Add Unit 3 to bottom of Unit 2 to complete block. Make 80 of Block B.
**4.** For Block C, join units 1, 2, and 3 in the same manner as for Block B. Add Unit 4 to bottom to complete block. Make eight of Block C.

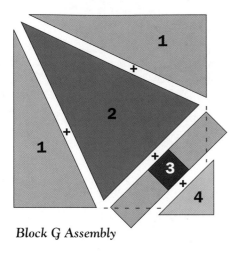

*Block G Assembly*

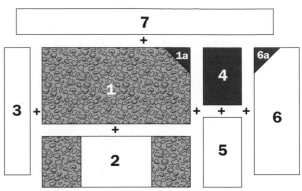

*Block E Assembly*

**5.** For Block D, fold and cut 4¾" x 6¼" pieces of Fabric VII in the same manner as for small trees. Trim ½" from tip of 12 D-2 triangles. Assemble Block D in the same manner as for Block B. Make 12 of Block D.

**6.** For Block G, use designated pieces of fabrics IV and V to make a miniature Strip Set 3 (3a). From this, cut four 1¾"-wide segments for Unit G-3.

**7.** Fold and cut 4⅞" x 7⅜" pieces of Fabric VII in the same manner as for other trees as shown in Diagram 1. Trim ¾" from tip of four G-2 triangles.

**8.** Referring to Block G Assembly diagram, join Unit 1 triangles to both sides of Unit 2, aligning points. Next, join Unit 3 to bottom of Unit 2, centering trunk. Press seam allowances toward Unit 3; then trim sides of Unit 3 even with Unit 1 triangles as shown in assembly diagram. Add Unit 4 as shown. Join Unit 5 to top and bottom edges; then add Unit 6 to sides to complete block. Make four of Block G.

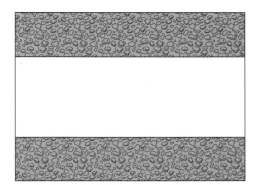

*Strip Set 4—Make 2.*

## Piecing the Cow Blocks

**1.** Referring to Block E Assembly diagram, use diagonal-corner technique to make one each of units 1 and 6. (If using scraps for faces, be sure to coordinate units 1a and 6a with Unit 4.)

**2.** To make Unit 2, refer to diagram of Strip Set 4. Join strips of fabrics VIII and X as shown. Make two strip sets. From these, cut thirty-six 2½"-wide segments for Unit 2. Join one Unit 2 to bottom of Unit 1.

**3.** Cut a 4" length of embroidery floss and tie a knot at each end. Pin one knot in side seam allowance at top left corner of Unit 1. Join Unit 3 to left side of 1-2 unit, catching tail in seam. Back-stitch over tail to secure it.

**4.** Join units 4 and 5 as shown in assembly diagram; then add this to right side of 1-2 unit.

**5.** Join Unit 6 to right side of 4-5 unit. Add Unit 7 to top to complete block. Make 18 of Block E.

**6.** Block F is made in the same manner as Block E, but it is a mirror image. Units are made exactly the same as for Block E, but positions of units 1a and 6a are reversed. Follow Block F diagram on page 270 carefully to assemble blocks. Make 18 of Block F.

## Piecing the Fence Sections

**1.** Referring to diagram of Strip Set 1, follow instructions given in Step 2 of Piecing the House Blocks to make eight more of Strip Set 1.

**2.** From these strip sets, cut the following segments:

◆ Eight 4⅞"-wide segments for First Round.

◆ Sixteen 5⅛"-wide segments for Third Round.

◆ Thirty-two 3¾"-wide segments for Fifth Round.

◆ Twenty-two 4½"-wide segments for Tree rows.

**3.** Referring to Quilt Assembly diagram and photograph, join posts (Unit 21) onto fence segments as shown for each round. All four sections of each round are assembled in the same manner.

## Quilt Assembly

**1.** Referring to Quilt Assembly diagram and quilt photograph, join A blocks at top edges.

**2.** Join each First Round fence section to a Unit 22. Press seam allowances toward Unit 22; then join one B block to both ends of each fence.

**3.** Cut two 1" x 42" strips of Fabric VI in half. Aligning one end with side of Block B, join one half-strip to bottom of a First Round section. Trim strip even with patchwork. Repeat with remaining First Round sections.

**4.** Referring to Quilt Assembly diagram and quilt photograph, join a First Round section to top and bottom of combined house blocks. Note that tree tops always point into quilt center. Join Unit 19 squares to ends of remaining First Round sections; then add these to sides of center section.

**5.** Join an E block and an F block to sides of one Block D for each section of Second Round. Referring to Quilt Assembly diagram, join a Second Round section to top and bottom of First Round, again positioning tree tops toward quilt center. Join Unit 20 squares to ends of remaining Second Round sections and add these to First Round sides.

**6.** Join 1½"-wide sashing strips of Fabric VI to top and bottom of Second Round. Press seam allowances toward sashing; then trim sashing even with patchwork sides. Join sashing strips to sides in the same manner.

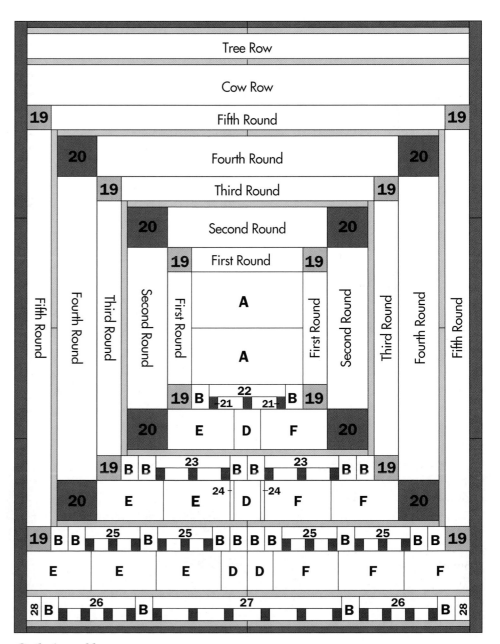

*Quilt Assembly*

**7.** Referring to Quilt Assembly diagram for number and placement of blocks, assemble Third Round sections in the same manner as for First Round, adding 1"-wide strips of Fabric VI to bottom of each section. Join Third Round sections to quilt.

**8.** Make Fourth Round sections in the same manner as for Second Round, adding Unit 24 strips to sides of D blocks as shown in Quilt Assembly Diagram. Join Fourth Round sections to quilt.

**9.** Join two 1½"-wide Fabric VI sashing strips end-to-end for each side of quilt. Matching centers of sashing strips and quilt, join sashing to Fourth Round in the same manner as Second Round sashing.

**10.** Referring to Quilt Assembly diagram, assemble Fifth Round sections. Join two 1"-wide Fabric VI strips end-to-end to make a sashing strip for bottom of each section. Join Fifth Round sections to quilt.

**11.** For each Cow Row, join three of Block E, two of Block D, and three of Block F as shown in Quilt Assembly diagram. Join Cow rows to top and bottom of quilt.

**12.** Join two 1½"-wide Fabric VI sashing strips end-to-end. Matching centers, join sashing to top edge of quilt. Press seam allowance toward sashing; then trim sashing ends even with quilt sides. Repeat to join sashing to bottom edge of quilt.

**13.** For each Tree Row, join fence sections with four B blocks as shown in Quilt Assembly diagram. Add a Unit 28 to both ends of each row. Join assembled rows to top and bottom of quilt.

**14.** Join two 1"-wide Fabric VI sashing strips end-to-end; then join two 1¾"-wide strips of Fabric XI in the same manner. Matching center seams, join strips. Matching centers, join combined strip to top edge of quilt. Press seam allowances toward sashing; then trim sashing ends even with quilt sides. Repeat to join sashing to bottom edge of quilt.

**15.** For each side inner border, join three 2¾" x 32" strips of Fabric XI end-to-end. Matching centers, join borders to quilt sides. Press and trim borders.

## Piecing the Checkerboard Borders

**1.** Referring to diagrams of strip sets 5 and 6, join strips of fabrics IV and XI as shown. Make five of each strip set. From Strip Set 5, cut sixty-two 3"-wide segments. From Strip Set 6, cut sixty-five 3"-wide segments.

**2.** Select two Strip Set 5 segments and one Strip Set 6 segment. Use a seam ripper to remove stitching from these segments to get squares to add to tree blocks (Block C).

**3.** To make bottom border, begin with a Strip Set 6 segment. Add two more segments, alternating between strip sets 5 and 6 as shown in quilt photograph. For fourth segment, join a Fabric XI square to top of one C block and join this to border. Add 14 more segments to border, alternating fabrics as before. For next segment, join a Fabric IV square to bottom of a C block and join this to border. Add 10 more segments to complete border.

**4.** Make top border in the same manner, this time using 28 segments and one C block as shown in photograph.

**5.** Assemble right border in the same manner, using 35 segments and two C blocks. Assemble left border with 34 segments and three C blocks. Note that each border begins and ends with a Strip Set 6 segment.

**6.** Join a corner tree block (Block G) to both ends of each side border, positioning trees as shown.

**7.** Join top and bottom borders to quilt, easing as necessary. (See page 19 for tips on easing.) Join side borders in the same manner.

**8.** Join three 2" x 42" strips of Fabric XI end-to-end for each side border. Matching centers, join borders to quilt. Press seam allowances toward borders; then trim excess border fabric at ends.

**9.** Join a 2" x 42" border strip to both ends of each 10½"-long strip to make top and bottom borders. Join these to quilt in the same manner as for sides.

## Quilting and Finishing

Mark desired quilting designs in Fabric XI borders and corner squares. The quilt shown has little houses quilted in corner squares and cross-hatching in borders and center section. Outline-quilt patchwork and add other quilting as desired.

Make 11⅜ yards of binding. See page 30 for directions on making and applying straight-grain binding.

*Strip Set 5—Make 5.*

*Strip Set 6—Make 5.*

# A **Moo**-vable Feast

*Inspired by the motifs in Till the Cows Come Home, this cheery tablecloth sets a happy tone for a party, picnic, or holiday meal. Select fabrics to represent your favorite breed—you can make a herd of Holsteins like ours, or use black fabric for Angus or tan and cream prints for Jerseys and Guernseys.*

**Quick-Piecing Techniques:** Strip Piecing (see page 20)
Diagonal Corners (see page 20)

**Finished Size**
Blocks: 12 cow blocks, 6" x 10"         Tablecloth: 60" x 90"
        14 tree blocks 4" x 6"
         4 fence blocks, 6" x 11"
         4 corner tree blocks, 7" square

## Materials

| | | |
|---|---|---|
| | Fabric I (black solid) | ⅛ yard |
| | Fabric II (black-on-white spotted print) | ⅜ yard |
| | Fabric III (light brown plaid) | ⅛ yard |
| | Fabric IV (assorted green prints) | scraps |
| | Fabric V (black-on-green small check) | ⅜ yard |
| | Fabric VI (brown solid) | ⅛ yard |
| | Fabric VII (dark apple red) | 5¾ yards |
| | Black embroidery floss | 1 skein |

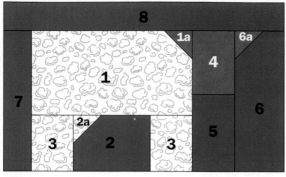

*Block A—Make 6.*

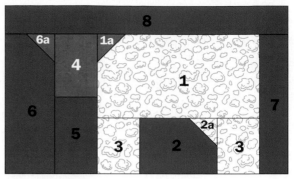

*Block B—Make 6.*

## Cutting

### From Fabric I (black), cut:
* One 2" x 42" strip.
  From this, cut:
  • Twelve 2" x 2¾" (A-4, B-4).
* One 1½" x 42" strip.
  From this, cut:
  • Twenty-four 1½" squares (A-1a, A-6a, B-1a, B-6a).

### From Fabric II (spotted print), cut:
* One 6¼" x 42" strip. From this, cut:
  • Twelve 3½" x 6¼" (A-1, B-1).
* Two 2" x 42" strips.
  From these, cut:
  • Twenty-four 2" x 2½" (A-3, B-3).
* One 1½" x 42" strip.
  From this, cut:
  • Twelve 1½" squares (A-2a, B-2a).

### From Fabric III (light brown plaid), cut:
* Two 1" x 42" strips for Strip Set 1 (C-2).
* Two 1¼" x 42" strips.
  From these, cut:
  • Twelve 1¼" x 4½" (C-1).

### From Fabric IV scraps (green), cut:
* Fourteen 4¾" x 6¼" (D-2).
* Four 5¾" x 8⅝" (E-2).

### From Fabric V (green check), cut:
* Two 3¼" x 42" strips.
  From each of these, cut:
  • One 3¼" square. Cut both squares in half diagonally to get four E-4 triangles.
  • Two 1½" x 36½" strips for grass strips.
* Two 1½" x 42½" strips for grass strips.

### From Fabric VI (brown), cut:
* One 1" x 18" for Strip Set 2 (D-3).
* One 1¼" x 6" for Strip Set 3 (E-3).

### From Fabric VII (dark apple red), cut:
* One 42½" x 72½" for center.
* One 42" x 72½" strip.
  From this, cut:
  • Two 9¾" x 72½" and two 9¾" x 60½" for facings.
  • One 2½" x 57½" for border.
  • One 8¼" x 16⅜" (E-1).
    Cut this as shown in Cutting diagram (page 269) to get eight triangles. Trim ¾" from narrow tip of each triangle. Each rectangle yields four triangles that point to the right and four that point left.
* Nine 2½" x 42" strips.
  From these, cut:
  • Six 2½" x 31" and two 2½" x 29" for borders.
  • Four 2½" x 12½" (C-3).
  • Twelve 2½" x 3¼" (A-2, B-2).
  • Twelve 2" x 3¼" (A-5, B-5).
* One 13¾" x 42" strip.
  From this, cut:
  • Four 5¼" x 13¾" (D-1).
    Cut these as shown in Cutting diagram (page 269) to get a total of 28 (and four extra). Trim 1⅛" from narrow tip of each triangle. Store righties and lefties separately.
  • Six 2¼" x 21" strips.
    From these, cut:
    • Two 2¼" x 18" for Strip Set 2 (D-3).
    • Twelve 2¼" x 5½" (A-6, B-6).
* Six 1½" x 42" strips.
  From these, cut:
  • Twelve 1½" x 10½" (A-8, B-8).
  • Twelve 1½" x 5½" (A-7, B-7).

* Three 1½" x 42" strips for Strip Set 1 (C-2).
* From scraps, cut:
  • Two 2¾" x 6" for Strip Set 3 (E-3).
  • Eight 1½" x 6½" (9).

## Piecing the Cow Blocks

**1.** Referring to Block A diagram, use diagonal-corner technique to make one each of units 1, 2, and 6. *Note:* If desired, eliminate Unit 2a from some blocks to mix some bulls into the herd.

**2.** Join a Unit 3 to both sides of Unit 2. Join 2-3 unit to bottom of Unit 1.

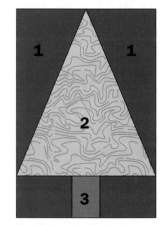

*Block D—Make 14.*

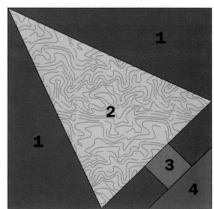

*Block E—Make 4.*

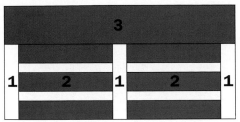

**Block C—Make 4.**

**3.** Join units 4 and 5. Add Unit 6 to right side of 4-5 unit. Join this to right side of cow body.

**4.** Cut a 4" length of embroidery floss and tie a small knot at each end. Pin one knot in side seam allowance at top left corner of Unit 1. Join Unit 7 to left side of cow body, catching tail in seam. Backstitch over tail to secure it.

**5.** Join Unit 8 to top edge to complete block. Make six of Block A.

**6.** Block B is made in the same manner as Block A, but it is a mirror image. Units are the same as for Block A, but positions of diagonal corners are reversed. Follow Block B diagram carefully to assemble six of Block B.

## Piecing the Fence Blocks

**1.** Referring to diagram of Strip Set 1, join three 1½"-wide strips of Fabric VII to two 1"-wide strips of Fabric III. From this strip set, cut eight 4⅞"-wide segments for Unit C-2.

**2.** Join two segments with three of Unit 1 as shown in Block C diagram; then add Unit 3 to top of fence. Make four of Block C.

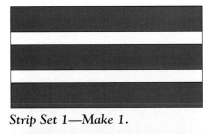

**Strip Set 1—Make 1.**

**Strip Set 2—Make 1.**

## Piecing the Tree Blocks

**1.** Referring to diagram of Strip Set 2, join 2¼" x 18" strips of Fabric VII to both sides of 1" x 18" strip of Fabric VI. From this, cut fourteen 1¼"-wide segments for Unit D-3.

**2.** Fold and cut each 4¾" x 6¼" piece of Fabric IV as described in Step 2 of Piecing the Tree Blocks for *Till the Cows Come Home* (page 271). Trim ½" from tip of each triangle. Assemble block following instructions given in Step 3 of those instructions. Make 14 of Block D.

**3.** To make Strip Set 3, join 2¾" x 6" pieces of Fabric VII to sides of 1¼" x 6" piece of Fabric VI in the same manner as shown for Strip Set 2. From this, cut four 1¼"-wide segments for Unit E-3.

**4.** Fold and cut 5¾" x 8⅝" pieces of Fabric IV in the same manner as for other trees. Trim ⅝" from triangle tips. Assemble block following instructions given in Step 8 of Piecing the Tree Blocks for *Till the Cows Come Home* (page 272). Make four of Block E.

## Tablecloth Assembly

**1.** Referring to Tablecloth Assembly diagram, join one A block, one B block, five D blocks, and two of Unit 9 to make a row for each end of tablecloth. Join a 42½" strip of Fabric V to bottom of each row.

**2.** Join remaining A, B, C, and D blocks to make side rows as shown.

**3.** Join two 36½"-long Fabric V strips end-to-end to make a grass strip for each side. Matching center seams, join grass strip to bottom of each long row.

**4.** Referring to Tablecloth Assembly diagram, join side rows to center section.

**5.** Add E blocks to ends of short rows as shown. Join rows to tablecloth ends.

**6.** Join 57½"-long border to one end of cloth. Press seam allowances toward border; then trim excess border fabric. Join two 29"-long strips to make another 57½" border and join this to opposite end in the same manner.

**7.** To make a border for each side, join three 31" strips end-to-end. Join these to sides of cloth.

**8.** On one long edge of each facing strip, press under a ¼" hem. On longer strips only, turn under another ¼" and press.

**9.** With right sides facing, join ends of long facings to hemmed edge of short facings as shown in Facing diagram. Press seam allowances toward short facings. Topstitch hemmed edges.

**10.** With right sides facing, pin facing to tablecloth and stitch around outer edge. Clip corners; then turn facing to back and press.

**11.** From right side, stitch in-the-ditch in patchwork seams through both layers to secure facing.

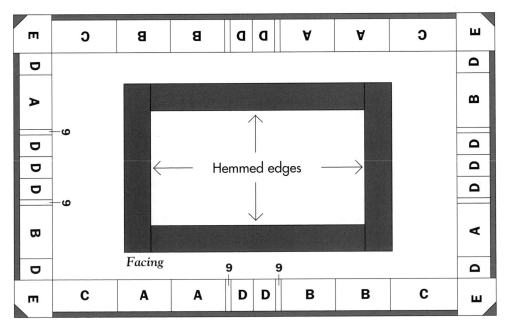

**Tablecloth Assembly**

# Seminole Flower Bed

*This quilt admirably demonstrates how Seminole Patchwork erases the difficulty of working with lots of little pieces. The clever combination of strip sets creates a design that looks intricate but is remarkably quick to sew. In this quilt, one floral print fabric has dramatic effect set amidst coordinating solids and subtle tone-on-tone prints.*

**Quick-Piecing Techniques:**   Strip Piecing (see page 20)

## Finished Size

Blocks: 20 blocks, 16" square          Quilt: 83" x 101"

## Materials

| | | |
|---|---|---|
| Fabric I (pink-and-green floral print) | 2 yards |
| Fabric II (dark mauve solid) | 1½ yards |
| Fabric III (pink-on-pink print) | 4¼ yards |
| Fabric IV (dark green-on-green print) | 1⅝ yards |
| Fabric V (white-on-ivory print) | 5 yards |
| Fabric VI (medium purple-on-purple print) | 5 yards |
| Backing fabric | 7½ yards |
| Square acrylic ruler, at least 12" square | |
| Spray starch | |

# Cutting

### From Fabric I (pink-and-green floral print), cut:
* Twenty $1\frac{1}{8}$" x 42" strips for Strip Set A.
* Ten $1\frac{1}{4}$" x 42" strips for strip sets D and G.
* Eight 2" x 42" strips for Strip Set E.
* Six $1\frac{1}{8}$" x 42" strips. From these, cut:
  * Eighty $1\frac{1}{8}$" squares (2b).
  * Eighty $1\frac{1}{8}$" x $1\frac{3}{4}$" (2c).
* Two $1\frac{1}{4}$" x 42" strips.
  From these, cut:
  * Forty $1\frac{1}{4}$" x 2" (G-1).

### From Fabric II (dark mauve), cut:
* Ten $1\frac{5}{8}$" x 42" strips for Strip Set A.
* Twenty $1\frac{1}{4}$" x 42" strips for strip sets B, D, F, and G.

### From Fabric III (pink print), cut:
* Ten $1\frac{5}{8}$" x 42" strips for Strip Set A.
* Twenty $4\frac{1}{4}$" x 42" strips for Strip Set A.
* Fifteen $1\frac{1}{4}$" x 42" strips for strip sets B, F, H, and L.
* Eight 2" x 42" strips for Strip Set C.
* Three $1\frac{1}{8}$" x 42" strips.
  From these, cut:
  * Eighty $1\frac{1}{8}$" squares (2a).
* Two $1\frac{1}{4}$" x 42" strips.
  From these, cut:
  * Forty $1\frac{1}{4}$" x 2" (F-1).

### From Fabric IV (dark green print), cut:
* Twenty-five $1\frac{1}{4}$" x 42" strips for strip sets B, D, H, J, and K.
* Eight $1\frac{1}{8}$" x 42" strips.
  From these, cut:
  * Eighty $1\frac{1}{8}$" x $1\frac{3}{4}$" (2d).
  * Eighty $1\frac{1}{8}$" x $2\frac{3}{8}$" (2e).
* Ten 1" x 42" strips for inner border.

### From Fabric V (white-on-ivory print), cut:
* Ten $3\frac{3}{8}$" x 42" strips.
  From these, cut:
  * 120 $3\frac{3}{8}$" squares. Cut each square in quarters diagonally to get 480 triangles (7).
* Three 3" x 42" strips. From these, cut:
  * Forty 3" squares. Cut each square in half diagonally to get 80 triangles (8).

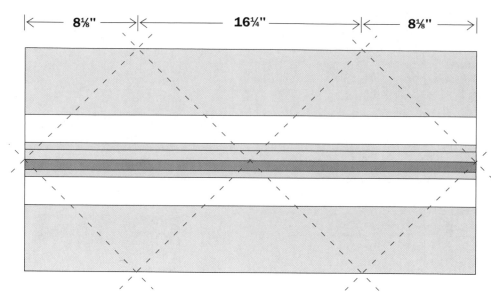

*Strip Set A—Make 10.*

* Twenty $2\frac{7}{8}$" x 42" strips for Strip Set A.
* Thirty-seven $1\frac{1}{4}$" x 42" strips for strip sets B, C, D, E, H, and L.
* Five 2" x 42" strips for strip sets I and K.
* Ten $1\frac{1}{2}$" x 42" strips for middle border.

### From Fabric VI (medium purple print), cut:
* Nine 3" x 42" strips for binding.
* Eighteen $1\frac{1}{4}$" x 42" strips for strip sets H, I, J, K, and L.
* Five 2" x 42" strips for strip sets I and L.
* Four $2\frac{3}{4}$" x 42" strips for Strip Set J.
* Sixteen $2\frac{1}{2}$" x 42" strips for sashing units.
  From 12 of these, cut:
  * Twenty-four $2\frac{1}{2}$" x $14\frac{1}{4}$" for horizontal sashing.
* Twenty-seven 1" x 42" strips.
  From these, cut:
  * Forty 1" x $11\frac{1}{2}$" (3).
  * Forty 1" x $12\frac{1}{2}$" (4).
* Ten 3" x $42\frac{1}{2}$" for outer border.

## Piecing and Cutting the Strip Sets
Before beginning, review page 20 for general instructions on strip piecing .
**1.** Referring to diagram of Strip Set A, join strips of fabrics I, II, III, and V as shown. Make 10 of Strip Set A.

**2.** Starting at one corner of each strip set, measure and mark $8\frac{1}{8}$" along one side as shown in diagram of Strip Set A. Measure and mark another $16\frac{1}{4}$" and then another $8\frac{1}{8}$" as shown. Repeat on opposite side.

**3.** Align square ruler with center seam and marked points to cut Strip Set A as shown. Cut two $11\frac{1}{2}$" squares from each strip set for block centers (Unit 1).

**4.** Referring to diagrams of strip sets B–L, join designated strips to make strip sets as shown.

**5.** From *each* of strip sets B, C, D, and E, cut 240 segments, each $1\frac{1}{4}$" wide. (To avoid confusion, store segments from each strip set in a zip-top plastic bag as described on page 17. Label each bag with strip set letter.)

**6.** From *each* of strip sets F and G, cut forty $1\frac{1}{4}$"-wide segments.

**7.** From *each* of strip sets H and I, cut twenty-four $1\frac{1}{4}$"-wide segments.

**8.** From Strip Set J, cut 129 segments, each $1\frac{1}{4}$" wide.

**9.** From *each* of strip sets K and L, cut 105 segments, each $1\frac{1}{4}$" wide.

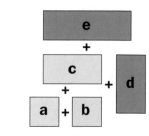

*Unit 2 Assembly*

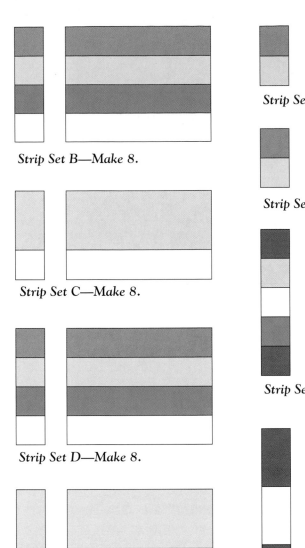

*Strip Set B—Make 8.*

*Strip Set C—Make 8.*

*Strip Set D—Make 8.*

*Strip Set E—Make 8.*

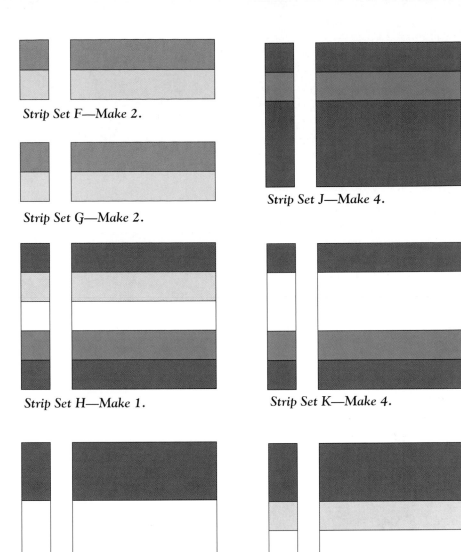

*Strip Set F—Make 2.*

*Strip Set G—Make 2.*

*Strip Set J—Make 4.*

*Strip Set H—Make 1.*

*Strip Set K—Make 4.*

*Strip Set I—Make 1.*

*Strip Set L—Make 4.*

## Piecing the Blocks

The Seminole Flower block is made with pieces designated for units 2, 3, and 4, and segments from strip sets A–G.

### To make the block center:

1. Referring to Unit 2 Assembly diagram, join 2a through 2e in alphabetical order as shown. Make 80 of Unit 2. Press under ¼" on Fabric IV edges only.

2. Aligning raw edges, position a Unit 2 at corners of Unit 1 squares. Topstitch or appliqué turned edges in place as shown in Block Assembly diagram.

3. Join a Unit 3 strip to top and bottom edges of each block. Press seam allowances toward Unit 3. Join Unit 4 strips to block sides in the same manner.

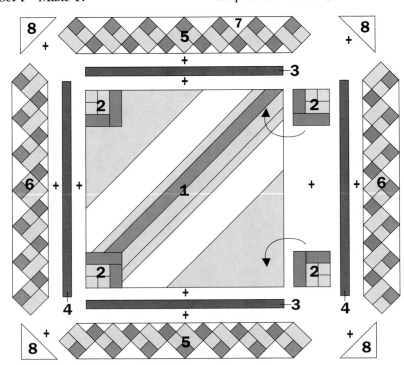

*Block Assembly*

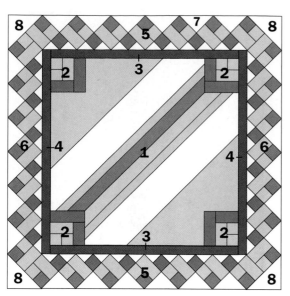

*Seminole Flower Block—Make 20.*

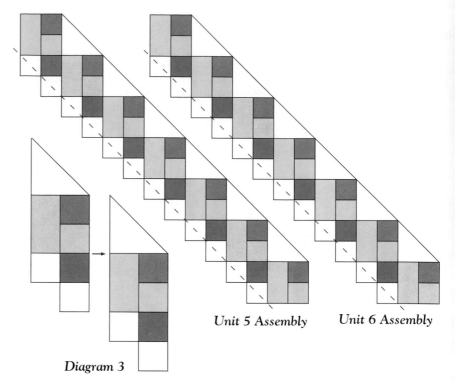

Unit 5 Assembly     Unit 6 Assembly

*Diagram 3*

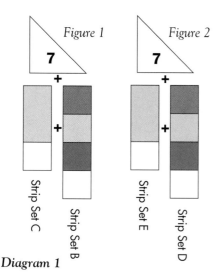

Figure 1     Figure 2

7     7

Strip Set C   Strip Set B     Strip Set E   Strip Set D

*Diagram 1*

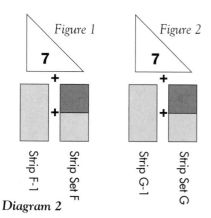

Figure 1     Figure 2

7     7

Strip F-1   Strip Set F     Strip G-1   Strip Set G

*Diagram 2*

### To make the Seminole-pieced block borders:

**1.** Referring to Diagram 1, Figure 1, join one segment of Strip Set B to one from Strip Set C, aligning top edges and seam lines. Make 12 B-C flower

units for each block. On 10 of these, add a Unit 7 triangle to top as shown. Referring to Diagram 1, Figure 2, make D-E flower units in the same manner.

**2.** Referring to Diagram 2, Figure 1, join Strip Set F segments with F-1 pieces. Add a Unit 7 triangle to top as shown to complete flower unit. Make two F units for each block. Referring to Diagram 2, Figure 2, make G flower units in the same manner.

**3.** Referring to Unit 5 Assembly diagram, join flower units in a row, aligning edges and seams as shown in Diagram 3. Make two of Unit 5 for each block. Referring to Unit 6 Assembly diagram, join flower units to make two of Unit 6 for each block. Press units 5 and 6, using a light spray of starch to prevent stretching bias edges when cutting.

**4.** Referring to assembly diagrams, trim bottom edges of each unit 5 and unit 6 strip, being careful to leave ¼" seam allowance below each seam.

**5.** Join a Unit 5 to top and bottom edges of each block, beginning and ending seams ¼" from each corner. Backstitch to secure. Join Unit 6 to block sides in the same manner. Join units 5 and 6 at each corner, stitching from outer edges to inside corners. Press mitered seams open.

**6.** Join Unit 8 triangles to corners to complete blocks. Completed blocks should measure 16½" square.

## Piecing the Sashing

Separate units are assembled for horizontal and vertical sashing. Horizontal sashing is made with segments from strip sets H, I, J, and 2½" x 14¼" pieces of Fabric VI. Vertical sashing is made with segments from strip sets J, K, L, and remaining 2½"-wide strips of Fabric VI.

### To make horizontal sashing:

**1.** Referring to Diagram 4, Figure 1, join segments of strip sets H, I, and J to make one flower unit, aligning seams as shown. Make 24 flower units. Press units with spray starch as before.

**2.** Align ruler with edges and trim flower units as shown in Diagram 4, Figure 2. Be careful to leave seam allowance below each seam.

**3.** Referring to Diagram 5, measure and mark 6⅜" from bottom left corner of each 2½" x 14¼" piece of Fabric VI. Next, measure and mark 5⅜" from top right corner as shown. Align ruler on diagonal line between marks and cut as shown to get two sashing units from each piece.

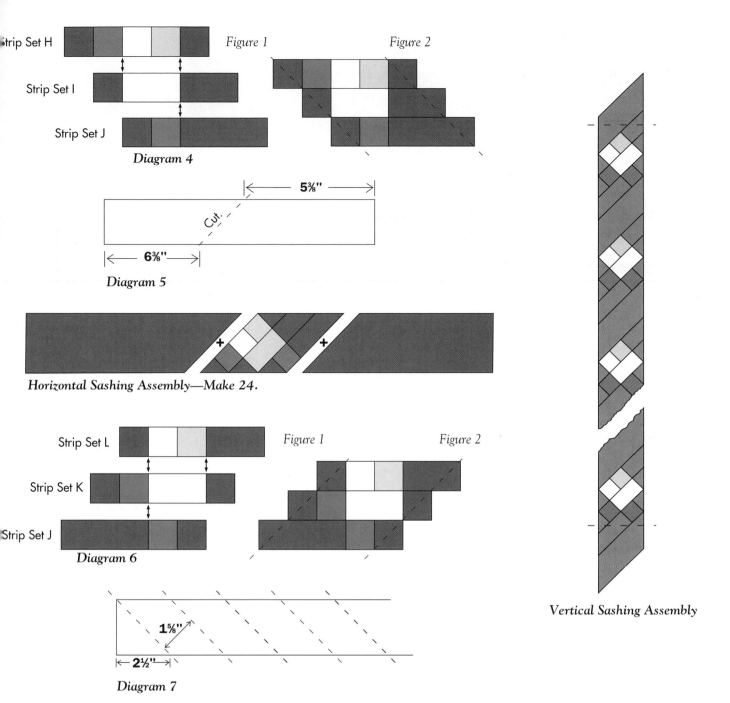

Strip Set H

*Figure 1*

*Figure 2*

Strip Set I

Strip Set J

**Diagram 4**

5⅜"

Cut.

6⅜"

**Diagram 5**

+          +

*Horizontal Sashing Assembly—Make 24.*

Strip Set L

*Figure 1*

*Figure 2*

Strip Set K

Strip Set J

**Diagram 6**

1⅝"

2½"

**Diagram 7**

*Vertical Sashing Assembly*

**4.** Referring to Horizontal Sashing Assembly diagram, join sashing units to flower unit sides. Make 24 horizontal sashing strips. Each strip should measure 16½" long.

**To make vertical sashing:**
**1.** Referring to Diagram 6, Figure 1, join segments of strip sets J, K, and L to make one flower unit, aligning seams as shown. Make 105 flower units. Press units with spray starch as before.

**2.** Align ruler with edges and trim flower units as shown in Diagram 6, Figure 2. Be careful to leave seam allowance below each seam.
**3.** Referring to Diagram 7, measure and mark 2½" from bottom left corner of each remaining 2½"-wide strip of Fabric VI. Align ruler on diagonal line between mark and top left corner as shown and cut. Discard trimmed triangle. Align ruler with cut edge and cut 1⅝"-wide segments from remainder of strip. In this manner, cut a total of 110 sashing units.

**4.** Referring to Vertical Sashing Assembly diagram, join 21 flower units in a vertical row with sashing units between them. Add sashing units to top and bottom of row. Make five vertical sashing rows.
**5.** Trim bottom and top of each sashing row as shown, leaving seam allowances beyond flower seams. Each trimmed sashing row should measure 92½" long.

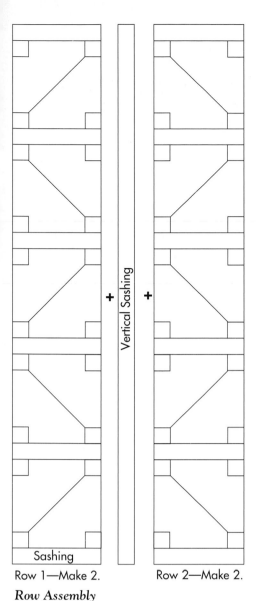

Sashing

Row 1—Make 2.    Row 2—Make 2.

Vertical Sashing

*Row Assembly*

## Quilt Assembly

**1.** Referring to Row Assembly diagram, join five blocks and six horizontal sashing units as shown to make one of Row 1. Pay careful attention to diagram for correct positioning of diagonal center of each block. Ease blocks to fit sashing units as necessary. (See page 19 for tips on easing.) Make two of Row 1. Repeat to make two of Row 2.

**2.** Join rows in 1-2-1-2 order as shown in Row Assembly diagram, with a vertical sashing row between block rows. Ease block rows to fit vertical sashing rows as necessary. Add remaining vertical sashing rows to quilt sides.

**3.** Join two 1" x 42" strips of Fabric IV end-to-end for top inner border. Repeat for bottom border. Join two 1½" x 42" strips of Fabric V in the same manner for top and bottom middle borders. Join two 3" x 42½" strips of Fabric VI in the same manner for top and bottom outer borders.

**4.** Matching center seams, join three strips for top border. Aligning centers of border and quilt, join border to top edge, starting and stopping seam ¼" from each corner. Repeat for bottom border.

**5.** Join three 1" x 42" strips of Fabric IV end-to-end for each side inner border. Join strips of fabrics V and VI in the same manner for middle and outer borders. Matching seams, join three strips to make one border for each side. Trim 8" or 9" from both ends of each strip.

**6.** Aligning centers of border and quilt, join border to one side edge, starting and stopping seam ¼" from each corner. Repeat for opposite side.

**7.** Miter border corners.

## Quilting and Finishing

Hand quilting is recommended for this quilt to minimize stretching all the bias edges. Quilt in-the-ditch in diagonal seam lines of all Seminole Patchwork. Continue the diagonal lines of the patchwork by quilting into solid areas of sashing units and triangle units 7 and 8.

Make 10½ yards of binding. See page 30 for directions on making and applying straight-grain binding.

# Blue Stars

Three simple blocks combine to make a galaxy of stars framed with a two-strip border. The monochromatic color scheme makes this quilt an ideal project in the color of your choice.

**Quick-Piecing Techniques:** Diagonal Corners (see page 20)
Triangle-Squares (see page 22)

**Finished Size**

Blocks: 165 blocks, 6" square
        52 half blocks, 3" x 6"          Quilt: 78" x 102"

**Materials**

| | Fabric | Yards |
|---|---|---|
| | Fabric I (medium blue solid) | 3½ yards |
| | Fabric II (dark blue mini-print) | 3¼ yards |
| | Fabric III (dark blue mini-print) | 1¾ yards |
| | Fabric IV (light blue print) | 2 yards |
| | Fabric V (medium blue print) | 1¾ yards |
| | Fabric VI (light blue check or print) | 2 yards |
| | Backing fabric | 6 yards |

## Cutting

Refer to diagrams on page 288 to identify blocks and units designated in cutting list.

**From Fabric I (medium blue), cut:**

✳ Eighteen 6½" x 42" strips.
  From these, cut:
  • Eighty-two 6½" squares (C-1).
  • Twenty-eight 3½" x 6½" (D-1).

**From Fabric II (dark blue mini-print), cut:**

✳ Nine 2½" x 42" strips for border.
✳ Nine 2½" x 42" strips for binding.
✳ Nine 6½" x 42" strips.
  From these, cut:
  • Thirty-five 6½" squares (B-1).
  • Twenty-four 3½" x 6½" (E-1).
✳ One 6" x 10" for half-square triangles (F).

**From Fabric III (dark blue mini-print), cut:**

✳ Twenty-eight 2" x 42" strips.
  From these, cut:
  • 576 2" squares (A-1a, C-1a, D-1a).

**From Fabric IV (light blue print), cut:**

✳ Nine 1½" x 42" strips for inner border.
✳ Four 3½" x 42" strips.
  From these, cut:
  • Forty-eight 3½" squares (A-1).
✳ Eighteen 2" x 42" strips.
  From these, cut:
  • 192 2" squares (A-3a).
  • Ninety-six 2" x 3½" (A-2).

**From Fabric V (medium blue print), cut:**

✳ Twenty-six 2" x 42" strips.
  From these, cut:
  • 192 2" squares (A-2a).
  • 192 2" x 3½" (A-3).

**From Fabric VI (light blue check or print), cut:**

✳ Sixteen 3½" x 42" strips.
  From these, cut:
  • 188 3½" squares (B-1a, E-1a).
✳ One 6" x 10" for half-square triangles (F).

## Piecing the Blocks

1. Referring to Block A Assembly diagram, use diagonal-corner technique to make one of Unit 1, two of Unit 2, and four of Unit 3 for each Block A. Join units in horizontal rows as shown; then join rows. Make 48 of Block A.

2. Using diagonal-corner technique, make blocks B, C, D, and E as shown.

3. To make Block F, see page 22 for instructions on half-square triangles. On wrong side of the 6" x 10" piece of Fabric VI, draw a 1 x 2-square grid of 3⅞" squares. With right sides facing, match marked fabric with the 6" x 10" piece of Fabric II. Stitch grid as directed on page 22. Cut 4 triangle-squares from this grid.

## Quilt Assembly

1. Referring to Row Assembly diagram, join blocks in rows as shown. Make two edge rows, eight of Row 1, and seven of Row 2.

2. Starting with a Row 1, join all rows 1 and 2, alternating row types.

3. Referring to photograph, add an edge row to top. Turn remaining edge row upside down and join it to bottom.

4. For side inner borders, cut in half one 1½"-wide strip of Fabric IV. Stitch one of these short strips between two full-length strips to make a 104"-long border strip for each side. For top and bottom borders, join two full-length strips end-to-end for each border.

5. Join long borders to sides of quilt. Press seam allowances toward border and trim excess border length. Add top and bottom borders in same manner.

6. Assemble 2½"-wide strips of Fabric II in same manner to make outer borders. Join outer borders to quilt in same manner as inner border.

## Quilting and Finishing

Outline-quilt patchwork and borders or quilt as desired.

Make 10¼ yards of binding. See page 30 for directions on making and applying straight-grain binding.

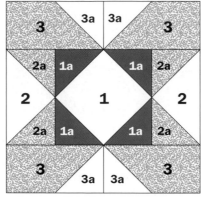

Block A—Make 48.

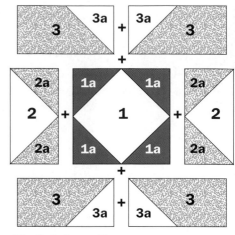

Block A Assembly

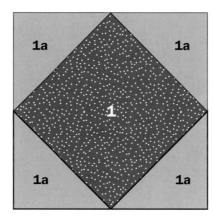

Block B—Make 35.

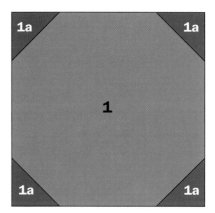

Block C—Make 82.

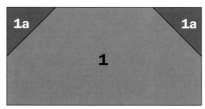

Block D—Make 28.

Block F—Make 4.

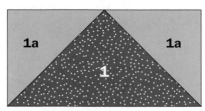

Block E—Make 24.

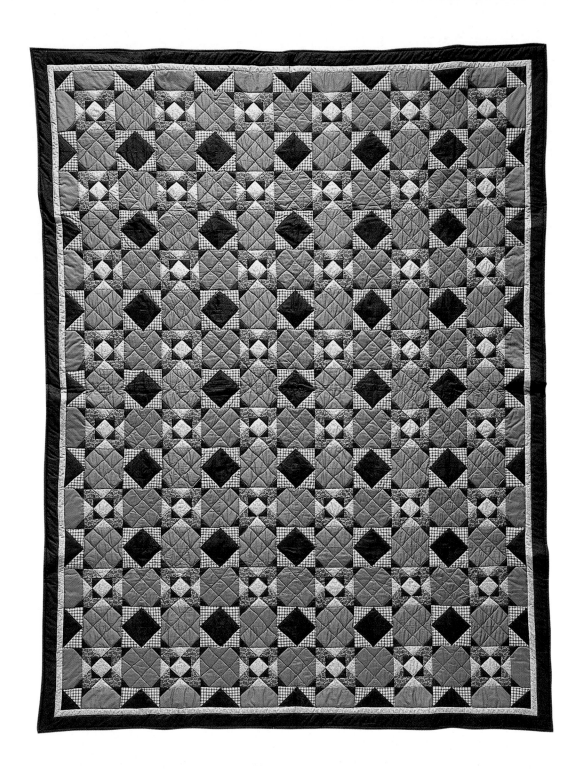

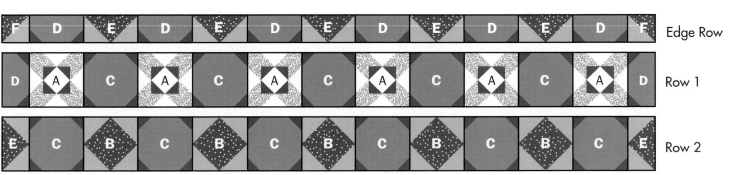

Edge Row

Row 1

Row 2

*Row Assembly*

# Formal Garden

A medley of four colors harmonizes in this patchwork interpretation of the elaborate landscapes of stately homes. The fabrics—in pastels or another theme of your choice—create a lovely diversity that disguises how easy this quilt is to make. Because this quilt uses just two basic quick-piecing techniques, we recommend it for beginners.

**Quick-Piecing Techniques:**　Diagonal Corners (see page 20)
Triangle-Squares (see page 22)

**Finished Size**

Blocks: 90 flower blocks, 6" x 10"　　　　Quilt: 92" x 116"
　　　20 half blocks, 6" square
　　　　8 corner leaf blocks, 6" square
　　　　8 nine-patch blocks, 6" square
　　　　4 checkerboard blocks, 10" square

**Materials**

| | | |
|---|---|---|
| Fabric I (blue print) | ¾ yard |
| Fabric II (light blue solid) | ¾ yard |
| Fabric III (yellow print) | ¾ yard |
| Fabric IV (light yellow solid) | ¾ yard |
| Fabric V (lavender print) | ¾ yard |
| Fabric VI (light lavender solid) | ¾ yard |
| Fabric VII (pink-on-pink print) | ¾ yard |
| Fabric VIII (light pink print) | ¾ yard |
| Fabric IX (light green texture-look print) | 2⅝ yards |
| Fabric X (dark green solid) | 3⅞ yards |
| Fabric XI (white solid) | 6⅝ yards |
| Backing fabric | 8½ yards |
| ⅛"-wide dark green double-faced satin ribbon | 12 yards |

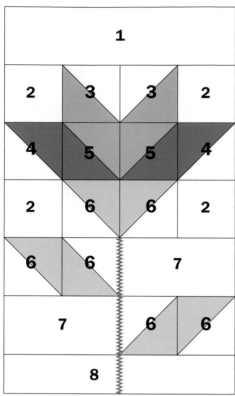

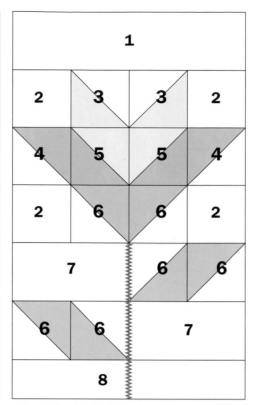

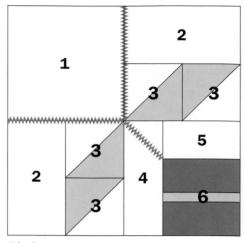

Block C—Make 8.

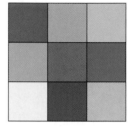

Block A—Make 19 with Fabrics I/II.
Make 26 with Fabrics V/VI.

Block B—Make 27 with Fabrics III/IV.
Make 18 with Fabrics VII/VIII.

Block D—Make 8.

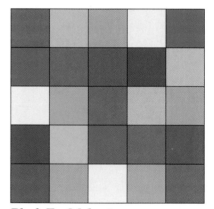

Block E—Make 4.

## Cutting

**From *each* of Fabrics I through VIII, cut:**
* One 11" x 42" strip. From this, cut:
  • Two 11" x 18¼" for triangle-squares (A-3, A-4, A-5, B-3, B-4, B-5).
* Two 2½" x 42" strips. From these, cut:
  • Eighteen 2½" squares (Blocks D and E).
* Three 1½" x 42" strips. From these, cut:
  • Ten 1½" x 10½" (outer border sashing).

**From Fabric IX (light green), cut:**
* Six 11" x 42" strips. From these, cut:
  • Twelve 11" x 16" for triangle-squares (A-6, B-6, C-3).
* Nine ¾" x 43" strips for Strip Set X.
* Eighteen 1" x 42" strips for Strip Set Y.

**From Fabric X (dark green), cut:**
* Eighteen 1⅜" x 42" strips for Strip Set X.
* Thirty-six 1¾" x 42" strips for Strip Set Y.
♦ Eleven 3" x 42" strips for binding.

* Two 2½" x 42" strips. From these, cut:
  • Twenty-eight 2½" squares (Blocks D and E).
* Two 1½" x 42" strips. From these, cut:
  • Eight 1½" x 10½" (outer border sashing).

**From Fabric XI (white), cut:**
* Ten 11" x 42" strips. From these, cut:
  • Eight 11" x 18¼" for triangle-squares (A-3, A-4, B-3, B-4).
  • Twelve 11" x 16" for triangle-squares (A-6, B-6, C-3).
* Ten 3½" x 42" strips. From these, cut:
  • 196 2" x 3½" (A-7, B-7, C-2).
  • Eight 3½" squares (C-1).
* Fifteen 1½" x 42½" strips. From these, cut:
  • Ninety 1½" x 6½" (A-8, B-8).
  • Eight 1½" x 2½" (C-5).
  • Eight 1½" x 3½" (C-4).
* Thirty 2" x 42" strips. From these and scraps, cut:
  • 110 2" x 6½" (A-1, B-1).
  • 440 2" squares (A-2, B-2).

## Piecing the Flower Blocks

1. See page 22 for complete instructions on half-square triangles. On wrong side of one 11" x 18¼" piece of Fabric II, draw a 4 x 7-square grid of 2⅜" squares. Repeat with 11" x 18¼" pieces of fabrics IV, VI, and VIII.
2. With right sides facing, match each marked fabric with an 11" x 18¼" piece of second fabric in the same color family (fabrics I, III, V, and VII). Stitch each grid as directed on page 22. Cut 56 triangle-squares from each grid for units A-5 and B-5.

**3.** On wrong side of each 11" x 18¼" piece of Fabric XI, draw a 4 x 7-square grid of 2⅜" squares. With right sides facing, match one marked piece with each remaining 11" x 18¼" piece of colored fabric (fabrics I–VIII). Stitch grids as before and cut 56 triangle-squares from each grid for units A-3, A-4, B-3, and B-4.

**4.** On wrong side of each 11" x 16" piece of Fabric XI, draw a 4 x 6-square grid of 2⅜" squares. With right sides facing, match marked pieces with corresponding pieces of Fabric IX. Stitch grids as directed on page 22. Cut 48 triangle-squares from each grid to get 572 triangle-squares (and four extra) for units A-6, B-6, and C-3.

**5.** Referring to Block A Assembly diagram, join blue triangle-squares and white units in horizontal rows, turning triangle-squares as shown. Join rows to complete one each of sections A and B.

**6.** Add ribbon stem to Section B before joining sections. (A walking foot or even-feed foot is helpful for applying ribbon.) Center ribbon over Section B center seam (between units 6 and 7), extending ribbon to bottom of Unit 8. Topstitch down one side of ribbon; then lift presser foot, pivot block, and stitch opposite side.

**7.** Join sections A and B to complete one block. Make 19 of Block A with blue triangle-squares and 26 blocks with lavender triangle-squares.

**8.** The flower part (Section A) of each Block B is exactly the same as for Block A. Section B is made with the same units, but Unit 6 (leaves) positions are reversed. Following block diagram carefully, make 27 of Block B with yellow triangle-squares and 18 blocks with pink triangle-squares.

**9.** Use remaining units to make half blocks. Referring to Block A Assembly diagram, make Section A only. Make nine blue half blocks, one yellow half block, one lavender half block, and nine pink half blocks. Before beginning quilt assembly, you should have 90 blocks and 20 half blocks.

## Piecing the Corner Blocks

**1.** Referring to Strip Set X diagram, join two 1⅜" strips of Fabric X to both sides of each ¾" strip of Fabric IX. Make nine strip sets. From these, cut four 36½ lengths, four 30½" lengths, and four 12½" lengths. Set these aside for inside borders. From remainder, cut eight 2½" lengths for Unit C-6.

**2.** To assemble top half of corner leaf block, begin by joining two of Unit 3 as shown at top right of Block C Assembly diagram. Join Unit 2 to top of Unit 3 pair. Add Unit 1 to left side of combined unit.

**3.** Before joining bottom half of Block C, add ribbon to Unit 4 as follows. Cut 2½" of ribbon. Starting at top left corner of Unit 4 piece, center ribbon at a 45° angle across width of unit. Topstitch both sides of ribbon.

**4.** To assemble bottom half of corner leaf block, begin by joining two of Unit 3 as shown at bottom left of Block C Assembly diagram. Join Unit 2 to left side of Unit 3 pair; then join Unit 4 to right side. Join units 5 and 6; then join this to right side of combined unit.

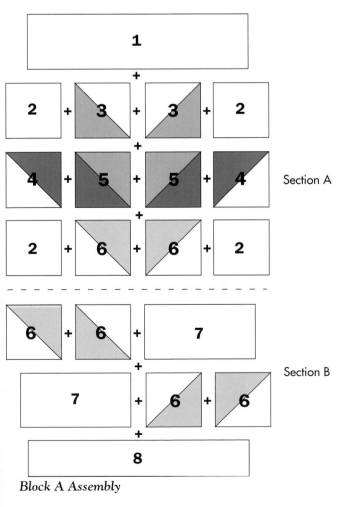

*Block A Assembly*

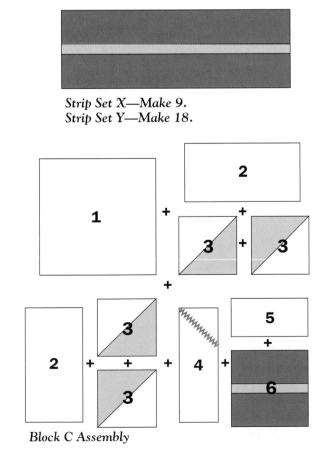

*Strip Set X—Make 9.*
*Strip Set Y—Make 18.*

*Block C Assembly*

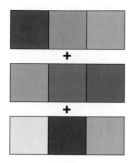

**Block D Assembly**

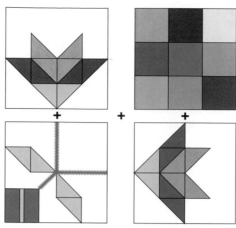

**Corner Assembly**

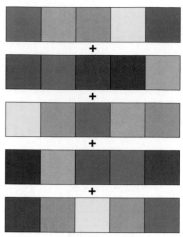

**Block E Assembly**

**5.** Join top and bottom sections to complete block. Make eight of Block C.

**6.** Cut 6¾" of ribbon for each C block. Topstitch ribbon in place atop Unit 1 seam, mitering ribbon at corner.

**7.** Referring to Block D Assembly diagram, join 2½" squares of fabrics I–VIII in three horizontal rows of three squares each, placing a Fabric X square in middle of center row as shown. Join rows to complete Block D. Make eight of Block D.

**8.** Referring to Corner Assembly diagram, join pink and blue half blocks with C and D blocks. Make eight corner blocks.

**9.** Referring to Block E Assembly diagram, join twenty-five 2½" squares of colored fabrics in five horizontal rows of five squares each, placing Fabric X squares in rows as shown. Make two of Block E as shown. Make two more blocks in the same manner, reversing placement of light and dark values of each color family.

## Quilt Assembly

**1.** Referring to Quilt Assembly diagram, join four remaining half blocks as shown to make center square. (Arrows on diagram indicate color and direction of each flower.)

**2.** Join a lavender block to right sides of four yellow blocks. Add 12½" lengths of Strip Set X to bottoms of all four pairs. Matching strip-set edge to center square, join two pairs to sides of center square. Join assembled corner blocks to sides of both remaining pairs, aligning seams of strip-set units. Referring to Quilt Assembly diagram, join these to top and bottom of center square.

**3.** Starting with a yellow block, join six blocks in a horizontal row as shown in Quilt Assembly diagram, ending with a lavender block. Make four rows. Join a 36½" length of Strip Set X to bottom of each row, easing blocks to fit as necessary. (See page 19 for tips on easing.)

**4.** Matching strip-set edge to center section, join two rows to sides of center square as shown in Quilt Assembly diagram. Join corner blocks to ends of both remaining rows. Referring to Quilt Assembly diagram, join these rows to top and bottom of center section.

**5.** Join two 30½" lengths of Strip Set X end-to-end to make 60½"-long top and bottom borders. Matching center seams, join borders to top and bottom of center section.

**6.** Referring to top of Quilt Assembly diagram, join 10 blocks in a horizontal row, starting with a pink block and ending with a lavender block. Matching top of block row with top border, join row to top of quilt.

**7.** Referring to bottom of assembly diagram, join 10 more blocks in a row, starting with a blue block and ending with a yellow block. Join this row to quilt bottom, again matching top of block row to border.

**8.** For Strip Set Y, join two 1¾" strips of Fabric X to sides of 1" strip of Fabric IX. Make 18 strip sets.

**9.** Join two of Strip Set Y end-to-end to make an 84½"-long border. Join these to quilt sides, easing quilt to fit border as necessary. From four of Strip Set Y, cut four 33½"-long strips. Join

two of these end-to-end to make a 66½" border for top and bottom edges. Matching center seams, join borders to top and bottom of center section.

**10.** Join yellow 1½" x 10½" sashing strips in pairs. Join one pair to each remaining yellow block, matching lighter sashing strip to *right side* of block. Using pink sashing strips, repeat with all but two pink blocks. Join each of the four remaining pink sashing strips to Fabric X strips.

**11.** Join lavender sashing strips in pairs. Join one pair to each remaining lavender block, matching lighter sashing strip to *left side* of block. Using blue sashing strips, repeat with all but two blue blocks. Join each of the four remaining blue sashing strips to Fabric X strips.

**12.** Referring to right side of Quilt Assembly diagram, join 11 blocks in a vertical row, starting with a yellow block and ending with a pink block. Note arrow directions for positioning of blocks. Add blue/green and pink/green sashing strips to row ends as shown. Join this row to right side of quilt. Referring to left side of assembly diagram, join blocks for left side of quilt as shown.

**13.** Use remaining blocks to assemble horizontal rows for top and bottom of quilt as shown in Quilt Assembly diagram. Add blue/green and pink/green sashing strips to row ends as shown; then join E blocks to row ends, positioning diagonal rows of Fabric X squares as shown. Join these rows to top and bottom of quilt.

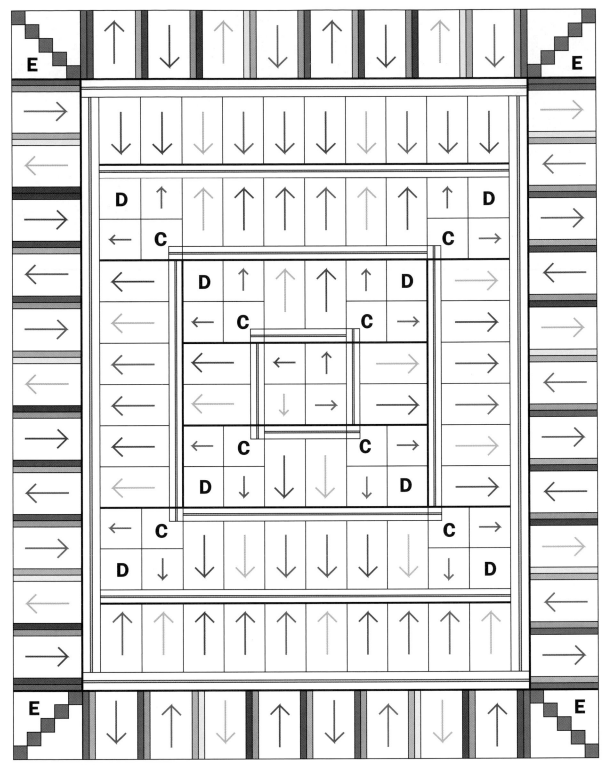

*Quilt Assembly*

**14.** From remaining Y strip sets, cut six 37½" lengths, four 38½" lengths, and four 9" lengths. Join three 37½" lengths end-to-end to make 111½"-long borders for each side. Matching centers of border and quilt side, join one of these to each side of quilt. For each of the top and bottom borders, join two 38½" lengths end-to-end and then add a 9" length to each end. Join these to top and bottom of quilt in the same manner as for side borders.

## Quilting and Finishing
Outline-quilt patchwork or quilt as desired.

Make 12 yards of binding. See page 30 for directions on making and applying straight-grain binding.

# South of the Border

Add a little salsa to your home decor with a quilt that says, "Olé, amigos!" A palette of colors from the American desert enhances four classic southwestern motifs that you can assemble with just two quick-piecing techniques. See page 303 for a spicy tablecloth made with the same chili blocks.

**Quick-Piecing Techniques:** Diagonal Corners (see page 20)
Diagonal Ends (see page 21)

## Finished Size

Blocks: 24 chili blocks, 7" x 9"        Quilt: 87" x 105"
     12 cactus blocks, 7½" x 12"
     4 coyote blocks, 10" x 11¾"
     102 border blocks, 4" x 6"

## Materials

| | | |
|---|---|---|
| Fabric I (orange-and-brown sunset-look print) | ¼ yard |
| Fabric II (dark brown print) | ¼ yard |
| Fabric III (light rust solid) | 2¾ yards |
| Fabric IV (light peach solid) | 1¾ yards |
| Fabric V (dusty green solid) | ¼ yard |
| Fabric VI (light dusty green solid) | ⅜ yard |
| Fabric VII (pink print) | 2¾ yards |
| Fabric VIII (burgundy print) | 1⅛ yards |
| Fabric IX (green texture-look print) | ½ yard |
| Fabric X (mauve solid) | 2½ yards |
| Fabric XI (dark turquoise solid) | 2¾ yards |
| Backing fabric | 8 yards |

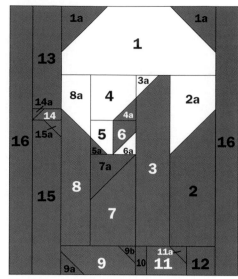

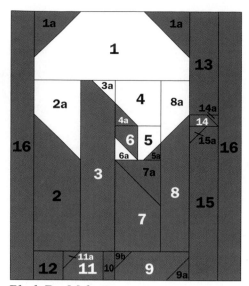

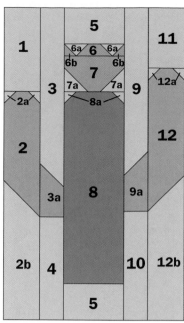

Block A—Make 2.

Block B—Make 2.

Block C—Make 12.

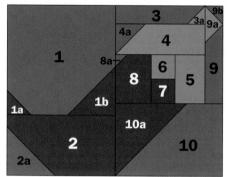

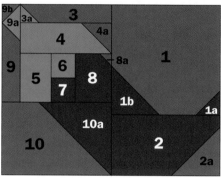

Block D—Make 12.

Block E—Make 12.

Block F—Make 102.

## Cutting

### From Fabric I (sunset print), cut:

✶ One 3½" x 42" strip.

From this, cut:

- Four 3½" x 7¼" (A-1, B-1).
- Four 1¾" x 3¼" (A-8a, B-8a).
- Eight 1½" squares (A-3a, A-6a, B-3a, B-6a).

✶ One 2½" x 42" strip.

From this, cut:

- Four 2½" x 4" (A-2a, B-2a).
- Four 2½" squares (A-4, B-4).
- Four 1½" x 2" (A-5, B-5).

### From Fabric II (dark brown print), cut:

✶ One 2" x 42" strip.

From this, cut:

- Four 2" x 8" (A-3, B-3).
- Four 1½" x 2" (A-6, B-6).

✶ One 2½" x 42" strip.

From this, cut:

- Four 2½" x 4½" (A-7, B-7).
- Four 1¾" x 2¼" (A-11, B-11).

✶ One 1¾" x 42" strip.

From this, cut:

- Four 1¾" x 6½" (A-8, B-8).
- Four 1¾" x 3¾" (A-9, B-9).

✶ From scraps, cut:

- Four 1" x 1¾" (A-14, B-14).
- Four 1½" squares (A-4a, B-4a).
- Four 1¼" squares (A-15a, B-15a).

### From Fabric III, (light rust) cut:

✶ Four 2½" x 42" strips.

From these, cut:

- Eight 2½" x 7½" (25).
- Four 2½" x 6½" (A-2, B-2).
- Thirty-six 2½" squares (A-1a, A-7a, B-1a, B-7a, D-2a, E-2a).

✶ Six 1¼" x 42" strips.

From these, cut:

- Thirty-six 1¼" squares (A-5a, A-9b, A-11a, B-5a, B-9b, B-11a, D-9b, E-9b).
- Twenty-four 1¼" x 4¼" (D-3, E-3).
- Twenty-four 1¼" x 3¾" (D-9, E-9).

✶ Seventeen 1¾" x 42" strips.

From these, cut:

- Sixteen 1¾" x 21½" (26).
- Eight 1¾" x 13½" (27).
- Eight 1¾" x 11½" (29).
- Four 1¾" x 10½" (17).
- Four 1¾" x 7¼" (A-15, B-15).
- Four 1¾" x 5" (A-13, B-13).
- Twenty-eight 1¾" squares (A-12, B-12, D-4a, E-4a).
- Four 1" x 1¾" (A-10, B-10).

✶ Nine 1½" x 42" strips.

From these, cut:

- Eight 1½" x 12¼" (A-16, B-16).
- Thirty-two 1½" x 7½" (24).
- Four 1½" squares (A-9a, B-9a).
- Twenty-eight 1" squares (A-14a, B-14a, D-8a, E-8a).

✶ Five 5" x 42" strips.

From these, cut:

- Twenty-four 5" squares (D-1, E-1).
- Twenty-four 3½" x 5" (D-10, E-10).

✶ One 2⅛" x 42" strip. From this, cut:

- Four 2⅛" x 10½" (21).

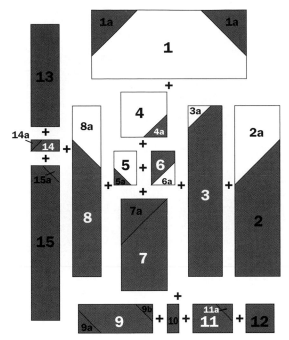

*Block A Assembly*

### From Fabric IV (light peach), cut:

✱ Five 2" x 42" strips.
  From these, cut:
  - Twelve 2" x 3½" (C-1).
  - Twelve 2" x 6" (C-12b).
  - Twelve 2" x 5½" (C-2b).
  - Twelve 2" x 2½" (C-11).
✱ Ten 1½" x 42" strips.
  From these, cut:
  - Twelve 1½" x 7½" (C-3).
  - Twelve 1½" x 7" (C-9).
  - Twelve 1½" x 4½" (C-10).
  - Twelve 1½" x 4" (C-4).
  - Twenty-four 1½" x 3" (C-5).
  - Twenty-four 1½" squares (C-7a).
  - Twenty-four 1" x 1½" (C-6a).
✱ Twelve 1" x 42" strips.
  From these, cut:
  - Six 1" x 35" and six 1" x 29" for middle borders.
✱ Seventy-two 1" squares (C-2a, C-8a, C-12a).
✱ One 12½" x 42" strip.
  From this, cut:
  - Ten 2½" x 12½" (22).
  - Four 3" x 12½" (23).

### From Fabric V (dusty green), cut:

✱ One 8½" x 42" strip.
  From this, cut:
  - Twelve 3" x 8½" (C-8).

### From Fabric VI (light dusty green), cut:

✱ Four 2" x 42" strips. From these, cut:
  - Twelve 2" x 6½" (C-12).
  - Twelve 2" x 6" (C-2).
✱ One 3" x 42" strip.
  From this, cut:
  - Twenty-four 1½" x 3" (C-3a, C-9a).

### From Fabric VII (pink print), cut:

✱ One 3" x 42" strip.
  From this, cut:
  - Twelve 2" x 3" (C-7).
✱ Fifty-seven 1½" x 42" strips.
  From these, cut:
  - 204 1½" x 4½" (F-1).
  - 408 1½" x 3½" (F-2).
✱ From scraps, cut:
  - Twelve 1" x 2" (C-6).
  - Twenty-four 1" squares (C-6b).

### From Fabric VIII (burgundy print), cut:

✱ Three 3" x 42" strips.
  From these, cut:
  - Twenty-four 3" x 5" (D-2, E-2).
✱ Two 3½" x 42" strips.
  From these, cut:
  - Twenty-four 3½" squares (D-10a, E-10a).
✱ Three 2½" x 42" strips.
  From these, cut:
  - Twenty-four 2½" squares (D-1b, E-1b).
  - Twenty-four 2" x 2½" (D-8, E-8).

✱ Two 4½" x 42" strips.
  From these, cut:
  - Twelve 4½" squares (19).
✱ From scraps, cut:
  - Forty-eight 1½" squares (D-1a, D-7, E-1a, E-7).

### From Fabric IX (green print), cut:

✱ Four 1¾" x 42½" strips.
  From these, cut:
  - Twenty-four 1¾" x 4¼" (D-4, E-4).
  - Twenty-four 1¾" x 2½" (D-5, E-5).
✱ One 1½" x 42" strip.
  From this, cut:
  - Twenty-four 1½" squares (D-6, E-6).
✱ Two 1¼" x 42" strips.
  From these, cut:
  - Twenty-four 1¼" squares (D-3a, E-3a).
  - Twenty-four 1¼" x 2" (D-9a, E-9a).

### From Fabric X (mauve), cut:

✱ Fifty-four 1½" x 42½" strips.
  From these, cut:
  - 408 1½" x 2½" (F-1a).
  - 816 1½" squares (F-2a).

### From Fabric XI (dark turqoise), cut:

✱ Ten 3" x 42" strips for binding.
✱ Thirty-two 2" x 42½" strips.
  From 20 of these, cut:
  - Six 2" x 31" for center quilt sashing.
  - Four 2" x 26" for center quilt sashing.
  - Six 2" x 30" for outer border.
  - Two 2" x 20" for outer border.
  - Two 2" x 16" for inner border.
  - Twelve 2" x 10" (28).
  - Five 2" x 10½" (18).
  - Two 1½" x 18½" (20).

## Piecing the Coyote Blocks

**1.** Referring to Block A Assembly diagram, use diagonal-corner technique to make one each of units 1, 3, 4, 5, 6, 7, 9, 11, 14, and 15 as shown.

**2.** Using diagonal-end technique, make one each of units 2 and 8.

**3.** To begin block assembly, join units 5 and 6 as shown. Then join Unit 4 to top of 5-6 unit and Unit 7 to bottom.

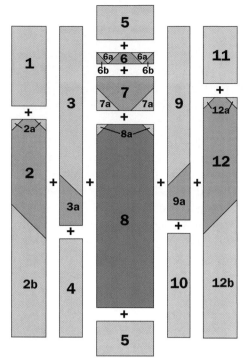

*Block C Assembly*

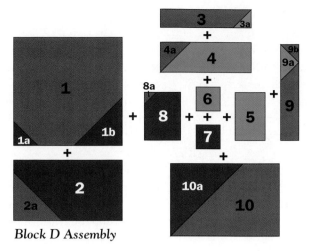

*Block D Assembly*

**4.** Join units 2 and 3 as shown; then join 2-3 unit to side of 4-5-6-7 unit. Join Unit 8 to opposite side.

**5.** Join units 9, 10, 11, and 12 in a horizontal row as shown; then join this to bottom of combined units. Join Unit 1 to top of combined units.

**6.** Join units 13, 14, and 15 in a vertical row as shown. Add 13-14-15 unit to side of combined units to complete block. Make two of Block A.

**7.** Block B is made in the same manner as Block A, but it is a mirror image. Units are made exactly the same as for Block A, but positions of diagonal corners and angles of diagonal ends are reversed. Make two of Block B, referring to block diagram carefully.

## Piecing the Cactus Blocks

**1.** Referring to Block C Assembly diagram, use diagonal-corner technique to make one each of units 7 and 8.

**2.** Using diagonal-end technique, make one each of units 3 and 9.

**3.** For Unit 2, use diagonal-corner technique to add 2a to piece 2. Use diagonal-end technique to join 2b to opposite end of piece 2. Make one of Unit 12 in the same manner.

**4.** To make Unit 6, add diagonal ends 6a to piece 6. Then add diagonal corners 6b to both ends of unit.

**5.** Referring to Block C Assembly diagram, join units in vertical rows as shown; then join rows to complete block. Make 12 of Block C.

## Piecing the Chili Blocks

**1.** Referring to Block D Assembly diagram, use diagonal-corner technique to make one each of units 1, 2, 3, 4, 8, and 10.

**2.** To make Unit 9, first join diagonal end 9a to piece 9; then add diagonal corner 9b to end of unit as shown.

**3.** Join units 6 and 7; then add units 5 and 8 to sides of 6-7 unit as shown.

**4.** Join units 3 and 4; then join 3-4 unit to top of 5-6-7-8 unit. Add Unit 9 to side of combined unit as shown. Join Unit 10 to bottom to complete half of block.

**5.** Join units 1 and 2 to make other block half. Join halves to complete block. Make 12 of Block D.

**6.** Block E is made in the same manner as Block D, but it is a mirror image. Units are made the same as for Block D, but diagonal corners and ends are reversed. Make 12 of Block E, referring to block diagram carefully.

## Piecing the Southwest Borders

**1.** Referring to Block F Assembly diagram, use diagonal-end technique to make two of Unit 1. Use diagonal-corner technique to make four of Unit 2.

**2.** Join two of Unit 2 to make two horizontal rows as shown. Join rows to complete block. Make 102 of Block F for Southwest borders 1–6.

**3.** Join F blocks end-to-end to assemble two of each border as follows. For each Border 1, join two blocks. Join five blocks for each Border 2, seven blocks for each Border 3, 10 blocks for each Border 4, 12 blocks for each Border 5, and 15 blocks for each Border 6.

**4.** Join Unit 19 squares to both ends of each of Border 2, Border 4, and Border 6.

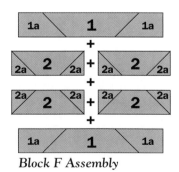

*Block F Assembly*

## Center Quilt Assembly

**1.** Join Unit 17 strips to top and bottom of one Block A and one Block B. Join these blocks head-to-head, sewing one Unit 18 between them as shown in Quilt Assembly diagram.

**2.** Matching centers, join Border 1 to opposite ends of center coyote blocks as shown. Trim ends of Border 1 flush with Unit 17. Then join a Border 2 to each side of center unit as shown.

**3.** Join Unit 20 strips to both short ends of center unit as shown in assembly diagram.

**4.** Join Unit 21 to top and bottom edges of both remaining coyote blocks; then add Unit 18 to each Unit 21 as shown. Join these blocks to ends of center unit, referring to diagram and quilt photograph for correct positioning.

**5.** Join four of Block C in a row, sewing Unit 22 strips between them as shown in Quilt Assembly diagram. Join Unit 23 strips to ends of row; then add another of Block C to each end. Complete row by adding a Unit 22 strip to both ends. Make another row of cactus blocks in the same manner. Referring to assembly diagram and photograph for positioning, join cactus rows to center section.

**6.** Join Border 3 to each short end of center section; then join Border 4 to sides, easing quilt to fit borders. (See page 19 for tips on easing.)

**7.** Join two 2" x 26" strips of Fabric XI end-to-end to make a border strip. Repeat to make second strip. Matching center seam to center of Border 3, join each border strip to center section as shown in assembly diagram.

## Outer Quilt Assembly

**1.** Referring to center bottom of Quilt Assembly diagram, join one D block and one E block, sewing a Unit 24 strip between them. Add Unit 24 strips to sides of joined blocks; then add Unit 26 strips to top and bottom edges. Make eight of these units in this manner.

**2.** On each of two D blocks and two E blocks, join Unit 25 strips to block sides; then add Unit 27 strips to top and bottom edges.

**3.** Referring to right side of Quilt Assembly diagram, join Unit 28 strips to sides of one double-chili unit. Add Block D unit to right end of row and Block E unit to left end of row. Repeat to make a second row. Join rows to ends of center quilt section as shown.

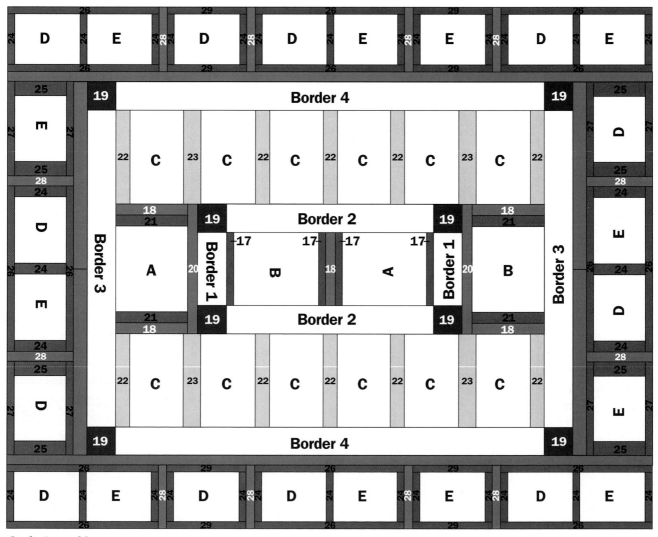

*Quilt Assembly*

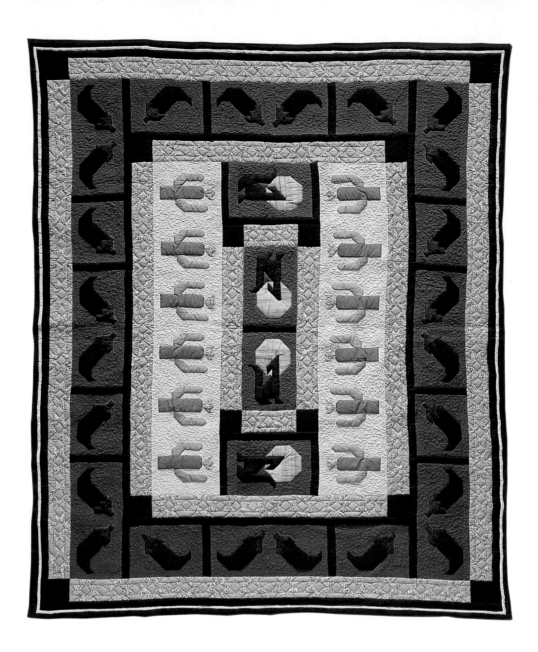

**4.** Join three 2" x 31" strips of Fabric XI end-to-end to make a 92"-long border for each quilt side. Matching centers, join borders to quilt. Press seam allowances toward borders; then trim excess border fabric at ends of strip.

**5.** On each remaining chili block, join a Unit 24 strip to both sides; then join Unit 29 strips to top and bottom.

**6.** Trim ¼" from 2" width of each remaining Unit 28 strip. Referring to bottom of Quilt Assembly diagram, join double-chili units and single chili units in a row, sewing Unit 28 strips between units as shown. Repeat to make a second row. Join rows to quilt sides as shown.

**7.** Referring to photograph, join Border 5 to ends of quilt, easing quilt to fit as necessary. Join Border 6 to quilt sides.

**8.** For each inner side border, join two 42½" strips and one 16" strip of Fabric XI. Matching centers of borders and quilt, join borders to quilt sides.

**9.** For each inner end border, join two 42½" strips end-to-end. Matching center seam with center of quilt, join borders to top and bottom edges.

**10.** For each middle side border, join three 1" x 35" strips of Fabric IV end-to-end. Join borders to quilt sides. For each middle end border, join three 1" x 29" strips and join borders to top and bottom edges in the same manner.

**11.** For each outer side border, join three 2" x 30" strips of Fabric XI. Join borders to quilt sides. For each outer end border, join two 42½" strips and one 20" strip of Fabric XI. Join borders to top and bottom edges.

## Quilting and Finishing

The quilt shown was machine quilted with outline quilting around patchwork and stippling around chilies, coyotes, and cacti. Quilt as desired.

Make 11⅛ yards of binding. See page 30 for directions on making and applying straight-grain binding.

# Chili Pepper Tablecloth

Use a southwestern theme to decorate for Christmas with this merry tribute to the great American chili pepper. A red-hot accent for any occasion, this easy-to-make tablecloth will make you the hostess with the spiciest parties in town!

**Quick-Piecing Techniques:** Strip Piecing (see page 20)
Diagonal Corners (see page 20)
Diagonal Ends (see page 21)

## Finished Size
Blocks: 28 blocks, 7" x 9"  Tablecloth: 66" x 84"

## Materials

| | | |
|---|---|---|
| | Fabric I (white-on-white print) | 4 yards |
| | Fabric II (bright red print) | 1¼ yards |
| | Fabric III (black-on-green print) | 1⅜ yards |
| | Fabric IV (dark green solid) | ¼ yard |
| | Backing fabric | 4 yards |

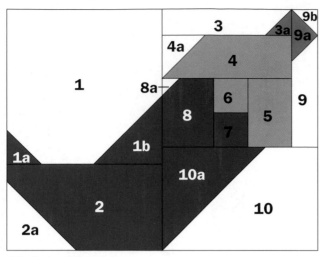

Block A—Make 12.

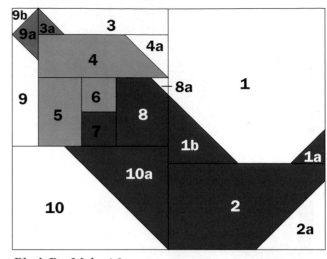

Block B—Make 16.

## Cutting

### From Fabric I (white), cut:
* One 23½" x 42" strip.
  From this, cut:
  • Two 20" x 23½" (12).
  • 28 1" squares (A-8a, B-8a).
* Four 11" x 42" strips.
  From these, cut:
  • Four 11" x 31½" (13).
  • Four 7½" squares (11).
* Six 5" x 42" strips.
  From these, cut:
  • 29 5" squares (A-1, B-1, C-1).
  • 28 3½" x 5" (A-10, B-10).
* Five 2½" x 42" strips.
  From these, cut:
  • 16 2½" x 7½" (15).
  • 28 2½" squares (A-2a, B-2a).
* Three 1¼" x 42½" strips.
  From these, cut:
  • 28 1¼" x 4¼" (A-3, B-3).
* 16 1½" x 42" strips.
  From these, cut:
  • 16 1½" x 31½" (inner borders).
  • Eight 1½" x 9½" (16).
  • 28 1¼" squares (A-9b, B-9b).
* From scraps, cut:
  • 28 1¾" squares (A-4a, B-4a).
  • 28 1¼" x 3¾" (A-9, B-9).

### From Fabric II (red print), cut:
* Two 5" x 42" strips.
  From these, cut:
  • 28 3" x 5" (A-2, B-2).
* Three 2½" x 42" strips.
  From these, cut:
  • 28 2½" squares (A-1b, B-1b).
  • 28 2" x 2½" (A-8, B-8).

* Four 1½" x 42" strips for Strip Set 1.
* Three 3½" x 42" strips.
  From these, cut:
  • 28 3½" squares (A-10a, B-10a).
  • Four 1⅝" squares (C-3).
  • Eight 1½" squares for outer border.
* Two 1½" x 42" strips.
  From these, cut:
  • 56 1½" squares (A-1a, A-7, B-1a, B-7).

### From Fabric III (black-on-green), cut:
* Eight 2" x 42" for binding.
* Four 4½" x 42" strips for Strip Set 1.
* Two 1½" x 42" strips.
  From these, cut:
  • Four 1½" x 5½" (C-2).
  • Six 1½" x 2½" (14).
  • 28 1½" squares (A-6, B-6).
* Five 1⅞" x 42" strips.
  From these, cut:
  • 28 1⅞" x 4¼" (A-4, B-4).
  • 28 1⅞" x 2½" (A-5, B-5).

### From Fabric IV (dark green), cut:
* One 1⅝" x 42" strip.
  From this, cut:
  • Two 1⅝" x 7¼" (C-4).
  • Two 1⅝" x 9½" (C-5).
* Three 1¼" x 42" strips.
  From these, cut:
  • 28 1¼" squares (A-3a, B-3a).
  • 28 1¼" x 2" (A-9a, B-9a).

## Piecing the Blocks
1. Refer to Piecing the Chili Blocks instructions for *South of the Border* quilt

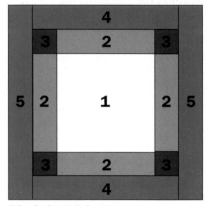

Block C—Make 1.

on page 300. Following those instructions and referring to diagrams above, make 12 of Block A and 16 of Block B.
2. Referring to Block C diagram, join two C-2 strips to opposite sides of C-1. Join C-3 squares to ends of remaining C-2 strips; then add these to top and bottom of C-1. Join C-4 strips to top and bottom of block. Join C-5 strips to sides to complete block.

## Tablecloth Assembly
1. Join a B block to top and bottom of Block C, turning each chili so its stem is adjacent to Block C.
2. Join a Unit 11 square to both sides of two B blocks. Referring to Tablecloth Assembly diagram, join these rows to sides of center unit, positioning chilies with stems pointing toward Block C.
3. Join Unit 12 to sides of center unit.
4. Join two of Unit 13 end-to-end; then add this strip to top of center unit. Repeat at bottom.

*Strip Set 1—Make 2.*

**5.** To make Strip Set 1, join two 4½" x 42" strips of Fabric III and two 1½" x 42" strips of Fabric II as shown. Make two strip sets. From these, cut fifty 1½"-wide segments.

**6.** Join three segments end-to-end. Make three more three-segment strips in the same manner. Join two of these strips with one Unit 14 between them, *always sewing red fabric to green fabric.* Repeat to make a second strip. Join assembled borders to Unit 13s at top and bottom of center section as shown in assembly diagram. (*Note:* Shaded areas of Tablecloth Assembly diagram indicate strip-pieced borders. Seams shown indicate strip-set segments.)

**7.** For each side border, join five segments end-to-end. Remove green fabric from bottom of last segment so border has a red square at both ends. Join borders to sides of cloth, easing cloth to fit. (See page 19 for tips on easing.)

**8.** Referring to bottom of Tablecloth Assembly diagram, join three A blocks and three B blocks as shown, sewing Unit 15 strips between them (except for center seam).

**9.** Join 1½" x 31½" strips of Fabric I in pairs to make eight 1½" x 62½" strips. Join one of these to top and bottom of chili pepper row. Complete row by joining Unit 16 strips to both ends.

**10.** Join two sets of three strip-set segments. Add a 1½" square of Fabric II to green end of last segment so there is a red square at both ends of each strip. Join these strips end-to-end, sewing one Unit 14 between them. Join border to bottom of chili pepper row.

**11.** Repeat steps 8, 9, and 10 to make three more rows in the same manner.

**12.** Join one completed row to bottom of tablecloth. Repeat at top of cloth.

**13.** Join one strip-set segment to ends of both remaining chili pepper rows. Join these rows to tablecloth sides.

## Quilting and Finishing

Outline-quilt chili peppers and quilt in-the-ditch in Block C to secure backing. Add additional quilting as desired.

Make 8⅝ yards of binding. See page 30 for directions on making and applying straight-grain binding.

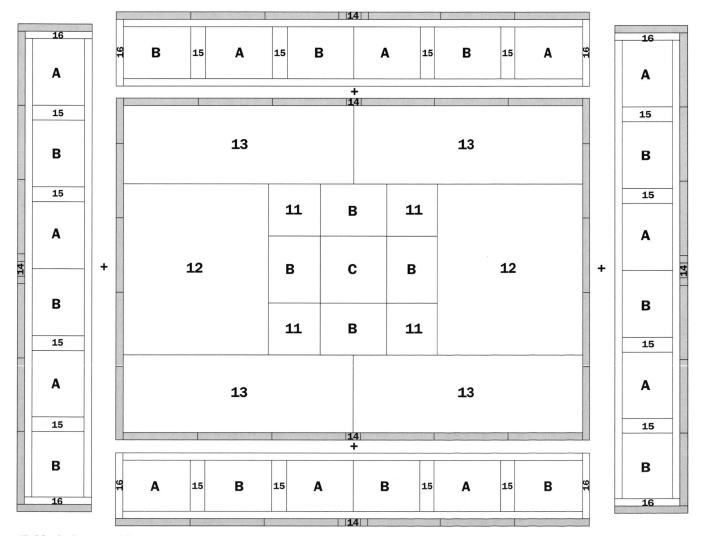

*Tablecloth Assembly*

# Amish Triangles

*Looking for a small, easy project? Here it is—a strip-pieced wall hanging that blends tradition with today's quick techniques. The design and fabrics, adapted from classic antique Amish quilts, have a strikingly contemporary appeal. For a different look, try nontraditional fabrics such as pastel prints on an ivory background.*

**Quick-Piecing Techniques:**   Strip Piecing (see page 20)
Diagonal Corners (see page 20)

## Finished Size

Blocks: 44 Triangle blocks, 6" square     Quilt: 60" x 60"
      4 Arrow blocks, 6" x 8"

## Materials

| | | |
|---|---|---|
| | Fabric I (black solid) | 2 yards |
| | Fabric II (purple solid) | 1⅝ yards |
| | Fabric III (yellow solid) | ¼ yard |
| | Fabric IV (teal solid) | ¼ yard |
| | Fabric V (red solid) | ¼ yard |
| | Fabric VI (gray solid) | 1 yard |
| | Fabric VII (aqua solid) | ¾ yard |
| | Backing fabric | 3¾ yards |

## Cutting

Refer to diagrams on page 308 to identify blocks and units designated in cutting list.

**From Fabric I (black), cut:**
* Six 3" x 42" strips for binding.
* Two 3½" x 42" strips.
  From these, cut:
  * Sixteen 3½" squares (2a).
  * Four 3½" x 4½" (6).
* Four 6⅞" x 42" strips.
  From these, cut:
  * Twenty-two 6⅞" squares. Cut squares in half diagonally to get 44 triangles (1).
* One 2½" x 42" strip.
  From this, cut:
  * Eight 2½" squares (4).
* Six 1¼" x 42" strips for Strip Set Y.

**From Fabric II (purple), cut:**
* Six 2½" x 42" strips for borders.
  From four of these strips, cut:
  * Four 2½" x 29".
  * Four 2½" x 11".
* Two 6½" x 42" strips.
  From these, cut:
  * Eight 3½" x 6½" (2).
  * Eight 6½" squares (9).
* One 4½" x 42" strip.
  From this, cut:
  * Eight 4½" squares (8).
* One 3½" x 42" strip.
  From this, cut:
  * Four 3½" x 4½" (7).
* Fourteen 1⅛" x 42" strips for Strip Set X.

**From each of fabrics III, IV, and V (yellow, teal, and red), cut:**
* Seven 1⅛" x 42" strips for Strip Set X.

**From Fabric VI (gray), cut:**
* Seven 1⅛" x 42" strips for Strip Set X.
* Six 2⅛" x 42" strips for Strip Set Y.
* One 4½" square (5).
* Four 2½" squares (3).

**From Fabric VII (aqua), cut:**
* Seven 1⅛" x 42" strips for Strip Set X.
* Six 2⅛" x 42" strips for Strip Set Y.

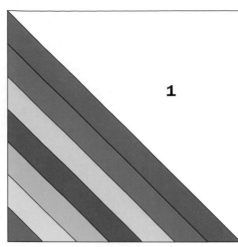

Block A—Make 24.

Block B—Make 20.

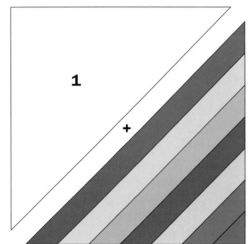

Block A Assembly

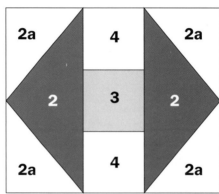

Block C—Make 4.

Strip Set X—Make 7.

Strip Set Y—Make 6.

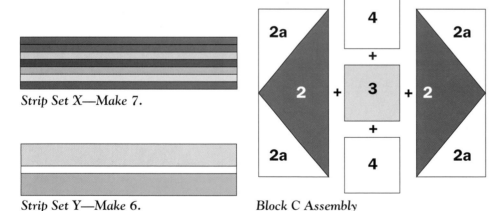

Block C Assembly

## Piecing the Blocks

**1.** Referring to diagram of Strip Set X, join all 1⅛" strips as shown. Make seven of Strip Set X. Square off left edge of each strip set.

**2.** Measuring from bottom left corner of strip set, cut a 45° angle as shown in Strip Set X Cutting diagram. If your acrylic ruler does not have a marked 45° angle, find the angle by measuring the strip set width (which, ideally, is 4⅞"); then measure the same distance along top edge. Cut from bottom left corner to marked point on top edge. Discard cut portion.

**3.** Make next cut perpendicular to diagonal edge. Cut triangles from each strip set as shown, cutting four triangles for A blocks and three for B blocks. See page 13 for tips on stabilizing bias edge of triangles.

**4.** Referring to Block A Assembly diagram, join Unit 1 to striped triangles. Make 24 of Block A and 20 of Block B. Press seam allowances toward Unit 1.

**5.** Using diagonal-corner technique, make two of Unit 2 for each Arrow block. Referring to Block C Assembly diagram, join units 3 and 4 in a vertical row as shown. Join rows to complete each block. Make four of Block C.

## Center Section Assembly

**1.** Referring to Center Section Assembly diagram, join two pair of units 6 and 7. Positioning blocks as shown, join A blocks to top and bottom edges of combined 6-7 units. Join remaining units 5, 6, and 7 in a vertical row as shown. Join rows to complete center section.

**2.** Referring to diagram of Strip Set Y, join 2⅛" strips of fabrics VI and VII to sides of 1¼" strip of Fabric I. Make six strip sets. Cut two of Strip Set Y in half.

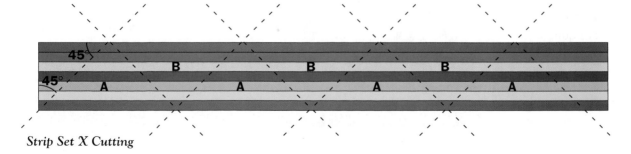

Strip Set X Cutting

**3.** Measure all sides of center section. Trim four Y half-strip sets to match *shortest* measurement. Join trimmed strips to top and bottom edges of center section, easing as necessary (see page 19 for tips on easing).

**4.** Join a Unit 8 to ends of two remaining half-strip sets. Join these to sides of center section.

## Middle Section Assembly

**1.** Referring to Quilt Assembly diagram, join four of Block A in a row as shown for each side section. Join rows to sides of center section.

**2.** For top and bottom edges, join two rows of four B blocks as shown. Add one of Unit 9 to each end of these rows; then join rows to quilt.

**3.** Measure all sides of assembled quilt. Trim remaining Y strip sets to match shortest measurement. Join trimmed strips to top and bottom edges of quilt, easing as necessary.

**4.** Join a Unit 8 to ends of two remaining strips. Join these to quilt sides.

## Outer Section Assembly

**1.** Referring to Quilt Assembly diagram, join six of Block A and one of Block C in a row as shown for each side section. Join rows to quilt sides.

**2.** For top and bottom rows, join six of Block B and one of Block C as shown; then join one Unit 9 to each end. Join rows to top and bottom edges of quilt.

**3.** Join two 29"-long border strips end-to-end. Matching centers of border and quilt, join border to top edge. Repeat for bottom edge.

**4.** Join an 11" border strip to ends of each 42" strip. Join borders to quilt sides.

## Quilting and Finishing

Outline-quilt patchwork or quilt as desired.

Make 7 yards of binding. See page 30 for directions on making and applying straight-grain binding. To make a hanging sleeve, see directions on page 138.

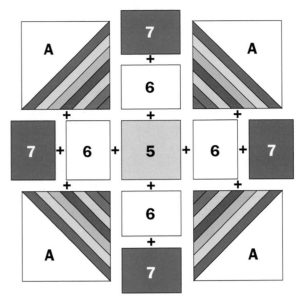

*Center Section Assembly*

*Quilt Assembly*

# Safari Path

*Elephants parade around a trio of exotic animals in this delightful tribute to our favorite beasts of the African plains. Each animal is made with a combination of three quick-piecing techniques, and strip piecing creates paths that connect one critter to another. The fabrics are solids and subtle prints that allow one bold print to stand out. Because there is so much piecing in this quilt, we recommend it for experienced quiltmakers.*

**Quick-Piecing Techniques:**  Strip Piecing (see page 20)
Diagonal Corners (see page 20)
Diagonal Ends (see page 21)

## Finished Size

Blocks: 14 elephant blocks, 12⅜" x 18¾"          Quilt: 101½" x 109"
      2 turtle blocks, 6¾" x 12"
      4 lion blocks, 11⅝" x 17⅝"
      4 giraffe blocks, 8⅝" x 23¼"

## Materials

| | | |
|---|---|---|
| Fabric I (pale yellow print) | | 2⅜ yards |
| Fabric II (gold mini-stripe) | | 2¾ yards |
| Fabric III (rust solid) | | 1 yard |
| Fabric IV (dark brown solid) | | 2⅝ yards |
| Fabric V (brown-on-cream print) | | 1¼ yards |
| Fabric VI (rust-on-dark brown print) | | 1¾ yards |
| Fabric VII (dark brown check) | | 2 yards |
| Fabric VIII (medium brown print) | | 1⅛ yards |
| Fabric IX (tan solid) | | 1⅛ yards |
| Backing fabric | | 9 yards |

## Cutting

**From Fabric I (pale yellow print), cut:**

✱ Eighteen 2" x 42" strips.
   From these, cut:
   • Twelve 2" x 35" for middle border.
   • Four 2" x 25" (30).
   • Four 2" x 12⅛" (27).
   • Four 2" x 9½" (H-1).
   • Four 2" x 8⅜" (E-13, F-13).
   • Four 2" x 4¼" (C-21, D-21).
   • Thirty 1¼" x 2" (A-3a, A-6a, A-8, B-3a, B-6a, B-8, C-16, C-18a, D-16, D-18a, E-2a, E-9a, F-2a, F-9a).
   • Two 1⅝" x 2" (A-10, B-10).
   • Six 2" squares (A-11, B-11, C-8b, D-8b).
   • Four 2" x 2¾" (E-10, F-10).

✱ Two 1¼" x 42" strips.
   From these, cut:
   • Fifty-eight 1¼" squares (A-2b, A-9a, B-2b, B-9a, C-11a, C-13a, C-19a, D-11a, D-13a, D-19a, E-12a, E-15b, F-12a, F-15b).
   • Four 1¼" x 2⅜" (C-10, D-10).

✱ Two 3⅛" x 42" strips.
   From these, cut:
   • Four 3⅛" x 11" (C-4, D-4).
   • Four 3⅛" x 4¼" (C-20, D-20).
   • Four 3⅛" squares (C-1a, D-1a).
   • Two 2⅜" squares (A-5a, B-5a).

*continued*

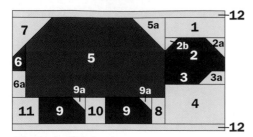

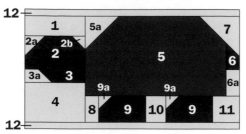

**Block A—Make 1.**

**Block B—Make 1.**

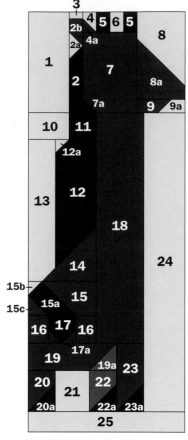

**Block E—Make 2.**

* Seven 1⅝" x 42" strips.
  From these, cut:
  * Four 1⅝" x 25" (31).
  * Four 1⅝" x 18⅛" (C-22, D-22).
  * Four 1⅝" x 9⅛" (E-25, F-25).
  * Four 1⅝" x 7¼" (26).
  * Two 1⅝" x 3⅞" (A-1, B-1).
  * Two 1⅝" squares (A-2a, B-2a).
  * Eight 1¼" x 1⅝" (E-4, E-6, F-4, F-6).
* Two 4⅝" x 42" strips.
  From these, cut:
  * Four 4⅝" x 12⅛" (28).
  * Four 3⅛" x 4⅝" (E-8, F-8).
  * Four ⅞" x 20".
    From these, cut:
    * Four ⅞" x 12½" (A-12, B-12).
    * Four ⅞" x 1¼" (E-3, F-3).
* Four 2¾" x 42" strips.
  From these, cut:
  * Four 2¾" x 17" (E-24, F-24).
  * Two 2¾" x 9⅛" (29).
  * Four 2¾" x 6⅛" (E-1, F-1).
  * Two 2¾" x 3⅞" (A-4, B-4).
  * Two 2¾" squares (A-7, B-7).
  * Four 2⅜" x 2¾" (E-21, F-21).
  * Twelve 1¼" x 2¾" (C-14, D-14).

**From Fabric II (gold mini-stripe), cut:**
* Nine 1¼" x 42" strips.
  From these, cut:
  * Fourteen 1¼" x 11¾" (G-15).
  * Fourteen ¼" x 5" (G-13a).
  * Thirty-four 1¼" x 2" (C-15, C-18, D-15, D-18, G-9a).
  * Eighteen 1¼" x 2⅜" (C-12, D-12, G-5).
  * Twenty-two 1¼" squares (C-13b, D-13b, G-12).
* Twenty-two 2" x 42" strips.
  From these, cut:
  * Eight 2" x 32" and twelve 2" x 29" for elephant section borders.
  * Four 2" x 12⅞" (33).
  * Four 2" x 12½" (C-17, D-17).
  * Sixteen 2" x 3½" (C-19, D-19).
  * Twenty-eight 2" x 3⅛" (G-6, G-10).
  * Eighteen 2" squares (C-8a, D-8a, G-2c).
* Six 3⅛" x 42" strips.
  From these, cut:
  * Fourteen 3⅛" x 5⅜" (G-16b).
  * Fourteen 3⅛" x 9⅛" (G-17).
  * Fourteen 2¾" x 3⅛" (G-19).
* Two 2⅜" x 42" strips.
  From these, cut:
  * Twenty-eight 2⅜" squares (G-14, G-16a).

* One 12⅞" x 42" strip.
  From this, cut:
  * Four 3½" x 12⅞" (35).
  * Six 3" x 12⅞" (34).
  * Four 4⅝" x 6⅛" (C-9, D-9).

**From Fabric III (rust), cut:**
* Four 2" x 42" strips.
  From these, cut:
  * Fifty-six 2" squares (G-3a, G-4b, G-7a, G-8a).
  * Fourteen 1¼" x 2" (G-5a).

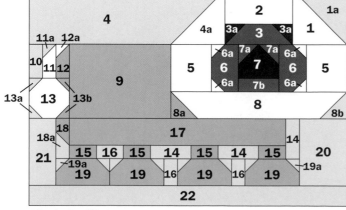

**Block C—Make 2.**

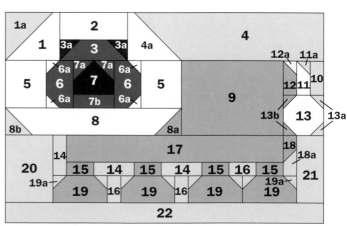

**Block D—Make 2.**

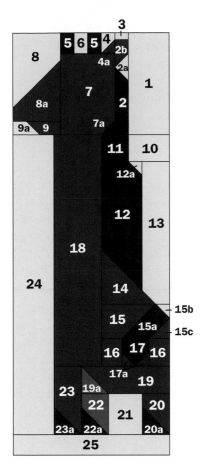

*Block F—Make 2.*

* Two 8¾" x 42" strips.
  From these, cut:
  • Fourteen 5" x 8¾" (G-2).
  • One 7" square.
    From this, cut:
    • Four 3½" squares (32).
    • Four 1⅝" x 8¾".
      From these, cut:
      • Four 1⅝" x 4¼" (C-3, D-3).
      • Eight 1⅝" squares (C-7a, D-7a).
* Five 1¼" x 42" strips.
  From these, cut:
  • Fourteen 1¼" x 8⅜" (G-13).
  • Four 1¼" x 2¾" (C-7b, D-7b).
  • Twenty-eight 1¼" squares (G-10a, G-11).
  • Fourteen 1¼" x 3½" (G-15a).

**From Fabric IV (dark brown), cut:**

* Four 2¾" x 42" strips.
  From these, cut:
  • Four 2¾" x 8⅜" (E-12, F-12).
  • Fourteen 2¾" x 3⅞" (G-4).
  • Fourteen 2¾" x 3⅛" (G-7).
  • Four 2⅜" x 2¾" (C-7, D-7).
  • Four 2⅜" x 3⅛" (E-15a, F-15a).
  • Four 2" x 3⅛" (A-9, B-9).

* Eleven 3" x 42" strips for binding.
* One 1¼" x 42" strip.
  From this, cut:
  • Two 1¼" x 3⅞" (A-3, B-3).
  • Two 1¼" x 3½" (A-6, B-6).
  • Four 1¼" x 4¼" (E-2, F-2).
  • Four 1¼" squares (E-7a, F-7a).
* One 1⅝" x 42" strip.
  From this, cut:
  • Eight 1¼" x 1⅝" (E-5, F-5).
  • Eight 1⅝" squares (C-3a, D-3a).
* One 2" x 42" strip.
  From this, cut:
  • Twenty 2" squares (E-11, E-17, E-20a, E-22a, E-23a, F-11, F-17, F-20a, F-22a, F-23a).
* One 2⅜" x 42" strip.
  From this, cut:
  • One 2⅜" x 20" for Strip Set 1.
  • One 2⅜" x 12" for Strip Set 3.
  • Two 2⅜" x 3⅞" (A-2, B-2).
* One 4¼" x 42" strip for Strip Set 4.
* Four 2⅜" x 42" strips for Strip Set 5.
* Ten 2" x 42" strips for Strip Set 6.

**From Fabric V (brown-on-cream print), cut:**

* Twelve 2½" x 42" strips.
  From these, cut:
  • Twelve 2½" x 36" for outer border.
  • Four 2" x 4¼" (C-2, D-2).
  • Four 1¼" x 2⅜" (C-11, D-11).
  • Twenty 1¼" squares (C-6a, C-12a, D-6a, D-12a).
* One 3⅛" x 42" strip.
  From this, cut:
  • Eight 3⅛" x 3½" (C-1, C-4a, D-1, D-4a).
* One 2" x 42" strip. From this, cut:
  • Four 2" x 10¼" (C-8, D-8).

* One 2¾" x 42" strip.
  From this, cut:
  • Eight 2¾" x 3⅛" (C-5, D-5).
  • Four 2¾" squares (C-13, D-13).

**From Fabric VI (rust-on-dark brown print), cut:**

* One 5" x 42" strip. From this, cut:
  • Two 5" x 8⅜" (A-5, B-5).
  • Four 5" squares (36).
* One 3½" x 42" strip.
  From this, cut:
  • Four 3½" x 5" (E-7, F-7).
  • Four 3½" squares (E-14, F-14).
* Two 3⅛" x 42" strips.
  From these, cut:
  • Four 3⅛" x 13¼" (E-18, F-18).
  • Four 3⅛" x 3⅞" (E-8a, F-8a).
* Two 2" x 42" strips. From these, cut:
  • Four 2" x 2¾" (E-20, F-20).
  • Four 2" x 4¼" (E-23, F-23).
  • Eight 1⅝" x 2" (E-16, F-16).
  • Four 2" x 5⅜" (E-19, F-19).
  • Four 1¼" x 2" (E-2b, F-2b).
  • Four 1⅝" squares (E-15c, F-15c).
* From scraps, cut:
  • Four 2⅜" x 3½" (E-15, F-15).
  • Four 1¼" x 2⅜" (E-9, F-9).
  • Twelve 1¼" squares (E-4a, E-17a, F-4a, F-17a).

**From Fabric VII (dark brown check), cut:**

* Five 3⅛" x 42" strips.
  From these, cut:
  • Fourteen 3⅛" x 10⅝" (G-16).
  • Fourteen 2" x 3⅛" (G-18).
* One 2⅜" x 42" strip. From this, cut:
  • Fourteen 2⅜" squares (G-2b).

*continued*

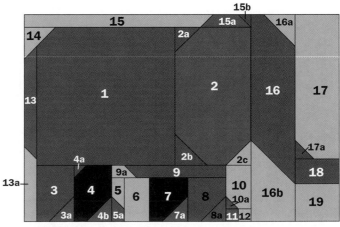

*Block G—Make 14.*

* Four 8¾" x 42" strips.
  From these, cut:
  • Fourteen 8¾" squares (G-1).
  • Three 2¾" x 24".
    From these, cut:
    • Fourteen 2¾" x 3⅞" (G-3).
    • Four 2" x 2¾" (E-22, F-22).
    • Seven 2¾" x 7".
      From these, cut:
      • Fourteen 2¾" x 3⅛" (G-8).
* Three 1¼" x 42" strips.
  From these, cut:
  • Fourteen 1¼" x 6½" (G-9).
  • Fourteen 1¼" squares (G-15b).
* One 2" x 42" strip.
  From this, cut:
  • Eighteen 2" squares (E-19a, F-19a, G-2a).
* From scraps, cut:
  • Fourteen 1⅝" squares (G-17a).
  • Fourteen 1¼" squares (G-4a).

### From Fabric VIII (medium brown print), cut:

* One 2⅜" x 42" strip.
  From this, cut:
  • One 2⅜" x 20" for Strip Set 1.
  • One 2⅜" x 15" for Strip Set 2.
* One 4¼" x 42" for Strip Set 4.
* Four 2⅜" x 42" for Strip Set 5.
* Ten 2" x 42" strips for Strip Set 6.

### From Fabric IX (tan), cut:

* One 2⅜" x 42" strip.
  From this, cut:
  • One 2⅜" x 15" for Strip Set 2.
  • One 2⅜" x 12" for Strip Set 3.
* One 4¼" x 42" for Strip Set 4.
* Four 2⅜" x 42" for Strip Set 5.
* Ten 2" x 42" strips for Strip Set 6.

## Piecing the Turtle Blocks

**1.** Referring to Block A Assembly diagram, use diagonal-corner technique to make one each of units 2 and 5 and two of Unit 9.

**2.** Using diagonal-end technique, make one of Unit 3.

**3.** Join units 6 and 6a as shown.

**4.** Join units 1, 2, 3, and 4 in a vertical row as shown in assembly diagram to complete head section.

**5.** Join Unit 6 to Unit 5 as shown. Use diagonal-corner technique to add Unit 7 to 5-6 unit.

**6.** Join units 8, 9, 10, and 11 in a horizontal row. Join this row to bottom of 5-6 unit to complete body section.

**7.** Join head and body sections as shown. Add Unit 12 to top and bottom edges to complete one of Block A.

**8.** Block B is a mirror image of Block A. Units are made exactly the same as for Block A, but positions and angles of diagonal corners and ends are reversed. Make one of Block B, referring to block diagram carefully.

## Piecing the Lion Blocks

**1.** Referring to Block C Assembly diagram, use diagonal-corner technique to make two of Unit 6, four of Unit 19, and one each of units 1, 3, 8, 11, 12, and 13. To make Unit 7, add diagonal corners as shown; then add piece 7b to bottom of unit.

**2.** Using diagonal-end technique, make one each of units 4 and 18.

**3.** To assemble Section A, begin by joining units 2 and 3. Add units 1 and 4 to sides of 2-3 unit as shown in assembly diagram to complete Section A.

**4.** To assemble Section B, begin by joining two of units 5 and 6 and one Unit 7 in a horizontal row as shown. Add Unit 8 to bottom of 5-6-7 unit. Join Unit 9 to left side of combined unit. Next, join units 10, 11, and 12 in a row as shown; then join 10-11-12 unit to top of Unit 13. Join combined unit to side of Unit 9 to complete Section B.

**5.** To assemble Section C, begin by joining two of Unit 14, four of Unit 15, and one Unit 16 in a horizontal row as shown. Join this row to bottom of Unit 17. Add a Unit 14 to right side of combined row and Unit 18 to left side. Next, join two of Unit 16 and four of Unit 19 in a row as shown. Join this row to bottom of combined unit. Add

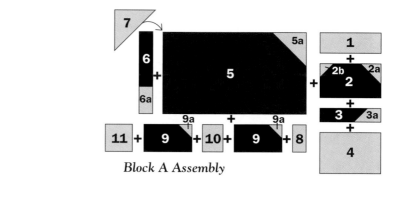

*Block A Assembly*

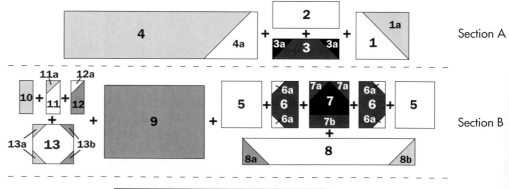

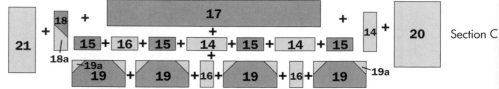

*Block C Assembly*

units 20 and 21 to sides of unit as shown to complete Section C.

**6.** Join sections A, B, and C. Add Unit 22 to bottom to complete Block C. Make two of Block C.

**7.** Block D is made in the same manner as Block C, but it is a mirror image. Units are made exactly the same, but diagonal corners and diagonal ends are reversed. Make two of Block D, referring to block diagram carefully.

## Piecing the Giraffe Blocks

**1.** Referring to Block E Assembly diagram, use diagonal-corner technique to make one each of units 4, 7, 12, 17, 19, 20, 22, and 23.

**2.** Using diagonal-end technique, make one each of units 8 and 9.

**3.** To make Unit 2, add diagonal end 2a to piece 2; then add 2b to combined unit as a second diagonal end.

**4.** To make Unit 15, add diagonal end 15a to piece 15; then add diagonal corners 15b and 15c.

**5.** To assemble Section A, begin by joining units 2 and 3. Add this to side of Unit 1. Next, join units 4 and 6 and two of Unit 5 in a horizontal row as shown. Join this row to top of Unit 7; then join combined unit to side of 2-3 unit. Join Unit 9 to bottom of Unit 8; then join this to side of combined unit to complete Section A.

**6.** To assemble Section B, begin by joining Unit 10 to Unit 11 and Unit 12 to Unit 13. Join 10-11 to top of 12-13. Add Unit 14 to bottom of this unit as a diagonal corner. Join Unit 15 to bottom of combined unit. Next, join two of Unit 16 to Unit 17 as shown; then join 16-17 unit to bottom of Unit 15. Join Unit 18 to right side of combined unit to complete Section B.

**7.** To assemble Section C, begin by joining units 20, 21, and 22 in a row as shown. Join this row to bottom of Unit 19. Add Unit 23 to right side of combined row to complete Section C.

**8.** Join sections B and C. Join Unit 24 to side of combined sections as shown; then add Section A to top. Join Unit 25 to bottom to complete Block E. Make two of Block E.

**9.** Block F is made in the same manner as Block E, but it is a mirror image. Units are made exactly the same, but positions and angles of diagonal corners and diagonal ends are reversed. Make two of Block F, referring to block diagram carefully.

## Piecing the Elephant Blocks

**1.** Referring to Block G Assembly diagram, use diagonal-corner technique to make one each of units 2, 3, 4, 7, 8, 10, and 17.

**2.** Using diagonal-end technique, make one each of units 5, 9, and 13.

**3.** To make Unit 15, add diagonal end 15a to piece 15; then add diagonal corner 15b to end of combined unit.

**4.** To make Unit 16, add diagonal corner 16a to top of piece 16; then add diagonal end 16b to bottom of piece 16.

**5.** Join Unit 1 to Unit 2 and Unit 3 to Unit 4. Join units 11 and 12; then join 11-12 to bottom of Unit 10. Set these units aside.

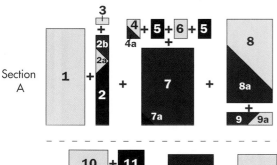

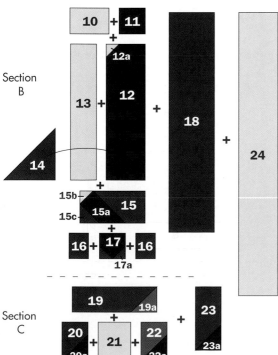

*Block E Assembly*

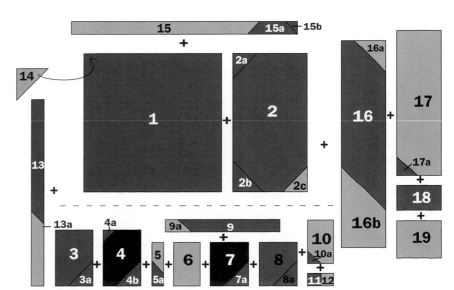

*Block G Assembly*

**6.** Join units 5, 6, 7, and 8 in a horizontal row as shown. Join this row to bottom of Unit 9. Join 3-4 unit to left side of combined row; then add 10-11-12 unit to right side.

**7.** Join row (units 3–12) to bottom of 1-2 unit to make body section.

**8.** Join Unit 13 to left side of body section. Using diagonal-corner technique, join Unit 14 to top of body. Add Unit 15 to top to complete body section.

**9.** Join Unit 16 to right side of body section. Next, join units 17, 18, and 19 in a vertical row as shown. Join 17-18-19 to Unit 16 to complete block. Make 14 of Block G.

## Center Quilt Assembly

**1.** Referring to diagrams of strip sets 1, 2, and 3, assemble designated strips as shown to make one of each strip set. From these, cut 2¾"-wide segments. Cut seven segments from Strip Set 1, five segments from Strip Set 2, and four segments from Strip Set 3.

**2.** Referring to Block H Assembly diagram, join four segments as shown. Add Unit H-1 to top and bottom of joined segments to complete Block H. Make two of Block H for center path.

**3.** Referring to Center Quilt Assembly diagram, join one Block H to nose side of each turtle block, sewing a Unit 26 strip between blocks. Add remaining Unit 26 strips to tail sides of turtles.

**4.** Join Unit 27 strips to face sides of each lion block; then add Unit 28 strips to tail sides.

**5.** Referring to assembly diagram and quilt photograph for correct placement, join lion blocks to top and bottom of turtle sections.

**6.** Referring to Center Quilt Assembly diagram, join remaining strip set segments to make vertical center path.

**7.** Join animal blocks to sides of vertical path to complete Section A.

**8.** Referring to diagrams of strip sets 4 and 5, join designated strips as shown. Make one of Strip Set 4 and four of Strip Set 5. Cut nine 2⅜"-wide segments from Strip Set 4. Cut thirty-eight 3½"-wide segments from Strip Set 5.

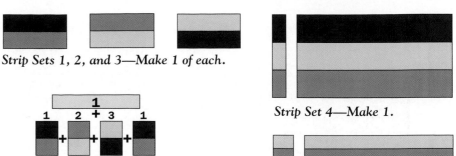

*Strip Sets 1, 2, and 3—Make 1 of each.*

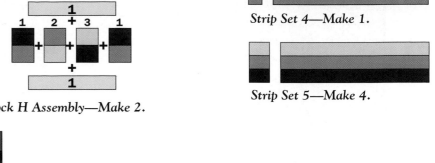

*Strip Set 4—Make 1.*

*Strip Set 5—Make 4.*

*Block H Assembly—Make 2.*

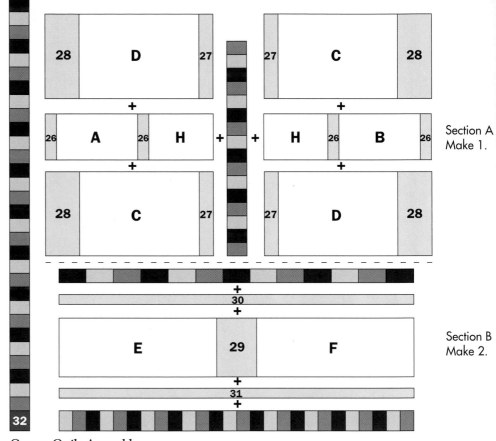

*Center Quilt Assembly*

**9.** To assemble Section B, begin by joining five Strip Set 4 segments end-to-end to make first horizontal path. Pull out seam to remove last two fabric pieces. (Use removed portion later to begin path for second Section B.)

**10.** Join two 2" x 25" strips of Fabric I end-to-end to make one Unit 30. Use two 1⅝" x 25" strips to make one of Unit 31 in the same manner.

**11.** Matching centers, join Unit 30 to horizontal path as shown.

**12.** Join two giraffe blocks head-to-head as shown, sewing one Unit 29

strip between blocks. Join giraffe section to bottom of Unit 30; then add Unit 31 to bottom of giraffe section.

**13.** For bottom horizontal path, join nine Strip Set 5 segments end-to-end. Pull out seam to remove last fabric piece. (Use removed portion later to begin outside vertical path.) Join this path to bottom of Unit 31 to complete Section B.

**14.** Join Section B to the bottom of Section A.

**15.** Repeat steps 9–13 to make a second Section B. Turn this section upside down and join it to top of Section A.

**16.** Use remaining Strip Set 5 segments to assemble two side vertical paths as shown in Center Quilt Assembly diagram. Add a Unit 32 square to both ends of each path. Join these to sides of center section, easing patchwork as necessary to fit paths. (See page 19 for tips on easing.)

## Adding the Elephant Section

**1.** For each side row, join three elephant blocks (Block G), sewing Unit 35 strips between blocks as shown in Outer Quilt Assembly diagram on page 318.

**2.** Join two 2" x 32" strips of Fabric II end-to-end to make a border for these rows. Make four border strips. Matching centers, join border strips to long edges of both rows.

**3.** Referring to assembly diagram and quilt photograph, join side rows to center section.

**4.** For top row, join four elephant blocks, sewing Unit 34 strips between blocks. Repeat for bottom row. Add Unit 33 strips to ends of both rows.

**5.** Join three 2" x 29" strips of Fabric II end-to-end to make a border for these rows. Make four border strips. Matching centers, join border strips to top and bottom edges of both rows.

**6.** Referring to assembly diagram and quilt photograph, join top and bottom rows to center section.

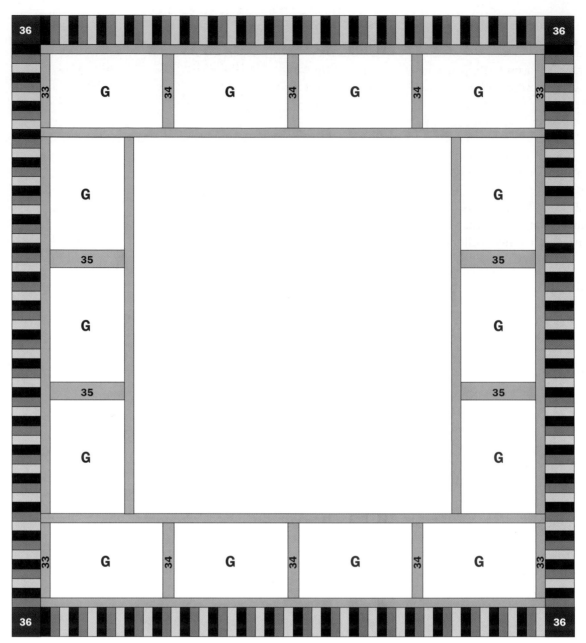

*Outer Quilt Assembly*

## Adding Borders

**1.** Referring to diagram of Strip Set 6, join designated strips as shown. Make 10 strip sets. From these, cut seventy-six 5"-wide segments.

*Strip Set 6—Make 10.*

**2.** For each side, join 20 segments end-to-end. Remove one fabric piece from bottom of last segment. Join borders to quilt sides, easing quilt to fit border.

**3.** Join 18 segments end-to-end for top border. Add a Unit 36 square to both ends. Join border to top of quilt, easing quilt to fit. Repeat for bottom border.
**4.** For each middle border strip, join three 2" x 35" strips of Fabric I end-to-end, making four 104"-long border strips. Matching centers of border and quilt, join one strip to each long side of quilt. Press seam allowances toward borders; then trim excess border fabric at ends. Join remaining borders to top and bottom of quilt in the same manner.
**5.** For each outer border strip, join three 2½" x 36" strips of Fabric V

end-to-end, making four 107"-long border strips. Join these to quilt in the same manner as middle border.

## Quilting and Finishing

Mark quilting designs as desired. The quilt shown was machine-quilted with meandering lines of free-style quilting worked in the open areas around the animals. Outline-quilt patchwork; then add other quilting as desired.

Make 12 yards of binding. See page 30 for tips on making and applying straight-grain binding.

# World Wide Marketplace

Quiltmakers love to shop for fabric. Modern technology enables you to shop all over the country at the touch of a button. These are just some of the internet fabric vendors we found. We've included a mailing address and telephone number where available. For mail-order catalogs, see page 24.

Remember that fabric lines are created and discontinued seasonally. Buy plenty of fabric to make your quilt because you can never be sure of finding it again. Oxmoor House is not responsible for availability of fabrics nor can we guarantee that information presented here will remain up-to-date.

### Fabrics and Notions

Batiks, Etcetera
200B W. Main Street, Wytheville, VA 24382
(800) 228-4573
www.Batiks.com

Batiks by Mail
1995 Murcer Lane, Elgin, IL 60123
(877) 797-0433
www.FrieStyle.com

Beaver Creek Fabrics
P.O. Box 400, Chelsea, MN 48118
www.BeaverCreekFabrics.com

Big Horn Quilts
P.O. Box 566, Greybull, WY 82426
(877) 586-9150
www.BigHornQuilts.com

Born to Quilt
1685 Branham Lane, Suite 254, San Jose, CA 95118
(877) 485-6320
www.BornToQuilt.com

Contemporary Quilting
P.O. Box 3307, Bridgeport, CT 06605
(203) 576-0591
www.ContemporaryQuilting.com

The Craft Connection
P.O. Box 762, Conifer, CO 80433-0762
(888) 204-4050
www.QuiltConn.com

www.equilter.com
(877) FABRIC-3

Fabric Loft of New England
(specializing in one-piece backing fabrics)
P.O. Box 43, East Hampton, CT 06424
(860) 365-0102
www.FabricLoft.com

Hancock's of Paducah
3841 Hinkleville Road, Paducah, KY 42001
800-845-8723
www.Hancocks-Paducah.com

Lunn Fabrics
317 E. Main Street, Lancaster, OH 43130-3845
(800) 880-1738
www.BatiksOnline.com
www.HandDyed.com
www.LunnFabrics.com

Main Street Cotton Shop
141 E. 2nd Street, Redwood Falls, MN 56283
(800) 624-4001
www.MainStreetCottonShop.com

Pinetree Quiltworks
585 Broadway, South Portland, ME 04106
(207) 799-7357
www.Pinetree.Quiltworks.com

Quilt Basket
872 Route 376, Suite B, Wappingers Falls, NY 12590
(845) 227-7606
www.QuiltBasket.com

The Quilted Garden
9061 West Lake Road, Lake City, PA 16423-2102
(814) 774-1161
www.TheQuiltedGarden.com

Quilter's Garden
P.O. Box 81555, Bakersfield, CA 93380
www.efabricstore.com

Quilters' Resource
P.O. Box 418850, Chicago, IL 60614
(800) 676-6543
www.efabricstore.com

Scrap Bag Quilt Company
8741 PennyFoot Court, Sacramento, CA 95828
(916) 689-9546
www.ScrapBagQuiltCompany.com

### Quilting Designs and Stencils

Golden Threads
2 S 373 Seneca Drive
Wheaton, IL 60187
(630) 510-2067
www.goldenthreads.com

### Acid-free Storage Boxes

The Craftgard Company
P.O. Box 472, Tustin, CA 92781
(888) 878-1212
www.craftgard.com

## Design Credits

*Amish Triangles:* Lynn Isenberg
*Baby Buggies Crib Set:* Mindy Kettner
*Baby Bunnies Crib Set:* Pam Bono
*Black-Eyed Susan:* Lynn Isenberg
*Blue Stars:* Pam and Robert Bono
*Breezing By:* Pam Bono
*Cabin in the Stars:* Robert Bono
*Celtic Rose:* Lynn Isenberg
*Chains of Love:* Pam Bono
*Chili Pepper Tablecloth:* Pam Bono
*Counting Sheep:* Pam and Robert Bono
*Country Hearts:* Pam and Robert Bono
*Crows in the Corn:* Mindy Kettner
*Don't Sit Under the Apple Tree:* Mindy Kettner
*Field of Flowers:* Pam Bono
*Field of Flowers Wall Hanging:* Pam Bono
*Flowerpot Wall Hanging:* Mindy Kettner
*Flowers in the Cabin:* Pam and Robert Bono
*Flying Home:* Mindy Kettner
*Formal Garden:* Lynn Isenberg
*Friends, Best-Friend Doll:* Pam Bono
*Grandmother's Violets:* Pam Bono, Robert Bono, Mindy Kettner
*High Summer:* Lynn Isenberg
*Intersection:* Robert Bono
*It's Okay to Be Different:* Mindy Kettner
*Keep On Truckin':* Mindy Kettner
*Moo-vable Feast:* Lynn Isenberg
*Mountain Greenery:* Lynn Isenberg
*Nine Lives:* Mindy Kettner
*Old Bones:* Pam Bono, Dallas Bono, Mindy Kettner
*Oriental Desire:* Lynn Isenberg
*Paw of the Bear:* Lynn Isenberg
*Pinwheels:* Pam and Robert Bono
*Primrose:* Pam Bono
*Safari Path:* Pam Bono
*Santa Claus Tree Skirt:* Pam Bono
*Seminole Flower Bed:* Pam and Robert Bono
*South of the Border:* Pam Bono
*Stained Glass Floral:* Pam Bono
*Stars & Stripes:* Lynn Isenberg
*Sunflowers:* Pam Bono, Robert Bono, Mindy Kettner
*Sweet Dreams:* Mindy Kettner
*Tea for Two:* Mindy Kettner
*Till the Cows Come Home:* Lynn Isenberg
*Trellis:* Pam and Robert Bono
*Tuxedo Cats:* Pam and Robert Bono
*Water Lily:* Pam and Robert Bono
*Which Came First?:* Pam Bono

## Contributors

Amish hand quilting by Quilting Plus
Nancy Birger
Janet Frane
Curé of Ars Quilt Group
Judy DeVries
Dotty's Quilt Shop
Cindy Jochims of Iowa Quilting
Debbie McCormac
Barbara Morgan, Animas Quilts
Mother of the Universe Quilt Group
Melissa Mullgardt
Wanda Nelson of Knit One, Quilt Too
Barbara Roddy
Ella Ross
Elizabeth Smith
Fern Stewart
Julie Tebay of Quilting Plus
Gail Thomson
Marguleta Westbrook

## Photography Credits

All photographs by **John O'Hagan** except the following:
**Keith Harrelson:** pages 54, 64, 71, 88, 112, 128, 144, 160, 164.
**Brit Huckabay:** pages 49, 76, 81, 100, 106, 154.

## Special Thanks

• To The Brass Bed of Homewood, Alabama, for use of the bed pictured on page 33
• To Lord & Lockridge of Birmingham for use of the bed pictured on page 310.